LOVE ME,
HATE ME

LOVE ME,

BARRY BONDS AND THE

HATE ME

MAKING OF AN ANTIHERO

JEFF PEARLMAN

HarperCollinsPublishers

HarperCollins books may be purchased for educational, business, or sales promotional use. For information, please write: Special Markets Department, HarperCollins Publishers Inc., 10 East 53rd Street, New York, NY 10022.

FIRST EDITION

Designed by Elliott Beard

Printed on acid-free paper

Library of Congress Cataloging-in-Publication Data is available upon request.

ISBN-10: 0-06-079752-5

ISBN-13: 978-0-06-079752-2

06 07 08 09 10   ❖/RRD   10 9 8 7 6 5 4 3 2 1

For the five who have been here all along . . .

Dad—the guru

Mom—the nurturer

David—the big heart

Daniel—the philosopher

And Uncle Marty—who attended a good Hebrew school

The Barry I know is a quiet, caring, giving individual.

—ERIC DAVIS, FORMER SAN FRANCISCO GIANTS OUTFIELDER

Personally, I hope Barry dies.

—PETE DIANA, FORMER PITTSBURGH PIRATES TEAM PHOTOGRAPHER

Love me, hate me—I don't give a fuck.

—BARRY BONDS

CONTENTS

LOVE ME,
HATE ME

PROLOGUE

IT BEGINS HERE. NOT the life itself, but the sense of attitude and entitle-ment. Here, on a tan couch in a white living room in the San Carlos, California, home of Marlene Rossi, housewife, mom, and—against her bet-ter judgment—den mother of Cub Scouts Troop 53.

They sit quietly, a group of seven- and eight-year-old boys decked out in the plaid pants and screen-printed T-shirts of the early 1970s, engrossed in their latest task: knot tying. To the die-hard Scout, the assignment is an opportunity to edge closer to the coveted title of Webelos. To the happy-go-lucky Scout, it's a fun, moderately meaningful activity.

To Barry Bonds, age eight, it's a huge pain in the ass.

Young Barry is, in many ways, the royalty of Troop 53. He is, hands down, the best athlete—the fastest, the strongest, the biggest. His father, Bobby Bonds, is a star outfielder for the San Francisco Giants who occasionally stops by to pick up his boy and sign a few autographs. Barry lives in one of the nicest houses, owns some of the hippest clothes, slings some of the clev-erest trash talk, meets all the coolest people. But there is one sizable dent in his armor: He cannot tie a knot.

To Barry's left, Sam Rossi, Marlene's son and Barry's longtime pal, deftly loops square and overhand knots. Across the octagon coffee table, Scotty, Jeff, and Michael progress with graceful ease. But not Barry. He stews. He pouts. He glances jealously toward Sammy, then looks away when he's caught peeking. From the corner of her eye, Marlene observes all this and sighs. "The other kids were always so enthusiastic and eager," she would say years later. "But with Barry, it was always a challenge to get him to do his projects. He was always like, 'Oh crud, I have to do *this*?'"

With time running short and Barry's patience wearing thin, Marlene beckons to the handsome boy with the miniature Afro and whispers reassuringly into his ear. "Don't worry," she says. "We'll just mark down that you did the knots correctly. It'll be our little secret."

This, Barry Bonds never tells anyone.

Fast-forward 32 years—to September 13, 2005. The San Francisco Giants have just defeated the San Diego Padres, 5–4, at SBC Park. Sitting alone by his locker, Barry Bonds looks bored. He fidgets with a bottle of green Gatorade. He checks his cell phone. He scratches himself.

I decide the time has come to approach Bonds about this book.

As any baseball writer knows, confronting Barry Bonds in the clubhouse is often akin to sidling up to a lion while holding 10 pounds of raw meat. Throughout the preceding months, I have tried my best to get Bonds to sit down with me. I have sent dozens of e-mails. I've had multiple exchanges with his publicist. I've called his manager, his agent, his former agents, his friends.

Nothing.

As Bonds relaxes on a folding chair, reporters circle nearby and an army of personal assistants awaits his next command. Finally, with little to lose, I speak up.

"Barry," I say. "My name is Jeff Pearlman. I used to write for *Sports Illustrated*. I've communicated with your publicist quite a bit, but I'm not sure what she's told you. I'm writing a biography of your life. I'm trying my best to be fair. And even though I've been told you likely won't cooperate, I felt that, journalistically, I had to ask if you'd want to sit down and talk."

Bonds grins, detecting a timidity he's seen in countless others. "I'd rather not," he says. "But thanks for asking." He sticks out his hand, and I shake it.

Not so bad, I think.

"Just so you know," I add. "I've interviewed everyone. Five hundred people. Your Little League teammates, your high school pals, even your Cub Scouts den mother."

Bonds scowls. Have I gone too far?

"Dude," he barks derisively, "I was never in the Cub Scouts."

With this he rises and walks away, pretending not to hear as I tail him to the exit shouting, "Marlene Rossi! Marlene Rossi! Marlene Rossi!" I am momentarily shaken. Was my research wrong? Have I screwed up the most basic of facts?

A few minutes later I relay my exchange to Pedro Gomez, the ESPN reporter whose assignment for the season is to shadow Bonds. Gomez sighs, nodding knowingly. "Let me tell you something," he says. "A few months ago I went up to Barry and told him that my neighbor in Arizona is Jose Rodiles." Rodiles had been Bonds's teammate at Arizona State for two seasons. "Barry said, 'I don't know that name,'" recalls Gomez. "I said, 'Man, you played with him at ASU.' But Barry insisted he had no idea."

A few days later, Gomez called Rodiles and told him of Bonds's apparent amnesia. "That's funny," said Rodiles. "Because the guy was *in my fucking wedding*."

ONE

70

IN THE INSULAR WORLD of Major League Baseball, there is no greater sin than disrespect. Most players can tolerate inflated egos. They can tolerate boredom (a job requirement). They can tolerate pain, indifference, softness, absentmindedness, excessive brutality, disregard for the rules, large men dressed as sausages, 12-minute renditions of the national anthem.

Disrespect, however, is the ultimate no-no. You don't show up the opposing pitcher. You don't spit on an umpire. You never act the coward.

That was the word running through the dugout of the San Francisco Giants on the night of October 4, 2001. *Coward*. Actually, it wasn't the only word. Some preferred *pussy*. Others, *chicken-shit. Wuss, wimp, softie*. Pick an adjective—any derisive adjective—and it was applied to Houston Astros manager Larry Dierker. With good reason.

For nearly three full games, Dierker had refused to allow his pitchers to face Barry Bonds, San Francisco's left fielder and powerful number three hitter. In any other series at any other time, few Giants would have batted an eye. Throughout the past few seasons, Bonds had been pitched around more than any man since the game's inception in the 1880s. One hundred seventeen walks in 2000. A major league record 172 (and counting) in 2001.

It was a running joke among the San Francisco beat writers. How many hittable balls will Barry see today? *One? Two? Three, if he's lucky?*

Now, circumstances were different. With his solo blast against the San Diego Padres less than a week earlier, Bonds entered the series at Houston's Enron Field needing one home run to tie Mark McGwire's single-season record of 70. It was a mythical year for Bonds, who had to somehow overcome the death of a close friend and, along with the rest of America, the devastation of the September 11 terrorist attacks. Just weeks earlier in—of all places—Houston, the FBI had informed Bonds that someone had threatened to shoot him. *Keep hitting homers—and you die.*

How had it come to this? Once a spindly 185-pound leadoff hitter, Bonds had reinvented himself as the second coming of Babe Ruth. Three years earlier he had been an afterthought in the race between McGwire and Sammy Sosa to break Roger Maris's single-season home run mark. Now he was altering the modern definition of power hitter. Entering the series, both teams had six games remaining. The Giants were two back of Arizona in the National League West, and Houston was tied with St. Louis in the National League Central. No matter. Few thoughts were on the playoff races.

This was about history.

In anticipation of a magical moment, more than 250 media outlets requested credentials for the Giants-Astros series. All three games were sold out. Aware that opposing pitchers were fearful of going down as *the guy* who allowed a historic homer, Bonds used his pre-series press conference to try to goad Dierker and the Astros into presenting him with hittable baseballs.

"I've played against Houston a long time and I've never known them to bypass anybody," he said. "They have too many quality pitchers on that side, back to Nolan [Ryan] and Mike Scott and all the rest of them. They have pride, too. They have always been up for the challenge. When you look at some of the other teams, you can probably say, 'Sure, they won't pitch to you.' But when you look at a staff like [Houston's], it would be kind of odd if they [pitched around me]."

Of course, the Astros were no more likely to pitch to Bonds than were the Mets, the Braves, the Brewers, or any other major league team. But with just six games remaining in the season, Bonds wanted Dierker to take the bait. *Needed* Dierker to take the bait. This record meant everything to Bonds. It was a symbol of unparalleled greatness—of being the absolute best in a sport steeped in legend. Throughout the early portion of his career, Bonds was often overshadowed by the legacy of his father, Bobby Bonds, a talented major league outfielder whose stardom was derailed by alcoholism. Even later, in forging his own identity as a multiple MVP winner, Bonds struggled to separate himself from Ken Griffey Jr., baseball's other mega-watt star. This, too, induced bitterness. Now, the opportunity was at hand for Barry Bonds to elevate his status to an all-time, one-of-a-kind icon. He did not simply want the home run record. He *craved* it.

Before the first game of the series on October 2, Mike Krukow, the Giants color commentator, was walking behind the cage during batting practice when he bumped into Harry Spilman, Houston's hitting coach. The two had been teammates with San Francisco in the late 1980s, and maintained a friendship. Spilman flashed a disappointed expression. "Sluggo ain't pitching to Barry," Spilman said in reference to Dierker. "Your guy ain't gonna get squat to hit."

To Krukow's dismay, Spilman was right. In that night's 4–1 San Francisco win, Bonds saw 17 pitches (in five at-bats), only five of which were strikes. The next evening was even worse. In the Giants' 11–8 triumph, Bonds saw 18 pitches, four of which were strikes. After the games an enraged Bonds retreated to the clubhouse, where Willie Mays—traveling with the team to witness history—calmed him down. "You'll get your chance, Barry," Mays told his godson. "Just be patient." So dire was the situation that Bonds's 10-year-old daughter, Shikari, took to holding a poster that read PLEASE PITCH TO OUR DADDY!

Though Dierker remained steadfast in his belief that pitching to Bonds was foolish, few in the ballpark agreed. As it became increasingly clear that Bonds would not be allowed to hit his 70th, the hometown fans turned on their skipper. Dierker, a former Astros pitcher and TV commentator whose uniform number, 49, had been retired by the franchise, was booed whenever he walked to the mound or stuck his head out of the dugout. "Larry didn't realize the significance of how much Houston fans were *baseball* fans, not

Astros fans," says Jose De Jesus Ortiz, who covered the team for the *Houston Chronicle*. "He thought everyone was saying, 'We're filling this stadium to see you *not* give up the 70th home run.' It was actually the opposite."

Bonds's biggest enemy was not Dierker, but the scoreboard. Through the first two contests, he rarely stepped to the plate when the game was out of reach. One home run could have impacted the outcome, and that was too much for Houston's manager—concerned more with standings than public opinion—to risk. "When the games were close, you just *couldn't* pitch to Barry," says Astros outfielder Lance Berkman. "If our fans were more astute they would have realized our manager was trying to win."

On October 4, everything changed. With his team leading 8–1 in the sixth inning, Bonds sauntered to the plate with a runner on second and one out. Two times he had already been walked, and two times those in attendance had booed lustily. Now, up by seven runs, Bonds was certain to enjoy a legitimate opportunity to swing the bat. On the mound was Ricky Stone, an unassuming rookie right-hander who had bounced around the Dodgers minor league system for seven years before landing in Houston. Stone's stuff was mediocre—an OK changeup, a less-OK curve, and a slick sinker—but his attitude was all bulldog. That's the by-product of spending too much time in the bush leagues, sleeping on buses and eating out of a White Castle bag. You want an opportunity—any opportunity.

Stone prepared to face Bonds, running the possibilities through in his mind, when he peeked into the dugout and saw Dierker ordering an intentional walk. Stone nodded, but he wasn't happy. As catcher Tony Eusebio stood to the side of the plate, arm extended, boos rained down from the crowd of 43,734. A handful of fans in the Diamond Club, an executive seating area behind home plate, orchestrated a middle-finger salute in protest. "When the people paying $20,000 to $30,000 for their seats turn on you," says Ortiz, "you know you've violated something." In the Astros dugout, straight-faced players quietly muttered disapproval under their breaths. Giants first base coach Robby Thompson screamed insults toward Houston's bench. Sitting in the press box, Giants general manager Brian Sabean shook his head in disgust. "Now I'm really starting to get fucking pissed," he said to Josh Suchon, the *Oakland Tribune* beat writer. "This is bullshit." The rage spread to the Giants dugout. "I don't care if the guy's the best hitter in the world—when I'm out there pitching, I want to try and get him out," says Jason Schmidt, a Giants starting pitcher. "You're in the big leagues for a reason. There's a code of decency that was broken."

Bonds accepted the walk with a smirk, dropped his bat, and jogged to first base. Giants second baseman Jeff Kent followed by grounding into an inning-ending double play, but nobody cheered. The crowd had come to watch Barry Bonds make contact, not the Astros make the playoffs.

The Giants added another run in the eighth, and when the top of the ninth inning rolled around, San Francisco led 9–2. Maybe it was the booing. Maybe it was the disappointed expressions on the faces of his own players. Maybe he was simply tired of his starring role as baseball wimp. Whatever the case, for the first time in three days, Dierker prepared to face Bonds, who was scheduled to lead off.

The Astros had just the pitcher for the job.

When Wilfredo Rodriguez was 15 years old, his mother bought him a new pair of sneakers. This was hardly an everyday occurrence in San Felix, one of Venezuela's largest, poorest, and most dangerous cities, where size 12 Nikes are usually out of financial reach. "It's a rough place to live," says Wilfredo, the third of Ginaro and Delvalle Rodriguez's six children. "People doing crime, robbing, stealing, knifing each other."

Young Wilfredo learned this the hard way. On his walk home from the store he was confronted by a man who demanded that he hand over his shoes. When Rodriguez momentarily paused, the man pulled out a .38-caliber revolver and fired two shots. Rodriguez crumpled to the ground, one bullet lodged behind his right knee, the other in his right thigh. The scars are still visible.

Until that moment, Rodriguez had been one of his city's top young baseball talents. Uninterested in academics, he spent his mornings, afternoons, and evenings either fishing or on the sandlots, positioning himself in right field and dreaming of the colorful uniforms and cathedral stadiums of the United States. It was his mental escape from a rough life. At home, Rodriguez, his parents, and his five siblings shared two beds in a house the size of a coffee table. "When I was shot, I thought I was done," he says. "I thought the dream was done. For a year I didn't play baseball. I just sat around and tried to get better. It was very sad."

After returning from his injury in 1995, Rodriguez went back to the outfield. One day in a pickup game at nearby Porto Das, a scout from the Houston Astros saw him rifle a throw from right field to home plate. "Do me a favor," the scout said. "Pitch the next inning and see what you can do." When Rodriguez took the mound, everything clicked. He felt a calm, and as the ball left Rodriguez's hand, the scout couldn't believe the radar gun—91, 93, 94, 92, 93, 92. Within days, 16-year-old Wilfredo Rodriguez signed a contract for $25,000 and was shipped to the Astros baseball academy in Valencia. He used the money to buy his parents a new home. With plenty of beds.

Over the ensuing six years, the Astros meticulously transformed Rodriguez from a hard-throwing-yet-erratic gunslinger into the organization's top pitching prospect. He was a big kid—6-foot-3, 210 pounds—with unusually long arms and an unconventional way of whipping the ball toward home plate like a slingshot. By the start of the 2001 season, Houston GM Gerry Hunsicker believed Rodriguez, age 22, was on the threshold of becoming a top-tier major leaguer. On September 15, after he posted 94 strikeouts in 92 innings and was clocked as high as 98 mph at Double A Round Rock, Rodriguez's dream turned reality. The Astros were calling him up.

"He was one of those mystery players," says Ortiz. "We knew he was some Venezuelan kid who threw hard and didn't have much control. But that was it."

The Houston coaches learned quickly. In his first bullpen session before pitching coach Burt Hooten, Rodriguez unleashed a torrent of fastballs that cut and hummed and slid with frightening unpredictability. He was the type of pitcher nobody wanted to face; the type never quite sure where his own ball was heading. When Spilman, the Astros hitting coach, assured Krukow that Bonds would be pitched around, he added a caveat.

"If we're ever crazy enough to go after him," he said, "we've got the ultimate secret weapon."

•••●●

As the Giants piled on the runs, Rodriguez sat in the bullpen and wondered, "Why are we so scared?" Back in San Felix, such cowardly behavior was unheard of. Rodriguez loved challenges. Survive two gunshot wounds, and the fear of failure erodes. Late in the game, Astros reliever Octavio Dotel suggested to Rodriguez that he might be brought in to face Bonds. "If that happens," said Dotel, "go after him. Pitch like a man."

The call came in the bottom of the eighth inning—the call Wilfredo Rodriguez had been waiting for. He stood to loosen up and began throwing some of his most wicked stuff in weeks. Since his promotion 19 days earlier, Rodriguez had appeared in only one game, a less-than-stellar two-inning, four-run debacle against the Cubs. Now he was fresh, rested, and anxious to make good. He thought about his parents; about his five siblings; about his small house and crowded bed.

"You're pitching to Barry Bonds," Dotel told him. "Not God."

At the end of the eighth inning Rodriguez strolled onto the field and took his eight warm-up pitches. The first one went over the catcher's head and to the backstop. In the on-deck circle, Bonds calmly sized up the young kid's stuff, eyes focused solely on the mound. Catcher Tony Eusebio threw down to second and trotted to the rubber.

"Acabenlo," he told Rodriguez.

Finish him.

As Eusebio retreated to his spot behind the plate, a chant began: *"Bar-ree! Bar-ree! Bar-ree!"* It grew louder. *"BAR-ree! BAR-ree! BAR-ree!"* And louder. *"BAR-REE! BAR-REE! BAR-REE!"* By the time Rodriguez reared back for his first pitch, it was as if a Boeing 727 had flown through the stadium. Nothing could be heard. Not the popcorn vendors or the PA announcer. Not Rodriguez, grunting as he fired a 95-mph heater.

Bonds cocked back and uncoiled a powerful swing that met nothing but air. The crowd oohed. Flashbulbs exploded.

Strike one.

On the Giants bench, veteran Shawon Dunston laughed aloud. "Man," he shouted, "this kid thinks he can get some cheese by the rat!"

Rodriguez peeked in for the sign, and the noise again reached maximum decibel. *"BAR-REE! BAR-REE! BAR-REE!"* In the Astros dugout, Dierker looked angry. *Who are these people rooting for?* By not pitching to Bonds he'd brought the raging stadium to a boil. Rodriguez fired another fastball, this one 96 mph and high out of the zone. Bonds didn't swing.

Ball one.

What the baseball fans of Houston were witnessing was classic theater. Rodriguez would never back down. Bonds would never back down. Rodriguez threw heat. Bonds pounded heat. Rodriguez wanted to be known as the guy who mastered the mightiest slugger. Bonds wanted the record. "The concentration Barry had at that moment was unparalleled," says Giants outfielder Eric Davis. "He was as locked in as we'd ever seen him."

With the count one ball, one strike, Rodriguez threw his third pitch of the inning, a 93-mph heater that crossed the meat of the plate. Bonds's swing was absolutely perfect—sliced through the zone, slight uppercut, arms straight, head down.

Rodriguez whipped his torso around, just quickly enough to catch sight of a white baseball soaring 454 feet into Enron Field's second deck. Bonds flipped the bat aside and triumphantly raised his arms.

The noise. Oh, the noise. *WHOOOSSSHHH!*

As he rounded first base Bonds pumped his index finger and shook his fist, a relieved smile crossing his face. The other Giants stormed out of the dugout and surrounded home plate, anxious to greet the new coholder of baseball's single-season home run record. After Bonds completed his trot and was mobbed, manager Dusty Baker embraced him in a tight bear hug. The Enron Field crowd remained on their feet. Smiling widely in the dugout, Bonds then stepped to the field for a curtain call as fans chanted his name. He waved, blew a kiss, and descended the steps back into the dugout. A half minute later he returned to the field, again acknowledging the roaring fans.

Television cameras flashed to Liz Bonds, Barry's wife, as she wiped the tears from her cheeks. His two daughters, Shikari and two-year-old Aisha Lynn, jumped up and down, crying with joy. ("I'll never forget that," Bonds said later. "[Shikari] is one of the toughest cookies in my household.") When the inning ended, Bonds jogged to left field and was hugged by a stream of San Francisco relievers exiting the bullpen. In a classy tribute, Giants manager Dusty Baker had outfielder Dante Powell enter the game as Bonds's replacement. The legendary slugger walked across the diamond and into the dugout, a conquering hero bathed in love and adulation.

Across the United States, a nation of fans didn't know how to feel or whom to root for. This wasn't 1998, when the face-off between the cuddly Mc-Gwire and the even cuddlier Sosa created a baseball lovefest that brought joy to millions. Back then, we were allowed to peek behind the game's curtain and see that large men with unimaginable power could laugh and cry and hug and exult in the mythical splendor of the home run. Now, nobody truly knew what to make of Bonds. He was, on the one hand, as blessed a talent as the sport had ever seen—a merging of speed, strength, discipline, instinct, and power that elicited comparisons to everyone from Mickey Mantle and Willie Mays to Rickey Henderson and McGwire. Over the course of his 16-year career, Bonds had compiled a broader résumé of accomplishments than any ballplayer since Ruth. He stole a career-high 52 bases with the Pittsburgh Pirates in 1990, and now shared the title of single-season home run king. He began as a subpar center fielder, then moved to left and won eight Gold Gloves. He struck out 102 times as a rookie, but never cleared the century mark again. "I've seen a lot of amazing baseball players through my life," says Brian Johnson, Bonds's former teammate with the Giants. "But Barry is a man who decides he's going to do something, then does it. If he wanted to hit 100 home runs, I'm pretty sure he could. If he wanted to steal 100 bases, he could have done that, too. He's playing on one level, and everyone else is a step or two or three behind."

Yet Bonds the ballplayer has always been obscured by Bonds the human being—an oft-guarded, oft-snarling, oft-difficult enigma of a man whose bursts of joy are overshadowed by lengthy periods of antagonism and anger. The word *jerk* frequently accompanies Bonds's name, but when you consider his complicated upbringing, the adjective seems staggeringly simplistic. Bonds was raised in a bubble—the son of a major league star who lavished material gifts upon his offspring but, thanks to alcoholism and ego, fell short in all measurements of fatherhood. Bobby Bonds had urged his son to be not just guarded, but aloof and antagonistic. The result was a child who craved fame but feared it; who sought friends but turned away those with the potential to grow too close; who needed warmth and affection but refused to show even the slightest bit of vulnerability. Raised in the exclusive white San Francisco suburb of San Carlos, Bonds never knew what it was to blend in with the crowd. He was the black athletic phenomenon with the ungodly talent; the kid destined to be a star. He was royalty, and he was expected to act the part. This does not merely weigh on a youngster. It crushes him.

Had Bonds ever decided to convey this side of his story, to tell the world, "Hey, I'm as messed up as the next guy," people would have understood and, in all likelihood, embraced him. But there is a reason Barry Bonds generates more fascination than any other superstar of his generation, and it is that nobody has been allowed access. We know Michael Jordan was cut from his high school basketball team. We know Peyton Manning was groomed by a loving father to be an elite quarterback. We know LeBron James was raised by a devoted mother in the Akron housing projects. But what do we really comprehend about Barry Bonds? And how does baseball's greatest slugger maintain such mystery?

Why would a man with such natural gifts cheat by using performance-enhancing drugs? Will he stick around long enough to break Hank Aaron's all-time home run record of 755? Will the day come when Bonds finally opens up to the world?

There is more at stake here than detective work. Well before most baseball gods retire, we can assume how their tombstones (and Hall of Fame plaques) will read. Not Bonds. Buried beneath the swirling dramas of his life is the daunting question of legacy. Too complex to pin down; too controversial to grasp—what do we really know of Barry Bonds? Baseball star or baseball brat? Excellence or enigma? Hero or cheater? Legend or liar?

I interviewed more than 500 subjects for this book, most of whom were unsure where, exactly, I should begin. Then I came upon Dickie Jackson, one of Bobby Bonds's childhood friends. A talkative man with a keen memory, Jackson answered all my questions, but paused when asked, "Where can I locate the soul of Barry Bonds?" After a half-minute delay, he responded.

"Find Riverside, California," he said, "and I bet you'll find Barry Bonds."

TWO

BIRTH OF A BALLPLAYER

BARRY BONDS ARRIVED AT Burton Field in San Carlos, California, on a warm March afternoon in 1975, 10 years old and a hero in the making. Just like a young Superman, who appeared out of nowhere (well, Smallville) to save the day, little Barry initially looked like just another kid, decked out in a T-shirt and shorts and lined up along a fence with 30 or so other freckle-faced boys. A handful of coaches from the San Carlos Little League had come to evaluate the talent pool before the following week's new player draft. As one child after another took a turn in the batting cage, then fielded fly balls in the outfield, all adult eyes focused on the skinny black kid with the confident stride.

"He didn't run," says Lloyd Skjerdal, head coach of the Lions Club Yankees. "He flew. He didn't just make contact with the ball. He crushed it. He didn't just . . ."

Skjerdal can go on for an hour. The boy before him was no ordinary ballplayer. In the outfield, he tracked down baseballs with unrivaled dexterity. At the plate, he turned on fastballs—*adult fastballs*—and walloped them into faraway pockets. When he threw a ball, the inevitable *pop!* induced goose bumps. Most 10-year-old boys are gawky assemblages of elbows and knees. Not this kid.

Word quickly spread, whispered from coach to coach and parent to parent. "That's Bobby's kid."

Who?

"Bobby Bonds. *That's Bobby Bonds's kid.*"

Skjerdal could smile. His Yankees possessed the first selection in the draft. There was no mystery. A lottery winner never turns down the pot. "Barry was 10, going on 15 or 20," says Skjerdal. "The best talent I've ever seen in a young baseball player. He was this magnificent collection of skill, and it was as if he had appeared out of nowhere—just showed up one day, ready to be a star."

Barry Lamar Bonds was born on July 24, 1964, in Riverside, California, and he was born to be a Major League Baseball player. That's the cliché, anyway, made more real with the passing of time and the accumulation of Hall of Fame–worthy statistics. Major leaguers are rare specimens, the best of the best. They are focused and determined from a young age, a perfect merging of physical brilliance, implacable grit, and furious concentration. But if you look past the praise—the confident, he-was-destined-to-do-this tone that became ingrained among Bay Area journalists over the past decade and a half—it could just as easily be said that Barry Bonds was born *not* to be a Major League Baseball player. Not with his teenage parents, and certainly not with his father's raging alcoholism.

Most everyone on the Eastside of Riverside knew that the Bonds bloodline, though blessed with otherworldly athletic gifts, was poisoned by the dual curses of an insatiable desire for alcohol and the inability to handle the stuff. Those traits were pioneered by Barry's grandfather, Robert Bonds, a short-tempered plaster contractor with a substance abuse problem that made life in the Bonds household miserable. Tall, with dark skin, thick shoulders, and an ironworker's worn hands, Robert arrived in Riverside from Texas in 1934, armed with a sixth-grade education and desperate for work. The mantra he repeated to his kids—"If God wanted you to go backward, he'd have turned your feet around"—was an inspirational one, but it was dulled by volatility. Drunk or sober, Robert was never one to spare the belt buckle. He was a man much of the community avoided, and with good reason. In his spare time, he was either drinking or blowing his dough at the nearest pool hall. Oftentimes both. "Just stayed drunk all the time," recalls Johnnie Baker, a family friend, neighbor, and the father of Dusty Baker, the future major league outfielder and manager. "I'd bet he didn't see a day sober in his life. I had a rule with my family, and it was this: Stay away from Robert Bonds. He was married to the bottle."

The same would turn out to be true with the youngest of Robert and Elizabeth Bonds's four children, a local schoolboy star named Bobby Bonds. For sports fans living on the Eastside of town in the 1950s and '60s, there were the Bonds children, and there was everybody else. Bobby's oldest brother, Robert Bonds Jr., went on to play football at San Jose State and was later drafted by the Kansas City Chiefs. The middle brother, David, was a splendid high school football player until he broke his left collarbone in an automobile accident. Sister Rosie was a U.S. record holder in the 80-meter hurdles, and reached the finals at the 1964 Tokyo Olympics. But Bobby— well, Bobby was divine. "The first time I saw Bobby walk onto a field, it was like he had a presence," says Roy Hale, who coached Bobby in Little League. "When he was 12 years old, he averaged a home run per game for me. He was stronger than anyone, faster than anyone, more powerful than anyone."

Located 50 miles southeast of Los Angeles, Riverside was known throughout California for the long rows of boxcars that carried fruits and vegetables to the rest of the state. Within the city confines—and especially on the multicultural Eastside—residents embraced an open-minded attitude well ahead of their time. As millions of American blacks were still being forced to drink from separate water fountains and ride in the rear of the bus, Riverside was a model of community and togetherness. Bobby's pals formed a rainbow coalition of blacks, Hispanics, and whites, and as they rode their bicycles across town, the all-too-familiar American taunts of "Nigger!" or "Spic!" were nowhere to be heard. "All the parents knew all the kids," says Paul Boykin, a childhood friend of Bobby's. "They saw them during the day, they saw them run to and from school. If you did something wrong at another kid's house, his parents would spank you, then call your parents. You'd get home and be spanked again. We were being raised the right way."

During summers, Bobby and his buddies would ride their bikes to Patterson Park, play baseball for a couple of hours (the goal was to hit a ball over Mrs. Pia's house beyond the left-field fence), stop by Alan's Sweet Shop for some gumballs, then dive into the community pool at Lincoln Park. Or they'd head to a field behind Bobby's house and play baseball with rocks or rolled-up tube socks. "Or those little red berries off the bushes," Bobby once recalled. "We had a system: As long as you hit the berry back when it was pitched to you, you kept batting." There was a storefront between Eleventh and Twelfth Streets called Wholesome Bakery, and when the owner closed up at night he would leave a bounty of leftover cookies and cakes on the back stoop. "I remember the dock between the bakery and the Union Pacific train," says Dickie Jackson, Bobby's childhood pal. "We'd stand there as the trains would go by, eating cookies and letting the wind fill our shirts."

"I wouldn't want to change my childhood for anybody else's childhood," Bobby once said. "At times we were middle class and at times we were poor. There were times I could get things and times I couldn't get diddley. I'd have holes in my shoes, and both soles would be flapping." Unlike his own children years later, Bobby was forced to understand the value of money. Little was handed to him. He caddied at a local golf course, hauled bags of cement at his father's construction site, and combed Riverside in search of recyclable bottles.

Meanwhile, sports consumed Bobby, and he became the pride of the Eastside, an area that approached athletics with grave seriousness. When he was 12, he started playing baseball at Evans Park, in a recreational summer league with future major leaguers like Tom Hall, Mike Corkins, and John Lowenstein, as well as future PGA star Gary McCord. When too few kids showed up, Bobby would allow a pesky little tagalong—Johnnie Baker's son—to stand in left field. He was three years younger than Bobby, and his nickname was Dusty. "There's no logical reason a 16-year-old would let this kid join in," recalls Dusty Baker. "But Bobby had a soft spot."

By the time he was in high school, at Riverside Polytechnic, he was becoming something of a local legend. Here was a youngster who once started in center field *and* participated in a track meet at the same time. Poly was facing rival Chaffey High School in both sports on a spring afternoon, and

Bonds's reputation was such that, when the long jump and 100-yard dash were set to begin, a time-out was called in baseball. Bobby quickly hopped over the center-field fence, dashed to the track, and competed. "He had his baseball uniform on and no time to warm up—and he ran the 100 in 9.8 seconds in baseball cleats," recalls Jackson, who witnessed the spectacle. "Then he climbed back over the fence, played a few innings, returns to the track and broad jumps 24 feet, 11 inches. That was in baseball cleats, too. I swear to God that happened. He was *that* good."

Prior to his freshman year at Poly, Bobby began what would turn into a near-lifelong partnership with alcohol. He did not drink heavily at first, and in the early years the habit never hampered his results. Bobby once scored six touchdowns in three quarters of play for the Poly varsity football team, and on the track he excelled as a 25-foot long jumper and 9.5-second sprinter in the 100-yard dash. He was so dominant on the baseball field that in 1960—Bonds's *freshman* year—a Cleveland Indians scout named Evo Pusich sent raving reports back to the big club about a kid outfielder from Riverside. In the 1963 edition of the *Koala*, Poly's yearbook, there is a photograph of Bobby soaring to the hoop in a basketball game against rival Ramona. The caption reads, "The Ramona Rams stand in awe as Bobby Bonds scores again." This was not hyperbole; the five cropped-haired white kids trying to defend Bobby's drive appear genuinely shocked.

Midway through his sophomore year, Bobby began stuffing bottles of wine and cans of beer into his bag and toting them along to athletic events. Were he a lesser specimen, the impact would have been obvious. But Bobby was so good, so strong, so powerful, his performance never fell off. On June 6, 1964, at the Los Angeles Coliseum, Bobby won the state long jump championship with a leap of 25 feet, 3 inches, just 1 foot, 3 inches short of the national mark. Twenty minutes earlier he had ducked behind a bleacher and chugged a beer. "He used to do the same thing before he ran the 100," says Johnnie Baker. "Whenever Bobby went behind the bleachers, you knew what he was doing."

Though boozing didn't diminish Bobby's level of play, it also didn't go completely unnoticed. "I had to talk to Bobby a million times about drinking when he was in school," says Johnnie Baker. "He would always say, 'Mr.

Baker, I don't do this.' And 'Mr. Baker, I don't do that.' I would use his dad as an example, and say something like, 'Is that the path you want to lead for yourself?' Bobby told me he would never wind up like his father. Promised me. But I wasn't so confident." Baker was terrified the area's most gifted athlete would junk everything. Along with the drinking, he was the first of his peers to start smoking cigarettes; the one with the quickest temper and the fastest fists. There was a certain attitude to Bobby—a don't-fuck-with-me aura that worked in his favor on a ball field but was not ideal for general society.

Bobby's cavalier attitude didn't deter Evo Pusich, who by Bobby's senior season was scouting for the San Francisco Giants and infatuated with the outfielder's explosiveness. Nor did it repel Patricia Howard. The daughter of Flo and Thurmond Howard, Patricia was lithe and attractive, an engaging girl with short hair and brown eyes. She had been an object of Bobby's affection since 1960, when her family moved into the neighboring house on Vasquez Place. "Man, everybody in town loved Pat," says Dusty Baker. "She was one of the finest things around. Everybody had a crush on her." It was Pat—not sports—who inspired Bobby to lift weights well before pumping iron was the norm. He kept a crude set of dumbbells in his garage and dreamed of the day Pat would see his long, sinewy body rippling with muscles. The physique never materialized (Bobby's 6-foot-1, 190-pound build was less Rocky Marciano, more Tommy Hearns), but the girl next door was smitten. Bobby and Pat were a celebrity item at Poly, the jock and the beauty, walking hand in hand through the hallways. "My mom's family put restrictions on when he could see her," Barry would later say. "So he started sneaking in her bedroom window at night to get some." What Pat loved in Bobby was that—unlike most of the other kids in their graduating class—he had a plan. He was going to be a baseball player. A great one.

On May 3, 1963, against the protestations of his parents, Bobby and Pat were married in a hometown ceremony. Within a few months she was pregnant. With a boy.

The summer of 1964 was a momentous one for Bobby Bonds. At the age of 18, he became a father. And, almost simultaneously, his career in pro-

fessional sports began. At the conclusion of his senior year Bobby had accepted an offer from Pusich and the San Francisco Giants. In addition to
an $8,000 signing bonus, the deal guaranteed Bonds a $500 monthly salary.
The Giants also agreed to underwrite his tuition at the college of his choice.
After the figures were established, Pusich broke out his you-can't-resist card:
"By the time you get to the big team, Willie Mays will have two or three years
left," Pusich told Bobby. "He'll be your teacher." Nothing more needed to be
said. Bobby signed on August 4, 1964—just 11 days after Barry had been
born at Riverside Community Hospital.

Seven months later, after briefly attending Riverside City College, Bobby
reported to the Giants' minor league spring training camp at Casa Grande,
Arizona, where 450 ballplayers were fighting for 150 minor league spots.
It was his first experience with cutthroat baseball, where peers rooted for
you to fail. Though Bobby had no problem with the physical demands, his
entry into the minors was psychologically bruising. Bobby was assigned to
the Giants Class A affiliate in Lexington, North Carolina, a town of 16,000
people located 21 miles south of Winston-Salem. Lexington was the self-
proclaimed "Barbecue Capital of the World," but as in many North Carolina hamlets, the barbecue was served only to those blacks who were willing
to eat behind the restaurant. Lexington was home to segregated schools
and segregated buses. At first, Bobby was confused by the hostility. "Listen,"
he'd say to the owner of a whites-only restaurant. "I'm playing ball. This
shouldn't be." (With a stern "Get the hell out, nigger," Bobby learned that in
the South the color of a baseball uniform didn't matter nearly as much as
the color of the man wearing it.)

Bobby spent much of the season as the only minority on manager Max
Lanier's roster, and his skills failed to win over a prejudiced crowd. The road
games were the worst. Be it in Gastonia, Rock Hill, or Greenville, Bobby
was everything to everybody—a nigger. A coon. A watermelon-eating dar-
kie. One time, after he singled in a game against Rock Hill, he heard a taunt
from his own dugout. "Get off that white base and stand on the brown dirt!"
a teammate screamed. "That's where you belong!"

Like Jackie Robinson, Roy Campanella, and Willie Mays before him,
Bobby was usually able to block out the hatred. But when, in the middle of

the season, Pat arrived with baby Barry for four weeks, she was taken aback by the anger and self-doubt within her husband. Pat had married the happy-go-lucky, self-assured Bobby Bonds. Now he'd become a man who feared for his life, and who wondered whether it was all worth it. Why not just go back to Riverside and live with pride? Why put up with this? The answer Bobby found was the same one Barry provided, some 40 years later, when asked why—in the midst of swirling steroid allegations—he continued to come to the ballpark: the love of baseball.

That's what kept Bobby afloat, though barely. When Pat and Barry returned to Riverside in mid-July, Bobby spent his free time drinking alone at his Lexington apartment, sitting in front of the TV, and playing records. At times he would go to the nearby pool and watch people swim; blacks were not allowed in the water. Near the middle of the season, Bobby walked into Lanier's office and told him he was done. "I can't take this anymore," he said.

Lanier begged his right fielder to reconsider. "With your ability, you'd be crazy to quit," he said. "You can be a major league ballplayer. But if you leave now, you'll end up with nothing. What you're hearing down here is something you're going to have to be hearing the rest of your life. You're going to have to get used to it."

He tried. Through 122 games at Lexington, Bobby was hitting .323 with 25 home runs and 33 stolen bases. Then, in August, the Giants gave Bonds a present better than any new car or wad of cash. He was promoted to Fresno of the California League, 2,500 miles away from North Carolina. No matter where his career led him, Bobby never forgot the bitterness of Lexington. He retold the stories, first to Barry, then to his other sons. Although his children would grow up spoiled in an upper-crust community, they were aware that the hardships their father faced in North Carolina were real. "I wouldn't want to go through that kind of thing again," Bobby said years later. "But I wouldn't run from it, either."

Back in Riverside, Pat and little Barry were learning how to cope with an absentee father. While Bobby was on the road, Pat lived at home with her parents on Vasquez Place, raising her son. Pat read to Barry, took him on strolls around the neighborhood, woke up with him at all hours, and rarely complained. "Pat was outstanding," says Dickie Jackson. "She was very nurturing. But Bobby wasn't ready to be a dad. You have to remember, his only world was athletics. That's how he was wired. So I wouldn't say being a father came naturally to him."

"Bobby was looked at as a man when he was still a boy," adds Dusty Baker. "At 16 he looked like he was 26. I think people had mature expectations for him when he probably wasn't at that level yet."

In Bobby's absences, his hometown of Riverside stepped in to help. There were Pat and her parents. There was Bobby's mother, affectionately known by the community as "Momma Bonds," and famous for her homemade chili and corn bread. There was the nearby Settlement House on Bermuda Avenue, a community center with dozens of volunteers willing to offer assistance. There was the beauty shop, where Ms. Coleman and Ms. Davis styled hair and talked gossip. There was the Park Avenue Baptist Church. "Barry was the baby of a very, very tight-knit community," recalls Alvin Davis, a future major league All-Star who grew up down the block on Vasquez. Only four years his senior, Davis remembers Barry as a toddler. "I can picture him waddling around when we were playing ball," says Davis. "Just a little guy doing his thing."

In the ensuing two and a half seasons, Bobby established himself as the Giants' top offensive prospect—a five-tool star-in-the-making with Mays-like skills. He spent the entire 1966 season at Fresno, where his 26 home runs and 91 RBIs placed him among the California League leaders. The following year the Giants promoted him to Double A Waterbury of the Eastern League. While Bobby's statistics were not eye-popping, his 15 home runs and 68 RBIs ranked second in a league dominated by pitching (Williamsport's C. B. Smith led all hitters with a .306 average). Noted one Giants scout in a report sent to the club: "Bonds has come into full bloom."

Bobby reported to spring training in February 1968 convinced he was he ready to help the Giants. So he was crushed when the club optioned him to Triple A Phoenix to begin the season. Sensing his disappointment, San Francisco manager Herman Franks promised Bobby, "Have two good months and we'll bring you up to the big team."

By the third week of the season, Bobby was batting .350 for manager

Clyde King, who unwittingly revolutionized the game by placing Bobby in the leadoff spot. Pre–Bobby Bonds, the standard idea in baseball was to stick powerful bats in the middle of the lineup and swift, slap-hitting gnats up top. King, however, was intrigued by Bobby's rare merging of speed and pop. He was Rickey Henderson before there was a Rickey Henderson. In his first game batting leadoff, Bobby went 5-for-5 with a home run.

Toward the end of June, the Giants decided Bobby's time had arrived. Before leaving for the big leagues, Bobby was called into King's office for one last visit. "You've paid your dues," the manager told him. "Now do us proud." Bobby was overcome by emotion. He hugged King and called his wife and mother.

Bobby Bonds was coming to San Francisco.

On the day Bobby made his major league debut, Barry was one month shy of his fourth birthday and, already it seemed, destined to be an athlete. He was an early walker and an early thrower; at age two, he hit a Wiffle ball hard enough to shatter a window in the family's living room. (Pat became a regular customer at the W. J. Bank glass store, where the concerned owner would call if she went longer than six months without having to replace a window.) While other parents would brag about their toddler's ability to, say, pedal a Big Wheel, Barry was slicing a miniature wood baseball bat through the strike zone and throwing a ball hard enough to leave a welt.

Like most fathers of the time, Bobby was a limited partner in the raising of his children. (Barry's younger brother, Ricky, was born in 1965, and a third, Bobby Jr., came along in 1970. A daughter, Cheryl, was adopted.) Though he did not change many diapers or spoon-feed pureed pears, nothing exemplifies Bobby the dad better than his frustration watching Barry eat his diced peaches with the *wrong* hand. "A lefty?" Bobby thought. "I don't think so." Left-handedness limited the positions a ballplayer could man on the field. How many left-handed catchers were there? How about left-handed third basemen or shortstops? So Bobby routinely swatted Barry's left hand, insisting he go with the right. *Swat! Swat!* Bobby wanted a ballplayer.

At San Francisco's Candlestick Park, Bobby was an immediate sensation.

In a 9–0 win over the visiting Los Angeles Dodgers on June 25, 1968, he became the first rookie since Philadelphia's William Duggleby in 1898 to hit a grand slam in his debut. Bobby received a standing ovation, but was too frazzled to relish the moment. It wasn't until the next morning, when he opened the sports page of the *San Francisco Chronicle* to see the headline BONDS SLAMS GIANTS TO VICTORY! that the achievement sunk in. "Wow!" he shouted aloud in an empty room. "Was *that* what I did?"

Back in Riverside, Bobby's feat was treated like a civic holiday. That night Paul Boykin, five years Bobby's junior, was competing for the Crushers in a Colt League game at Evans Park. In the middle of the seventh inning, play was stopped and an announcement made. "Ladies and gentlemen, Riverside's own Bobby Bonds has just hit a grand slam in his first game with the San Francisco Giants!" For a full five minutes the approximately 150 people in attendance stood and cheered. "There wasn't a whole lot else going on in Riverside at the time," says Boykin. "Bobby Bonds *was* Riverside."

Bobby enjoyed a good—not great—rookie year for the second-place Giants, batting .254 with nine home runs, 35 RBIs and 16 stolen bases in 81 games. But his talent was bountiful. "The man was built like a greyhound," says Jack Hiatt, a first baseman and catcher with the club from 1965 to 1969. "If he wasn't the fastest player in the NL when he came up, he certainly was one of them. But what was truly amazing was the power. When you thought of sluggers back then, it was big guys like Hank Aaron and Willie McCovey. Bobby was wiry thin, and he'd still hit the ball a mile."

The season marked Barry's first foray into a major league locker room. The boy was immediately drawn to the 37-year-old Mays, the legendary center fielder who, as the team's star, leader, and most prominent black player, showed Bobby the dos and don'ts of big league life. Mays was the guy who slipped Barry pieces of Beechnut chewing gum; who'd humor him with a game of catch and soft-punch boxing matches; who let the him sit in the front seat of his pink Cadillac. Unless he was in the company of Bobby or a handful of other players, Mays was not especially gregarious. By age 37, the Say Hey Kid had morphed into a man short on trust and long on bitterness. Mays always believed the Giants were ripping him off and that he was unappreciated by San Franciscans. He mostly kept to himself in the Giants clubhouse, and those who broke into his sphere of privacy risked his wrath. "An awful lot of people took advantage of Willie throughout his career, and he resented that," says Charles Einstein, Mays's biographer. "He had a raft of problems that he didn't think were anyone's business. He went through a divorce, he had financial problems. That probably led to a pretty big wall he built up around himself."

Bobby was allowed in, partially because Mays saw a younger version of himself and partially because Mays resented those already tagging Bonds "the next Willie Mays." It was a negative for both players—Mays deserved more respect, and the 22-year-old Bobby didn't need the burden. "He didn't want to hear the next Mays stuff," said Mays. "He wanted to establish himself."

Mays made it his priority to protect Bobby. He liked the kid's inquisitiveness—he was full of questions other players never asked. (Though many were simply too intimidated to approach, Mays saw the younger players' lack of curiosity as a sign of disrespect.) When the Giants went on the road, Mays took Bobby to dinners and movies. One day during batting practice a coach was teaching Bobby a new way to hold the bat. Mays went ballistic. "Leave him alone!" he screamed. "You're just screwing him up!" The coach slunk away. Aware of Bobby's penchant for the bottle, Mays urged him to focus his attention on the game. "Watch out for yourself first and foremost," he would tell Bobby. "Winning is great. But look out for Number One."

Appreciative of the way his son gravitated to his mentor, Bobby asked Mays to serve as Barry's godfather. (Though it has often been assumed that Mays was *literally* Barry's godfather—the man who sponsored him at baptism—the title was in fact merely honorary.) Like his father, Barry watched Mays and learned. He witnessed the way Mays turned a wind-twisted fly ball into an easy catch; the way his cap flew off as he rounded first and dug for second; the way he hit home runs and everyone—his teammates, his opponents, the fans—stood in awe. As Ira Berkow of the *New York Times* wrote, "No matter how many times you watched Willie Mays play, there was always something new and fresh and purely pleasurable about it, like a root beer float." Barry also saw the bad Willie—blowing off the media, blowing off teammates; sarcastic comments that stung like a snakebite. Mays knew he was royalty, just as he knew those frumpy-looking men with inkstains on their sweaters weren't of his ilk.

Barry soaked it in.

In 1969, with Bobby entrenched as the Giants' leadoff hitter and starting right fielder, he and Pat moved with their two children, four-year-old Barry and three-year-old Ricky, from Riverside to the outskirts of San Francisco. The change was heartbreaking for a family that had been an integral part of the Riverside fabric, and equally hard for those in Riverside who had helped nurture Bobby from a baby to a budding star. A hero was moving on.

The Bonds family settled on a quaint beige house on the corner of Barford and Lyndhurst avenues in the hills of San Carlos. Whereas Riverside was a multicultural conglomeration of accountants and plumbers, San Carlos—a part of the 40-mile stretch of land from San Francisco to San Jose known as The Peninsula—was elite. This was the home of doctors and lawyers, corporate executives and college presidents. In 1969, some 93 percent of San Carlos was Caucasian, with minorities scattered throughout the area, many of them members of the local sports teams: the Giants, the Oakland Athletics, the San Francisco 49ers, the Oakland Raiders, and the San Francisco Warriors.

What Bobby and Pat liked about San Carlos—besides the stunning mountain landscape outside their back window—was what it seemed to share with Riverside: an innocence perfectly suited to raising children. Just down the street from the family's new abode was a local hangout nicknamed "The Rocks"—a sizable vacant lot dotted with a dozen boulders. This overlooked Arguello Park, home to a baseball field and a 4H farm. Several of Bobby's teammates, including pitcher Gaylord Perry and infielder Jim Davenport, lived nearby, adding to the homey feel.

"It was a town where you'd ride your bike everywhere and never feel unsafe," says Ron Galatolo, a San Carlos native who played Little League ball against Barry. "As little kids, we'd say, 'Let's go see Jimmy Davenport! We'd ride up the street, knock on his door, and he'd say, 'C'mon in, guys.' He'd show us his Gold Glove, a few bats, and give us Cokes to drink. I can't picture a better place for a kid to be."

If Pat and Bobby were concerned about their children losing their racial identity, it didn't show. In Bobby's seven seasons in San Francisco, during which time he became a two-time All-Star and one of the game's most feared hitters, Barry mixed in with the white kids of San Carlos. He was Troop 53's only black Cub Scout. He delivered newspapers to one white neighbor after another (Pat drove Barry house to house in the family station wagon). His romantic interests were mostly white girls with blond hair. His favorite baseball player (alongside Mays) was Mickey Mantle. His best friend was an Irish-Italian kid named Bobby McKercher, whose mother, Carol, stuffed Barry with pasta and sweets before sending him home.

Shortly after the move, Barry entered kindergarten at Arundel Elementary School, where he was one of three black students. Teachers were immediately struck by the youngster's athleticism and his competitiveness. This was not a child who played kickball in the spirit of good fun. "In the classroom, he was very reserved and smiled all the time," says Martha White, Barry's first-grade teacher. "But on the playground he was so good that he would sometimes take advantage of the other kids." If a classmate kicked into an easy out, Barry sternly lectured him on proper kickball procedure. Occasionally, this would result in a fight. "We ended up coming up with a good idea," says White. "We'd place Barry in charge of the games, instead of as a participant. That way he felt important, and other kids could coexist peacefully."

"I don't think Barry was a bad kid," adds Betty Kendall, his fourth-grade teacher. "But some of the kids were afraid of him. He was just so active on the playground, and so physically strong. I didn't think of him as a bully, but I know some students and teachers did. It's just that whatever he was playing—Four Squares or dodgeball—he played to win."

The derivation of Barry's competitiveness was no mystery. During the off season Bobby occasionally picked his son up from Arundel. Before leaving the classroom, he would command Barry to put on a performance. "His dad would say, 'Son, show how you do push-ups!'" says Colleen Dyer, Barry's second-grade teacher. "And in front of me, Barry would get down and do 50. Most of the other kids couldn't do one." With Bobby's own father lost in a drunken haze, he often resorted to crude parenting techniques. His sons were show dogs, and they'd better learn how to compete and obey. If Barry received a B+ on a book report, Pat would greet the news with a hug and a smooch on the cheek. Bobby, if he even heard the news, would shrug and crack, "Boy, a B+ ain't an A."

As a result, Barry became a card-carrying mama's boy. "I would rather watch my mom put on her makeup," Barry once said, than spend time with his dad. "Or I would put on a wig and dance with her." It was Pat who regularly took Barry to school and attended parent-teacher conferences, and it was even Pat who took in almost all of Barry's baseball games. A myth that has gathered steam over the years is that Bobby attended most of Barry's Little League events, too, hiding behind a tree or sitting in the family car, so as not to siphon attention away from his son. On the rare occasions he showed up, Bobby did remain concealed. But this was not to allow Barry the spotlight. It was so that Bobby could drink in peace.

As Barry completed the fourth grade at Arundel, the school district put the finishing touches on a busing program to balance out the ratio of white to minority students at nearby Sequoia High, which was greater than 100-to-1. Although the busing would not affect Barry for another five years, panic overtook San Carlos. Swarms of parents removed their children from the public school system, turning to the numerous private Catholic academies located throughout the surrounding towns. While San Carlos's mostly liberal denizens wore their NO NIXON and NOW pins with pride, allowing unruly kids from East Palo Alto to infiltrate the pristine classrooms of Sequoia was, for many of them, intolerable.

Though their motivation is unclear, it was at this point—in the fall of 1974—that Pat and Bobby transferred Barry from Arundel to a private institute in neighboring San Mateo: the Carey School, which had been founded in 1928 by a husband and wife, James and Mary Kehoe Carey. When Barry arrived, Carey's emphasis was on intimate classrooms—enrollment was kept between 150 and 300 students—and hands-on learning. Although the school taught sports, Carey was primarily a place to educate. Which is why Barry, a substandard student at Arundel, was not initially accepted.

"We felt Barry was below grade level, and so we tested him," says Clare

Carey Willard, the founders' daughter, who, with her sister Mary Therese, served as the school's coheadmaster. "It turns out he was well below grade level, and that it probably wouldn't work out." Before Barry was turned away, a conversation took place that the 78-year-old Willard still remembers. As she was about to make a final decree on Barry, she called a principal at Arundel for a second opinion. "Barry's not that bright," the principal said, "but you know how *those people* are." That sealed it. "What a horrible thing to say," says Willard. "It turns out there he was a very smart boy—a B student at our school. It's just that everyone was so convinced he was an excellent athlete, nobody ever showed an interest in his academics."

On his first day at Carey, Barry chose a desk in Mrs. Swanson's fifth-grade class, sat down, and scribbled his name atop of a piece of paper. Sitting at the neighboring desk was Clarke Nelson, who peeked at the signature and excitedly yelped, "I bet you're Bobby Bonds's kid!" Though he was but 10 years old, Barry had already begun to resent the you're-Bobby-Bonds's-kid! theme to his life. "Yeah." He responded. "So what?"

"Hey, that's cool," said Nelson. "I love baseball. And your dad's great." Later that day the two played a spirited game of Ping-Pong, won by Nelson. "For the next few weeks Barry practiced nonstop," says Nelson. "I never beat him at anything again."

Though the school wasn't especially diverse—there were three blacks, two Jews, and one child, a boy named Edward Huang, who was 80 percent deaf—Carey was a good place for Barry in that it offered lessons in open-mindedness. To stress the values of diversity, Willard and her sister hired a dwarf as the school's physical education teacher.

As a man who topped out at 4 feet, 6 inches, Dennis Calonico knew there would be problems earning the respect of your average 12-year-old. On Calonico's first day at Carey, a group of students was playing handball against an outdoor wall when they spotted their new PE teacher and laughed aloud. Calonico challenged them to a game. The laughing didn't last long. "Kicked all their butts," he says with a proud chuckle. Barry was among those on the receiving end of the slaughter, and though he wasn't above mocking his teacher, he became one of Calonico's favorites. "People say Barry is cocky now, and he could be back then, too," Calonico says.

"And sometimes his cockiness affected the people around him; made them feel a little uncomfortable. But for the most part he was a nice kid. A really nice kid."

As Barry progressed through Carey, developing into the school's top athlete, Bobby's life was freefalling in an opposite direction.

On the Giants, Bobby's devotion to beer was relatively unnoticed. Back in the 1970s, baseball and drinking went together like the hit and run. You arrived, you played, you won or lost, you returned to the clubhouse, you got sauced. "It was seen as a badge of honor to get drunk at night, then come back the next day and perform at a high level," says Sam McDowell, Bobby's former Giants teammate and, 32 years later, a recovering alcoholic. "Back then it was truly considered normal and natural that as soon as the game ended, you drank two, three beers. Then we'd all hurry out to the bar and have another two, three, four drinks. Most of us were having eight or nine drinks per night."

Like his coworkers, Bobby drank to excess, but unlike many of them, he was unable to measure himself. Though undiagnosed at the time, he had an allergy to alcohol that caused him to become intoxicated after one or two beers. "It never took a lot to get him drunk," says Dusty Baker. "And that's how you figured something was off." In his seven years with the Giants, Bobby was one of the National League's most potent offensive weapons. He posted two 30-home run, 30-stolen base seasons, drove in 102 runs as a leadoff hitter in 1971, and five times ranked in the top 10 in at-bats, a total that spoke to his durability. Yet Bobby was an off-the-field headache, and the front office grew tired of wondering whether their star would wind up in the newspaper for hitting a home run with his bat or for hitting a tree with his car. Twice in 1973 he was involved in traffic incidents, one a highly publicized drunk driving arrest that resulted in jail time and a $360 fine. Shortly thereafter he pleaded to *Sports Illustrated*'s Ron Fimrite, "I'm no troublemaker. I'm no drunk."

On February 16, 1973, after nearly 10 years of marriage, Pat filed for divorce, an action that later was withdrawn. According to friends, Pat had tired of Bobby's drinking. There were also rumors of on-the-road affairs with this groupie in Philadelphia, or that one in Atlanta, as well as drunkenness at home. It's fair to surmise that, by this point, Bobby's mounting drinking and marital problems had a dramatic influence on Barry—the boy more than the ballplayer. "If you want to delve into Barry's childhood and how it impacted him," says a close associate of both Barry and Bobby, "imagine having to drag your dad off your mom after he came home from downing a few too many. That'll change your outlook on things."

As has been written repeatedly, Barry spent a good amount of time at Candlestick Park alongside his father. What's less well known is that Barry often went to Candlestick grudgingly, urged by his mother to enjoy the afternoon with Bobby. Though Barry was happy to roam the stands during the game, wolfing down popcorn and cheering for the team under Pat's watchful eye, he was more than just embarrassed by Bobby—he viewed him as a bad father and a miserable role model. "I resented him," Barry would later say. "Not that he was abusive [to me]. I can't say that. I can say he whupped my butt plenty of times, and sometimes I didn't feel I deserved it. Most of the time he would give you the benefit of the doubt, but sometimes he'd hit you with his hand. Smack your leg.

"We always bitched that we never got to see him. But when he wanted to do something, I'd be whining, 'Mom, I'm not going.'"

Then, on October 22, 1974, Bobby was traded to the New York Yankees for Bobby Murcer. It was baseball's first one-for-one swap of $100,000 ballplayers, and it involved one man who had been labeled "the next Willie Mays" and another, "the next Mickey Mantle." By the time the deal was finalized, Bonds's reputation in San Francisco had been battered. He was not only widely known as a drunk, he was falsely rumored to be a recreational drug user. "The Giants were certain his career would end prematurely because of the drinking," says Glenn Dickey, a *Chronicle* sportswriter since 1963. "So they wanted him gone." Bobby expressed happiness at leaving San Francisco, but Barry's first experience as the son of a traded ballplayer proved traumatizing. At least when Bobby played for the Giants, he was home enough to chaperone an occasional class trip; attend a Little League game here or there. Now he'd be living in New York, available only via telephone.

Ironically, the trade meant that the two Bonds ballplayers would share something in common. Bobby played for the New York Yankees, Barry for Lloyd Skjerdal's Lions Club Yankees. A 10-year-old among mostly older boys, Barry enjoyed a brilliant first season of Little League, batting .430 and leading his team in several categories. He also proved himself to be—in the words of Dan Skjerdal, Lloyd's son and the team's star pitcher—"a cocky little fucker."

"No one ever really liked him," says Dave Pellegrini, also a Yankees teammate. "He was arrogant and self-centered. Barry would catch the ball in the outfield and then do a flip, and it'd really piss people off." Like his athleticism, his confidence was a hand-me-down from Dad. Bobby learned from Mays that to be a superstar, one must carry himself like a superstar. That meant being occasionally difficult with the press. It meant making the clubhouse attendant fetch him a cup of coffee, even when the percolator was within arm's reach. It meant seeking out the rival team's star during BP, just for the photo op. It meant carrying himself with an air of distance and danger. Barry watched and adopted Bobby's swagger at a young age.

Not that the attitude always translated to performance on the field. Well before Barry earned a reputation as a playoff choker for his three appearances with the Pittsburgh Pirates in the National League Championship Series, he acquired a similar tag in San Carlos. Much like Bobby's 1975 New York Yankees, who finished third in the American League East with 83 wins, the Lions Club Yankees were a strong club. They won the city title with a 20–1 record and advanced to the finals of the district championship, where they met a less talented squad from neighboring Half Moon Bay. In a game played at San Carlos and televised locally on KQED-Channel 9, the Yankees and Half Moon Bay took a 1–1 tie into extra innings. When Lloyd Skjerdal ran out of eligible pitchers he summoned Barry, who had spent the game in center field and rarely pitched. The first batter hit an easy grounder to Barry, who threw the ball past the first baseman and into right field. The base runner was rounding second and headed for third when Barry received the throw from the right fielder. He turned, spun, and whipped the ball over the third baseman's head. "He faced one batter," recalls Tim Pellegrini, Dave's brother and also a teammate. "He made two errors. We lost. End of story."

Following the game, a dejected Barry walked toward his mother's car, tears streaming down his cheeks. Bobby was nowhere to be found.

Leader is a word rarely used to describe Barry Bonds. Not in high school. Not in college. Certainly not with the Pirates and Giants. Yet during Barry's eighth-grade year at Carey, that's what Dennis Calonico found his star athlete to be. On the Carey basketball team, he played point guard, delivering the ball to Clarke Nelson, Calonico's best shooter, without hesitation. "He was Magic Johnson," recalls Nelson. "And I was Doug Collins." In baseball, he was a gritty catcher (yes, catcher) who blocked balls with his bare hand to save runs. "All the other players would unanimously agree he was our MVP," Calonico says. "He had the respect of all his peers." Even as he performed in the school operetta, a compulsory annual ritual at the June commencement, Barry stepped up and sang with all his out-of-key might.

On graduation day, Barry presented Nelson with a baseball autographed and thumbprinted by his father. It was a gesture of friendship. At Carey, Barry was just another kid. Athletic, sure. Black, sure. But one who enjoyed singing and art, and who received much greater commendation for acing a math test than shooting a basket.

Although this was fine for Pat, who would've been thrilled had Barry grown up to be happily anonymous, Bobby wanted his oldest son to take sports to the next level. In his final two seasons with the Lions Club Yankees, Barry batted above .400 and hit balls to the far reaches of Arguello Park. Bobby was especially thrilled by the report of a game the Yankees played against the Royals, when Barry bet a teammate $1 that he could hit the opposing pitcher in the leg with a ball. In his first at-bat, Barry swung and nailed a kid named Ron Jackson on the hip. *A B+ in history? Who cares, kid. A black-and-blue welt on Ron Jackson's hip? That's my boy!*

Down the road from San Carlos, in the town of San Mateo, there was a high school perfectly suited to Bobby's philosophy. In the fall of 1978, Barry enrolled in Junipero Serra High—the jock school to end all jock schools.

THREE

SERRA

FOR NORTHERN CALIFORNIA PARENTS who saw their sons as the next Willie
Mays or Cliff Branch or Rick Barry, there were few places like Junipero
Serra High, a private, all-boys school in San Carlos. Located just a few miles
down El Camino Real from the Bonds residence, Serra was to athletes what
Cal Tech is to theoretical physicists. Featuring top-of-the-line facilities and
a coaching staff dedicated to victory at any cost, the school was steeped in
the unofficial belief that success in sports was as noteworthy as success in
the classroom. Maybe even more so.

When Barry arrived, Serra's most famous alum was Pittsburgh Steelers
receiver Lynn Swann, who graduated in 1970 and went on to a Hall of Fame
career. Serra produced two other NFL players, Chargers quarterback Jesse
Freitas and Seahawks running back Jim Walsh, and four major leaguers, including Jim Fregosi, an All-Star shortstop for the Angels. (Today, along with
Bonds, the best-known Serra athlete is Patriots quarterback Tom Brady, a
1995 graduate and two-time Super Bowl MVP). In the Bay Area, it was well
known that if your kid had the makings of an athlete, Serra was the place to
be. And if he wasn't that bright, well, they'd find a way to make it work.

One day early in his freshman year, Barry turned to classmate Chris
Conway during a history lesson and casually proclaimed, "Ya know, I'm

gonna be a superstar." This was no exaggeration. Barry started as a small forward on the freshman basketball team that winter—a quick slasher with decent court vision, a mediocre outside shot, and no right hand to speak of. But the athleticism was otherworldly. Whereas many of his peers struggled to touch rim, Barry dunked and swatted shots off the backboard. He was unlike anyone Serra had seen in years. And this was his *second* best sport.

That spring, Tim Walsh, Serra's freshman baseball coach, was eagerly awaiting the new outfielder with the notable last name. It took only 10 minutes of team tryouts to see that this would be his starting center fielder. Barry was the fastest, quickest, strongest, most instinctive, most confident schoolboy athlete Walsh had ever seen. "In hindsight, he should have been playing varsity as a freshman," says Walsh. "We won a lot of games 19–2 and 21–1, and I'd be taking him out in the fourth inning to keep us from embarrassing the other teams. What I recall about Barry is that he wanted to be great. A lot of kids just wanted to play. That wasn't enough for him."

In his first home game, played at nearby Central Park, Barry hit a home run so far and high that it was met with a moment of awed silence from the crowd. A few weeks later, he hit another blast—this one even longer. He led the team in home runs, but what Walsh remembers most is that the shots often came late in close games. "I never saw him sweat," says Walsh. "Never saw him get nervous." Reports of Barry's heroics made their way from student to student. He was 14 years old and already leaving a mark.

Along with the talent, what made Barry stand out was attitude. It wasn't enough for his teammates to know he was special. He had to *show* them. If Serra's 19 other freshmen ballplayers wore Converse cleats, he wore Brooks. If the other players sported three-quarter-length sleeves on chilly days, he wore long sleeves. Most players were taught to sprint on and off the field between innings. Barry walked leisurely. He was the lone Serra ballplayer to wear double wristbands; to have someone bring him his glove to the outfield. On practice days, Barry was never shy about breaking out one of his father's old major league jerseys. The other players wore T-shirts.

Behind the bravado, however, Barry suffered pangs of loneliness and isolation. Founded in 1944 to provide for the Catholic educational needs of the boys of San Mateo County, Serra initially had a student body comprising 86 freshmen and sophomores, none of whom was black. It was a place, according to the Serra mission statement, where "mature Christians" could be developed to "live lives of faith and service and . . . find Christ in and bring Christ to the people with whom they live, work and serve."

By the time Barry arrived in the fall of 1978, Serra remained all-male and as white as new snow. In a class of 229 students, three blacks—Barry, Terrence Hall, and Arthur Jarrett—walked the long gray halls. Although Serra prided itself on inclusiveness and open-mindedness, such talk went only so far. In 1981, a history teacher named Peter Gort helped Serra's minuscule African-American population organize a black student union. When the proposal was brought before the administration, it was dismissed as too controversial.

To be one of a handful of blacks in an otherwise all-white school is to fill a perverse societal need. Especially in the late 1970s and early 1980s, the token black student was—of course—the great athlete and dancer. He made you feel cool, because—of course—blacks were cool and hip and down with the latest trends. When Serra teachers had a question about mathematical equations or the American Revolution, they turned to Walter Bankovicth or Chris Ruetz. When the 49ers were battling the Jets, there was no one better to talk football with than Barry Bonds.

"As the only black student, or one of a small number, you're the person they'll find when everyone needs their fix of black culture," says Howard Bryant of the *Washington Post*. The author of *Shut Out: A Story of Race and Baseball in Boston*, Bryant grew up on Cape Cod, the lone black in Plymouth-Carver High's class of '86. "The white people who are going to be your friends make it seem like they're doing you this great favor by treating you like a human being," Bryant says. "Like, 'Boy, see how cool I am? I can actually treat you like everybody else.'

"That wears on you after a while. And when you're around a crowd of black people they're mad because they think you're trying to assimilate outside the black community. You're never part of any society. Now add being the son of a baseball player and add having more talent than anyone around you—that has to create a very different personality."

At Serra in the late 1970s and early 1980s, words like *nigger* and *coon* were dispensed with alarming regularity. Behind his back, Barry was called "Black Barry" or "Black Barry Pie" in the same way Swann had been targeted a decade earlier. To their faces, Barry and Swann were "man" and "big guy." Epithets that were normally off limits were used in an "only kidding" context. From the precarious position of the outsider, the African-American student is supposed to laugh off being called a nigger, the Mexican being called a spic. "I was the only black kid at parties," Barry recalled. "Always. It was hard. Friends are laughing at different comedies, and I'm offended. I held it in and tried to be bigger and stronger."

Barry found Serra to be a mostly good place. A safe place. But even at a school known for athletics, Barry was *The Jock*—as long as he excelled in sports, teachers gave him a free pass. Barry wants to roll his shirtsleeves up on a hot day? Fine. Barry's talking during a lesson? OK. "If you were running late for class, you got yelled at," says Scott Kockos, a Serra classmate, "But not Barry. I remember the looks on the faces of teachers when Barry did something wrong. They knew there was no point going to the dean, because nothing was going to happen. He could get away with anything."

Barry largely kept to himself at Serra, remaining cocooned in a group of four friends from San Carlos who accompanied him to the school. This provided Barry with a layer of comfort, but it also initiated his lifelong reputation for being a self-centered prima donna. On the first day of classes in the fall of 1978, Barry found himself sitting next to a fellow freshman named Ray McDonald, who had been an excellent middle school ballplayer at All Souls. After introducing himself, McDonald asked Barry if he played baseball. "Yeah," said Barry. "What position are you?"

When McDonald responded with "shortstop," Barry didn't mince words. "Well, not here you don't. That's my friend Bob McKercher's position, and he's better than you."

"I liked Barry immediately after that," says McDonald, who played two years of varsity baseball—as a first and third baseman. "He was cocky, and I was cocky. He believed in himself, and so did I. He had an interesting reputation at the school—liked, disliked, envied, emulated. He was a lot of things."

Not a student. Beginning his freshman year, Barry spent little time paying attention in class, and even less time studying. Serra was a long way from the Carey School. Here, it wasn't about making the honor roll, but about scoring high enough to stay athletically eligible. As a result, when presented with the opportunity Barry enrolled in the easiest courses. "He was a mediocre student," says Randy Vogel, the school's director of admissions, "with average abilities." Long before he was accused of cheating baseball with steroids, Barry cheated at Serra, looking over the shoulders of smarter classmates during tests and copying the notes he failed to take. Some got mad. Others were excited to be used by the star athlete. Russ Bertetta, a former Serra English teacher, recalls catching Barry taking a vocabulary quiz with the answers scribbled on his hand. The incident was laughed off, and Barry went unpunished. "He was one of those guys who'd always come a little late, and he'd tap me on the shoulder, reach over, and grab my paper," says Kockus. "I take part credit for getting him through high school. I'm not saying Barry wasn't smart, but he had a priority. He was practicing until 8 P.M., and there was no time for homework. I think the school understood. If there was cheating with Barry Bonds, they'd look the other way."

Michael Peterson, Serra's principal from 1978 to 2003, denies that Barry had it easy. "You have to qualify academically to get into Serra," he notes, "and you're not going to get out of here unless you perform." Even so, in April of Barry's junior year, an editorial appeared in the student newspaper, the *Serra Friar*, criticizing the administration for hiring teachers and coaches focused more on sports than studies. John Dilts, author of the piece, was called into Peterson's office and reprimanded. "When the wrestling coach whose motivation in life is wrestling winds up teaching English, it makes you wonder what the priority of things is," says Dilts. "That was the Serra way."

As his son was adjusting to Serra, Bobby Bonds was going through a metamorphosis of his own. No longer the star-in-the-making whiz kid with a limitless future, Bobby was now a 32-year-old journeyman, sent by the Yankees to the Angels at the end of the 1975 season, then traded again on December 5, 1977, from California to the Chicago White Sox. He still ran well, still hit, still made the thrilling play in the outfield. But with Bobby

Bonds came baggage, and most everyone in baseball knew it.

By the late 1970s, Bobby struggled to conceal his drinking problem. He would arrive late for games, oftentimes hung over or still intoxicated. His hands shook and his attention wavered. While playing right field for Texas on July 18, 1978 (he had been unloaded by the White Sox in May), Bobby was yanked after stumbling around the outfield. "In my entire career," says Jim Sundberg, the Rangers catcher, "that was the only time I ever smelled alcohol on a teammate's breath around the batting cage in the morning." On the team flight that night, Bobby took a swing at manager Billy Hunter. "Bobby was wrong," says Sundberg, "and we all knew it."

Although the media reported on his alcohol-related automobile accidents only twice—one incident in 1973 and another in 1975—throughout the late 1970s Bobby was repeatedly pulled over for erratic driving. Sometimes the officer would let Bobby go in exchange for an autograph. Other times Bobby's agent, Rod Wright, would find a way to get his client off and keep it out of the news. "Bobby was a good man with a bad issue," says Wright. "At one point I finally said to him, 'This is your career and your life on the line. I don't want to see you going to jail. I don't want to see you die.'"

Instead of acknowledging that his problems were alcohol-related, Bobby convinced himself his career would be better if only he were white. Years later, this logic would be embraced by his son, when Barry blamed the steroid-related controversy on race. But unlike Barry, Bobby was partly correct. Because he was a black man willing to speak his mind, Bobby's rough edges and quick tongue gave him a bad reputation. "When you didn't take shit from nobody and didn't give a fuck who they were, they classified you as militant," says Dock Ellis, Bobby's longtime friend and former teammate with Texas. "It was like, 'You're a black ballplayer and you should just be glad you're here.' You know what Bobby and I said to that? 'Fuck you.'

"Bobby was an angry dude," continues Ellis. "He resented being traded by the Giants, and that resentment grew in him. Festered. The shit me and Bobby would say and do, white players wanted to say and do the same thing. But they weren't gonna do it. That didn't help our reputations, but we didn't care. We were honest black men at a time when you were just supposed to keep your mouth shut."

Barry maintained an emotional distance from Bobby. Like most high schoolers, he feared his father might embarrass him. The concern was understandable. In a late-season freshman baseball game between Serra and St. Ignatius, Barry and his teammates were taking the field when an inebriated Bobby arrived at Central Park. For the first hour or so, he stood to the side, barking slurred insults at the umpire. In the fifth inning, he sat down on the bench next to one of the coaches, alcohol oozing from his breath. Barry's teammates kept trying to act as if nothing strange was transpiring. But everyone knew.

The great Bobby Bonds was wasted again.

In the fall of 1979, Barry Bonds allowed his friends to coerce him into playing for Serra's junior varsity football team. This was not something the boy had dreamed of. Barry possessed many fine athletic qualities, but toughness was not one of them. The last time he had played competitive tackle football had been during an eighth-grade field trip to Blackberry Farm in Cupertino, California, when a bunch of boys from the St. Pius School challenged the Carey School kids to a game. Not much is remembered from the battle, except that Barry talked a lot of trash, then received the opening kickoff and was drilled into the ground by a kid named Kevin O'Brien. He did not get up for 10 minutes.

"I had never played anything but mud football," Bonds recalled years later. "The first time I was given pants and pads, I put on the pants and thought that you taped the pads on the outside of the pants. And I had no idea what to do with the shoulder pads."

After a stellar freshman baseball run Barry was bursting with confidence. A week before the gridiron season opener, a couple of varsity players pulled a prank by hiding his helmet in an empty locker. Most members of the JV squad would have fallen victim to the gag, awkwardly searching here and there as everyone in the room laughed it up. Not Barry. Without batting an eye, he turned to Kevin Griffin, a seldom-used varsity reserve, and snapped "Gimme your helmet. The team doesn't need you anyway."

Barry's first season of football was a resounding success. At the same time the Serra varsity team posted an unspectacular 5–4 mark, the JV lost only one game en route to the West Catholic Athletic League title. Quarterback Rob Leary, one of Barry's pals from San Carlos, used his favorite target often. Barry was a wiry 6-foot-1, and he could out-jump most defensive backs. "I was not a good QB," says Leary, "so my favorite pass pattern was the fade, where I took a three-step drop and threw it high. Barry could have been an outstanding college receiver, maybe even in the NFL." Leary laughs. "But I don't think he'd ever survive the contact."

Barry went on to play one more year of football, starting as a junior on a varsity team that finished 2–7. It was a miserable season, hitting its nadir in a Saturday afternoon game against Bellarmine in which the opposing team's fans chanted, *"Five-oh-two! Five-oh-two! Five-oh-two!"* The number was the police code for "driving while intoxicated"—a mockery of Bobby Bonds that pierced Barry's heart. "People sometimes forgot," says Gort, "that he was just a kid."

If Barry was considering returning for his senior season, the idea was squashed in a game against Sacred Heart, when he crossed the middle of the field to catch a fluttering Leary pass and was crunched by a pair of linebackers. "Big guys," recalls Bertetta. "One nailed him high, one nailed him low. Barry was lying there on the field, and the Sacred Heart sideline was going crazy. He was a wanted man."

As Barry grew entrenched at Serra, his ego went unchecked. This was best personified by Barry's prep basketball career. In the winter of 1979–80, Barry's JV basketball coach was Peter Gort, the popular history teacher who tried organizing the black student union. Gort was thrilled at the prospect of having Serra's top athlete as his starting small forward, but that changed as soon as practice began. Barry was disrespectful and sleeping-dog lazy. Everyone on the team knew basketball was Barry's excuse to hang with his friends. Frustrated, Gort nearly cut Barry in favor of Rick Bruno, a dive-for-every-ball type with scraped knees and minimal talent. When Gort lost his nerve and Bruno wound up not making the squad, Bruno's parents complained that their son was beaten out by a kid with no heart. "I had this idea that everybody should give 100 percent," says Gort, whose team finished 20–5 with Bonds as its second-leading scorer. "Barry rarely did, and it frustrated me. I was never able to communicate to him the idea of competing against yourself."

To Gort, Barry seemed eager to jump on any opportunity to humiliate a coach or teammate. At the end of the season, when it was customary for Serra athletes to purchase their head coach a gift, Barry stood up in a team meeting and said, "Why should we get Gort anything? What did he do for us?" The following year, when he was an assistant coach with the varsity team, Gort gave a pair of players, Barry and Jeff Prothro, a ride back from a game. Along Highway 280, the engine in Gort's 1964 Volkswagen Beetle froze, and the three had to push the vehicle. As Gort and Prothro pushed, Barry stayed to the side, laughing hysterically. "Gort," he said, "your car is a total piece of shit!"

"Maybe," countered the teacher, "but at least I have a car."

"Yeah, I've got a car, too," said Barry. "Except it's not like yours." It was a new purple Dodge B200 van—fully customized and paid for by his parents.

"That," says Gort, "was typical Barry."

Barry was able to get away with anything, and he knew it. He could call his coach's Volkswagen a piece of shit. He could loaf through practices and games, as he did for one year of JV basketball and two more of varsity. He could cheat. He could lie. He could even commit a felony on school property—sans retribution.

The incident came near the beginning of Barry's senior year, and it involved a fellow basketball played named Greg Parry, a 5-foot-9, 130-pound guard who fulfilled the mandatory Everytown High School casting call for unlikable wise-ass. Parry was the back-of-the-classroom kid who had a smart-aleck remark for everything. As a senior Parry ran unopposed to become the school's rally commissioner (job description: boost school spirit)—and lost, failing to garner the required 50 percent support. "He was an asshole," recalls Kockus. "Almost everyone hated him."

But Parry was more insecure than evil, and his slurs and insults served mostly as a shield against those who made fun of his snazzy clothes and froufrou haircut. Parry was a good-looking kid who'd done some modeling; that, too, serving as a great source of ridicule. But Parry did not cower in the face of taunts. He taunted right back—harder and fiercer than the others.

After religion class one day, Kockus asked Bonds if—in exchange for continued help with his studies—he would shut up that damn Parry kid. In a game of one-on-one following practice, Parry was being Parry, taking shots at Barry, telling him he was overrated and soft and nothing more than a squeaky-voiced punk. On his left arm he wore a cast from a recent accident, and he was shoving it at Barry's body, blocking his path to the hoop. Twice, Barry urged Parry to cut it out. Twice, Parry ignored him. *Jab. Poke. Jab. Poke. Jab. Poke. Jab. Poke. Jab. Poke. Jab.*

POP!

Barry clenched his left fist, spun, and unloaded a punch that walloped into Parry's mouth and sent him sprawling. With blood dripping onto the court, teammates gathered around, not one reaching down to help. "I don't think anyone was offended," says David Petroff, a classmate. "It was more like, 'Nice shot, dude. And good riddance.'" Parry was no more popular with his teachers, many of whom quietly celebrated as he was rushed to Mills Hospital in San Mateo with a shattered jaw. For the next four weeks Parry suffered the humiliation of having his jaw wired shut. His face black and blue, he took his meals through a straw. Bonds, meanwhile, went unpunished. On page 40 of Serra's student-parent handbook, it says one will be suspended for "serious violations including fighting." Was this not serious?

"If Barry were not a star athlete and he'd hit me like that, he'd have been kicked out of school," says Parry. "There's no doubt. Instead the administration did nothing to discipline him. The only thing they did was *say* he was on probation." Parry took action. He filed an assault charge against Barry, one Parry says was triggered by his outraged father. The case was settled out of court, with Parry receiving a couple of thousand dollars. Amazingly, Rod Wright, Bobby's attorney, was able to manipulate the family's homeowner's insurance into footing the bill. Bobby and Pat never forced their son to apologize to Parry, and he never did. It was yet another important lesson in Barry's life: Do right and you'll be celebrated; do wrong and you'll be covered.

•••● ●

Were he just an ordinary student who cheated and shattered jaws, Barry certainly would not have survived Serra's disciplinary code. But Barry was prized: He was the best baseball player the school had ever seen.

This was saying something. Since 1948, when a pitcher/infielder named Dan Miller signed with the Philadelphia Phillies, 21 Serra graduates had gone on to careers in professional baseball. But Barry was different. During the 1978–79 academic year, when Barry was playing on the freshman baseball team, Serra's varsity coach, Dave Stevens, would check in for updates. One day Walsh pulled Stevens aside with his mouth agape. "You're not gonna believe this," Walsh said, "but the Bonds kid launched a ball over El Camino." El Camino Real was the street that bordered Central Park, and to reach it entailed not just hitting the baseball more than 350 feet, but projecting it high enough to soar above a row of 25-foot pine trees. According to Serra lore, Bonds's shot cleared the right field wall, the pine trees, six lanes of traffic, and hit the third story of a building. Barry was a *freshman*. "I've heard it hit cars, I've heard windows, I've heard people," said Joe Kmak, a former Serra star. "It's just one of those great Paul Bunyan stories."

The next year Stevens promoted Barry to the varsity alongside McKercher, his best friend from San Carlos. Barry was euphoric. His happiest times at Serra—*in life*, he later maintained—came on the diamond, where he was playing the game he loved with the peers he trusted. Whereas in football and basketball he halfhearted his way through workouts, here Barry was relatively serious. He and his pals would stay late after practices and take fly balls or hit off the tee. "The perception was that he was cocky," says Stevens. "And maybe he was. But I remember the Barry who would work on the little things, like getting his lead off first just right, like making the break for second. He knew he was good, but he also knew he could get a lot better."

Barry played center field and batted leadoff for the 1980 Padres, who went 16–8–1 and won the West Catholic Athletic League (WCAL) championship. In the title game, a 3–2 victory over Sacred Heart of San Francisco, Bonds led off the bottom of the seventh inning of a 2–2 tie with a triple to center and moments later scored the winning run. His performance led to a glowing headline in the next day's *San Francisco Examiner*, HEREDITY AND

HEART EARN A TITLE FOR SERRA. Wrote Merv Harris:

> You don't have to know the name of Serra High's center fielder
> to become excited about his baseball future. He is only 15 years
> old, but he stands nearly 6-foot-2, he runs swiftly and with that
> easy grace all outstanding athletes own and, when he comes to
> bat, he utilizes a quick, level swing that seems to generate noth-
> ing but line drives.

Barry led the WCAL in homers as a sophomore, and was named second-
team all-league. After the season, Marty Pletkin, a senior pitcher and DH
for Serra, asked Barry if he had any thoughts on college. "I'm going to
Arizona State!" he exclaimed. Pletkin laughed. ASU was the best baseball
school in the country—home to Reggie Jackson, Floyd Bannister, and a
mass of others. "I thought, 'He's great, but he's gonna have to get a lot greater
to go there,'" says Pletkin. "That's exactly what he did."

If Barry's sophomore year was excellent, his junior season was so breathtaking that, by the end of 1981, it was debatable who was the best player in
the Bonds household. At the same time Barry was again leading the WCAL
in home runs, Bobby was in his final days as a major leaguer. His body
wracked by alcohol abuse and two packs of cigarettes per day, Bobby spent
much of '81 either searching for a job or slumming in the minor leagues
with the Triple A Wichita Aeros of the American Association. When he
was finally called up by the Chicago Cubs in June, the results were disastrous. He broke his finger fielding the first ball that came his way and batted
.215 in 45 games before being released. It was a pathetic showing, made
even more so by his insistence that his ever-declining reputation was un-
deserved. "It's easy to start a rumor, but where is the verification?" he told
Sports Illustrated. "I'd like to meet the individual who has ever seen me take
drugs. Yet a thousand people write that I do. I can't say I'm perfect. There
are days in everybody's life that shouldn't be remembered. But I ask you,
how could I have accomplished what I have if I'd done what people say I've
done? First of all, I'd be dead." Shortly after the publication of the *SI* article
Bobby was pulled over near San Carlos for erratic driving and arrested on

charges of DWI. At the time Barry was receiving a ride home from school with a friend. He saw his father's vehicle on the side of the road and said nary a word.

Barry spent a good deal of time in the offices of his coaches, unloading his mental baggage. With each incident involving his father, Barry's shell grew more impenetrable. He wouldn't talk publicly about Bobby; sometimes wouldn't even acknowledge he had a father. The worst moments came when Barry (whose large purple Dodge was nicknamed "The Love Van" by friends) was called to pick up his intoxicated father up and ferry him home. "That started before Barry even had his license," says one friend. "It was horrible for him. It ate him up." When someone would accidentally refer to Barry as "Bobby"—look out. The rage would creep across Barry's face, and he'd snap. "My name is Barry, not Bobby!"

To Barry's credit, Bobby's ongoing problems did not keep him from baseball dominance. In a junior year win against Sacred Heart, the opposing manager ordered his hurler to pitch Barry high and tight and leave nothing over the plate. On the first pitch, Barry hit an estimated 400-foot home run. "The coach ran out of the dugout to remove the pitcher," recalls Tim Walsh, "and Barry jogged around the bases shaking his head, as if to say 'How could you throw me *that*?'"

A few weeks later, however, his season nearly came to an end. While sprinting through the hallways after gym class, Barry caught his school ring on a metal locker and pulled one of the fingers out of the socket. He was taken to nearby Mills Hospital, and underwent three hours of surgery. "It just about ripped his finger off," says Dave McAdam, a Serra pitcher. "I visited him at the hospital, and I thought he was really in trouble. A short time later he was back on the field, and the only thing visible was a little hole on his finger. You knew there was something special about him if he could heal that fast and get back to playing that well."

Midway through Barry's junior year, scouts began attending Serra games en masse—seven or eight men in straw hats and collared shirts sitting in the stands, jotting notes and nodding appreciatively. On a warm Saturday afternoon in late March, they watched Barry slam two mountainous home runs in a 5–4 win over Sacred Heart. In May, he compiled four hits—two of them homers—and six RBIs against El Camino ace Andy Leonard, whose fastball reached the low 90s. The scouts who had come to clock Leonard's pitches found themselves turning their attention toward Barry. Even in a 7–3 loss to St. Francis in the WCAL title game, Barry doubled twice. "There was nothing he couldn't do," says Mark Gonzalez, who covered Serra for the *Peninsula Times-Tribune*. "He had a body like his dad, he could run like his dad, he could hit like his dad, he was lefthanded and he was confident. He's the best I ever saw at that level."

By his senior year, Barry no longer pretended to listen to his instructors, study for exams, or even arrive at practice on time. "Barry," says a high school teammate, "thought he treaded water." This was most evident on the field, where he would infuriate opposing coaches by refusing to slide while stealing a base or standing at the plate long enough to watch his home runs fly off. He was a trash talker in a sport where trash talk was uncommon, and during batting practice he enjoyed lounging on the outfield grass and taking a quick snooze. A vintage moment came in a playoff win against St. Francis. A few days earlier, it had been announced that St. Francis first base-man Mark Locatelli—not the more-deserving but less-respected Bonds—had been named the league MVP. As he rounded first base after hitting yet another homer, Bonds glared up at Locatelli and shouted, "There's your MVP, baby!"

This sort of behavior prompted one National League scout to scribble a single word under the heading "Attitude/Personality" on his report: "Ass-hole." The assessment was shared by many, outweighed only by one other word, listed below "Talent/Ability": "Awesome." Using his dented orange Tennessee Thumper bat, Barry hit .467, led Serra with 14 homers and 42 RBIs, and seemed to collect a clutch hit in every important game. His performances for the scouts were awe-inspiring. One clocked him at 9.5 seconds in the 100-yard dash. Another timed him from home to first in 3.94 seconds, which would have made him one of the fastest players in the major leagues. Before a game at St. Ignatius, a St. Louis Cardinals scout badgered Stevens into letting Barry try a wood bat, as opposed to the aluminum models used in the league. On the third pitch of his first at-bat, Barry hit a ball that landed 50 feet beyond the right-field fence. By the time the inning had ended, most of the 20 scouts in attendance were gone. It was all they needed to see.

Barry was a no-brain first-round pick. Even though he had committed to Arizona State after visiting the school with McKercher (whose father was a Pacific-10 basketball official), money and a high spot in the draft would have enticed him to turn pro immediately. There was just one problem. As the June amateur draft approached, Bobby began to play a larger role in his son's career, calling himself Barry's "advisor" and talking up his own negotiating prowess. "In my 14 years," he said at the time, "I've always negotiated my own contract." Though not entirely true (Bobby's agent, Rod Wright, handled his contract negotiations beginning in 1977), the talk spooked a number of major league clubs who could deal with an arrogant kid, but not an arrogant kid and his alcoholic, militant, pain-in-the-ass father. As a result, on June 7 the San Francisco Giants made Barry their *second*-round pick, following a power-hitting first baseman from the University of Nebraska named Steven Stanicek. The news was a blow to father and son, neither of whom believed Barry would slip so low.

As the Giants were debating how much to offer, another incident bruised Barry's reputation even further. During mid-June tryouts at UC Berkeley for the Northern California High School All-Star Team, Barry spent part of the afternoon asleep in the left-field bullpen. "There was no doubt he could play," says Mike Lafferty, coach of the team. "But he already had a bad image, and then this happened." At the ensuing coaches' meeting, Barry was not voted onto the roster (which included six future major leaguers, including a gawky left-handed pitcher named Randy Johnson), and the news spread throughout baseball that the Bonds kid was up to his old tricks again.

What few people knew at the time was that Barry had spent the previous night at the Palo Alto Hills Golf & Country Club, home to what is still considered the wildest senior prom in Serra history. "It was our first foray into the dinner-dance format," says Bertetta. "What's best representative of the night is our senior class president vomiting into his salad." Bonds and his San Carlos friends proceeded to a Holiday Inn in Burlingame, where they partied into the early morning. "If he had told us at the time that he was up all night at the dance, we would have understood and let him sleep," says Larry Quirico, the director of the All-Star Game. "But he said nothing, and we knew about his other problems. I think in this case Barry was a victim of his reputation."

The Giants offered Barry a take-it-or-leave-it $70,000, refusing to budge when Bobby demanded $5,000 more. Many in the organization felt they could do without another Bonds headache; some regretted drafting the kid in the first place. When Barry learned that his hometown team would not meet his needs, he shrugged his shoulders and moved on with the confidence of a kid certain his talent would take him far.

Forget the Giants. Barry Bonds was heading to Arizona State.

FOUR

ARIZONA STATE

THE HIGH SCHOOL GRADUATION gift was Bobby's idea.

Now at the end of his baseball career and hoping to make amends for his failings as a father, Bobby purchased his eldest son a fully loaded black Trans Am. Costing nearly $14,000 after taxes, it was an eye-catcher, with leather seats and gold stripes painted along the side. As much as Barry disdained his dad, he had to admit, the ride was sweet. "Bobby thought he was doing the right thing," says Dickie Jackson, Bobby's lifelong friend. "He felt like he had money to help his children, and he wanted to spend it."

The elder Bonds didn't understand the impact the car would have on the son of *the* Bobby Bonds. When so much of your life is spent in the cozy confines of a major league clubhouse, having your shoes shined and your coffee stirred, you lose perspective. Barry was about to enter a world where he was already prejudged, and the last thing he needed was a sleek new vehicle. "I yelled at Bobby," recalls Jackson, "'Who buys a new Trans Am for a freshman? Do you know what kind of pressure that'll put on him?' That boy was doomed."

As Jackson predicted, Barry rolled up to the ASU campus with a bull's eye on his back. "I was driving around in a Ford courier truck with more than 100,000 miles on it," says Kendall Carter, a junior starting pitcher in

1983. "And here's this guy." The instant Barry's new teammates saw the vanity license plate (BBSTA, for "Barry Bonds's Trans Am"), the designer jeans, and the $100 sneakers, they formed a decisively negative opinion.

The Sun Devils players could laugh at Barry's audacity because they knew what was in store for him. Though the Arizona State campus is framed by a mountainous terrain and breathtaking sunsets, it was anything but serene for baseball players. The program was the personal fief of head coach Jim Brock, whose three favorite training tools were pain, suffering, and humiliation—especially the last one. To humiliate a player was to tattoo into his soul the idea that *you should never, ever, ever make a mistake*. Though Brock died of cancer in 1994, ASU baseball alums rarely speak of him fondly. "I couldn't stand Brock," says Dave Graybill, a former ASU pitcher. "It was all about winning and nothing else. Not building character, not forming bonds, not having fun, not trying your best. It was you win, or you're a failure."

Born and raised in Phoenix, Brock stuttered so severely as a boy that he had difficulty saying his own name. His childhood was spent trying to meet the expectations of a father he once described as "spitting and snarling at the world." Although his teenage son was 5-foot-10 and built like a toothbrush, Bill Brock believed Jim was destined for the major leagues. He had a mound constructed in the family yard so that Jim could develop his arm, but the results were never good enough.

When it became clear the young Brock had no future as a player, he entered coaching. After 12 years of guiding American Legion teams, in 1966 he was named Mesa Community College's first-ever baseball coach. Brock attributed his achievements at Mesa—two national junior college championships and one runner-up finish in six seasons—to a ruthless coaching style. He didn't merely yell at players; he lashed out with sharp-tongued rants intended to denigrate. "If my team won, my job was just to stay out of the way," Brock wrote in his autobiography, *The Devil's Coach*. "If they lost, my job was to make it such a miserable experience they would never want to do that again." His tactics took a toll on his reputation. "Jim had no friends," says Jim Frye, an assistant coach to Brock at Mesa and ASU. "He kicked his players' asses and never thought a second about it."

Following the 1971 season, the Sun Devils needed to replace Bobby

Winkles, a coaching legend who had been offered a job managing the California Angels. Winkles enjoyed a startling run at ASU: a 524-173 record and three NCAA crowns. In accepting the position, Brock wasn't merely graduating to a Division I team; he was inheriting the New York Yankees of college ball.

It quickly became apparent that Brock was unaccustomed to the pressures of managing in front of 3,000 fans at Phoenix Municipal Stadium—each comparing him to his predecessor, one of the greatest minds in college baseball history. As a result, the Sun Devils coach turned sinister. Throughout the 1970s and early 1980s, Brock contrived a series of punishments, one more lethal than the next. Players were forced to run six miles in 95-degree heat—without water. Latecomers to practice were denied entrance with a Master Lock on the field's main gate. It made no difference if team drills conflicted with an important study session; players were expected to arrive on time or suffer the consequences. On repeated occasions Brock bad-mouthed his junior stars to professional scouts, hoping that a player's stock would fall enough to force him to return for another season in Tempe. Don Wakamatsu, an ASU catcher in the early 1980s, was the final pick of the 1984 June draft following an All-Pac-10 junior season. Why so low? Brock had spread false rumors among scouts that Wakamatsu was demanding a $100,000 signing bonus.

Brock took youthful cockiness and pounded it into the ground. His players were humble workhorses, no pizzazz allowed. If you fell short, there was no place for you at Arizona State. This was the person Barry Bonds was coming to play for, and the match seemed doomed to failure. "The one man I thought would never succumb to treating some players differently than others was Jim Brock," says George Lopez, an ASU third baseman from 1983 to 1985. "He was consistently mean."

But Brock didn't merely tolerate Barry—he embraced him, even before Bonds committed to his school. The coach had already fallen under the athlete's spell the previous year. While recruiting Barry, Brock violated NCAA rules by paying for an airplane ticket to Tempe for Barry's girlfriend, and by allowing Bobby and Pat to stay in his house for two days. Clearly, Barry could be arrogant and annoying, but his talent was magnificent. During one of his first batting practice sessions at Arizona State, he hit 15 consecutive balls over the left-center-field scoreboard. To a coach fixated on winning, that kind of skill proved irresistible.

According to the sacred tradition of the ASU baseball program, freshmen were uniformly treated as worthless beating boys. Barry would have none of it. On the first day of practice he parked his Trans Am in a spot at the activities center reserved for Brock. Though the coach quietly fumed, he said nothing. This was only the start. "All the freshmen had duties with the team," says Lew Kent, a catcher at ASU in 1983 and '84. "We had to pick up balls and make sure the equipment was put away. Not Barry." On road trips, freshmen were responsible for hauling bags from the team bus into the hotel lobby. "Barry never carried a single bag," says Wakamatsu. "Not one." Instead, he exited the bus with the upperclassmen, picked up his room key, and took a nap. Or had a snack. Barry was rarely shy about making such activities known to his fellow freshmen. "See y'all later," he'd say with a sly grin. "It was preferential treatment, plain and simple," says Kent. "And it pissed a lot of us off." When the team traveled to Omaha for the College World Series, freshmen Charles Scott, Greg Shirley, and Gilbert Villanueva lugged the team luggage for the final time. To celebrate, Scott went to Barry's room, placed him in a headlock, and began choking him, forcing his head under a sink. The two had to be separated.

To the extent Barry was unaware of how much he was despised, it was due to a lack of basic social skills. His conversations were awkward and revolved mostly around himself. A classic moment came in a game against UCLA, when Barry signaled for a time-out in the middle of an inning and sprinted from left field toward the dugout. Was Barry ill? Did he need aid? Brock sent a player into the clubhouse to find out. "Coach," he reported, "Barry's got a bad stomachache and he had to go to the bathroom." Ten minutes later Barry reemerged and returned to the game as Brock's face turned deep red. "Hey," Bonds told his coach, "it was either call time or shit in my pants."

"That," says Lopez, "sums up Barry perfectly." Years later, Brock told *Sports Illustrated*: "I never saw a teammate care about [Barry]. Part of it would be his being rude, inconsiderate and self-centered. He bragged about the money he turned down, and he popped off about his dad. I don't think he ever figured out what to do to get people to like him."

More revealing of Barry's poor social antennae than Brock's assessment, however, was a collegiate-era quote from the player himself. "I'm so proud the guys we have are so close," he said. "We're like a big family." With or without Barry, the ASU team wasn't built on camaraderie. The pitchers went one way, the hitters another. Whites stuck with whites and blacks stuck with blacks. If the players shared anything, it was the belief that Barry was a pampered baby.

College might have provided Barry a chance to mature into a man, if not for the influence of his dual role models—a mean, win-at-all-cost coach, and an intrusive, alcoholic dad who made sure his son was treated like royalty. Before Barry arrived in Tempe, Bobby explained to Brock that his son would not listen to Frye, the team's hitting coach. When it came to batting, it was Bobby's way, or nobody's way. "Barry showed up with a terrible attitude," says Frye. "I had no interest in changing things, because he had a beautiful swing. But he was a spoiled, arrogant kid. When people ask me about being Barry's hitting coach, I correct them immediately. I was the hitting coach at Arizona State when Barry was there. But I sure didn't coach *that guy*."

Beginning early Barry's freshman year, Bobby made several unannounced trips to Tempe, where he sat in the stands during practices. If Bobby didn't like what Brock was teaching, he would loudly berate the coach. Sometimes Bobby was sober, but more often than not he held a bottle (obscured by a paper bag) in his hand. It was embarrassing for Brock, and worse for Barry. "My dad would call me in college," Barry said, "and I'd just pray he didn't show up."

Why didn't Brock fight back? Two reasons. He was a classic bully, tough until somebody comes along and smacks him in the teeth. But mostly, he was blinded by Barry's potential. As the third freshman ever to start at Arizona State, Barry led the team with 11 home runs (a freshman record), 54 RBIs, and a .568 slugging percentage. He saved his most exceptional performance for the postseason. In an NCAA West II Regional game against Brigham Young University at Packard Stadium, the Sun Devils trailed by eight runs to a team featuring six future major leaguers. ASU clawed its way back, and late in the game Barry hammered a grand slam over Packard's Green Monster—a 30-foot wall located 5 feet beyond the stadium's center-field wall—to win 19–11 in 100-degree heat. "That was the biggest hit of our season," says Romy Cucjen, an ASU shortstop. "I can't remember ever seeing a ball go further, and it was in the absolute clutch. Barry just had that ability; he'd get hot exactly when we needed it."

The Sun Devils advanced to the College World Series against Oklahoma State, where Barry hit a home run that traveled more than 400 feet in a must-win 6–5 triumph. It was his fifth home run in six games. "The wind was blowing," says Chris Beasley, an ASU pitcher, "and he cleared the fence by a couple of football fields." Although Arizona State was eliminated two days later, leaving the Sun Devils with a third-place finish, Barry's performance had been nothing short of awesome.

Barry spent most of his summer in Tempe, living in the apartment of Mylie Davis, an old family friend from Riverside. This went against the wishes of Brock, who strongly encouraged his troops to hone their skills in a summer league. Barry eventually complied by joining the Fairbanks Goldpanners of the Alaska League for their final six games of the season—all at the National Baseball Congress tournament in Wichita, Kansas.

"I couldn't believe how much power such a little guy had," says Lindsay Meggs, a Goldpanners infielder. "He was a physically undeveloped guy who just crushed the ball." Barry's performance as an outfielder and first baseman was mediocre (he batted .222 with no homers and two RBIs), but memorable to teammates. Thirteen members of the '83 Goldpanners reached the major leagues, and four of them (Bonds, Oddibe McDowell, Shane Mack, and Mark Davis) bunked together in the same room. "Everyone called it the 'Gold Room' because we knew the guys in it would become stars," says Don Dennis, the Goldpanners general manager. "The hotel wasn't so nice, and I remember Barry saying to me, 'Man, it ain't the Gold Room. It's the 'Mold Room.'"

Brock looked forward to Bonds's sophomore season with mixed feelings. Though ASU's roster would be its most talented, Barry was a social leper. In the weeks before the start of 1983–84 academic year, Brock telephoned

George Lopez and strongly suggested that he room with Barry. This wasn't a coach trying to forge friendships, but a response to a dilemma: Nobody wanted to live with his star. There was good reason.

As a freshman, Barry boarded with first baseman Reggie Mosley in an apartment on Orange Street. In the neighboring pad lived another two players, pitcher Jose Rodiles and third baseman Bert Martinez, who hailed from the nearby town of Chandler. Every week Martinez's mother, Helen, would bring her son large bags filled with her homemade specialty, green chili. "One day I come back from class and the window to my apartment is cracked and there's a hole," says Martinez. He searched high and low but found nothing missing. He then opened the refrigerator. "My mom's food was gone," he says. "All of it." Martinez confronted Mosley, who ratted out Barry. "He knew my mom brought this food for me," he says, "and here he is, driving a new Trans Am, cracking *my* window."

Brock had been told of Bonds's crime and ignored it. Now he was encouraging Lopez to take Barry in. Was he insane? "I did it, but only because I was intimidated by Coach Brock," says Lopez. "There were about four of us on the team who had a somewhat friendly relationship with Barry. But it wasn't easy. He had the ability to get under somebody's skin and just not care. We could lose 10–2 and he would let us know that at least he'd done his job."

Lopez and Barry lived in an apartment on Rural Road, near a popular bar named After the Gold Rush. In a rare display of charisma that several teammates still chuckle over, Barry once arrived at the saloon for an unofficial team function and did a spot-on Michael Jackson impersonation, break-dancing across the floor to "Billie Jean." (He was equally adept at mimicking Stevie Wonder.) "He could be like that," says Lopez, "and you'd think, 'Really, he's not so bad.'"

Most of the time, Barry and his girlfriend, a pretty blond named Leslie, kept to themselves. This wasn't unusual behavior for the Sun Devils, a team with four married players and minimal social interaction. But Barry was different. He would sit alone in front of the TV every morning, watching the cartoon *He-Man and the Masters of the Universe* and giggling hysterically. He would sneak into Lopez's closet and swipe his new Ralph Lauren shirts without asking. ("Guy sweated like a pig," says Lopez.) He would write the odometer reading from his Trans Am on a scrap of paper, convinced teammates were taking his vehicle without permission. ("Confession," says Lopez. "We were. It was the nicest car around, and when he went home for Thanksgiving or Christmas we'd cruise around in that thing like rock stars.") At times, Barry could be warm and outgoing—as when he would cradle Danielle Henry, teammate Doug Henry's baby daughter, in his arms—but those moments didn't come often.

Barry posted strong numbers (.360, 11 home runs, 55 RBIs, 30 stolen bases) for a team that went 55–20 and was ranked number one in the nation for much of the season, but his attitude was terrible. He missed a bus trip, arrived late to several practices, often took BP with halfhearted intensity, and turned in lukewarm efforts in the outfield that infuriated the pitching staff. "He would never attempt to throw a guy out at home if it was going to be a close play," says Randy Rector, a pitcher. "There'd be 15 scouts in the stands, and he didn't want them to see that he had no arm."

In the ensuing years, Barry would deflect Pittsburgh- and Bay Area–based media hostility by noting, "Hey, my past is clean." The intent would be to imply, "OK, maybe I'm not always that nice. But there's no real dirt to dig up." Were this actually true, it would be a fine defense. In 1984, however, Barry committed a pair of acts that would have lost a lesser player his scholarship. First, he spent several hundred dollars using a calling card that belonged to the university. Second, there was the incident that, in one humiliating blow, officially killed the ASU reputations of Bonds *and* Brock.

In March 1984, the Sun Devils flew to Honolulu for a four-game series against the University of Hawaii. This trip was troubled to begin with. On the seven-hour flight an ugly exchange took place when Rector—who earlier in the season had supposedly made an ill-advised comment about placing bombs in the lockers of black teammates—referred to black outfielder Mike Devereaux as a "nigger." The mild-mannered Devereaux barked back at Rector, and shoves were exchanged. "That was a total misunderstanding," says Rector. "Mike and I were friends. I was just joking around. I liked almost all of the colored guys on the team."

Brock punished Rector by sentencing him to six miles of running, but by the time the team had landed and checked into their hotel, the players had a filthy taste in their mouths. That night Brock set an 11 P.M. curfew, to be enforced by the team's tri-captains, outfielder Oddibe McDowell, shortstop Romy Cucjen, and pitcher Kendall Carter. Four players, including Barry, did not return to their rooms on time.

At the stadium the following afternoon, McDowell gathered the four night crawlers together. "We're trying to win a national championship, and you guys are just killing us," he said. "So when we get back to Tempe, y'all are gonna have some serious punishment running to do." Three of the four nodded in agreement. Barry did not. He looked McDowell in the eyes and said, "Who do you think you are? You're not the coach here. Jim Brock is. You can't make me fucking run."

The taunt was a bad idea. The 5-foot-9, 165-pound McDowell was beloved as a player and a peer. During his junior year at McArthur High School in Hollywood, Florida, McDowell suffered a ruptured spleen when his bicycle collided with a moving van. Doctors said he would never play baseball again, but he returned to sports six weeks later. Ignored by Division I schools, he spent two seasons at Miami-Dade North Community College, then received a scholarship offer from Brock to play center field. McDowell hit .352 as a junior at ASU, and would bat a team-leading .405 during the '84 campaign. He was Bonds's polar opposite: humble and hardworking; the son of a tile setter; a leader. "Oddibe was the most respected and well liked person I ever played with," says Graybill. "We'd go out and have a few drinks, and Oddibe would always be drinking orange juice. He was just that type of man."

A former state high school wrestling champion, McDowell could have grabbed Barry and tossed him into the nearest ball bin. Instead, he nodded, walked away, and seethed. Barry resented McDowell's abilities and leadership, and everyone knew it. *He* was supposed to be the star of the team. That's what Brock had told him during the recruiting period—that this would be "Barry's ship." But it wasn't, and Barry pounced on every opportunity to chip away at McDowell's reputation. Now Barry had crossed the line. Upon returning to Tempe, Brock suspended Barry and held a team meeting. Barry was not invited.

"It's been brought to my attention that a lot of you think Barry is causing more harm than good," Brock told his players. "And I don't believe I can excuse his actions any longer. So here's the deal—I'm going to give you boys the authority to vote on Barry's future. Do you want him to continue on the team, or do you want him off? Keep in mind, our ultimate goal here is to win a national championship, and he's obviously a big part of that. But it's your decision." Brock walked off, and his troops retreated to the players' lounge to talk. He was certain that, with enough thought, Barry would be asked to apologize and stay. Nobody wanted to lose one of the team's brightest stars—not over a late curfew. Right?

But this wasn't about a curfew. It was about the calling card and the indifference, about the way he referred to himself in the third person during interviews and the way he always made excuses for misplays. "He was missing practices, showing up late, leaving early," says Louie Medina, the Sun Devils first baseman. "He would say, 'Oh, I have a stomach virus,' and it would be allowed. I can't speak for everyone, but I was tired of his act."

"It wasn't a white thing or a black thing or a star or bench warmer thing," adds Graybill. " It was about the value of a team—about loving to play, and doing it together."

When McDowell informed Brock of the team's decision, the coach got what he had expected—a strong consensus. But shockingly, the majority had voted *against* Barry continuing as a Sun Devil. Only two players, outfielders Devereaux and Todd Brown, were in favor of Barry's return, and their support was tepid. The rest had decided that he was finished. "I'd never seen the expression on Jim Brock's face that I saw right there," says Jeff Pentland, the team's hitting coach. "Absolute shock. It was obviously a plan to have the vote come out in favor of Barry, and it backfired."

For a moment, Brock earned the grudging respect of his players. He had asked them to vote, and they voted. He was willing to lose the club's most talented offensive weapon— a wonderful lesson for young men on the true meaning of responsibility. Good for Jim Brock.

It didn't last. Brock told the team that because the vote wasn't unanimous, he could not—"with a good conscience"—expel Barry. "The players might have thought they were voting," explains Pat Brock, the coach's wife.

"Jim was just asking for their input." Instead, Brock ordered Barry to run 10 miles (Bonds never did it). Unreported at the time was that immediately following the Hawaii trip, Brock had received a threatening visit from Bobby Bonds, demanding that he revoke Barry's suspension—or else. The incident took place during a closed practice, when Bobby drove his Mercedes onto the field, parked in front of the dugout, and bull-rushed Brock. "If you mess with my son," he yelled, veins bulging from his neck, "I'll own this school!"

The Sun Devils went on to have a fabulous year, but the injustice of the Hawaii affair stained the season. In the past, Brock's irrationality had been grudgingly accepted as part of the ASU package. Medina had been temporarily kicked off the team after tearing his forearm muscle and being unable to play. Graybill was forced to run 20 miles in his cleats. Brown, an outstanding walk-on outfielder from upstate New York, had to wait until his final season to receive a scholarship. Before Hawaii, such behavior from a cruel, victory-obsessed coach was taken in stride. But no more. The Sun Devils would play hard, but they would not play for their coach. When Arizona State was eliminated by eventual champion Cal-State Fullerton in the College World Series, players consoled one another as if there had been a loss in the family. But few consoled Bonds, who set a world series record with seven consecutive hits. And none consoled Brock.

After the season ended, Barry passed up a chance to hang out with his childhood pals back home to spend time in what might be the most boring town in America. OK, maybe Hutchinson, Kansas (population: 40,787), isn't *that* bad. But when the place where you're whiling away your summer days is best known as the home of poet William Stafford, well, the U2 concert ain't coming anytime soon.

Other than the acres of cornfields, central Kansas's only attraction for Barry was the Hutchinson Broncs, members of the Jayhawk League. The team's owner, Nelson Hobart, had known about Barry for two years and was strongly encouraged by his manager, Cal-State Fullerton assistant coach Dave Snow, to recruit Arizona State's left fielder. When Barry flew to Kansas, he immediately teamed up with Oklahoma State's Pete Incaviglia and Mississippi State's Rafael Palmeiro to form perhaps the greatest summer league outfield of all time. "For a lot of us it was the first taste of what professional baseball was like, playing every night, traveling on a bus for four hours to play the next series," says Palmeiro, who went on to a 20-year major league career also burdened by substance abuse charges. "It made you feel like you were someone special."

When the Broncs were involved in important games, Barry was the best player on the diamond. In a 13–10 exhibition loss to the U.S. Olympic team at Hobart Detter Field, Barry hammered a two-run home run off Mike Dunne, a future teammate with the Pittsburgh Pirates. Another two-run homer came in the National Baseball Congress tournament, during which Barry went 6-for-17 with two doubles, a triple, two homers, three stolen bases, and nine runs scored. Though his stats were impressive, Barry's effort on the field came and went like a Midwest breeze. "Whenever scouts were watching, he played his ass off," says Hobart. "He could hit a home run anytime he wanted to. But a lot of the time, he didn't really care."

Upon arriving in Hutchinson, members of the Broncs were assigned to live with local families. That's how Barry wound up spending much of his time on the north side of town on Waldron Street, dwelling in the modest home of Virg Navarro. Her experience hosting the young star is yet another layer to the Bonds enigma.

According to Virg, Barry was a dream—polite, respectful, helpful around the house. He would teach Jared, her teenage son, how to make omelets in the morning, and then allow him to tag along to practice in the afternoons. He affectionately referred to Virg as "Mom," and whenever Barry hit a home run, the family would throw a party. "He loved my cooking," says Virg, "so I always made him tacos and enchiladas. That man could eat." On weekends, Virg would take Barry to the local bar on Main Street and buy him a few beers. "Nobody believes me," she says, "but Barry was a very loving young man. He became a part of my family."

Based largely on the golden memories of the summer of '84, when Jared was ready for college he chose Arizona State. He graduated in 2001, and works for a financial institution in Tempe. Barry paid part of his tuition. "He was just that type of guy," says Virg. "Pure goodness. I still love him like a son."

•••●

Upon returning to Tempe in late August, Barry believed his time had finally arrived. Oddibe McDowell, the Sun Devils star center fielder, was now a member of the Texas Rangers organization, having been selected in the first round of the June draft, and Barry took over his outfield position and his unofficial designation as The Man. Despite McDowell's departure, to Barry, ASU's baseball talent appeared to be as deep as ever. Surely a third appearance in the College World Series was in the cards. Maybe even a national championship.

Nothing could possibly go wrong—except *everything*.

In November the team was placed on two years' probation by the Pacific-10 Conference for violating the work-study program in a way that granted disproportionate financial aid to five players. Though the missteps were the result of confusion more than malice (the NCAA's work-study regulations are slightly less convoluted than Nietzsche's *Thus Spoke Zarathustra*), the Sun Devils forfeited their 1984 Pac-10 title, surrendered 14 scholarships, had five players declared ineligible for 25 percent of the season, and were banned from postseason play for one year. Brock's optimistic declarations of resiliency ("Our big goal is to end the year as the top-ranked team, as always") couldn't stave off a debacle. The Sun Devils finished 31–35, the first losing season in school history. "That year sucked for all of us," says Rector. "Nobody liked Brock, there were fights between players, the effort was weak. And we knew we weren't playing for anything."

Barry, one of the season's few bright spots, was named a second-team All-American after hitting .368 with 23 home runs and 66 RBIs. Most noteworthy was a show he put on before the annual Sun Devils Alumni Game. With a handful of major leaguers surrounding the batting cage inside Packard Stadium, Barry stepped in and smoked liner after liner off of a machine throwing 85 mph. Between pitches, Barry inched closer and closer to the machine. Step—*thwack!* Step—*thwack!* Step—*thwack!* Finally, he was 30 feet away. "None of the big leaguers even thought about trying it," says Medina. "Barry was superhuman."

After beginning the season 5–3, Brock's club dropped five in a row and three of four to Grand Canyon College, an NAIA school. Times were as rough as they had ever been at ASU, and following a 14–4 loss to Grand Canyon, Brock noted, "It can't get any worse than this." It did. On March 22, the *Arizona Republic* reported that Dr. James Gough, a psychiatric consultant for the university's sports program, had prescribed Nardil, an antidepressant, to two unnamed baseball players and had recommended it to six others. Manufactured by Parke-Davis Co., the drug Nardil was for those suffering from severe neurotic depression, and could result in potentially fatal blood pressure elevation. Dr. Robert Voy, chief medical officer of the U.S. Olympic Committee, said Nardil should be used only as a last resort in cases of severe depression. But Gough believed that Nardil would combat the kind of tension resulting in batting slumps. "Coach Brock had the whole team seeing [Gough]," says Wakamatsu. "He'd talk about mental imagery and positive thinking. Most of us thought it was kind of silly, but harmless. But when you start talking medication, that's a whole different level."

Brock himself was a regular Nardil user. He was so enamored of its power to induce tranquillity that he strongly urged his players to take the drug—even though a member of the coaching staff had suffered a seizure while using it. One player Brock encouraged was George Lopez, a third baseman who had fathered his first child during his sophomore season. "Coach wanted me to play without all the pressure on top of me," says Lopez, who refused the drug. Two others, Rector and infielder Drew Siler, also said no to Nardil and found their on-field time drastically reduced. Siler wound up transferring to UNLV. "When Brock took it, he became a a lot more mechanical and mellow in the way he talked," says Lopez. "When the story about Nardil broke, it made a lot of sense to us because Brock was damn near falling asleep on the bench."

Nardil wasn't merely intended for average players. Among those urged to utilize the drug were a handful of standouts, including Barry Bonds. In many ways, Brock considered Barry an ideal Nardil recipient. If he was this good without Nardil, imagine how potent he would become with the enormous chip removed from his shoulder. There was just one problem: When Bobby Bonds learned that his son had taken an antidepressant he immediately telephoned Brock. "If you give my son anything medical again without checking with me first," he said, "I will come down there and snap your neck." That put a stop to Barry's use of Nardil.

"That whole situation was just too weird," says Royal Clayton, an ASU pitcher. "Brock was taking it. Barry was taking it. I was like, 'What's everyone taking pills for?' I was in college, running around, feeling great. What was there to be depressed about?

"But Jim Brock could make you crazy. The pressure he put on you to perform at the highest level was unhealthy. It caused a lot of guys to put too much pressure on themselves. I'm sure Barry felt it, because he was the best player in the nation on a team that always won. And we weren't winning anymore."

When the Nardil story went public, Brock panicked. He called a team meeting—not to apologize to his players, but to instruct ASU's pitchers to start taking batting practice so that, if suspensions were handed out, they would be prepared to hit for themselves. The school's athletic director, Dick Tamburo, resigned under pressure. Brock retained his job but became fodder for editorial cartoonists—a depressed baseball pharmacist on a sinking ship.

This was the lowest moment in Arizona State baseball history, but it was also one of the first times Barry Bonds displayed resiliency. With his team crumbling and under the scrutiny of scouts at every game, Barry went on a tear. He hit a two-run homer in a 13–12 loss to Arizona on April 5, then another one a week later versus USC and one after that versus UC-Berkeley. On May 9 he drove in seven runs against Stanford with a grand slam and a three-run homer. He even seemed to be having fun. After each victory, ASU's three outfielders—Bonds, Devereaux, and Brown—would meet in center field for a leaping high five. They called themselves "The Soul Patrol."

Before the program was put on probation Barry had all but decided he would turn pro after his junior year. Now, he was definitely gone. Barry believed he would be the top pick in the nation and proceed on to a life of fame and fortune. Several major league franchises, however, had concerns. Many a top prospect had been sidetracked by a poor attitude, and clearly this kid was not easy. The Milwaukee Brewers, which had the top choice in the first round, ruled out Bonds, as did the Chicago White Sox, holders of the fifth selection. But one team was not deterred. Beginning with his junior season at Serra High, the Pittsburgh Pirates had been sending scouts to watch Barry on a regular basis, and the reports grew more positive by the year. Angel Figueroa, a longtime scout for the Pirates, first watched Barry at ASU as a freshman. By Barry's junior year he was sitting in the stands for every game. "He's the type of guy who will rise to the occasion," Figueroa reported. "You get a bunch of guys around who are good or better and he wants to prove he's as good or better. There are guys with more power, there are guys who can run better, guys who can throw better, guys who can hit better. But there's only one guy who can carry the mantle for all of them and that's Barry."

On June 3, 1985, the Pirates made Barry Bonds the sixth pick in the first round of the amateur draft, following B. J. Surhoff (Brewers), Will Clark (Giants), Bobby Witt (Rangers), Barry Larkin (Reds), and Kurt Brown (White Sox). Pittsburgh had actually preferred Larkin, the University of Michigan shortstop who would have a Hall of Fame–worthy career. But once he was gone the choice was a no-brainer. "I'm sure there are a lot of people who regret not taking Barry Bonds," says Jerry Gardner, a former Pirates scout. "The kid was can't-miss. And we weren't about to miss."

That week, the Pirates flew Bonds to Pittsburgh so he could take a few swings during batting practice at Three Rivers Stadium. With Pirates coaches Jim Leyland and Don Zimmer watching from behind the cage, Barry hit 11 of 15 pitches into the right-field stands. "Any lefty can do that," cracked Leyland. "But can you go the other way?"

Barry, looking intently at his coach, replied coolly, "Watch this." He drove the next five pitches into the left-field stands. His final hit sailed over the center-field wall.

"My God," said Zimmer. "What in the world are we doing sending this kid out to the minors?"

FIVE

A PRODIGY TURNS PRO

ONE OF THE PIRATES' fears about drafting Barry Bonds was that he would become a nightmare to sign. It's not that Barry had submitted a pre-draft list of outrageous demands. What scared Gardner and his colleagues was the prospect of having to negotiate with Bobby Bonds.

Now in his second year as a hitting coach with the Cleveland Indians, Bobby's reputation was in ruins. He made little effort to conceal a bar-to-bar path of infidelity, and it was not unusual for him to arrive at Cleveland's Municipal Stadium with liquor on his breath and a cigarette between his lips. On road trips, he would load up on booze before boarding the plane and then inevitably cause a scene. On more than one occasion Pat Corrales, the Indians manager, instructed a stewardess to leave the vodka out of Bobby's favorite drink, a vodka tonic. "Bobby never knew the difference," says John Goryl, the Indians third base coach. "After a couple of drinks it still looked like he had a buzz on."

Few players respected Bobby as a hitting guru, and Corrales wanted him fired (Cleveland management refused, insisting they needed a minority on the staff). In one ugly incident, before a team flight to Oakland Bobby loaned his tie to pitcher Ernie Camacho, who feared he would not be al-lowed to board the plane. Corrales then turned to a bewildered Bobby and accused him of violating the team dress code. "You can't fly with us," Corrales said. "Not without a tie." After cursing out the manager, Bobby returned with a piece of cardboard cut in the shape of a tie dangling from his neck. "Pat made him wear that the entire flight," says Sheldon Ocker, who covered the Indians for the *Akron Beacon-Journal*. "It was degrading."

In the midst of his drunkenness, Bobby was aware enough to see that—after a career of superstardom—he was now as vital to baseball as an autographed Otto Velez jersey. The only card he held was his eldest son.

"I remember getting into a long discussion with Bobby when we were coaching together," says Dennis Sommers, the Indians bullpen coach. "His contention was that in order for Barry to succeed, he was going to have to be short with people and aloof. He hammered that into his head. Bobby said that's the way he'd raised his son, and it was on purpose. I told him, 'I've met Mickey Mantle, I've met Stan Musial. And they're not like Barry. They're nice guys.'"

In the months before the draft, Bobby and Gardner came to a friendly agreement on the range of Barry's signing bonus. As soon as the date approached, however, Bobby's number skyrocketed. When his father had to leave town, Barry dealt with Gardner one-on-one, and they agreed peacefully to a $150,000 signing bonus. In the end, Bobby had little to do with it.

Barry signed with Pittsburgh on June 5, 1985, and was assigned to the Prince William Pirates of the Class A Carolina League. Located 27 miles outside Washington, D.C., Prince William, Virginia, was to the East Coast what Hutchinson, Kansas, was to middle America—an outpost of suburban nothingness. "Not a bad place," says former outfielder Van Evans, "but zero to do except play baseball." As is the case with most first-round selections, Barry's arrival was greeted by teammates with skepticism. "Number one picks are marked men on whatever team they start with," says Jim Neidlinger, a pitcher with Prince William. "There are more 43rd-round picks and 28th-round picks and 14th-round picks than there are first-round guys, and they all feel overlooked. Everyone knew about Barry because of his success at Arizona State and his father. So he stepped into a rough situation."

On his first day with Prince William, Barry was introduced to Branch Rickey III, the organization's vice president in charge of minor league clubs.

Rickey stood alongside Prince William manager Ed Ott and catcher Burk Goldthorn while Barry made his batting practice debut. The kid was 20 years old, with no more than 175 pounds on a Twizzler-thin 6-foot-1 frame. Only the smallish black mustache kept him from looking 15. As line drive after line drive sprayed off Barry's bat, Rickey turned to Goldthorn. "I really hope we didn't make a mistake with this Bonds kid," he said. "He looks like he's gonna be a gap hitter. I don't think he'll develop much power."

When Rickey walked away, Goldthorn and Ott laughed aloud. "No power?" says Goldthorn. "The guy was phenomenal."

In his debut game, an away contest against the Peninsula Pilots, Barry started in center-field and hit cleanup, going 2-for-5 with a double off the left-center-field wall. Ten days later he hit two home runs in a game against Kinston, then blasted three more in a win at Durham. On July 26 against Durham, he hit a home run that traveled nearly 500 feet—one of the longest in league history. Although he played in only 71 games, Barry led Prince William with 13 home runs and a .299 average. "As soon as I saw him, I knew he was unlike any player I'd ever seen," says Terry Adkins, a Prince William pitcher. "The biggest transition most players had to make was adapting to the wood bat. But Barry just crushed the ball."

In Ott, Barry was gifted with the anti–Jim Brock. Unlike the Arizona State skipper, Ott refused to bow down to a pimply-faced rookie with a cocky strut. This doesn't mean he was excessively hard on the newcomer. But as a man who had spent eight seasons in the major leagues and won a World Series as the starting catcher for the '79 Pirates, he knew that attitude, even more than skill, was the key to succeeding at the top level.

Barry's first lesson in this regard came when he reported to Prince William, entered Ott's office unannounced, and proclaimed, "I'm Barry Bonds, the number one draft pick." Ott spun around in his chair. "I'm Ed Ott and I'm your manager," he said. "Now get your fuckin' ass out that door and don't come in until you knock." In a game against Lynchburg several weeks later, Ott went haywire when Barry attempted a shoestring catch, missed, then jogged after the ball. At the play's conclusion Barry found himself yanked. Waiting for his young star at the lip of the dugout, Ott was prepared to let his center fielder have it. He didn't get the chance. "Skip," Barry said, "that will never happen again." The next day Ott received a call from Rickey, furious that he had embarrassed a top pick. "If that's the way you want him to play, fine," said Ott. "But you better fire me then, because I'll do the exact same thing again." Rickey backed down.

Although Barry's play was a breathtaking boost for a team that finished 29½ games out of first, the rookie's off-the-field attitude wore on his teammates. Occasionally Barry received cardboard boxes stuffed with wristbands, batting gloves, and bat donuts. The packages were from Bobby, who was part owner of a San Francisco sporting goods store. Teammates would hover around Barry's locker, hoping to score one of the 30 batting gloves peeking from the box. "Most of us were low-level players making very little money," says Prince William infielder Brian Jones. "Barry knew that, and he was a bonus baby. But he'd only give you a glove if you paid him $8. It was petty." Scott Knox, a scrappy blond outfielder, was the lone teammate to openly defend Barry's stinginess. In return he received a 50 percent discount.

"Some of us were being paid $600 a month," adds Neidlinger. "Barry probably should have understood that."

Frank Klopp, a 23-year-old Prince William outfielder, offered Bonds a room in the house he shared with his wife, Marla; his infant daughter, Nicole; and another couple in nearby Dale City, Virginia. After two weeks with Barry, the Klopps moved out. "The house was rented in our name, the utilities were in our name, but we had to leave," says Klopp. "We didn't have the heart to kick Barry out, but we just couldn't get along with him. He knew everything at 21. He was never wrong, and he couldn't accept being wrong. He was a first-round pick, he was Bobby Bonds's son, he was Willie Mays's godson—and he reminded us of that every single day."

Near the season's conclusion, Ott called Barry into his office for a one-on-one conversation. What was supposed to be a 20-minute chat turned into a two-hour marathon. Ott wanted to discuss the pressures that were inseparably attached to Barry's high-profile last name. He assumed he would do most of the talking. Instead, Barry bared his soul. "I don't like being the son of Bobby Bonds," he said. "I don't always like my dad, I know what people say about him, and I definitely don't like when people call me 'Bobby.' That's not my name, and they should know it."

Ott urged Barry to not try to live up to his father's achievements. He also offered a tip that—years later—Barry clearly forgot. "I didn't like the way he always treated the local media," says Ott. "He could come off the wrong way. So I told him that the media could be his best friend, and that he should embrace the whole process. I wanted him to know that he could really develop a positive persona, where the world would love Barry Bonds."

In February 1986, Barry was invited to major league spring training. Though he arrived in Bradenton, Florida, as a nonroster player, he was no ordinary prospect. Instead of being assigned the traditional high uniform number designated for nobodies, he was presented with number 7. "James Bond was agent 007," said Pirates publicist Greg Johnson, "so we thought Barry Bonds should be our No. 7." Despite his youth and inexperience, Barry *knew* he would make the Pirates, and grew only more certain when he sized up the team's aging roster. The Pirates were coming off a 104-loss season, and the few veterans he recognized were has-beens like Steve Kemp and Lee Mazzilli. Upon boarding a team bus one day, Barry turned to Jim Leyland, Pittsburgh's new manager, and boasted, "Dude, you're gonna need me around here." *The nerve! The audacity!* Leyland smiled. "You're probably right," he replied. The rookie had the type of attitude the skipper craved.

Still, Barry was young and raw. When, late in spring training, Leyland sent him to the minor league camp with the promise that "You'll be up here very soon," Barry wept in his locker. In a game against the Kansas City Royals that afternoon he smoked a line drive past the opposing pitcher's head and screamed, "Just missed!" It was the type of bush league garbage Leyland hated, and Tommy Sandt, the manager at Triple A Hawaii, pulled Barry aside and reprimanded him. "Don't show up the pitcher!" said Sandt. "Next time he'll bean you in the head."

"Aw," laughed Barry. "They can't hit me."

In his ensuing at-bat, Barry received a first-pitch fastball to the ribs.

For players banished to the minor leagues, there was no better destination than Honolulu—home of the Triple A Hawaii Islanders. Sure, drawing 4,000 fans per game in 50,000-seat Aloha Stadium could be lonely. But while the

Pirates were losing night after night in the dreary Steel City, members of the Islanders could spend their free time lying on the beach, a piña colada in one hand, a bottle of suntan lotion in the other. Some members of the team actually preferred *not* to be called up.

Barry wasn't one of them. The moment he was assigned to the Islanders, he became determined to join the Pirates ASAP. Though he struggled initially, striking out 21 times his first 87 at-bats, the slump didn't last long. In 44 games with the Islanders, Barry hit .311 with seven home runs, 37 RBIs, and 16 stolen bases. "His hands were just so quick," says Sandt. "All his home runs were to left center. I never saw another guy hit the ball that far the other way." On a Monday night in early May, he drove in seven runs in an 18–8 win against Calgary, including four on a ninth-inning grand slam down the right-field line. The next afternoon, his bases-loaded triple in the ninth was the game-winning hit in a 9–6 triumph.

On May 19, the Islanders traveled to Phoenix for a five-game series against the Firebirds. Meeting the team in Arizona was the Pirates general manager, Syd Thrift, who was returning from California after signing the organization's latest top draft pick, a 19-year-old outfielder named Moises Alou. Thrift had met Barry in spring training, and was struck by the kid's confidence. "Barry was way ahead of the group when it came to baseball aptitude," says Thrift. "That stood out to me." Now Thrift was here to evaluate Barry's progress and determine his major league readiness.

Several hours before the night's game, Thrift asked Sandt whether he believed Barry was prepared for the big time. "I do," Sandt replied, "but he still has areas where he could improve."

"OK, put it this way," Thrift said. "If you were the manager of the Pirates, who would you rather have starting in the outfield, Steve Kemp or Barry Bonds?" It was a no-brainer, but if the general manager needed further confirmation, it came an hour later. With Thrift sitting in the Islanders dugout, Barry took batting practice. The first three pitches were hit over the right-field wall. Barry turned to Thrift and yelled, "What do you think of that?" Thrift grinned. "Very nice," he said. "But any left hander can hit the ball to right. That's nothing new." In a display reminiscent of his introductory session at Three Rivers Stadium a year earlier, Barry returned to the cage and laced the next three balls to left field—one after the other after the other. In Thrift Speak, it was the *darndest thang* he'd ever seen. In the third inning of that night's game, Thrift entered the Islanders dugout, tapped Sandt on the shoulder, and whispered, "Take him out. After this thing ends, he's coming with me."

Not wanting to distract his star, Sandt waited until the conclusion of the game to deliver the good news. The third person to know was actually Carlos Ledezma, the team equipment manager, who was instructed to pack Barry's gear. Benny Distefano, an Islanders infielder, happened into the clubhouse as Ledezma was completing the task. When Distefano later saw Barry in the shower, he offered a hearty "Congratulations, man!"

"Benny," Barry asked, "what the hell are you talking about?"

Oops.

"Um, for having a great game," he said. "Nice job."

Two minutes later, Sandt gave him the good news. The first person Barry called was his father.

In 1986, there was no worse place to be a Major League Baseball player than Pittsburgh. Not Milwaukee. Not Detroit. Not Montreal. Nowhere. Just seven years earlier, the Pirates had won the World Series with a lovable cast of characters who, thanks to a ubiquitous Sister Sledge song, came to be known as "The Family." Those were the halcyon days of Steel City baseball, when larger-than-life superstars like Willie "Pops" Stargell and Dave "Cobra" Parker ruled Three Rivers Stadium. Throughout the 1970s, the Pirates owned the National League with six division titles, and the good times seemed certain to continue well into the next decade.

Beginning in 1980, however, several Pirates developed a cocaine habit that would gut the team and taint the apple-pie image of the sport. A year removed from World Series glory, the Pirates dropped from 98 to 83 wins. The ensuing strike-shortened '81 season was even worse, with Pittsburgh finishing 46–56. Rumors of coke binges and late-night buys swirled around the team, but little came to light until September 1985, when a Pittsburgh federal court played host to what was painfully known as the "Pittsburgh Drug Trial." The plaintiff was Curtis Strong, a former clubhouse caterer and drug dealer. Among the seven Pirates who admitted to purchasing cocaine were Parker, a popular pinch hitter named John Milner, and Dale Berra, the son of baseball icon Yogi Berra. As *Time* magazine's Ed Magnuson accurately surmised, "Not since the 'Black Sox' scandal of 1919 . . . has the national pastime suffered such a loss of public esteem."

In Pittsburgh, the impact was lethal. As the team's on-field play deteriorated and word of the drug abuse spread, fans stopped watching on TV, stopped listening to the radio, stopped talking at the water cooler. The '84 Pirates had drawn 773,500 paying customers—a new low for fan apathy, until the figure slipped to 735,900 the following season. (By comparison, the 1984 Los Angeles Dodgers led the National League with 3,134,824 spectators.) "I was overwhelmed by how horrible it was," says outfielder Mike Brown, who played for the team in 1985 and '86. "I remember one time early on in my career, a guy in the right-field stands was screaming at me, 'Guard the line! Guard the line! I know you guys are good at guarding the line!' It was a cocaine joke. The stadium was so empty everyone could hear him. Man, it was rough."

The team's owner, Dan Galbreath, didn't help matters when, in 1983, he sold 48 percent of his interest in the Pirates to Warner Communications. A rumor spread that Galbreath was plotting to air Pirates games only on pay-per-view TV, turning the once-popular public figure into public enemy number one. It was bad enough when Galbreath had threatened to move the team to New Orleans. This was too much. Finally, frustrated by a franchise and a city going nowhere, Galbreath placed the Pirates on the market in 1985, stoking rumors of an inevitable relocation.

Led by Pittsburgh mayor Richard Caliguiri, a group of local investors known as the Pittsburgh Associates rallied to purchase the franchise. The Pirates were staying. But it sure would help if they could find a superstar to lead the way back to respectability.

Barry Bonds made his debut with the Pirates on May 30, 1986, batting leadoff and playing center field in a home contest against the Dodgers. That night's game began at 7:35. At 7, Syd Thrift brought Barry into the clubhouse and ordered manager Jim Leyland to place him in the lineup. Leyland was not happy, but he understood. The Franchise had arrived.

In his first at-bat, Barry swung at an Orel Hershiser fastball and popped up to shortstop. He proceeded to walk, strike out (with two runners on and one out), line out, and strike out two more times. The Pirates lost 6–4, and 25,320 fans sat through yet another dreary setback. Even the premiere of a hotshot rookie couldn't spice things up. In recapping the game Pohla Smith of United Press International summed up the buzz by writing: "Bonds, 21, the son of former major-leaguer Bobby Bonds, went 0-for-5 and walked once in his major-league debut." Ho-hum.

The next day, Bonds led off the bottom of the first inning with a double for his first big league hit. The scoreboard flashed the achievement, the ball was saved, the fans cheered, Dodgers pitcher Rick Honeycutt nodded his head in acknowledgment.

Then Barry was picked off second base.

Leyland knew there would be days like this. Lots and lots of days like this. When he was hired to take over for Pirates manager Chuck Tanner the previous winter, it was understood that the task of rebuilding would be monumental. "The total environment had to be destroyed," says Thrift. "You couldn't give tickets away, couldn't give boxes away. Jim Leyland was the perfect guy. Everybody in Pittsburgh respects you if you work hard and tell the truth. And that was Jim in a nutshell."

Raised in Perrysburg, Ohio, Leyland was a classic small-town, three-sports star—athletic enough to impress at Perrysburg High but destined for a career in construction or restaurant management. A good-hit, good-field catcher, Leyland signed with the Detroit Tigers in 1963, attended spring training, and immediately understood his dream of reaching the majors was as unattainable as a date with Ann-Margret. "I went in there thinking that I was going to be the head of this household because I had been All Northern Lakes League," he said. "Then I got out there and . . . I was smart enough to know real early on I had no chance."

Leyland wandered the bushes for seven years before he was asked to manage the Tigers Class A club in Bristol, Virginia, in 1971. He was 26 years old. Over the next 11 seasons he toured a variety of minor league outposts before White Sox manager Tony La Russa hired him to come to

Chicago and coach third base in 1982. It was the ultimate learning experience. "[Tony] made the moves that, in his mind, gave his team its best chance to win," Leyland said. "No matter how they came out, or how they were perceived by other people, he made those moves."

Leyland's vagabond ways and blue-collar approach prepared him well for the Pirates. A chain smoker with a weathered sea captain's face, the new manager *looked* the part of hard-nosed Pittsburgh. He was perfect. The day after Barry arrived, Leyland called him into his office (this time, the rookie knocked) and explained that—sink or swim—he was the Pirates center fielder and leadoff hitter. "He was ready because the situation dictated he could be ready," says Leyland. "Would we have brought him up if we had a pennant winner that year? Probably not. But under the circumstances it was the perfect scenario for him to get his feet wet."

By the time Barry had begun playing at Prince William, his relationship with his father had improved markedly. Though Bobby was often dulled by an alcoholic haze, he knew what it felt like to be a hotshot rookie, and what it took to develop a thick skin. "I've stood 60 feet, 6 inches from Bob Gibson and Don Drysdale," said Bobby, who served as the Cleveland Indians hitting coach from 1984 to 1987. "There's no situation that comes up for Barry that I haven't gone through myself." While Barry's feelings toward his dad were still mixed, he needed someone to turn to whom he could trust. He started calling his father for advice. Bobby might have been a terrible dad, but he knew the mechanics of hitting. He also recognized what his son required to excel in the big leagues—a quick bat, a soft glove, and oodles of swagger. On the night after Barry's 0-for-5 debut, the two spoke. "Stay confident, stay arrogant, stay aggressive," Bobby told him. "Don't forget who you are and what you've accomplished. You belong there."

When Barry carried this attitude into the clubhouse, it did not go over well. Veterans welcomed him, and he reciprocated by ignoring their advice. He would walk past teammates without so much as a head nod, and made little secret of his plans for world domination. "I've never met anyone before Barry," says Pirates pitcher Bob Walk, "who had Hall of Fame ambitions as a rookie."

Immediately following Barry's second game, pitcher Jim Winn and outfielder R. J. Reynolds took him out for a night on the town and left him stranded in a Pittsburgh bar with an unpaid bill. Two nights later in Atlanta they repeated the prank. The remainder of Barry's evening was spent in the backseat of a taxi, going from hotel to hotel, trying to remember where the team was staying. "Barry thought he was the big dog, and R. J. and I didn't go for that," says Winn. "R. J. was a cool, laid-back guy, and he didn't want to be overshadowed and overlooked by some rookie." While still in Atlanta, Pirates pitcher Don Robinson, a respected veteran and team leader, treated Barry and a couple of teammates to drinks. Robinson had planned on paying for everything until he heard the bartender ask Barry why he was drinking for free. "Because I'm Barry Bonds," he said, matter-of-factly.

"I cut him off right there," says Robinson. "It was way too disrespectful, too arrogant, for a newcomer to say."

Regardless, Pittsburgh was a unique place for a brash rookie to find himself. Were he with the Mets, Barry would have had Keith Hernandez and Ray Knight beating him into a pulp. The same went for Philadelphia, where Mike Schmidt never took guff from a plebe. But the Pirates were rebuilding, and the few remaining veterans were either indifferent (Robinson, second baseman Johnny Ray) or mediocre (Kemp, Billy Almon). Years later Barry liked to spin the yarn about Mazzilli and Rick Rhoden forcing him to change in the middle of the clubhouse. "Maz had two lockers, and one was supposed to be mine," he told the *Washington Times*. "I had to dress on the floor." It made a nice story, if only it were true. Of the 17 members of the '86 Pirates interviewed for this book, none recall Barry changing on the floor, carrying bags, paying for meals, dressing up as a cocktail waitress, or anything else generally required of rookies.

"Barry rubbed everybody on that team the wrong way," says U. L. Washington, the longtime Kansas City Royals shortstop who was wrapping up his career with Pittsburgh. To this day, Washington angrily recalls asking the rookie to loan him a bat. "Sorry dude," Barry replied. "I've only got seven left."

To the delight of many of the Pirates, Barry's freshman year was not particularly impressive. He collected 17 hits in his first 100 at-bats. "It was like, 'OK, you've come up here and you're running your mouth a lot," says pitcher Mike Bielecki. "Let's see you do it on the field." In an effort to shield

the rookie from the pressures of having to drive in runs, Leyland hit Barry
leadoff. It was an awkward fit. The same guy whose batting practice home
runs drew the awe of opposing players was an easy out atop the order. Eighteen years earlier, during Bobby's rookie season, opposing pitchers threw
nothing but off-speed stuff, then watched the kid flail away. Now the same
strategy was being used against the son, and it worked. Barry hit 16 home
runs in 1986 (the most by a Pirates rookie since Al Oliver hit 17 in 1969),
but his .223 average and 102 strikeouts were the mark of an undisciplined
hack trying to crush every ball.

Bonds's most glaring inadequacy was on defense. In center field, he was
"truly horrible," according to Walk. He repeatedly ignored Leyland's instruc-
tions to play deep, only to watch balls soar over his head and roll to the wall.
It was part nobody-tells-me-what-to-do arrogance, part self-preservation.
Were he to position himself deep, his below-average throwing arm would
be exposed. "We used to tell him in batting practice, 'Boy, if you don't stop
playing shallow I'm gonna be seeing the back of your uniform all day long!'"
recalls Eric Davis, the star outfielder for the Cincinnati Reds. "But Barry
didn't hear none of that. He was stubborn." Instead of outs, deep fly balls
turned into doubles and triples. In private meetings with pitching coach
Ron Schueler, Pittsburgh's pitchers fumed.

At times, even Barry's apparent successes fell flat. In the first inning of
an August game against the Astros, Barry crushed a ball off Houston ace
Mike Scott and triumphantly posed to watch it sail off into the distance.
One problem: The baseball hit the top of the right-field wall. By the time
an embarrassed Barry turned for third, the ball had reached the cutoff man.
Many Pirates chuckled as their teammate was called out.

One month later, Barry hit a home run off Phillies closer Steve Bedrosian
in the bottom of the ninth to clinch a breathtaking 6–5 win. It was the finale
of a two-game series, and afterward the newspaper scribes in attendance
gathered around Barry's locker as he ate his postgame meal. "Move, moth-
erfuckers," Barry ordered. "Do I come to your house at suppertime and
bother you? Now get the fuck out of my house at suppertime and when I'm
done I'll talk to you."

Several coaches and teammates were horrified by the outburst. "He was a rookie," says Pirates bullpen coach Rich Donnelly. "A rookie! But you know what? All nine writers went like little sheep and just went away. And when he was done eating they all came right back."

Donnelly also recalls seeing another side of Bonds, however, during the off season. On the morning of January 18, 1987, the coach woke up, looked out the window, and cursed. It was snowing heavily, which meant the youth baseball clinic he was hosting at Brooke High School in Wellsburg, West Virginia, would surely be missing one key ingredient—Barry Bonds.

One month earlier, Donnelly had asked Barry to participate and was shocked to hear the young outfielder reply, "Absolutely." But with snowflakes blurring the landscape, there was no way Barry would show. Not for a measly $500 appearance fee and an audience of 25 rural kids. Donnelly arrived at the school at 8 A.M., hoping at least for a courtesy call from Barry. Instead, he received shocking news. "Rich, everything's fine," said the school's principal. "We've got coffee and donuts, and one of your players is already here." Donnelly expected it to be pitcher Stan Fansler or outfielder Trench Davis, but upon entering the gymnasium he spotted Barry, standing in the middle of a circle of coaches and telling one uproarious Jim Brock story after another. Once the kids showed up, Barry stayed for four hours, doling out autographed bats and gloves. Before leaving he tapped Donnelly on the shoulder and handed him the $500 check. "Rich, do me a favor," he said. "Keep this and write it over to the athletic fund here."

"That's a side of Barry I had never seen before," says Donnelly. "It's weird, but I don't think he wants many people to see it. It's his little secret, and he doesn't need it in the clubhouse."

In February 1987 Barry arrived in Bradenton, Florida, for spring training with a comforting sense of security. He was the starting center fielder on an up-and-coming Major League Baseball team. The Pirates had lost 98 games, but the talent was prime to bloom. No longer burdened by the contracts of worn-out veterans, Pittsburgh featured young, future stars like third baseman Bobby Bonilla, first baseman Sid Bream, and pitchers Doug Drabek and John Smiley.

With the season set to begin, Barry was in a good mood—a great mood.

Yet with a single transaction, his outlook went dark. On April 1, Thrift pulled off a masterful trade, sending veteran catcher Tony Pena to the St. Louis Cardinals in exchange for three young players: pitcher Mike Dunne, catcher Mike LaValliere, and a cocky, athletic 26-year-old named Andy Van Slyke—a center fielder.

In evaluating Barry, the Pirates brass agreed his unlimited offensive upside was coupled by a glaring lack of defensive ambition and instinct. "None of us trusted him," says Logan Easley, a Pirates reliever. "If a guy's on second base and the ball is hit to you, at least try throwing him out at home. Give it some effort. I mean, that's my flippin' run that just crossed the plate. But Barry was more concerned about his arm looking bad than winning a game."

The baseball fan in Barry loved center field. There was a glory to the post. Center field was Joe DiMaggio and Duke Snider. It was his two childhood idols—Mickey Mantle and Willie Mays. To be the Pirates third baseman or middle reliever was cool. To be the center fielder was awe-inspiring.

Van Slyke's arrival signaled that Barry's days at the position were numbered. Though significantly less talented, Van Slyke had one vital attribute Barry lacked: insatiable drive. In his four years with the Cardinals, Van Slyke was known as a player whose skin was never less than 30 percent turf burns. He dove for everything, and not because he wanted a spot on ESPN highlights. Van Slyke craved the baseball. "Andy's ability was average," says Pirates pitcher Bob Patterson. "But every day Andy would take fly balls and ground balls—every single day. On that AstroTurf you just wanted a day off for your back, because it pounded you. But not Andy. He went hard nonstop."

Van Slyke and Barry were polar opposites. White-black. Grinder-gifted. While Barry was standoffish, Van Slyke never met a postgame microphone he didn't ingest. When he was a second grader at St. John's in New Hartford, New Jersey, nuns forced young Andy to wear a scarlet cardboard tongue around his neck as punishment for excessive talking. In St. Louis and Pittsburgh, Van Slyke challenged himself by standing behind home plate and driving golf balls out of the stadium. As *Sports Illustrated*'s Steve Rushin once wrote, "If you can't have fun with Andy Van Slyke, well, Dr. Kevorkian has an opening next Tuesday. Fun? Van Slyke sees life's dribble glass as half full."

It was no surprise that the two men disliked each other from the beginning. Barry felt threatened. Van Slyke detested Bonds's demeaning swagger. For the first seven weeks of the season Leyland kept Barry in center and placed Van Slyke in right, hoping the arrangement would somehow work. It didn't. In the second game of the season, the Pirates and Mets were tied at 2 in the bottom of the seventh when Easley entered for his major league debut. The first batter he faced, New York slugger Darryl Strawberry, hit a shot to deep center that sailed over Barry's head and resulted in a double. Two batters later, Strawberry came around to score the decisive run.

Easley wasn't the only Pirate to notice Barry's slow-motion pursuit, but he was the most enraged. Weeks earlier the two had exchanged words during a heated spring training confrontation, and now Easley wondered whether Barry had dogged the play out of vindictiveness. "I've always believed Barry was saying, 'Screw you,'" says Easley. "It was the first loss of my career, and it really pissed me off."

On May 30 against Cincinnati, Leyland finally made the move much of his team had been clamoring for. Van Slyke started in center, Barry in left. To his credit, Bonds didn't whine. Even he seemed to recognize Van Slyke's defensive brilliance. It was the way two-thirds of the Pirates outfield would remain for the next five and a half years, as Pittsburgh rose to respectability and the trio of Bonds, Van Slyke, and Bobby Bonilla established itself as the best in the game.

"It was all an attitude issue with Barry," says Van Slyke. "He thought he was gonna be a great center fielder because he was Barry Bonds. Life doesn't work that way."

When baseball writers attempt to pinpoint Barry's breakout season, they often cite 1987, when his 25 home runs and 32 stolen bases helped the upstart Pirates improve to 80 victories. While Leyland was indeed encouraged by the development of his 23-year-old star, in the clubhouse Barry had begun to flash his future form by displaying a palpable dislike for the media.

In the ensuing years, Barry would recall a conversation he had with Leyland in 1987, in which manager urged player that his time with the fourth estate was detracting from his on-field performance. "I was too nice to the media," Barry has said. "Jim said I was talking too much." Leyland, though, doesn't remember any such conversation, and neither do other teammates and coaches. Dating back to Serra, Mark Gonzalez, who covered young Barry for the *Peninsula Times-Tribune*, recalls a kid who "you couldn't have a conversation with." *Too nice to the media?* Not Barry Bonds.

Now as the Pirates emerged as the cliché "feel-good" story of the season (goofy collection of youngsters learn to win under gruff manager), more and more attention was thrust upon Barry. Consequently more and more writers committed the ultimate sin—inadvertently referring to Barry as "Bobby." There was no greater culprit than the Associated Press, which filed game recaps to newspapers across the nation.

> Associated Press, March 21, 1987: "In Bradenton, Mike Greenwell had two hits, drove in two runs and scored one in Boston's six-run seventh inning as a split Red Sox squad defeated Pittsburgh. Bobby Bonds hit a two-run homer for the Pirates."

> Associated Press, May 18, 1987: "Cangelosi wishes he were playing more; he starts only occasionally, usually in center field for Bobby Bonds."

> Associated Press, July 11, 1987: "Earlier, Andy Van Slyke drove in four runs to help the Pirates take a 5–4 lead into the ninth. Van Slyke singled off Mark Davis in the seventh to score Bobby Bonds from second base and break a 4–4 tie."

> Associated Press, July 27, 1987: "Whitson, 9–7, who pitched his third complete game, had gone 0–1 since he went the route in his last victory June 23. The right-hander allowed seven hits, including consecutive second-inning home runs by Bobby Bonilla and Bobby Bonds."

Associated Press, September 18, 1987: "Gott ran into a bases-loaded jam with two out in the ninth, but Bobby Bonds made a skidding catch of Smith's bid for the game-winner."

"A kid comes up and all he wants is to sketch out his own identity," says R. J. Reynolds. "But Barry never had that chance. He'd read the paper and it'd be 'Pittsburgh's Bobby Bonds.' He'd step into the batter's box and hear, 'Now batting, Bobby . . . I mean, Barry Bonds.' You know how many times that happened? Countless. That'll put anyone in a bad mood."

During one-on-one interviews with Bonds, reporters would inevitably say "So Bobby . . ." and watch Barry stand up and leave. "Usually it takes time for guys to become wary of the media," says Jim Lachimia, the Pirates' media relations director from 1986 to 1994. "But Barry developed that immediately. It's like Roone Arledge once said of Howard Cosell—'He wanted the adulation, but he hated the people who gave it to him.' That summed up Barry." In the middle of the '87 season, Lachimia arranged a phone interview between Barry and a baseball writer for the *Los Angeles Times*. The next afternoon, Barry entered the clubhouse and walked up to Lachimia. "I never called that guy!" he yelled loud enough for everyone to hear. "So fuck it!"

Some have theorized that Barry's distaste for the press stems from the way his father was covered. Yet with few exceptions, Bobby was given a free pass. His alcohol arrests were never widely reported, and his vices—known to beat writers from city to city—were kept under wraps. In 1987, during his final season as Cleveland's hitting coach, Bobby famously engaged in a screaming match with a rookie Indians infielder named Tommy Hinzo. It took place in a hotel bar, and though no writers were present, it was the talk of the clubhouse the next afternoon (Bobby to Hinzo: "You couldn't hold Willie Mays's jock!" Hinzo to Bobby: "Neither could you!"). This likely would have immediately ended Bobby's already tenuous employment with the Indians—had it touched print.

Though Barry believed his father had been brutalized in the newspapers, that wasn't the main cause of his antagonism. What Barry refused to tolerate was the media obsession with determining what made him tick. Whose business was that? Certainly not some potbellied schlub in wrinkled khakis and a Super Bowl VII golf shirt. And what did these reporters know about hitting a Nolan Ryan fastball? About crashing into the outfield wall? Besides, who cared what the papers said? Barry had learned from his father that mystique was vital to success. Never get too close to teammates, never fall for a groupie, and never, ever let a member of the press get into your head.

These thoughts must have been running though Barry's mind when, midway through the 1987 season, a timid local radio reporter named Tom Gilbert stuck a microphone in his face and began to ask questions. *"Repetitive!"* Barry replied to the first. *"Repetitive!"* he said to the second. *"Repetitive! Repetitive,* man!" he said again, forcing Gilbert to slink away. "Barry just humiliated the guy loudly in the middle of the clubhouse," says John Perrotto, who covers the Pirates for the *Beaver County Times.* "He wasn't a regular beat guy, and Barry smelled the vulnerability."

Whenever Barry was the hero of a game, he knew the media would be waiting by his locker for some wisdom. So he hid. In the clubhouse kitchen. In the shower. He'd peek out, act like he was about to approach, then walk the other way. He'd read a newspaper with his feet up on a chair and dismissively wave his palm if a writer dared approach.

During his time in Pittsburgh, Barry would stand alone in center field before games, swinging a bright orange sledgehammer over his head. Yes, it served the purpose of loosening his muscles. But more to the point, it caused a stir. Cameras would click, writers would jot notes into their pads. He was untouchable, alone in the middle of an ocean of grass. When Alan Cutler, the color analyst for Pirates games on KDKA-TV, would ask Barry to appear on the postgame show, the response was always "Not today. Ask tomorrow." It wasn't an invitation, but a taunt. I will never, ever, ever go on with you—*but you'll keep begging.*

"I don't care," Bonds once told Dan Le Batard of the *Miami Herald,* explaining his treatment of the media. "I . . . don't . . . care. You see that light switch over there? That's me. I turn my emotions on and off. Click. Turn it on. Click. Turn it off. It's like any pain. If you scratch your arm, you can put on a Band-Aid and keep moving or you can sit there crying. I wrap my emotions in a Band-Aid and keep moving."

To his credit, Barry was as dismissive of the *New York Times* or ESPN as the *Greenburg Tribune-Review*. Also, he brought occasional flashes of humor to his media standoff. For more than half a season, he and Paul Meyer, the longtime *Pittsburgh Post-Gazette* scribe, held a contest to see who could flash the other with a middle finger first.

"That's what was so weird about him," says Perrotto. "He could be such a monumental pain in the ass, but he could also turn around and do something silly like that."

Perrotto pauses. "But mostly," he says, "he was just a pain in the ass."

To Thrift, Leyland, and the rest of the Pirates brain trust, it made no difference. Yes, Bonds was trouble. But Pittsburgh went 27–11 over the final six weeks of the season, winning 80 games for the first time in four years and drawing more than one million fans to Three Rivers Stadium.

"We were bound and determined to get better," says Leyland. "And Barry was the key. It was clear he was the type of player who could carry the organization to the next level. He was ready."

SIX

THE MONTREAL SUN

THEY MET IN A strip club.

That's the first thing one should know about the relationship between Barry Bonds and Sun Branco. Some couples meet at church. Others over cocktails. Bonds and his first wife met at a strip club—where she worked.

In early June 1987, the Pirates visited Montreal for a three-game series against the Expos. On the night of the second game, Barry headed out to Chez Parée, one of the best-known gentlemen's clubs on the major league circuit. Located on Stanley Street adjacent to the Le Centre Sheraton, Parée's private VIP rooms and "85 charming dancers" (as the club boasted) drew a constant stream of visiting athletes. The establishment catered to celebrities; an attentive staff made sure paparazzi and autograph-seeking fans remained outside. Former Yankees manager Billy Martin visited the club. So did Madonna. "Without trying to sound egotistical, we run a nice place," says John Barile, Chez Parée's owner. "It's clean, there's nothing shady going on, and we're best known for the breathtaking appearances of our employees."

That's surely what Barry noticed when he walked through the front entrance. Chez Parée offered a rainbow coalition of gorgeous women—its staff was black, white, Asian; Canadian, American. One young lady stood out: Susann "Sun" Branco, a 23-year-old bartender with sparkling eyes and a pinup body. A Swedish immigrant and aspiring cosmetologist who had recently passed her high school equivalency exam, Branco oozed sexuality. "Man, she was hot," Bonds bragged to friends. "You don't find too many like that."

When Bonds later mentioned the woman's name to teammates, they erupted in laughter. Sun Branco? The infamous Montreal Sun? "She was known as the chick to call when you were in Montreal," says one former Bonds teammate, echoing a familiar refrain. "She was a fun girl."

Although Branco did, in fact, date more than one ballplayer, her antics hardly warranted a nickname. "She had a reputation, and that's all it was—a reputation," says Floyd Youmans, a former Expos pitcher who dated Branco. "She was actually a pretty good girl who was nice to people. She definitely was not a typical hoochie." Youmans warmly recalls Branco's kindness when he suffered head injuries in a car accident while driving along the Trans-Canada Highway. "I didn't speak French and few people in the hospital spoke English," he says. "Sun stayed and took care of me. I hated what people said about her. It wasn't nice."

Isolated from the clubhouse scuttlebutt, Barry had no idea of Branco's reputation. All he knew was that the woman before him was beautiful, sexy, flirtatious, and seemingly interested. "I wound up going to another club and she went to the same place," Barry recalled in an interview with *Playboy*. "We danced, talked, had some fun. I wouldn't say it was love at first sight . . . but it was chemistry." The next afternoon, Sun invited Barry out for lunch. She attended that evening's Pirates-Expos game as Barry's guest, but—bored by baseball's slow pace—didn't arrive until the seventh inning. Later that night they had sex.

Over the course of the summer the two kept in regular contact. ("I had $700 phone bills," Bonds recalled.) Less than a half year after they first met, Bonds issued a challenge. "You show up at my door in Arizona," he said, "and I'll marry you." At the conclusion of the '87 season, Branco arrived at Bonds's home in Phoenix, where she stayed for 10 days. On a drive to Sedona, Branco called her mother from Barry's car and said, "I'm going to marry this man!" One month later, she moved in permanently with Barry and found a job waiting tables at a sports bar.

On November 14, 1987, Barry planned a dinner at a fancy nearby restaurant, inviting only Branco and a handful of close associates. When Barry proposed with a $5,200 diamond ring, Branco's mouth fell agape. "I didn't even say yes. I just didn't connect," she later said. Bonds's banker, one of the guests, jokingly spoke up, "If you don't say yes, I will."

"Yes!" she cried.

The news of Barry's engagement did not thrill Bobby and Pat Bonds, who were wise enough to recognize that five months of dating was hardly much time, and five months of dating a strip club bartender was, well—what parent would be happy? Plus, there was something about Branco that rubbed some people the wrong way. A high school dropout from the small Swedish town of Norrtalje, she was not especially warm or curious. Her passable English was obscured by a thick accent. Were Barry, say, a garbage man or elementary school teacher, would she be so enamored? Was it mere coincidence that she aspired to be a makeup artist for celebrities, or did she believe snagging a sports star would take her one step closer to her dream? Was she just another sexy gold digger in tight pants?

In a 1993 *Playboy* interview Barry was asked this question, and the answer is telling. Was the union based on love? Commitment? Shared values? "[I offered her] stability," Barry said. "I had a job. I had my own condominium. I was making a hundred thousand dollars."

Barry knew the concerns of his family; he had heard the cautionary tales of athletes bled dry by money-hungry vixens. On February 4, 1988, the day before they were to fly to Las Vegas and exchange vows, the couple allegedly stopped at a Phoenix office to meet with Barry's financial advisor, Mel Wilcox. In a conference room, Wilcox allegedly told Sun that Barry would not proceed with the wedding unless she signed an already-drafted 13-page prenuptial agreement. Sun did not argue, assuming her soon-to-be husband only wanted to maintain separate ownership of property obtained before the union. But she was surprised. Barry had never previously mentioned the idea of a prenuptial. Sun didn't even know what the word meant. Neither, for that matter, did her friend Margareta Forsberg, who had tagged along. Prenuptial? Sure, Sun would sign a prenuptial. Why not?

The next day, two weeks before the start of spring training, Barry and

Sun were married in a small Las Vegas ceremony with no caterer or written invitations. The guest list was limited—Barry's parents, Willie Mays, Forsberg, and a handful of other friends. The couple seemed genuinely happy. As a wedding present, Mays supplied a suite at Bally's Hotel. All of Barry's personal dreams were coming true. He had long desired a family of his own, so that he could be the type of husband and father Bobby had never been. This was just the beginning.

As word spread through the baseball world that Barry Bonds had married "Montreal Sun," the reaction was part befuddlement, part amusement. When Rod Wright, Barry's agent, told Expos third baseman Tim Wallach—also a client—about the union, Wallach's stunned response was "He married . . . *who*?" That was tamer than most of the Pirates, who took great pleasure reminding Bonds that his wife worked at a strip club. It was the ultimate payback for Barry's arrogance and insensitivity. "Even though it wasn't true, the joke around the clubhouse was that we'd all seen Barry's wife naked before he did," says Glenn Wilson, a Pittsburgh outfielder. "Everybody knew he met her at the strip club, and everyone thought it was the funniest thing ever."

If Barry was troubled by the wisecracks, he refused to let it show. He led off seven of the Pirates' first eight games of 1988 with hits, going 14-for-34 over the span. When asked by Pohla Smith of United Press International to explain his fast start, he hardly flinched. "I credit my wife," he said defiantly. On April 14, he smashed two home runs in a 4–2 win over the Phillies, completing a three-game sweep. Three days later his 475-foot home run off Calvin Schiraldi landed in the seldom-reached upper section of the bleachers in Wrigley Field. In 1987, many considered it a fluke when the Pirates finished strong. But now the team was off to a 19–10 start, and Barry was carrying the load. "Barry Bonds has got a chance to be one of the top five players in the league," Van Slyke said at the time. "I say that without question. In fact I'll put it in gold letters. And you can put that in capitals."

For the first time in Barry's major league career, people were witnessing the wide-ranging splendor that had been predicted by Dave Stevens at Serra, Jim Brock at Arizona State, and Ed Ott in Prince William. Though he was not yet the best all-around player on the Pirates (Van Slyke held that title), Barry had a looks-too-easy explosiveness few others could match. When Barry slid, it was smooth. When he hit the 400-foot home run, it was done without the fierce all-or-nothing swing of a Rob Deer or Mike Pagliarulo. Throughout his first two seasons, Barry wasted his at-bats trying to hit home runs and prove to Leyland he belonged in the middle of the order. But with hitting coach Milt May reminding him not to overswing, a game plan sunk in. "When he started just trusting his natural ability, it was magical," says May. "Barry had that beautiful quick, short, strong swing. You saw it once and knew this was a one-of-a-kind talent."

Unique to Barry was a tendency to raise or lower his game to the level of the opposing team's premier outfielder. If the Pirates were playing Cincinnati, Barry was determined not to let Eric Davis outdo him. In New York, he would be damned if Darryl Strawberry hit a home run while he didn't. On the other end, it was sometimes difficult for Barry to go all out when Houston came to town with an outfield alignment of, say, Kevin Bass, Gerald Young, and Billy Hatcher. "Barry's the only person I ever met," says outfielder R. J. Reynolds, "who could turn it on or off like a light switch."

The 1988 season was unique in that it was the first time Bonds placed genuine trust in his coaches. In Leyland, Barry had a manager who balanced sensitivity with toughness and knew how to read a player's mind and mood. May, meanwhile, was an intelligent, soft-spoken mentor who never felt threatened by Bobby's looming presence. Throughout much of his life, Barry had been brainwashed to believe there was one way to approach hitting—the Bobby Bonds way. Whenever he encountered trouble, the lone person Barry would confide in was his dad. Now, Barry was becoming more willing to trust himself, as well as the wisdom offered by those around him. "I've always felt that Barry had to distance himself from Bobby in order to become the player he is," says Scott Ostler, a columnist for the *San Francisco Chronicle*. "At some point Barry said, 'I'm not gonna fuck up like my dad did. I've got the same tools that he did and I'm not going to piss them away. I'm not gonna smoke, I'm not gonna drink, I'm not gonna take it for granted.' When he made that decision, it turned him into a truly unique ballplayer."

This was the season Barry learned the art of defense. With Van Slyke covering large swaths of turf, Barry dedicated himself to the left-field line, turning sure doubles into meek singles while piling up five assists. Barry's arm remained mediocre, but he reached balls swiftly and his release was lightning-quick. From the day Leyland handed Van Slyke the center-field job—*Barry's* center-field job—the relationship between the outfielders had been frosty. The two exchanged their fair share of barbs, fueled primarily by Barry's jealousy. Give up the center-field job? Fine. But Barry sure as hell wasn't going to be outdone.

Van Slyke paid close attention to the transformation, which became complete after the '88 season. That's when Van Slyke was named a Gold Glove recipient for the first time. "The trophy was shipped to me in the clubhouse," recalls Van Slyke. "I opened the box, and it was a very cool-looking piece of hardware." When Barry approached to admire the award, he wore the envious expression of a little boy inspecting a friend's Christmas presents. He looked the trophy up and down, rubbed his hand along its side. "Next year," he promised, "I'm gonna win me one of these."

"That just told me something about Barry Bonds," says Van Slyke. "When he decides to get something done, he gets it done. Up until around that point in his career, he decided he didn't need to be a very good outfielder. But when he changed his mind, he willed himself to become great."

Barry won his first Gold Glove in 1990. Over the ensuing eight seasons he would collect seven more.

The Pirates of 1988 were a wonderful tale, reviving the national pastime in a city that had all but abandoned it. The team finished in second place with an 85–75 mark, drawing a record-breaking 1,866,713 fans. Opened in 1970, Three Rivers Stadium was shaped like (and as charming as) a plain donut. The complaints from fans were endless: The field was too far from the seats, the hot dogs were mushy, the beer tasted like liquid Spam. When the "We Are Family" Pirates wowed the city in 1979, the problems with Three Rivers were overlooked. But when the team hit rock bottom, few desired to attend games. Who could blame them?

Now another revival was emerging. With the exception of the 29-year-old Reynolds, all the regular position players were 27 or younger. The team's ace, 15-game winner Doug Drabek, was 25, and number two starter John Smiley was 23. The Pirates were young, handsome, exciting, dashing, hard-nosed—and far removed from the cocaine era. Pittsburgh's clubhouse was a pie-in-the-face sort of joint, where the sounds of Twisted Sister and AC/DC blasted and a dozen players might dine together on the road. It was all for one, one for all—with one exception.

As more attention was lavished on Barry, he made more of an effort to distance himself from the unit. This was the year Barry began taking long naps before games, lounging across the clubhouse sofa until five minutes before start time. Was he tired? Perhaps. But what Barry was concerned with was the message it sent his teammates: *You go ahead and stretch and sprint and take BP. I don't need to.* "Barry was simply inept with social situations," says Van Slyke. "I think it was a condition that manifested itself because he never saw what it was to treat people with dignity."

In a moment of sweet revenge, one early evening Barry was napping on the clubhouse couch when Reynolds convinced an attendant to turn the clock forward from 6:10 P.M. to 7:40. All 23 Pirates snuck out of the room and stood in an adjacent hallway as the attendant shook Barry's shoulder. "Mr. Bonds, the game!" he yelled. "The game!" Barry looked at the clock, stumbled into his uniform, grabbed his glove, and sprinted out the door—where he was greeted by uproarious laughter. "He didn't talk to anyone for three weeks," says Rich Donnelly, one of Leyland's coaches. "Oh, he was mad."

Bonds lacked the self-confidence to be able to laugh off such incidents. He also often misread social cues and had an odd sense of humor. When the Braves came to Pittsburgh for a three-game series, Pirates team photographer Pete Diana was shooting Barry in center field as the Atlanta players entered the stadium. From afar, Barry spotted Willie Stargell, the legendary Pirates slugger who now coached with the Braves. "Get on out of here, you old man!" Barry hollered. "They forgot about you in Pittsburgh! I'm what it's all about now!" Stargell continued to walk, not uttering a word. Finally, Barry perceived that he had gone too far. "Pops! Pops!" he pleaded. "I'm just kidding. C'mon, Pops!"

Stargell stopped in his tracks. "Boy," he said, "you better get some more lines on the back of your baseball card before you talk to me like that." Two years later Barry committed a nearly identical faux pas when he bumped into former Pirates slugger Dave Parker at the All-Star Game and shouted, "What's an old man like you doing here?" The 39-year-old Parker was furious. "Listen, ass-wipe," he said, "I started making All-Star Games when you were in your daddy's stroller." With Stargell and Parker, Barry meant no harm. He was simply incapable of making jokes without hurting feelings. "He's totally befuddled by the most normal of situations," says Tim McCarver, the former major league catcher and longtime announcer. "I mean, you don't have to go out of your way to like somebody, to say, 'How ya doing?' or 'I'd rather not talk today.' But he's utterly incapable. In that regard I have pity for him."

As he entered Three Rivers Stadium before a game against the Mets in June 1988, Barry told a group of young autograph seekers to "Fuck off! Fuck off! Fuck off! Fuck off!" The scene was repeated often, once resulting in Reynolds lambasting his teammate in front of a group of onlookers. "Be a fuckin' man, Barry!" he said. "Treat people with dignity!" Barry's intolerance puzzled many Pirates. They couldn't understand why he openly complained of having to sign for "these pathetic losers," but then placed himself in accessible positions. On the road most players would wait for the bus to the stadium inside the hotel lobby. Yet Barry stood on the sidewalk, all but begging people to approach so he could ream them out. "He wanted the attention without anyone knowing it," says Reynolds. "That was the warped side of Barry."

Years later, when Barry was playing for the Giants, he once stormed into manager Dusty Baker's office dressed head to toe in a black leather outfit and motorcycle helmet. "When are people gonna leave me the fuck alone?" he griped. "Look at this. I'm dressed so nobody could recognize me with my visor down, but people still approach me and ask for shit. Why can't a person live a private life?"

"Barry," Baker said, "walk with me for a minute." The two strolled to the players' parking lot, where Bonds's motorcycle rested. On the side of the vehicle BONDS 25: THREE-TIME MVP was painted in large letters.

"Sorry dude," said Baker, "but you can't have it both ways."

During the '88 season, Barry hired Dave Tumbas, the Pirates assistant trainer, to answer his fan mail. Back in Ted Williams's heyday, the "Splendid Splinter" had a team employee sign autographs on his behalf. Barry did him one worse. Tumbas was instructed to sort through Barry's mail and weed out the important stuff (endorsement checks, potential business deals) from fan letters. When Pete Ottone, eight-year-old Pirates diehard from Mt. Lebanon, wrote Barry a 10-page love note, it almost certainly went right into trashcan. So did hundreds of other letters, many written by children. Eventually, Tumbas talked Barry into filling out small thank-you cards and sending them in return. But Barry wanted nothing to do with the process.

Such behavior made Van Slyke sick to his stomach. It was one thing to be a jerk to the media. But why treat fans like dirt? Throughout the season, the tension mounted until, as Donnelly recalls, "they only spoke to call each other off on fly balls." On the night of July 14, the bad feelings boiled over. In the fourth inning of a game against the Giants at Three Rivers, Van Slyke batted with one out, Barry at third base, and Pirates shortstop Rafael Belliard at first. Van Slyke hit a two-hopper to second baseman Robby Thompson, who immediately spotted Barry nonchalantly strolling toward home. Thompson threw a dart to catcher Bob Brenly, and Barry was easily tagged out.

"I was absolutely incredulous at what I saw," says Van Slyke. "I almost ran from first base to the dugout just to punch him in the face. But that would only embarrass the team." When rain later caused a suspension of the game, Van Slyke rushed into the clubhouse and camped himself next to Barry's locker. As the Pirates shuffled into the room, there was a palpable silence. "What the fuck do you want?" Barry said to Van Slyke.

The center fielder's fists were clenched. Furor creased his brow. "Barry, if you ever fuckin' do that again—embarrass me or this team while I'm in uniform and we're playing together—I'll punch you right on the spot," he said. "Play the game the way it's supposed to be played." Barry responded with a shove to Van Slyke's chest, an open invitation for an exercise in team stress release. Van Slyke pulled back his right fist and fired it into Barry's nose, then readied to throw another jab. That's when seven teammates pushed Van Slyke aside and jumped in to pummel Barry, too. "It was the funniest thing I ever saw," says Brian Fisher, a Pirates pitcher. "Everybody grabbed Barry and nobody grabbed Andy. I was like, 'Please throw one for me!'"

Leyland separated Barry from the mob. "If you guys wanna fight," he said, "take it into my office." Van Slyke walked toward the manager's quarters, turned around, and saw Barry standing still, his head down. "I just shrugged my shoulders and went back to my locker," he says. "It was over."

Word of the brouhaha never reached the media, and reporters continued to tell the story of the feel-good Bucs and their goofy, carefree clubhouse. But the incident was an eye-opener for Bonds. What did it say about his personality that not one teammate stepped in on his behalf? Maybe his jokes weren't that funny. Maybe he did rub people the wrong way. On multiple occasions Leyland had asked Bonds to tone down his clubhouse rhetoric, but was he really *that* bad? Bonds had been stung.

"Come sit at my locker and have nobody to talk to," he once told Dan Le Batard of the *Miami Herald*. "See how it makes you feel. It ain't that nice. Nobody comes around to talk to me. Stay here long enough and you'll see it. Every day, it's lonely."

Though the Pirates wound up 15 games behind the National League East champion Mets, the season was an enormous step forward. Barry put up solid numbers with 24 home runs and 58 RBIs while hitting a career-best .283.

"He's a great talent," Leyland said. "Sometimes people rush these kids. He's still a young player. People ask me when he's going to produce like he's capable, and I say he's been everything I've expected so far."

Despite not making the playoffs and being stuck as the leadoff hitter (a status the power-conscious Barry routinely griped to Leyland about), Barry Bonds was a happy man in the winter months of 1988–89. At his home in the Pittsburgh suburbs, Barry found Sun to be exactly what he desired in a spouse—attractive and seemingly understanding of the idea that, on the road, men will be men. Even when Sun accidentally drove their Porsche into the living room, Barry kept his cool. He knew what he had in his wife. "Sun has more patience than toilet paper," Barry once said. "Toilet paper just sits there and waits. . . . She knew exactly what she was getting when she married me. It's a package deal; she married public property." To Barry, Sun was the quintessential baseball bride—well dressed, big breasted, and contented to be seen and not heard.

Bonds failed to understand that, in fact, Sun was growing frustrated with her limited role. She longed to be more than eye candy. "He always told me that I was too opinionated," Sun would say years later, "that I didn't need to have an opinion. [He said] he was the man of the house and that I should shut up, that I was being childish and irresponsible in everything I did." When Sun broached the idea of employment, her husband bristled. "You are married to a professional baseball player," he said. "I'm Barry Bonds. You do not need to go back to work."

Barry possessed everything he wanted. Living in Pittsburgh year round, he had easy access to the Three Rivers Stadium weight room, where he would meet teammate John Cangelosi several times per week. At 5-foot-8 and 160 pounds, Cangelosi was Barry's physical opposite, but the star took to him. He was one of the first teammates to learn that if you didn't bow down, Barry Bonds not only backed off, he admired you for it. Leyland never allowed a player to question his authority, and Barry respected the manager. The same went for Cangelosi.

That winter, as they did squats and dumbbells, Barry would whine to Cangelosi about his treatment around the clubhouse. "If you have guys on the team who ain't liking you, change your fucking ways," Cangelosi would reply. "Let's face it—you're a great player. But that doesn't give you the right to treat people like shit."

As one of Barry's few friends, Cangelosi witnessed his softer side. When a pal named Frank Castro was holding a baseball card show that winter, Cangelosi convinced Barry to waive his fee and appear for free. "I was at the show," says Cangelosi, "and he was phenomenal." A few weeks before Cangelosi's wedding, Barry pulled up to his house and said, "Let's go buy motorcycles!"

"Motorcycles?" replied Cangelosi. "I've never been on a motorcycle in my life. I'll kill myself. Anyway, I don't have that kind of money to throw away." Barry waved him off, taking him to a nearby dealer and purchasing two Kawasaki Ninja 600s. "Those are the things people don't see," says Cangelosi. "Is he moody? Yes. Was he dumb in the way he worked the press? No question. But if you get inside, you'll see the compassion."

Another man able to break through Bonds's exterior was James Mims, a former baseball player at the University of Southern California who, in 1988, started his own wristband company, M&N Bandit. Two years earlier Dusty Baker had introduced Mims to Bonds, and the two remained casual friends. One days Mims and Bonds were talking when the topic of wristbands arose. "Do you need money?" Bonds asked out of the blue.

"Well," said Mims, "in order to purchase the machinery I'm trying to get at least four or five guys to loan me $5,000. But I'm not asking you to . . ."

"Five thousand?" interjected Bonds. "Pfft, that's nothing." Bonds wrote the check and immediately handed it over, no strings attached. Shortly thereafter he became one of Mims's first customers. Featuring the faces of players alongside the words SAY NO TO DRUGS, the wristbands exploded into a major league fad. "He didn't know whether the product was going to fly," says Mims. "But he took a chance on a young guy trying to make it. I'll never forget that."

Most Pirates weren't privy to the perspective enjoyed by Cangelosi and Mims, and many in the front office began to wonder whether Barry was a headache worth suffering. So when the Braves came calling in December 1988, the Pirates listened. Atlanta's system was stockpiled with talented youngsters like outfielders David Justice and Ron Gant, and pitchers John Smoltz and Tom Glavine. Pittsburgh general manager Larry Doughty, who had replaced Thrift in November, made it clear that there were six players the Pirates would not consider trading—Van Slyke, Drabek, Smiley, third baseman Bobby Bonilla, second baseman Jose Lind, and reliever Jim Gott. Barry Bonds, however, was on the table.

Braves GM Bobby Cox attempted to entice Doughty by dangling 25-year-old Andres Thomas, an up-and-coming star whose 13 home runs and 68 RBIs in 1988 led all National League shortstops. Pittsburgh was intrigued, but the man they insisted on was Jeff Blauser, another shortstop and, at age 23, a player young enough to build around. The previous season the Pirates' shortstop triumvirate of Rafael Belliard, Felix Fermin, and Al Pedrique combined for a league-worst 17 RBIs. The powerful Blauser would provide the remedy.

As Barry watched his name being bandied about in the local newspapers, he scratched his head. His father had been traded six times, each transaction more miserable than the prior one. How could anyone trade Barry Bonds? *The great Barry Bonds?*

The Pirates rejected Thomas, and Atlanta pulled Blauser off the table. Both went on to enjoy average big league careers. The Pirates had been wise. Either deal would have gone down as one of the worst trades in major league history.

The beginning of the end for Barry Bonds in Pittsburgh started on February 18, 1989, when the team signed Van Slyke to a $5.5 million contract to keep him in a Pirates uniform for the next three years. On the record, Barry was exceedingly polite to a teammate who, less than a year earlier, had punched him in the nose. "I am happy for Andy Van Slyke," Barry said. "He deserved what he got. He is the best center fielder in baseball."

In fact, Barry did not believe the center fielder warranted such a hefty contract. Sure, Van Slyke played some mean defense, and his 25 home runs and 100 RBIs in '88 were career highs. But the way Barry saw it, Van Slyke was not in his class.

Were he not facing his own financial dilemma, perhaps Barry could have ignored the contractual circumstances of his teammates. But at the same time Van Slyke (who as an unrestricted free agent was due the large contract) became a very rich man, the Pirates offered Barry a one-year deal for $360,000. The $140,000 raise from the previous season was generous on Doughty's part, considering Barry was 42 days shy of becoming eligible for arbitration. The team could have forced the left fielder to return for $60,000 less.

Barry didn't see it that way. Growing up, he would hear his father pout repeatedly over so-and-so player earning this and so-and-so earning that. Barry saw the mediocre Van Slyke making millions and the amazing Bonds making peanuts. "I never wanted to break the bank," Bonds said after receiving Pittsburgh's offer. "I never wanted more than what I worked for. It's our salary structure. You do well, you get paid. . . . This is not to take anything away from any other ballplayer, but the Pirates placed all the emphasis on time and service and none on my accomplishments."

For the remainder of the spring, Barry pouted. He was rude to the media and barely acknowledged Van Slyke. When Doughty entered the clubhouse, Barry wore the look of a man who had smelled spoiled milk.

His attitude crept onto the playing field. During exhibition play, Barry half-assed several balls, which only led to greater anger on the part of teammates. As the year wore on and the injury-plagued Pirates struggled to stay near .500, Barry's anger rose. It didn't help that Van Slyke was having a terrible season. By late June the center fielder was stuck at 21 RBIs, and a strained rib cage had sapped much of his speed. Barry, on the other hand, was emerging as a true virtuoso. His 19 homers ranked second on the team, as did his 58 RBIs. But unlike the other young up-and-coming stars around baseball (Oakland's Mark McGwire, San Francisco's Will Clark), the Pirates did not consider Barry a necessity. Doughty often thought, "Is this guy worth the trouble? Is he a player who wants to win?" In a July loss to the Dodgers, Barry dropped a routine fly ball that cost Pittsburgh the victory. In August, he misplayed a ball against the Expos in the 11th inning that led to another loss. Though the flubs were excusable, Barry's reaction was not. "He never took responsibility," says Reynolds. "There was always an excuse."

In July, Dodgers executive vice president Fred Claire approached the Pirates about a potential deal for Bobby Bonilla. Doughty laughed it off, then asked if Claire had any interest in Barry. "He's available," Doughty said, "for the right package." The Pirates GM knew Bonds would put up yet another stink about money and respect and the state of the organization. What was the point of running a baseball team if the best player made everyone's life miserable?

Though Los Angeles passed, Toronto stepped in, offering pitcher Dave Stieb and infielder Manny Lee in return for Bonds. Doughty thought long and hard about the deal, but in the end he turned it down. Stieb was 31 years old, and Lee was a mediocre talent. Barry could be traded, but not for mush.

On August 18, Doughty at last pulled the trigger on a swap, and though

Bonds was not part of the trade, it would certainly affect him. With little fanfare, the Pirates sent Glenn Wilson to Houston in exchange for outfielder Billy Hatcher. Leyland immediately announced that the newest Pirate would start in right field and lead off, and Barry would drop to fifth in the order. "All I've been hearing since Bonds got here is how he should bat lower," said Leyland. "Well, now we'll find out if he can drive in runs. It's time for him to show us that he can. "

Throughout his Pittsburgh tenure, Barry had whined to the manager, his teammates, and the media that he was being misused. Leyland was sick of it. Put up or shut up, kid.

The next night in Atlanta, Barry debuted as a middle-of-the-order threat. With Bonilla hitting cleanup in front of him, Barry went 2-for-4 with his 16th home run, a 420-foot blast off Smoltz. The Pirates lost 4–3, but Barry was euphoric. He was a run producer.

And run producers made the big bucks.

SEVEN

OF FINANCES AND
(PLAYOFF) FLOPS

TED POWER WAS A 35-year-old right-handed relief pitcher with no place to go when, on one of the first days of spring training 1990, he met Barry Bonds. Over the past few seasons, Power had heard things about Barry—few of them good. He was arrogant. He was abrasive. He was moody. "A jerk," says Power, a new free-agent signee. "A pretty big one."

In the midst of a brief discussion, Barry asked Power where he was staying in Bradenton. "Aw, I didn't know where to go," Power said. "So I'm in the team motel."

Barry stopped the conversation. "Absolutely no way," he said. "My wife and kids are leaving in four days. Why don't you move into my apartment with me?"

Power accepted, but on the condition that he pay rent.

"Screw that," Barry said. "If you wanna buy groceries, buy groceries. If you don't, don't. Just relax and make yourself at home."

This was a side of Barry Bonds Power had never heard of—an easygoing guy with a big heart. In 1990, Barry returned to the baseball field with a smile across his face. Four months earlier his first child, a son named Nikolai, had been born, and Barry could barely contain his giddiness, flashing pictures to teammates and bragging about his boy's stellar athleticism.

"Wow," thought Power, "this guy's great. It's gonna be a fun spring."

It was anything but.

Despite the new addition, Barry Bonds was mad. He had reported to past spring training camps with a chip on his shoulder, but his anger was always baseball related. *I'm better than Van Slyke. Leyland gives me no respect. You think Bonilla can hit? Watch this.* Now, it was personal. On February 18 an arbitrator named Raymond Goetz ruled the Pirates would have to pay Barry $850,000 in 1990, not the $1.6 million he had requested. Though upset about the figure, what set Barry off was the pit-bull tactics of Pirates general manager Larry Doughty, who used the arbitration hearing as a chance to air every conceivable grievance.

Bonds, Doughty contended, didn't play hard, didn't have a positive attitude, didn't hit well with runners in scoring position (a .211 average), and didn't drive in enough runs. He compared the 58 RBIs Barry compiled in 1989 with the totals of other young sluggers like Mark McGwire (95), Eric Davis (101), Will Clark (111), and Kevin Mitchell (125). "These guys hit me leadoff all year and then complain that I don't drive in runs," Barry complained to Rod Wright, his agent. "That's some dirty bullshit right there." It was the same tactic Doughty used in degrading Bonilla, a natural outfielder who played third base at the Pirates' behest. The team won its arbitration hearing against Bonilla by attacking his shoddy infield defense.

Barry was understandably distressed by the outcome of the hearing, but the way he handled its aftermath was childish. In the days following the ruling, Wright told the Pittsburgh media, "He's fed up. I talked with Barry, and he's so irritated with the organization he doesn't want to be a part of the Pirates. If he could be gone tomorrow, he would be happy." Wright contended that, should Leyland return Barry to the leadoff slot, he would refuse the assignment. Wrote Bob Hertzel in *The Sporting News*, "By flexing his jaws instead of his biceps, [Bonds] is doing nothing to enhance his image."

But Barry didn't care about his reputation. "It used to be I'd never think of playing for another team but the Pittsburgh Pirates," he said. "I wanted to be a Pirate for my whole career. But this makes you realize this is a business. If I stay here, OK, but if not, I'll work somewhere else. We're going to win a championship here, and it will be about the same time everybody becomes eligible for free agency. And we're going to say, 'You didn't care about us when we were second- and third-year players. You didn't care about us when we went to arbitration.'"

Instead of supporting a teammate in need, most of the Pirates wanted Barry to keep quiet and play ball. His closest ally was Bonilla, another arbitration loser. Among the team's eight arbitration-eligible players, the three who lost were Bonds, Bonilla, and R. J. Reynolds—all black. Meanwhile, three of the five victors were white. Barry couldn't help but reflect on his father's struggles throughout his career—first as a "nigger" minor leaguer in racist Lexington, North Carolina, then as an oft-traded star whose Afro and militant stance scared team executives. In private conversations, Bonds and Bonilla mused over racism in sports and, specifically, on the Pirates. Why were *they* the arbitration losers? Why was the team's most cherished player Van Slyke?

On the exterior, Bonilla was a gentle soul beloved by both white and black teammates (Wrote Hertzel: "Bonilla is sunshine, Bonds is smog; Bonilla is a smile, Bonds is a sneer"), but inside he, too, possessed an anger fueled by race and class. Raised in the South Bronx with his mother, father, twin sisters, and brother, Roberto Martin Antonio Bonilla saw firsthand that in America minorities got the short end of the stick. His father, Roberto, worked as an electrician, and often forced his youngest child to tag along. "Do you want to do this all your life?" his dad would ask. "Do you see any glamour here?" What Bobby saw was a good, humble man fighting the world to make a decent living. A good, humble Hispanic man.

Bonilla would recall the struggle his family had endured any time he felt lazy or indifferent. His jolly laugh was infectious, but behind it lurked a hidden furor. Many in Pittsburgh recall the time Bonilla, upset over the trivial matter of his wife's parking space at Three Rivers Stadium, grabbed a team employee by the neck and pushed him against the wall. Leyland spent many team flights massaging Bonilla's ego. "Bobby would accommodate you with a smile, but there was always the feeling that he was sort of full of shit," says John Perrotto, the longtime Pirates beat writer for the *Beaver County Times*.

"Bobby once said something to me that summed him up perfectly. He said, 'If you ask, 'Hey, pick me up tomorrow at 3,' Barry's the kind of guy who'll tell you to go fuck yourself. I'm the type who'll promise you I'll be there, then not show up.'"

Bonds and Bonilla formed the heart of the new Pirates lineup, and together they represented a strong voice of discontent. In a town that prided itself on a blue-collar, hardworking steel mill image, two outspoken, out-of-town minorities with large paychecks would inevitably wear out their welcome.

One thing saved the two stars—talent. In 1990, Bonds and Bonilla were *the* story in Pittsburgh. In the Pirates' third game of the season, a 6–2 win at the Mets, Barry drove in three runs, threw a runner out at the plate, and stole a base. Two weeks later, in San Diego, he had four hits and two home runs in a 9–4 victory, and the next day added three more hits and an RBI in another win. Bonilla was equally potent. In an opening-day romp of the Mets, he went 3-for-6 with a homer, two runs, and three RBIs. Eleven days later against the Cubs, Bonilla compiled three hits, two home runs, and three RBIs. On April 30, *Los Angeles Times* writer Bob Wolf began his profile of the 14–6 Bucs with "Any discussion of the Pittsburgh Pirates these days begins with the question, 'Are they for real?'"

The answer was an indisputable affirmative. Drabek emerged as the National League's best starter, winning the Cy Young Award with a 22–6 record. Van Slyke was once again hitting for a good average (.284) and driving in runs. Bonds and Bonilla were the top offensive duo in the National League—Willie Stargell and Dave Parker all over again. If Barry homered one day, Bonilla did so the next. If Barry collected two hits, Bonilla got three. "People talked about Canseco and McGwire in Oakland, but I'd have taken Barry and Bobby any day," says Van Slyke. "They did everything, and they did it great." On May 30, the Pirates thumped Los Angeles 5–3 behind Barry's two-run homer and three RBIs, improving their record to 29–17. After the game, Barry was uncommonly giddy as he reflected on his new position in the middle of the batting order. "Now everything's falling into place like it should have a long time ago," he said. "Everyone knows Andy Van Slyke and Bobby Bonilla are going to drive in runs, but it's hard to drive in runs when you're leading off and hitting homers with the bases empty. I've got a chance to drive in 80 runs now and I feel a whole lot better."

Not that Barry was suddenly admired. What especially bothered many of the Pirates was the way Barry treated rookies, journeymen, and the club's support staff of trainers, clubhouse managers, media relations specialists, and photographers. It was one thing to talk trash to Van Slyke or Drabek, stars who instinctively knew to tune the noise out. But Barry reveled in picking on the little guy. As his father did in his playing days, Barry intentionally tossed his used socks on the floor, just to make John Hallahan, the crusty equipment manager, scurry over to pick them up. "He was a rude, nasty, belligerent person," says Chuckie Cirelli, the assistant equipment manager from 1975 to 2003. "He'd be missing a shirt from his locker and he'd yell really loud, 'I don't want any white bastards in my locker!'" To Barry, this was not racism, just good old-fashioned clubhouse humor. Nobody laughed.

If Barry wanted a drink from the water fountain, he'd nudge the person in front of him and say, "Out of my way. You're not good enough to drink before me." When pitcher Mark Ross, a minor league journeyman, arrived one day wearing a shirt with a golf emblem sewn on the breast, Barry snuck into his locker and cut a hole in the garment. "Why would someone do this?" a distraught Ross said aloud after the game. "Who did I make mad?"

"Personally, I hope Barry dies," says Pete Diana, the former team photographer. "I hate him *that* much. I've seen him do stuff to people that goes beyond evil. I've seen him walk down a hallway and throw a whole bag of sunflower seeds at a security guard. I've seen him ride clubhouse employees to death and tip them close to nothing." When it came time to shoot the official 1990 Pittsburgh Pirates team photograph, 24 of the 25 players on the roster arrived on time, as did the batboys, trainers, and coaches. When Leyland ordered Diana to take the picture, the photographer noted that Barry was missing. "Fuck him!" said the manager. "Shoot the fucking thing without him." A local grocery chain named Giant Eagle was sponsoring the photograph, and when store executives were presented with the finished project, they went ballistic. "We can't hand this out without Barry Bonds," one CEO moaned. "Where the hell was he?"

Answer: Asleep in the clubhouse.

In July 1990 Barry was selected for his first All-Star Game, and upon arriving at Wrigley Field with his father, he bumped into Giants slugger Kevin Mitchell, the starting left fielder and reigning National League MVP. "Fuck Mitch, you shouldn't be starting ahead of me," he said. "You're just a fat fuck." As Barry chuckled, Mitchell's face went blank. A former San Diego gang member with a bullet still lodged in his back, this was not a man to mess with. He turned to Bobby Bonds and whispered with chilling sincerity: "Get your fucking son away from me, or I will beat down his ass and rip out his skull."

What frustrated Bonilla and two or three other Pirates was that, deep down, there was a soft side to Barry. When he let you in it was golden. But, says Jim Lachimia, "his wall of mistrust was so thick, it was hard to get a peek." Following a June game against the Mets in New York, Barry went to Greenwich, Connecticut, to meet up with a friend, freelance sports photographer Scott Clark. That night Clark's wife, Maxine, went into labor, and the three rushed to nearby Greenwich Hospital. "You can't get much whiter than Greenwich," says Clark. "And a white guy and a black guy charge into the emergency room, both claiming to be the father. The looks in that place were pretty funny." Barry stayed the night, signing autographs in the waiting room while anxiously awaiting the news. When Haley Clark was born the next morning, Barry was euphoric. "You should see the Christmas basket he sends us every year—a small family could live in it," says Clark. "I wish people could see that Barry Bonds, because he does exist."

On the morning of July 29, 1990, Barry entered the Three Rivers Stadium office of Jim Leyland, plopped himself down on the couch, and sighed. "I don't think I can play today," he said. "I've got a really bad migraine."

Leyland wasn't happy. The division-rival Phillies were in town. "What the fuck do you mean you've got a migraine? What kind of fuckin' bullshit is that?"

"No, I'm being serious," said Barry. "My family's visiting, and they're staying with us and they were up all night, driving me crazy. My head is killing me."

Leyland angrily stormed to the hallway, where he lit a cigarette and fumed. Migraine? *Migraine!* "You're not gonna believe this sonofabitch," he said to Rich Donnelly, the coach. "Barry says he's got a headache and can't play. I know the guy's fucking lying. He just doesn't wanna face a fuckin' lefty pitcher."

Donnelly chortled with delight. En route to the stadium that morning, he had run into a friend who owned The Mirage, a nightclub in nearby Steubenville, Ohio. "Hey, I'll tell you what," the club owner told Donnelly, "that left fielder of yours can dance his ass off!"

Donnelly's jaw dropped.

"Uhm . . ."

"Yeah," the owner continued, "he was at The Mirage until five or six in the morning, just doing his thing."

Donnelly relayed the story to Leyland and then watched as the manager returned to his office, where Barry remained lying on the couch, eyes closed. "You sonofabitch!" Leyland yelled. "You think you're gonna get into the Hall of Fame taking days off? If you wanna get into the Hall of Fame, you better play against right-handers, left-handers, junkballers, flamethrowers. . . . "

"But Skip," Barry interjected, "my head is killing me. I'm dying."

Leyland turned, headed for the door, and stopped short. "Yeah, your head," he said. "How was that dancing at The Mirage last night, anyhow?"

Bonds sat straight up and dashed into the clubhouse to grab his glove. "He never asked out of the lineup again," says Donnelly. "Thank God for us."

The 1990 season was the one that lifted Barry Bonds from star to superstar. Those who watched him with the Giants in the late 1990s and early 2000s believed they were witnessing the greatest baseball display in modern history. Yet Bonds was at his best not with San Francisco, but as a Pirate, when he brought power, speed, defense, and instinct to the game. In 1990, Barry compiled career-best numbers with a .301 average, 33 home runs, 114 RBIs, and 52 stolen bases. He won the National League Most Valuable Player award with 23 of 24 first-place votes. (Bonilla received the one other vote.) "He made everyone in the lineup better," says Leyland.

With Bonds batting behind him, Bonilla—hitting cleanup—posted 32 homers and drove in 120 runs. Though there was much debate in Pittsburgh over who was the better of the "Killer Bs," anyone with a baseball IQ acknowledged the obvious. "Barry was the only guy in the game who would come up to the plate and you just knew—and *he* just knew—that a home run was coming," says Jay Bell, the Pirates shortstop. Bobby Bonilla was fantastic. But Barry Bonds was blessed.

There was one problem. Barry Bonds was blessed until crunch time arrived. The Pirates and Mets were engaged in a late-season dogfight for the National League East title. Near season's end, Pittsburgh ran off seven straight wins to pull away and clinch the division (the Pirates wound up 95–67, four games ahead of New York). Yet as Drabek came up big and Van Slyke hit everything in sight, Bonds struggled. He batted .160 without a home run, a slump he publicly blamed on fatigue but should have attributed to nerves. Throughout his life, from high school to college to the minor leagues, Barry was so much better than the competition that stress was irrelevant. But come September and October in the big leagues, everyone is at his best. The pitchers throw harder, the umpires are sharper, the stadiums are more crowded, the TV lights are brighter. Entering the 1990 season, Barry's .109 career average with runners in scoring position in the late innings was the lowest ever documented by the Elias Sports Bureau. This wasn't mere coincidence.

"I think that boiled down to age and maturity," says Bob Patterson, a Pirates reliever from 1986 to 1987 and 1989 to 1992. "It takes learning not to do anything different than you've done all year. People can tell you that, but until you've actually had success doing it, you'll always try doing things extra. You start thinking about the largeness of the situation and you're done."

The Pirates met the Cincinnati Reds in the National League Championship Series, an even matchup of small-market teams with solid pitching; young, dynamic outfielders; and unyielding grit. Even though Pittsburgh took the opener with a 4–3 victory at Riverfront Stadium, the omens were not good for Bonds. He notched just one hit, a weak single. After the game, Leyland hailed Bonds for provoking seven pickoff attempts from Reds pitcher Jose Rijo. Were Barry a lesser player, perhaps the praise would be justified. But this was the National League MVP.

In a 2–1 game two loss, Bonds twice came to the plate with two men on base without driving in a run. In the fifth inning he lost a fly ball in the afternoon sun, turning a sure out into a run-scoring double for the Reds. In a surprising bit of insight, Bonds admitted to trying too hard. "I'm not kidding anybody," he said. "The pressure is there. We're chasing pitches we wouldn't normally go after. We're like [Bonds made a gurgling sound while grabbing his throat] choking right now. I've been patient all year. And now I'm chasing pitches I wouldn't chase all season."

As the Pirates lost the next two games at home, Bonds swung wildly at the plate and in the press, blaming the league for an early start time ("I think it's ridiculous to have games at 3 o'clock in the afternoon. The sun expanded the whole day."), the umpires for a too-wide strike zone ("What frustrated me is this: Can a pitcher throw a perfect pitch on the outside corner every time?"), and Pirates fans for not supporting the club ("I don't even want to tell you how I feel about it. I'm going to hurt someone's feelings.").

Teammates were surprisingly sympathetic to Barry's struggles until he crossed the line. In baseball, it's OK to rip an opponent or the playing conditions. Ripping a teammate, however, is treasonous. In the minutes before game five in Pittsburgh, Pirates third baseman Jeff King was scratched from the lineup because of lower back pain. King had suffered the injury in game two but played the next two contests with acute discomfort. While watching King scuffle through batting practice before game five, Leyland made the decision to move Bonilla to third. The Pirates won 3–2, and afterward Bonds went on the offensive. "Jeff King's supposed to be the everyday third baseman, but you've got to go out there all the time," he told a throng of reporters. "Hey, there's a lot of minor league third basemen who'd love to be up here playing every day, who'd play whether they're hurt or healthy.

"Jeff's a big asset to this ball club and we need that bat in the lineup. I'm not personally mad at Jeff. But when we play Friday, Bobby Bonilla will be playing third and Jeff King will be sitting there getting his back healthy. He'll be getting ready for spring training."

The humble, soft-spoken King refused to fire back, but he didn't have to. Not one Pirate sided with Bonds. "That bothered me a lot," says Jay Bell. "It was Barry feeling like he had something important to say and not thinking about the meaning behind the words. Jeff King was one of the hardest workers we had. If he wasn't playing, you knew he was really hurting. Everyone was angry." If Bonds had been batting .500 with three or four homers against the Reds, the outcry would have been muted. But how could a guy who would go on to hit .167 with no home runs and one RBI degrade another player? In the series-ending game six loss at Cincinnati, Bonds went 0-for-1 with three walks, taking a handful of pitches he would have swung at were it May or June. The Reds won 2–1 as three pitchers combined for a one-hitter. Yes, Bonilla and Van Slyke also slumped, the former hitting .190 and the latter .208, with not a home run between them. But neither player had the audacity to slam a hurting teammate.

"You wanna criticize someone? Fine, criticize," says pitcher Bob Walk. "But you better be able to walk the walk. Barry didn't even come close."

Upon boarding the charter flight for the trip home to Pittsburgh, Pirates players were greeted by a stack of 25 large pizza pies. When the plane reached cruising altitude, Bonds was the first to hop out of his seat and attack the spread. To the disbelief of the other Pirates, he grabbed three whole pies. R. J. Reynolds, who was sitting with his wife, Yolanda, was not happy. "Hey Barry," he shouted, "how 'bout throwing me one of those pizzas! You can't eat all of 'em!" Bonds's response was a terse "Fuck you."

In his five and a half years as a Pirate, Reynolds had earned much respect from teammates for his ability to tolerate the mercurial Bonds. He was a happy-go-lucky man from Sacramento whose superlative athleticism concealed a glaring lack of baseball instincts. What Reynolds possessed in bushels was empathy. "R. J. understood what was going on," says Jerry Weinstein, his baseball coach at Sacramento City College. "He was a caring person who tried to help others get along." Because he and Bonds were both black outfielders, many teammates assumed they were close. In reference to Barry, Reynolds often heard, "R. J., talk to your boy about his attitude." Truth be told, Reynolds only tolerated Bonds because, he says, "it just seemed like the right thing to do. He obviously was a social misfit. I felt like he needed guidance and support."

No more. Reynolds reached into Bonds's row, grabbed one of the pizza boxes, and began to open it when Bonds smacked it from below, flipping the entire pie onto Reynolds's brown suede sweater and leather pants. Cheese and tomato sauce flew everywhere. The airplane went silent. No chatter. No laughter. Silence. Many had been anticipating when Reynolds would finally snap and crack Bonds over the head. The moment appeared to be at hand.

Reynolds turned to Bonilla, who was sitting nearby, and said, "That's it. I'm done with this guy. All these years of taking his shit—for what? It's over." As he clenched his fists and stood up, Reynolds was tugged back down by Yolanda. "He's just a baby," she said. "It's not worth it."

"It was a fucked-up way to come at me," says Reynolds. "Our last flight together, and you do me like that? I don't hold a grudge, but I was hurt."

Three weeks later, Bonds and Reynolds were two of 26 players named to the U.S. All-Star team that would play an eight-game series in Tokyo against a collection of Japanese standouts. Reynolds barely spoke to Barry, and he felt vindicated as the other big leaguers blew him off as well. "It only took eight days," says Reynolds. "Eight days, and that entire team hated Barry."

In a 10–5 victory over the Japanese team on November 7 at Koshien Stadium, Bonds hit a soaring home run off Shinji Imanaka, tossed his bat 20 feet into the air, made a big loop toward the rival dugout, and hotdogged his way around the base paths. "All the goodwill between the two teams and the fans of Japan toward us—gone," says Reynolds. "Typical Barry."

In the hotel bar after the game, Bonds and Oakland A's pitcher Dave Stewart, a respected 10-year veteran and four-time 20-game winner, engaged in a heated exchange. In front of most of the team, Bonds tore into Stewart's career. "Look at your ERA—crap," Bonds said. "If we played in the same league, I'd take you apart every single time."

Like Reynolds, Stewart took the high road and walked away. "That's just Barry," Reynolds explained to the pitcher. "A fuckin' weirdo."

Despite the team's record attendance (2,049,908 paying customers in 1990), the Pittsburgh Pirates Baseball Club, Inc., was flailing. With total revenue of $44 million, the organization lost approximately $5 million in 1990, and there was little reason to feel optimistic. Between 1981 and 1990, the city's population had dropped 14 percent, to 370,000, and a recent census put the

Pittsburgh metropolitan area population at 2.2 million people, down from 2.4 million a decade earlier. The Pirates were hemorrhaging money in a decaying market.

On the day he was named the National League MVP, Bonds—still incensed by his arbitration experience of eight months earlier—made clear his frustration with the team's payroll slicing. "The Pirates can't keep crying, 'Broke,'" he said. "You can't own half of Pittsburgh and say you're on welfare." Three weeks later, free-agent first baseman Sid Bream signed a three-year, $5.6 million deal with Atlanta after offering to stay with Pittsburgh for $1 million less. Shortly thereafter, Bonds told the media he wouldn't sign with the Pirates "for $100 million" if the team didn't give him a $3 million-per-year contract before his February 15 arbitration hearing. "If I do leave," Bonds said, "I'll haunt the Pittsburgh Pirates. They'll be the one team I beat up on."

Such words did not play well in Pittsburgh, where blue-collar pride trumped athletic greed. In the *Pittsburgh Press*, columnist Gene Collier teed off in a piece that echoed the sentiments of many of the city's fans:

> The atrocities are almost unprintable. The Pirates, and Pirates president Carl Barger is specifically responsible, forced on young Barry a salary of $850,000. With no incentives. I mean, the ruthlessly imposed conditions agreed to in good-faith bargaining between the clubs and Bonds' union. Forced him to travel the better part of six months to first-class cities using only first-class air and hotel accommodations with first-class meal money. Clearly, if Judgment Day were tomorrow, you get the feeling the official agenda would read something like this: 1) Hitler. 2) Saddam Hussein's treatment of the Kurds. 3) Brunch. 4) Barger's treatment of Barry Bonds.

In February 1991, with the Pirates unwilling to negotiate a long-term deal and two more seasons remaining until unrestricted free agency, Bonds had no choice but to again file for arbitration. He put in a request for $3.25 million, countered by Pittsburgh's offer of $2.3 million. It did not go well.

On February 14, Drabek smashed the arbitration record when his salary tripled to $3.3 million.

On February 16, Bonilla lost his request for $3.475 million and was handed $2.4 million.

On February 17, Bonds lost his case.

On April 6, the Pirates signed Van Slyke to a four-year, $12.6 million extension.

When Bonds learned of the arbitration loss from his agent, Rod Wright, he was livid. He screamed at Wright, screamed at his wife, screamed at his parents. The arbitration case itself had been nothing short of a nightmare. Although it is common for the team representatives to degrade a player's worth, things had turned unusually ugly. Sitting mere inches from Bonds, Doughty bashed his wife, Sun, as a horrible influence and "terrible person to have around." At one point, Bonds lunged across the table, only to be held back by Wright.

How could the MVP be handed such a meager amount of money? At the same time a pitcher—*a pitcher!*—was awarded the big bucks? Why was it that once again the two black stars were kept in the cold? Upon arriving in Bradenton for spring training, Bonilla and Bonds teamed up for a boycott of the media, maintaining that speaking to the press was helpful to the organization. The Pirates? *Fuck the Pirates.*

The Pirates' relationship to Bonds hit bottom on the morning of Monday, March 4, when Barry engaged in a now-infamous shouting match with Leyland. The day began routinely enough, with Bonds and his fellow outfielders tossing on an out-of-the-way Bradenton field. Standing alongside Bonds was Scott Clark, his freelance photographer friend, who was casually leaning against his camera. When a pair of television crews began filming, Bonds snapped. "Get out of my face!" This caught the attention of Jim Lachimia, the team's media relations director, who told Bonds he lacked the authority to determine press access. "They're just doing their jobs," Lachimia said. "They have a right to be here."

"I will decide what cameras stay here!" Bonds barked. "Now get the fuck out of my face." Minutes later Pirates instructor Bill Virdon, an old-school baseball disciplinarian, advised Bonds to shut his mouth. More yelling ensued. "Barry's yapping and causing a big hubbub, raising hell and ranting and raving," said Virdon. "He says, 'Nobody's gonna tell me what to do,' and of course that hit me wrong."

"By that point," says Clark, "I packed up my camera and *slowwwwly* started to slink away."

Leyland arrived, having made a beeline from an adjacent field. For too long he had done his best to massage Bonds's ego, and for too long he had grown increasingly exasperated by the whole act. Leyland approached Bonds, stood inches from his face, and exploded.

Leyland: "Don't fuck with me!"

Bonds: "I'm not fucking with you!"

Leyland: "I said don't fuck with me! I've been kissing your ass for three years and I'm not gonna do it again! I'm the manager of this team and I'm gonna tell you what to do and you're gonna do it and if you goddamn don't like it you can go someplace else. I'm the manager of this fuckin' team!"

With that, Leyland rose from manager to legend. "It wasn't like we didn't already have a lot of respect for Jim," says Pirates catcher Mike LaValliere. "But it was just one more reminder that Jim was running the ship, and you didn't have to worry about him looking at Barry with special glasses."

In the spring of '91, only the most adept of managers could have handled the seething anger within the Pirates camp. Leyland was that guy. He was unafraid to talk trash to Bonds and was receptive when Bonds fired it back. "Hey Old Man, what do you know about playing in the majors?" Bonds would say, only to be swatted down with a quick, "Shut the fuck up, you spoiled Hollywood brat." At the same time, Bonds felt comfortable entering Leyland's office when he needed to pout; he knew the manager would listen. Bonds viewed Leyland as a father figure. "I come from a big family," says Leyland. "My dad was one of 16 and I was one of seven. You learn how to deal with people. I always tried to get to know the player, to see what made him tick. Being such a horseshit player really worked to my advantage as a manager, because I respected how difficult the game was and I respected the players. I was honest with them. I told them the truth. They didn't always like that, but it was the right thing. I also knew that you didn't treat every player the same. All people have certain unique needs."

During a game at San Francisco's Candlestick Park in the early 1990s, Leyland showed just how understanding he could be. Bonds hit a towering fly to center, where Giants outfielder Willie McGee positioned himself to make the catch. The wind took hold of the ball and blew it out of McGee's range. Because Bonds assumed it would be caught, he only reached first base. Pirates reserve outfielder Gary Varsho spent the rest of the inning waiting for Leyland to tee off on Bonds. Instead the manager held his tongue. The next day Varsho asked Leyland why he had remained quiet. "Lemme ask you something," said Leyland. "Who do you think was the most embarrassed person in the whole yard?"

"Barry," Varsho replied.

"Well, 40,000 people saw him be embarrassed, whoever was watching on TV saw him embarrassed," said Leyland. "Do you want me to make it even worse by having words? Is that gonna make Barry better?"

Varsho, the team's 25th man, nodded. This was one smart skipper.

"And one more thing," Leyland said with a grin. "If that was you, you'd be back in the minors quicker than the next flight went out."

The morning after the shouting match, Bonds approached Lachimia and *almost* apologized. Though the words *I'm sorry* never escaped his lips, he offered what—for Barry Bonds—was a mea culpa. "You know," Bonds said, "this morning I told Bobby Bonilla, 'Man, I shouldn't have yelled at Jim.'"

Lachimia nodded and shook Bonds's hand. As far as he was concerned, the embarrassing incident was over. (For Bonds, the grudge didn't die. In an interview with *Playboy* two years later, Bonds accused the Pirates of masterminding the altercation. "Why would a microphone and a TV crew be right there at that time?" he said. "Just to stir up shit. The funny thing is, my dad told me before I went to spring training, 'They're going to set you up when you get there.' He was right.") But not in the public's mind. As the altercation was broadcast nonstop across the country, Bonds (along with Oakland's Rickey Henderson, who spent most of spring griping about his paltry $3.3 million salary) emerged as the face of greed in sports. He was booed vigorously throughout spring training, and the harsh fan reaction brought repercussions. Rod Wright, Bonds's agent, had negotiated an endorsement deal with Pepsi. "As soon as they saw the tape of Barry screaming," says Wright, "they wanted nothing to do with him." Among the promotions planned at Three Rivers Stadium in '91 were Bobby Bonilla Wristband Night, Jay Bell Growth Chart Day, Doug Drabek Cy Young T-shirt Night, and Barry Bonds MVP Bat Day. Immediately after the outburst, the sponsor of Bonds's event pulled out.

Despite jeers both at home and on the road, Bonds and the Pirates enjoyed another banner season in 1991, finishing 98–64 and 14 games ahead of St. Louis for the National League East crown. Throughout the year the New York Yankees made repeated attempts to acquire Bonds, but their best offer (outfielder Jesse Barfield and a minor league center fielder named Bernie Williams) was not enough. Bonds remained in Pittsburgh, piecing together yet another monster season (.292, 25 home runs, 116 RBIs, 43 stolen bases). There were even signs of enlightenment. Bonds hired a New York–based public relations agency to help improve his image. He approached the Pirates about filming a public service announcement for the Children's Hospital of Pittsburgh, participated in a free baseball clinic for inner-city kids, and donated $100 for every home run he hit to a foundation for troubled youths. Bonds won the home run contest in an exhibition at Triple A Buffalo, then signed autographs for 35 minutes.

Within the clubhouse Bonds, along with the other Pirate players and coaches, participated in an ultra-competitive Nerf mini-hoop tournament nicknamed the "Rat Basketball Classic" (In a staggering upset, Bonds lost to LaValliere, the stumpy 5-foot-9 catcher, in the semifinals).

Who was this strange man? Some Pirates attributed Bonds's temporarily lightened demeanor to Nikolai, his son. An endearing young father by most accounts, Bonds bragged of changing diapers and waking up at all hours of the night to soothe his boy. Determined not to follow in his own father's footsteps, Bonds told those listening that there would be no drunken tirades or weeks without contact. When Nikolai was old enough, Barry installed bunk beds in the boy's room so the two could lie near each other and talk. "My son is everything to me," he said. "My life."

Indeed, Bonds's behavior with the children of friends and teammates was often remarkable. While Pirate players generally kept their distance from Bonds, their sons and daughters were more than welcome to climb on his chair, comb through his locker, and sneak pieces of Bazooka bubble gum from his pockets. Bonds's comfort with them made sense. Kids don't seek out your legal background or ask repetitive questions about a groin injury. They don't criticize that botched play in the outfield or whine about your salary. With children, Barry didn't have to put on a front. He could be himself.

In a professional career that would span beyond 20 years, this was the first time the media would wonder aloud whether we were witnessing a "new" Barry Bonds—a kinder, gentler, more giving man who had matured with age. On the July afternoon Varsho hit his first career home run in a game at Wrigley Field, the teammate most anxious to congratulate him was—of all people—Bonds, who slapped him hard on the back and, recalls Varsho, "had a smile as big as the sun." When Bonds drove in his 100th run with a single against the Cubs at Three Rivers in mid-September, the 18,152 fans in attendance saluted the accomplishment with a standing ovation, and teammates Lloyd McClendon and Gary Redus offered a Superman cape in the clubhouse after the game. Wrote Mark Maske of the *Washington Post*: "The stories about Bonds being the most hated person in the Pirates' clubhouse have been heard less often."

While Bonds's image might have temporarily improved, his reputation as prime-time choker would again be put to the test. By winning the National League East for a second straight season, the Pirates were scheduled to meet the Braves. One season removed from 97 losses and a third straight last-place finish, Atlanta rode its young, talented roster to 94 victories. What concerned Leyland most was the Braves' rotation. Led by 20-game winner Tom Glavine, 18-game winner Steve Avery, and 14-game winner John Smoltz, Atlanta's starters were confident, deceptive, and often unhittable.

"Anyone who wanted to see Barry at the plate in a big situation needed a lobotomy," says Mike Bielecki, a former Pirate who pitched briefly for the Braves in 1991. "I don't think we pitched to him all that differently. But our pitchers were very smart, and they were extra careful not to make mistakes with him at the plate."

Before game one in Pittsburgh, Bonds looked around at the mountains of TV cameras and notepads and decided the occasion called for some thoughtless verbal freestyling. First, he challenged Atlanta's baserunners to test his arm in left field: "That's my house out there, and you better be careful when you come into my house," he said. "Is there a left fielder in this league who compares to me? Nobody. That's speaking just defensively. Now offensively . . . well, there's nobody that compares to me either." Then he accused the Pirates of racism: "Everyone knows what's going on with this team," he said. "Open your eyes. Wipe your glasses. You know what's going on. You don't want to write it, you just want to goad Barry Bonds into saying it." Finally, he took Van Slyke and Bonilla and mixed them into his own racial stew: "Andy Van Slyke, he's the great white hope around here," he said. "Do you think Bobby Bonilla should make more money than Andy Van Slyke? You know why. Let's leave it at that."

The performance was stupefying. Why now, with the playoffs beginning, did Bonds have to speak up? "He had no sense of timing," says Van Slyke. "Of understanding that some things are better left unsaid."

In a seven-game Braves conquest, Bonds flopped. He batted .148 with no home runs or RBIs. The Pirates returned home to Pittsburgh with a 3–2 series lead, but they couldn't seal the deal. Atlanta's pitchers twice walked Bonilla intentionally to face Bonds in the fifth game, and he failed to produce. Together, the trio of Bonds, Bonilla, and Van Slyke went 1-for-36 with runners in scoring position. "Everybody's looking for me to do something great, to be a hero," Bonds said. "That's tough. Baseball teams can't depend on one person." This was a far cry from the brash Barry Bonds of the regular season.

One month later, Atlanta's Terry Pendleton was named the National League MVP, besting Bonds by a 274–259 margin, the closest vote in 12 years. No one could make the case that Pendleton was a more talented player than Bonds. But along with his excellent statistics, Pendleton was the emotional leader of the Braves. His drive and encouragement took them to the next level.

Barry Bonds, meanwhile, was stuck in neutral.

EIGHT

THE WRIGHT STUFF

THE FAMILY AND THE agent first found each other on a nondescript morn-ing in March 1977. While walking through the lobby of the Palm Springs Municipal Courthouse, an obscure 27-year-old public defender named Rod Wright was tapped on the arm by a despondent African-American man with muscular shoulders and an Afro. "Mr. Wright," the star outfielder for the California Angels said, "can I speak to you for a moment?"

Bobby Bonds had just watched Wright deftly handle an arraignment, and he needed legal advice. The ballplayer was in court for driving under the influence during the revocation of his license. A potential punishment was a year's jail time. "Bobby, I'm a public defender so I can't represent you," Wright said. "But I've looked at your case, and I think I can help."

As Bobby went before the judge, Wright sat in the nearby attorney's booth and instructed him to follow his signals. When Wright nodded yes, Bobby was also to nod. When Wright shook his head no, Bobby did so, too. Upon completion, the judge placed Bobby on probation—no jail.

When they reconvened in the lobby, Bobby embraced Wright in a bear hug and handed him a rolled-up wad of $100 bills. "Hey, I appreciate that," said Wright. "But I can't take it. I work for the county."

Impressed with Wright's integrity, one month later Bobby hired him as his agent, marking the beginning of a long, fruitful relationship that merged business and friendship. Wright and Bobby shared much in common—both were raised by strong Pentecostal mothers, and both had baseball in their blood (Wright played third base at the University of Florida before tearing his rotator cuff as a senior). When Wright joined his client on the road, they split a hotel room, sleeping in side-by-side beds and spending half the night talking about the game. Upon introducing Wright, Bobby often said, "Meet my brother."

That bond led Barry to Wright in 1985, when he was a junior at Arizona State and contemplating the future. "Hey Rod, you and I haven't gone over this, but I'm coming out and I'm gonna sign," Barry said. "Would you represent me?"

"Barry," Wright replied, "I'd be honored."

The young Bonds quickly discovered that Rod Wright wasn't like other agents. Neither slick nor sleazy, when Wright called to say, "How's everything going?" it was because he actually cared. His genuineness led to a small but impressive list of clients that included two Expos, an established third baseman named Tim Wallach, and a future legend, pitcher Randy Johnson. When, in 1990, Barry decided the 6,000-square-foot lot he had purchased on the Bear Creek Golf Club in Murrieta, California, wasn't large enough to build a house, Wright traded him the 11,000-square foot lot (on 1.3 acres) he and his wife, Barbara, had purchased months earlier for *their* dream home. "I would've done anything for Barry," says Wright. "Absolutely anything. I viewed him like I would a brother or son."

Prior to the 1992 season, Bonds and Wright sat down and devised a fiscal strategy. Given the Pirates' stinginess, there was no way Bonds would return once his contract expired. That December Bobby Bonilla, his closest friend, had left the Pirates to sign a five-year, $29 million deal with the New York Mets. Wright knew it was chump change compared to what Bonds would receive on the open market. "Just stay healthy and keep your comments in check," Wright told Bonds, "and you'll have a contract to set you up for life."

The words stuck with Bonds. After avoiding another arbitration hearing by signing a one-year, $4.7 million contract (the highest one-year deal in baseball history), the Pittsburgh left fielder was on his best behavior for much of the early season. At the MTV Rock and Jock Softball Challenge he was full of good cheer. A few weeks later, he sat and signed baseballs for free at a charity benefit. He funded a $5,000 scholarship for the Negro Educational Emergency Drive's adopt-a-student program and remained in close contact with Tyrone Hill, the 18-year-old Pittsburgh resident who would attend Penn State thanks to Bonds. In March, when the Braves nearly acquired the Pirates star in a trade for reliever Alejandro Pena and outfielder Keith Mitchell, Bonds informed those around him that it was great to remain in Pittsburgh.

"Pittsburgh has been good to me," he told *Sport* magazine during spring training. "No matter what happens, my heart will always go to the Pirates because they gave me my big break."

Bonds was smiling, laughing, and having fun. But once again, it didn't last.

The problems began at home, where—after several years of relative peace—Bonds's marriage to Sun was crumbling. During the off season, Bonds retreated to their Murrieta, California, house, where he hoped to unwind far away from the media glare of Major League Baseball. "The place they lived in was absolutely gorgeous," says Kevin Cook, who interviewed Bonds for *Playboy* in the winter before the '93 season. "A palace." With a chuckle, Cook recalls that Bonds took special pride in the yellowish-beige paint covering many of the walls. He had purchased so many gallons that Sherwin-Williams named the color "Bonds 103." The house featured a juice bar, a pizza oven, a pool with a waterfall, and two enormous stained glass windows to honor the occupants—one in the shape of a sun, the other a baseball diamond.

A beautiful house, however, does not equal a beautiful marriage, and the couple was arguing incessantly—about Nikolai, about their finances, about Sun's independence. With the shouting and door slamming, the abode was a place Bonds no longer enjoyed. He increasingly viewed the ballpark as his refuge. Friends recall visiting the Bonds residence and seeing broken furniture parts floating in the pool and a husband and wife barely on speaking terms. Sun was tired of her husband's refusal to see her as an equal partner.

In her six years in the United States, Sun had evolved from timid foreigner to strong American woman. Dissatisfied with the role of ballplayer's wife, she desired new adventures.

Though he had promised he would never become like his father, Bonds degraded Sun. He criticized her parenting skills, her appearance, her mannerisms. He dismissed her thoughts as irrelevant babble. On fleeting occasions, he was able to look into the mirror and see a less-than-ideal husband, but in the throes of emotion, he could not help himself: He was turning into Bobby. "Barry was broken up over Sun," says Gary Varsho. "You'd see him crying, and that was the reason why. His relationship with his wife was in trouble."

Bonds tried to behave in 1992, but the nonstop bickering apparently wore on him. When the Pirates' new general manager, Ted Simmons, traded 20-game winner John Smiley to Minnesota for a couple of minor leaguers and insisted falsely that it wasn't a financial move (Smiley made $3.44 million), Bonds couldn't hold his tongue. "Just don't insult anyone's intelligence by saying it wasn't because of anybody's contract," he said. "That's insulting to the intelligence of adults. Bobby Bonilla's gone, John Smiley's gone . . . is there light at the end of the tunnel?"

Through the end of May Bonds adhered to Wright's free agency plan by enjoying the best season of his life, batting better than .300 and leading the league in home runs, RBIs, and runs scored. On June 4 the New York Mets and Bonilla came to Pittsburgh. From the moment Bonilla emerged from the dugout, hostility rained down on him. When he stepped to the plate, the Pirates organist played "Take the Money and Run." Banners reading BOBBY BOOONILLA, DO YOU LIKE N.Y. MONILLA? and BOBBY BO-TRAITOR hung from the railings. In the eighth inning, Bonilla took to the field wearing a helmet after a golf ball pelted him in the leg. Although Bonds had a terrific night, collecting a double and a home run and scoring three runs in a 7–2 Bucs victory, the battering of his pal made him sick.

The next day, Bonds refused to hold back. "Don't kid yourself that it's about the money," he said. "It's a black thing." Bonds correctly noted that when, in 1991, Sid Bream returned to Pittsburgh for the first time as an opponent, he received a warm ovation. Unprovoked, Bonds proceeded to unload on Van Slyke. "Mr. Pittsburgh," Bonds snarled in reference to his white teammate. "Anyone touches Andy on this club and he gets released."

Although Bonds's harsh words made his agent wince, the outburst was justified. The standard rule of thumb in baseball media relations is to stay far away from prickly issues, but Bonds was merely echoing the sentiments of dozens of black Pirates before him—from Dock Ellis to Dave Parker to Bonilla to anyone present for the public harassment former second baseman Rennie Stennett received in the late 1970s when he married a light-skinned black woman. Why were Pittsburgh's fan favorites usually white? And when they were black, why did they have to be genteel and soft-spoken? "Hell, if I were white they would have built a shrine for me in front of the stadium," says Parker, a Pirate from 1973 to 1983. "There's a double standard where black players are always—*always*—given a shorter leash than whites."

"Racism certainly played a part in Barry's unpopularity," says Bob Smizik, the longtime Pittsburgh newspaper scribe. "This town does not like uppity black guys. They liked [Mean] Joe Greene and Willie Stargell because those guys were very humble. But black guys who strut take a beating."

The city's recent history casts a dramatic light on the complexities of race. On April 5, 1968, the day after the assassination of Martin Luther King Jr., riots broke out in Pittsburgh's Hill District neighborhood, once home to legendary jazz clubs like the Savoy Ballroom and the Crawford Grill. By the 1960s the Hill District's residents were mostly black, and the majority of buildings were dilapidated. Five hundred fires raged in the days following King's death, as much of white Pittsburgh observed the chaos from afar and thought, "What are *those people* doing to themselves?"

"When the riots took place, I was a sophomore in a high school that was 70 percent white and 30 percent black," says Lou Ransom, managing editor of the *New Pittsburgh Courier*, the city's black newspaper. "By the time I graduated it was the other way around. It was white flight—quick, dramatic, and widespread. The only white folks who didn't leave were the white folks who couldn't leave. It was a city divided."

Though attitudes had improved by the late 1980s and early 1990s, racial tensions remained. In June 1986 the Ku Klux Klan set fire to a cross and inducted new members at a weekend rally in Uniontown, Pennsylvania, a mere 50 miles outside the city. One year later, after a Pittsburgh-based pilot named Phillip Garland filed a discrimination suit against USAir, he received a letter that read, bluntly, "Nigger, go home."

Wright was less than thrilled by the uproar surrounding Bonds's remarks, but he still believed that with another MVP-caliber season, his client could hit free-agent paydirt. As the mid-season All-Star break approached and Bonds's future became a hot topic, Wright was contacted by Dick Schaap. The famed author and television personality wanted to host an ESPN special on a big-time agent and big-time player heading toward free agency. Wright excitedly called Bonds and told him they would sit down with Schaap on the eve of the All-Star Game at San Diego's Jack Murphy Stadium. Bonds agreed—and began acting very strangely.

Far from naive, Wright had considered the possibility of rival agents attempting to steal his star client. Bonds was on the verge of becoming the highest-paid free agent ever. Yet Wright's concerns were put at ease by thoughts of kinship. Sure, Barry was moody and arrogant and inconsiderate and often downright mean. But Wright and the Bonds family went way back. They got together for holiday dinners and exchanged gifts. Wright was the only nonrelative allowed to call Bobby's father "Pops." This wasn't blood, but it was awfully close.

On the day before the Schaap interview, Bonds arrived unannounced at his agent's house and asked what, exactly, Wright had been doing on his behalf. Over the ensuing eight hours, Wright presented mounds of documents, spelling out investment strategies and endorsement deals. "I set up a retirement portfolio for him to move all his money from endorsements into a personal service contract, and he could be president of his own corporation," says Wright. "That's what you do in estate planning." Throughout the session Bonds received phone calls from Sun, instructing him to "Look for this!" and "Ask him about that!" Wright did not trust her. "She would always ask me things about Barry's personal finances," says Wright, "and I would say, 'Sun, I do not represent you. He's my client.' She would get very irritated. I believe she was trying to get into Barry's pocket, and I considered it part of my job to protect him."

At the end of the night, with mounds of paper on the dining room table,

Bonds hugged Wright. "We're all right," he said. "I'm gonna go home and take care of this." The next morning, without explanation, he called Wright to say he was backing out of the Schaap segment. That same day, while standing on the field at Jack Murphy Stadium for the All-Star gala, Bonds ran into Dennis Gilbert, founder of the powerful Beverly Hills Sports Council, and asked, "How do you feel about being my new guy?" Gilbert was euphoric. His biggest clients were Bonilla and Jose Canseco, two of baseball's brightest young stars. Now he had landed Bonds. "I loved it," Gilbert says. "You're talking about a marquee player who wasn't getting good representation."

Wright has accused his rival of thievery, but Gilbert vehemently denies the allegations, calling Bonds's former agent, "a big baby" and "overmatched." True, the idea of moving to a new agent had first been floated by Bonilla, but Sports Council executives were quick to tell Bonds that he needed a powerful machine behind him, not a "one-trick weakling" like Rod Wright. A reputation for client swindling had even earned the agency a nickname: "Beverly Hills Sports Criminals."

"This is a business that's almost solely built on shame and humiliation," agent Matt Sosnick said. "How much humiliation can you give your competitors? That's the reason the Beverly Hills Sports Council, when they steal a guy, they write in the termination letter, 'I have decided to switch to Beverly Hills Sports.' They not only want to take the power from you. They want to humiliate you and basically say, 'Look, you can't stop us.'"

When Bonds finally told Wright that he was fired, the agent was stunned. "This is how I support my family," Wright pleaded. "I'm the one who's been with you for eight years, down in the battles. And now, right before the multiyear deal, you're going to leave me?" Wright called Bobby, asking him to talk some sense into his son. "This isn't something for me to get involved in," Bobby responded. The phone call was the last time Wright and Bobby Bonds would speak. Wright threatened a lawsuit, reminding Barry they had a binding exclusive representation agreement through free agency. "You can't just leave me like that," he told Bonds. "It doesn't work that way."

What took place next hit Wright like a Joe Frazier uppercut. According to Wright, Bonds spread the word that he was an ineffective, immoral, pathetic snake of a man. One by one, nearly all of Wright's clients dropped him. Chuckie Carr—gone. Randy Johnson—gone. Doug Henry—gone. When Bonds drove by Wright's house, he would honk the horn and wave mockingly—the ultimate taunt to a family he had loved. Wright reached out once, begging Bonds to at least contact his 13-year-old son, Brian, and explain that the move was strictly business. "Barry," says Wright, "was my child's idol."

Bonds agreed to make the call, but when Wright picked up the telephone he heard Barry telling the boy, "Your dad ripped me off and wasn't doing me right. So I had to do this."

"Barry, what has happened to you?" Wright yelled. "Who have you become?"

Click.

With his client roster in tatters (Wallach and journeyman pitcher Mark Lee were the only two to stick with him), his reputation trashed, his finances in disarray (he was counting on Bonds's impending payday), Wright saw that his career was finished. In the following years he lost his home, sold most of his possessions, contemplated suicide, and then moved the family to Florida, where he dedicated himself to Jesus. Although his lawsuit against Bonds was thrown out of court, Wright landed on his feet and is now a successful real estate developer in Destin. "I've been toying with the idea of writing a book," Wright says with a chuckle. "I'll call it, *I Invested in Junk Bonds*."

Looking back, Wright is astonished he was blind to Bonds's dark side. "Barry has trust issues," says Wright. "If someone gets too close, like I did, he automatically backs away. It's a terrible way to go through life, but it's who he is." Wright pauses, thinking back to the end of their relationship. "In hindsight, the funny thing is that I think Barry left me because he thought a large agency could turn him into a movie star," he says. "Barry was expressing an interest in acting, and I guess he believed the Beverly Hills Sports Council could take him to the next level." Wright smiles—not wickedly, but with a look of satisfaction. "How did that work out?"

Bonds appeared in a handful of TV shows, guest starring as baseball player "Barry Larson" in an episode of *Beverly Hills 90210*, and appearing as himself on *Everybody Loves Raymond*, himself on *Arli$$*, himself on *Between Brothers*, and himself in the baseball movie *Rookie of the Year*. In 1994 the Beverly Hills Sports Council hooked Bonds up with his big break, landing him a plum role as "Senator Wilson" in the made-for-TV movie *Moment of Truth: Broken Pledges*. One line from the April 11, 1994, *Daily Variety* review says it all: "Baseball superstar Barry Bonds, in what certainly rivals the stiffest [performance] in memory of an athlete-turned-reader, blankly portrays the New York legislator."

His interest in becoming a movie star waned shortly thereafter.

Without Bonilla and Smiley, Leyland miraculously managed to guide Pittsburgh to its third straight NL East crown in 1992. Stripped by free agency of much of its talent, Pittsburgh compiled 96 wins behind the potent bat of Bonds, who hit .311 with 34 home runs, 103 RBIs, and 39 stolen bases and won his second National League MVP trophy in three years. In an otherwise dream offensive season, Bonds suffered a jarring setback when, on June 23, a strained right side forced him to the disabled list for the first time. Outfielder Gary Varsho stumbled upon his teammate in the Three Rivers Stadium batting cages after he learned of his deactivation. "He was bawling like a baby because he couldn't play," says Varsho. "The game that he loved and cherished was being taken away from him."

The Pirates survived, thanks in large part to the play of journeymen like right fielder Cecil Espy and first baseman Orlando Merced. No pitcher won more than 15 games, no reliever saved more than 18. Still, they found a way.

Bonds's looming free agency might have served as a distraction, except there was no mystery about it: He was a goner. Team president Mark Sauer called Bonds's potential payday "in another solar system," and midway through the season Bonds had the audacity to take Mark Whicker of the *Orange County Register* through a survey of franchises where he might wind up.

The Braves: "They're a great team. My wife and I were just talking about that. Who wouldn't want to play for them?"

The Dodgers: "They've got that great history. But I don't know about Eric [Davis] and Darryl [Strawberry]. They're always getting hurt."

The Angels: "I really like Whitey [Herzog]. They've still got Hubie Brooks and Von Hayes, and good pitching."

The Mets: "I'd be with Bobby Bonilla, my best friend. He's a sweet guy."

The Yankees: "Sure. I know hitting .300 wouldn't be enough, but I can handle it. They'll give me enough money to handle it."

The Padres: "Put me between these two big ones [Gary Sheffield and Fred McGriff], man, and I might have 150 RBI."

For now, he was in Pittsburgh. And in trouble. By winning the division, the Pirates would again face the Braves in the National League Championship Series. Bonds dreaded the matchup. Atlanta still had the game's best pitching staff, and by now Bonds's status as a choke artist was widespread. In April and May, he was the most feared hitter in the game. In September, he was Tom Veryzer. One awful playoff series was bad luck. *But two in a row?* The label stuck to Bonds, so much so that when rivals wanted to take a shot at the Pirates star, they knew where to aim. "He's not done anything in the postseason," Dodgers slugger Darryl Strawberry said during the year. "I've got a [World Series] ring. What does he have? He's a joke."

Bonds assured his teammates that this postseason was different—he would carry them to the World Series. For the Pirates, everything was on the line. Bonds and Drabek were certain to leave as free agents, and rising stars like Jay Bell and Jeff King probably wouldn't last much longer, either. As the cheapest organization in baseball, unwilling to spend to win, the team would not see the playoffs in 1993. It was now or never.

On the morning of game one, Bonds woke up in his room at the Atlanta Ritz-Carlton and likely tugged the *USA Today* peeking out from under his door. There, in large type, was the headline BONDS PLAYS FOR PAY: POST-SEASON CAN AFFECT NEXT CONTRACT. "Barry Bonds has more at stake than anyone in the National League playoffs," the article read. "He also is playing for next year's salary. And the year after. And the one after that. The impression he makes in this seven-game set will be indelible and could have an impact on his potential earnings."

This kind of press was the last thing he needed.

Facing the pressure of an all-time classic playoff, the man nicknamed "Mr. Noctober" by Rick Hummel of the *St. Louis Post-Dispatch* hit .261

against the Braves, with one home run and two RBIs in 23 at-bats. Atlanta won the first two games in convincing fashion, taking a 5–1 decision in the opener and a 13–5 laugher a day later. The formula for Braves manager Bobby Cox was simple: Pitch great, score a couple of runs, and—with no Bonilla to worry about—don't let Bonds make the difference. Bonds went 1-for-6 in the first two games, often appearing clueless against Atlanta starters John Smoltz and Steve Avery. The 22-year-old Avery especially befuddled Bonds. In the first inning of game two, Bonds came up with a runner on second and two outs—then watched a wicked breaking ball float across the plate for strike three.

The vision of Barry staring at the ball, anxious to uncoil but somehow unable, is an appropriate representation of his playoff experiences. In his next at-bat, Bonds popped out, his face scrunched in anxiety. To the Braves, pitching Bonds carefully didn't mean not pitching to him. It meant getting in his head and reminding him that his legacy was slowly rotting away. The Braves fans did their part: When Bonds collected his first hit of the series, a single to lead off the seventh inning, he was saluted with a sarcastic stand-ing ovation. Bonds playfully tipped his cap, but inside he was humiliated. "Barry had put a lot of pressure on himself," Bream said after the second game. "He gets in these situations and thinks he has to be the one to do the job."

"The hardest part of the game is mental," added Avery. "When people start asking you what's wrong with you, you start to wonder if something *is* wrong."

Bonds maintained he was as focused as ever, but one had to wonder whether impending free agency was clouding his radar. On the afternoon of October 6, just hours before game one, Bonds was spotted house hunt-ing in northeast Atlanta. According to a city resident named Debbie Avery (no relation to the Braves pitcher), Bonds pulled up to her driveway on the corner of Mount Paran Road and Powers Ferry Road. "I'm Barry Bonds," he told her. "I play for the Pirates and I'm looking for a good-size house with a lot of land." Bonds spoke to Avery for 15 minutes, more or less trying to determine whether he should join the team now standing between his Pirates and the World Series.

In a sign of how low Bonds had sunk, Jerome Holtzman, the legendary *Chicago Tribune* baseball writer, focused his column after Pittsburgh's 3–2 game three win on Barry's "remarkable" mid-playoff turnaround. "Father knows best," Holtzman wrote. "Reaffirmation of this truism was evident again Friday night when the slumping Barry Bonds regained his batting stroke."

Whether Bonds had "regained" his stroke was never up for debate—he hadn't. In a game that saw Bonds go a familiar 0-for-3 (after receiving some tips from his dad), Holtzman was clearly looking for something Barry-related to write about. He took two deep fly balls as a good sign. But when a writer praises mediocre play, it says more about what the athlete *isn't* doing. When Bonds went 0-for-2 in the game four loss, putting Atlanta one win away from the Series, it was obvious Holtzman was wrong. Bonds's stroke wasn't back. His defining moment in game four was not a home run or even a bloop single. It came in the seventh inning, when the Pirates trailed 6–4 and Bonds walked to the plate with Van Slyke on second and one out. This was a situation the Three Rivers crowd had been begging for, and they roared in anticipation. Pittsburgh's slogan throughout the season had been "Right Now!," a nod to the Van Halen song that blasted through the stadium.

> *Right now, hey*
> *It's your tomorrow*
> *Right now,*
> *C'mon, it's everything*
> *Right now.*

The Braves brought in lefthander Mike Stanton, who easily struck Bonds out on four pitches. Right now, rally over. Right now, hype dead. The home crowd lustily booed its best player.

"Barry didn't hit in the playoffs, and I feel bad about that," says Leyland. "Because he was just so damn good the rest of the year. A lot of guys didn't hit in the playoffs, and you don't hear about them. But when you're the superstar, the expectations are higher and you have to accept the blame. Or at least some of it."

Bonds had bottomed out. His statistics were pathetic, and on the bench teammates were wondering whether the club would be better served if their star player took a day off. His fuel was confidence, and the tank was dry. When Leyland walked past Bonds's locker, he wrapped an arm around his slumped shoulders and asked him to enter his office, where the two sat for nearly an hour and a half. The media suggested the discussion was a managerial browbeating. In fact, Leyland assured Bonds he was the center of the offense; that whether he struck out 10 times or hit 10 home runs, the Pirates were behind him. "Whatever happens, when this all ends you'll make a lot of money and go on to a great career," he told Bonds. "So don't put any more pressure on yourself. It's just a game. Have fun. Play hard. Don't worry. Make these last few games count."

Leylands's soothing words were exactly what Bonds needed to hear. Later that night he spent two hours on the phone with Bonilla, who reiterated the it's-just-a-game pep talk. At the urging of Sun Bonds, Bonilla flew to Pittsburgh from his home in Bradenton, Florida, the next morning to surprise his friend. Having spent the season alone in New York being heckled by disappointed Mets fans, Bonilla knew the power of support (or the lack thereof). He took Bonds for lunch at the Clark Bar & Grill, a Pittsburgh institution where fans gathered. When he walked in, Bonds was greeted by cheers. "That made me feel great," Bonds said. "The fans kept saying, 'The jinx is going to be over, it's going to be over.'"

Pittsburgh's decisive 7–1 game five win wasn't one of those contests Bonds owned (35-year-old Bob Walk, a surprise playoff starter, played hero, throwing a complete-game three-hitter), but it was the first time he looked relaxed in a playoff setting. Bonds broke an 0-for-28 postseason slump with men on base by driving in the second run of Pittsburgh's four-run first; he had two hits and made an across-the-body running catch to snare a sinking line drive from Ron Gant. How great was the relief? After reaching second on a double, Bonds smiled toward the Pittsburgh dugout and yelled, "It's over! It's over!"

The good vibes continued in game six at Atlanta–Fulton County Stadium, another Pirate victory (by a 13–4 score) with more inspired play from Bonds. His first postseason home run led off the second inning, when he unloaded on a Tom Glavine fastball and sent it soaring over the center-field wall. Before the at-bat he turned to Varsho and said, "If he throws me a heater over the plate, I'm taking him deep."

Bonds had returned to form.

In the hours before game seven of the National League Championship Series, the Atlanta Braves clubhouse might have been confused for any number of libraries in metropolitan Fulton County. The room was eerily quiet, with a couple of outfielders speaking softly in one corner, a few relief pitchers drinking coffee in another. That's the way Braves manager Bobby Cox liked things. He was an old-school skipper who never believed much in pep talks or self-motivating trash talk. A player who wasn't thinking about the upcoming game wasn't thinking, and that was a huge no-no.

The Pirates clubhouse was, by comparison, a zoo. In the minutes before taking the field, the players lined up in front of the team's portable Nerf mini-hoop and performed a joyful lay-up drill, one man after the other. These weren't the most talented of the three modern-era Pirate playoff teams, but the confidence was stronger than ever. The Pirates had come back from a 3–1 deficit, and now they were convinced of inevitable victory.

"We had the better team," says relief pitcher Roger Mason. "When you know you're better and you've got the momentum, that makes you pretty confident."

The feeling was justified. The Pirates staked Drabek to a 2–0 lead, scoring one run in the first and another in the sixth. Although the former Cy Young winner wasn't dominant in 1992, on this night he was a bona fide ace. Drabek mixed his pitches with flair, throwing high when the Braves were expecting low, hard when they expected soft. Through the first five innings, he faced 16 batters. When the Braves threatened in the sixth with the bases loaded and no outs, he forced Jeff Blauser to line out to third baseman Jeff King, who stepped on the bag for a double play. Terry Pendleton then flew out to left field for the third out. "Doug was absolutely amazing," says first baseman Gary Redus. "The man was just flat-out dealing."

The Pirates entered the bottom of the ninth with a 2–0 lead, and though Drabek was worn after escaping two late-inning jams and throwing 120 pitches, Leyland had little confidence in his relief corps. When Pendleton opened the inning with a double into the right-field corner, reliever Stan Belinda began throwing in the bullpen. That's when playoff pressure took over. Braves slugger Dave Justice hit a routine grounder to second base, where Gold Glove winner Jose Lind prepared for the pickup and throw to first. Lind, however, took his eyes off the ball, and it rolled away. With no outs, runners stood on first and third. "Chico didn't boot one ball like that all year," says pitcher Bob Patterson of Lind. "Not one." Drabek was shaken. He walked Bream on four pitches to load the bases. Onto the field came Belinda.

"We're going to lose this game," Mark Sauer, the team president, thought in the stands. "I can't believe we're going to lose this game."

Twenty-six-years old and eight years out of State College Area High School, the Pennsylvania-born Belinda was a welcome sight for the Braves, who had tired of Drabek. Though Belinda was technically Pittsburgh's closer (he led the team with 18 saves), he was an ordinary right-hander with an average fastball and a hot-or-cold curve. Unlike elite firemen such as Lee Smith and John Wetteland, who thrived on an angry intensity, Belinda tiptoed into ballgames. "Is this the day I fail?" entered his mind too often for Leyland's liking.

The first batter he faced was Ron Gant, the powerful Atlanta left fielder whose game two grand slam was one of the series' biggest hits. This time, Gant again demolished the ball, sending a line drive *deep, deep, deep* to left, where Bonds sprinted back and caught it against the wall. Pendleton tagged up and jogged home, cutting the lead to 2–1. After walking catcher Damon Berryhill (on several perfect pitches umpire Randy Marsh inexplicably called balls), Belinda forced pinch hitter Brian Hunter into a popup for the second out, setting up a do-or-die moment for a most unlikely potential hero.

If there was one Atlanta position player Leyland wanted at the plate during crunch time, it was Francisco Cabrera, a 26-year-old reserve catcher who had experienced all of 10 at-bats with the Braves in 1992. Cabrera was a guy who'd hung around for a couple of years because he could block pitches behind the plate and every so often show a little pop. He was also one of the nicest men in the game. When Cabrera played with the Triple

A Syracuse Chiefs in 1989, he was the player who signed autographs until every fan left happy.

With the bases loaded and a pennant on the line, Cabrera was shocked to hear Atlanta batting coach Clarence Jones call his name. "Frankie!" Jones yelled. "Get ready to go hit!" Until that second, Cabrera's big playoff moment had come three and a half hours earlier, when he caught the ceremonial first pitch from Rubye Lucas, wife of a late Braves executive. Here—the ninth inning, the seventh game—was the kind of scenario Cabrera had dreamed of way back when he was a small kid with holes in his jeans, running around a patch of dirt in the Dominican city of Santo Domingo. Cabrera was signed in 1986 by the Toronto Blue Jays. But three days prior to his being scouted by Jays executive Pat Gillick, his father, Pablo, had to ask for a 75-peso advance from his boss so he could buy Francisco cleats. "I wasn't nervous," Cabrera said of his at-bat. "I was ready. I'd been ready my entire life."

Standing in left, Bonds felt ready, too. He positioned himself unusually deep, resolute in the philosophy that, should a ball get by him, the Pirates lose. From center, Van Slyke looked at Bonds and yelled, "Move in! Move in!" Van Slyke was nonplussed when his teammate responded with the middle finger.

"Typical Barry," says Van Slyke.

Belinda started Cabrera with a slider. Ball one. Then came a high fastball. Ball two. The next pitch, an inside fastball, was fouled off. In between pitches, Cabrera convinced himself that Belinda was done with the slider. "He's coming at me with gas," he thought. "He doesn't think I can hit it." The ensuing pitch was a fastball, up and over the plate. Cabrera made solid contact, lacing the baseball over shortstop and into left field. Justice jogged in easily with the tying run, but why in the world was third base coach Jimy Williams sending home Sid Bream? Slower-than-backward Sid Bream? "Anybody else who was running would have been across the plate, into the dugout, and up into the clubhouse by the time Barry's throw came home," says Bream. "But I'd had five operations on my right knee and I was wearing a big brace and I ran like molasses. So it was a pretty gutsy decision."

Bonds charged the ball to his left, picked it up, and threw a dart across his body toward home. The ball was in his glove before Bream reached third. Had he followed Van Slyke's positioning advice, Bream would have been out by 5 feet. But this dart began to drift left. Catcher Mike LaValliere caught the ball a couple of feet up the first base line and lunged toward Bream at home plate. "I've never understood how that play was even close," says LaValliere. "With Sid running, I thought he'd be out by a bunch. But Barry Bonds was not getting paid for his arm. People forget that."

"Should Barry have thrown Sid out?" adds Drabek. "Well—yes."

With the passage of time, the play becomes closer and closer. But Bream was indisputably safe, and as he lay sprawled across the plate his teammates piled on top. The Braves were returning to the World Series. This was the first time in a winner-take-all postseason game that a team that was leading was defeated on the last pitch. "This loss," wrote Tim Kurkjian of *Sports Illustrated*, "was perhaps the cruelest in baseball's long history of heartache."

Upon returning to the clubhouse, several Pirates spotted the trophy for the National League pennant as it was swooshed out the door. Technicians were ripping down a stage that had been built for the award presentation. "It was like someone had entered your house," says Rich Donnelly, "and taken your wife." Bonds sat at his stool, head in hands, and bawled. There was nothing he could say, and no one he could look at. Humiliation was etched in his face. Nearly everyone on the team knew of his stubborn refusal to move in. He had once again come up woefully short in a key postseason moment, and now the price was a trip to the World Series. Van Slyke hammered home the final dagger. He stood on a trunk and, looking directly at Bonds, announced, "It was my fault! I should have hit more, and I should have played much better defense. This loss is on me."

"Barry just sat there," says Jay Bell. "That's the biggest difference between those two. Andy took responsibility. Barry did not." This was the first time Van Slyke had ever cried after a loss, and he was not alone. Everyone in the room knew that, come 1993, the Pittsburgh Pirates would stink once again. There would be a youth movement. Empty seats. A town returning to indifference.

"I was pissed off," says LaValliere. "It was the writing on the wall. We lost Bobby Bonilla, and we knew Barry was gone. How do you replace that type of talent?"

"I knew in my heart that I would never be in that position again as long as I was a Pirate," says Van Slyke. "It was my saddest day in baseball. The end of the road."

Behind left fielder Al Martin, the 1993 Pirates went 75–87 and finished fifth in the National League East. They have yet to compile another winning record.

NINE

A HAPPY HOMECOMING

BY THE WINTER OF 1992, Barry Bonds had narrowed down the list of baseball teams he would consider signing with to eight—the California Angels, San Diego Padres, Los Angeles Dodgers, Atlanta Braves, Chicago Cubs, Chicago White Sox, New York Yankees, and New York Mets. Through his later years, as Bonds became the face of the San Francisco Giants, the media would often refer to his "lifelong dream" of playing for his father's old club. In fact, Bonds had many reasons for *not* wanting to return to the Bay Area. The Giants had finished the 1992 season in fifth place in the National League West, with a 72–90 mark. Candlestick Park was a charmless icebox, and taxpayers had four times voted down proposals for a new downtown stadium. There were mounting reports the team would soon be sold and relocated to St. Petersburg.

One consideration, however, trumped the others. Becoming a San Francisco Giant meant that Bonds would have to play in front of his father on a regular basis. This notion brought on an anxiety that dated back to Barry's early days in Pittsburgh. Several Pirates recall his routine on West Coast road trips. "We'd get to San Francisco and Barry would suddenly come up with some mysterious injury or illness," says R. J. Reynolds, the Pirates outfielder. "Maybe he'd play, but he wanted that excuse, because he knew he wouldn't step up with Bobby watching. It was in his head." In his seven years with Pittsburgh, Bonds batted .278 against the Giants, his third lowest average against a National League club. Most striking were his numbers *at* Candlestick—a .226 average, four home runs, and 12 RBIs in 119 career at-bats. When Bobby was unable to attend, Barry usually played well. Otherwise he was often a mess. "I don't think Bobby was doing it intentionally, but he really got to Barry," says Reynolds. "Barry would hit a home run and drive in four, and Bobby would not let him get the glory. Bobby would have to talk about the game when *he* hit *two* home runs and had *five* RBIs."

Two days after the Pirates' heartbreaking playoff loss in the '92 NLCS, Barry returned to his home in Murrieta, California, and set about finding a new team. Naive about the process, Bonds expected free agency to be a series of expensive dinners and private airplanes and sweet talk from rich white men desperate for the game's top performer. What team *wouldn't* want Barry Bonds?

A lot of teams, it turned out. The Atlanta Braves, one of Bonds's top choices, spent the off-season pursuing a different free agent, Chicago Cubs right-hander Greg Maddux (he would sign a five-year, $28 million deal with the club). Seattle star Ken Griffey Jr. offered to take a pay cut if his team signed Bonds, but the Mariners instead spent $1.7 million over two years on Mike "Tiny" Felder. The San Diego Padres, Bonds's top choice, never made an offer. Neither did the Dodgers or the Angels. The New York Yankees remained in the hunt, but faded after Bonds rejected a five-year, $36 million proposal. As agent Dennis Gilbert scrambled for suitors he was generally greeted by one of two responses: (a) Your client costs too much; (b) Your client isn't worth the trouble.

Come December there was only one man salivating over Bonds, which would have been good news had he been affiliated with a major league franchise. Peter Magowan, however, was not a team owner. He was a dreamer— a very rich dreamer. Which, in this case, was the next best thing.

Were the 50-year-old Magowan a typical business tycoon, he might have spent his entire career as the CEO of Safeway, an enormous supermarket chain that had been founded by his grandfather. Throughout his 20s, young Peter worked at Safeway as a checker, night stocker, produce clerk, assistant manager, and store manager. But Magowan longed for more than riches. He was a nephew of the famed American poet James Merrill, who had majored in American literature at Stanford, studied at Oxford, and attended the Johns Hopkins School of Advanced International Studies. He'd even worked two summers at the State Department, as part of a plan to figure out what to do with his life. "I'd been 13 years the CEO of Safeway," he said, "and while I loved what I was doing, it was going to be the same sort of thing. If ever there's a time to move, age-wise, I thought that was the time."

Magowan's midlife career crisis came just as Giants owner Bob Lurie decided to unload the franchise. Frustrated by the city's inability to build the team a new stadium, Lurie had agreed to sell the club to Tampa–St. Petersburg interests for $111 million. "Bob badly wanted to keep the team in San Francisco, but he had no financial options," says Duffy Jennings, the Giants public relations director from 1981 to 1993. "So when the sale to Florida was reported, the shit hit the fan and Bob was crucified as the most hated man in San Francisco. But baseball is a business, and he had no real choice." When Magowan and a group of 12 investors (including corporate heavyweights like Charles Schwab, Bill Hewlett of Hewlett-Packard, and Don Fisher, founder of the Gap) approached Lurie and major league commissioner Bud Selig about purchasing the Giants and keeping the team in San Francisco, there was a seismic shift. Major League Baseball nixed the Tampa–St. Petersburg deal and encouraged Lurie to peddle the franchise to Magowan for the bargain price of $100 million. As the drama played out in newspapers throughout the Bay Area, Selig assured Magowan the team was his. It was a deal, just not a done deal.

Meanwhile, Magowan and Larry Baer, a former Giants marketing director and a key point man in the potential ownership group, fantasized about building the roster. "If you could get one guy on your team, who would it be?" Magowan routinely asked Baer. The answer was always the same—"Barry Bonds." In November 1992, well before Magowan officially purchased the Giants, he and Baer placed a series of phone calls to Gilbert, whose standard response was "I'm glad you want Barry, but you guys don't *own* anything." After six calls, Gilbert finally presented Baer with Barry's telephone number. "You can't reach him between 10 A.M. and 4 P.M.," Gilbert warned. "That's when he's with his workout coach and running the steps of the football stadium at San Diego State."

"This," Baer told Magowan, "is the player for us."

Baer finally spoke with Bonds, and the response was everything he had hoped for. "If you guys are for real," Bonds told Baer, "it would be an amazing thing for me to come home. I think a lot about my dad and Willie Mays and growing up, and I'd like nothing more than to come back to San Francisco." Though Bonds omitted the fact that no other clubs were showing much interest, Magowan and Baer were elated. They arranged a meeting with Gilbert at the San Francisco Airport Hilton, and as Magowan, Baer, Gilbert, and Willie Mays (who attended at Magowan's behest) sat around a table in a conference room, everyone dug in for what would surely be a lengthy process.

"Dennis, we really want Barry to come back home and revitalize this franchise," said Magowan. "We think he's the best player in the game, and the best player ought to be the best paid." Gilbert nodded in agreement. "Right now the best-paid player is Ryne Sandberg," said Magowan of the Cubs second baseman. "He's signed for $7.1 million over four years. We propose for Barry $7.2 million and five years."

"Well," interjected Gilbert, "Barry has his heart set on seven years."

"How 'bout six?" said Magowan.

"Done," said Gilbert.

In less than five minutes, the man who didn't yet own the Giants had committed more than $43 million. The league would not be happy. In the spirit of self-preservation, later that week Magowan called Al Rosen, the Giants' lame-duck general manager, and asked his opinion on three of the team's incumbent left fielders. One by one, Rosen agreed that Cory Snyder, Chris James, and Kevin Bass were stiffs. "Well, what do you think about Barry Bonds?" Magowan asked. Dead silence. "Barry Bonds?" Rosen said. "Are you serious? Barry Bonds is the best player in the game. If you get him you won't need [star first baseman] Will Clark down the road."

"We took that as consent from the Giants that they'd have no disagreement with us signing Barry Bonds," says Magowan, smiling mischievously. "So we went and signed him immediately before the Yankees could make any more offers."

On the night of Saturday, December 5, just hours before the start of base-ball's annual winter meetings, Bonds inked a contract to join the Giants. A press conference was scheduled for 5 o'clock the next evening at the Galt House Hotel in Louisville, where the meetings were being held. Magowan arranged for Bonds's family to be flown in from the Bay. This was sure to be the greatest moment of Magowan's life.

On the afternoon of the big announcement, Magowan had just reached the hotel when the phone rang. It was Baer on the line. "Cancel the press conference!" he said. "We have a meeting with Bud Selig at the hotel ASAP. He's not happy." In a ballroom inside the Galt House, approximately 50 members of the media were already sitting in chairs, watching as Barry Bonds—resplendent in a fruit punch–hued sports coat—made his way to a podium. He was flanked by Mays, Bobby Bonds, and a team of agents.

This is where the ear-to-ear whispering began. Not only did the reporters get word of the news before Barry Bonds, but so did the catering staff, the woman sweeping the carpet, the bellhop taking a cigarette break. A major league representative approached Barry and said, "You've gotta get off the stage. It's not happening." Barry's expression went blank. *Not happening? What's not happening? The press conference or the homecoming?*

Magowan and Baer took the elevator to the 25th floor, where Selig was waiting in a suite alongside Lurie, Rosen, Major League attorney Bob Keel, and Jerry Reinsdorf, Chicago White Sox owner and head of baseball's own-ership committee. The mood in the room was tense. In Lurie's opinion, Barry Bonds was the last man who should be wearing a Giant uniform. Yes, Lurie was unloading the team. But as owner, his top priority was to bring in players with class and civility. He believed it meant something to sport the black and orange uniform, and the arrogant, moody, selfish Bonds didn't deserve such a privilege. Selig got straight to the point. "Gentlemen," he said, "your signing of Barry Bonds was a very bad thing for you to have tried and done. It is hereby canceled."

Baer and Magowan are both nice men; relatively soft-spoken and—as Bonds would prove countless times through the ensuing years—easy to push around. But this was something they desperately wanted, and neither was going down without a fight. The Giants were *not* going to start Kevin

Bass in left field in 1993. "I don't understand," said Baer, flashing a whoa-is-me facial expression. "We had permission from the Giants to do this."

"Permission from the Giants?" said Lurie. "Who in the hell gave you permission?"

"Why," said Baer, "Al Rosen did."

Within two seconds Rosen had leaped from his chair and was jabbing a finger into Baer's chest. "What in the hell are you talking about?" he barked. "I never told you to spend $43 million of Bob Lurie's money!"

Selig had heard enough. "You're going to have to work things out with Bob," he told Magowan. "Otherwise, as far as I'm concerned Barry Bonds is a free agent."

Over the next two days, Magowan and Baer convinced the partners in their group to agree that, should the sale not go through, Bonds would become a free agent and they would take responsibility for any money less than the $43 million that was promised. Selig and Lurie signed off on the conditions, as did Bonds, who responded to the completion of negotiations by hugging Magowan and Baer. "It's amazing how you guys have fought for me," he told them. "In Pittsburgh, I didn't even know who the owners were."

On the afternoon of December 8, one month before Magowan would officially purchase the franchise, a press conference was at last held. As Bonds stood at center stage, surrounded by his father, his agents, and the new Giants brass, the 28-year-old millionaire cried. "It's like a boyhood dream that came true for me," he said. "All I've ever wanted to do was share something with my father. This is the greatest moment in my entire life." With his voice cracking, Bonds continued. "Every time I step on that field," he said, "I know my godfather's in center field and my dad's in right field."

Just feet away, Jennings, the outgoing PR man, shook his head in disbelief. Minutes earlier, he had introduced himself to Bonds and explained how the press conference would unfold.

"You don't tell me how things will go," Bonds snapped back. "I say how things will go. This is my show."

A new era in Giants baseball had begun.

••●●

In the afterglow of the press conference, the Giants announced that Bonds would sport uniform number 24, which had been long retired in homage to the incomparable Mays (Bonds was also given the locker stall Mays had occupied at Candlestick Park). "I get to keep his dreams and what he accomplished alive," Bonds explained. "I'm not trying to fill Willie Mays's shoes. He's like a father to me, and he's part of my family. If you retire all the numbers, there won't be any numbers left."

This did not fly in San Francisco. The team's phone lines lit up, and Bonds meekly switched to number 25, Bobby's old digits. "I'd rather be in left field looking at [Mays's] number instead of wearing it on my back," he pleaded. "I'm not a spoiled rotten brat here." Judging by the ensuing letters to the *San Francisco Chronicle*, not all the fans were pacified.

Russ Christian of Martinez: "Barry Bonds is to be paid $43.75 million. For that kind of money you could present a free hand warmer to every Giant aficionado until the end of time."

Dennis Earley of Santa Cruz: "Congratulations, Barry. You have found a team where you will not have to worry about choking in the postseason."

John Callahan of Richmond: "This undeniably tops the list of half-witted moves by the Giants. Barry Bonds. Too much money for way too many years."

Despite a few contrary voices, the overwhelming response in the Bay Area was euphoric. Just months earlier, the Giants had been packing their bags for Florida. Now, thanks to Magowan and his crew of wealthy executives, not only was the team staying, but the reigning National League MVP was in left field, the new manager was the beloved Dusty Baker, and the new first base and hitting coach was, of all people, Bobby Bonds. "We wanted to bring a family atmosphere back to the Giants," says Magowan. "That's exactly what we did."

Bobby's return to the black and orange was especially meaningful, because it came with the renewed vigor of sobriety. When Bobby was fired as the Cleveland Indians hitting coach in 1987, he finally acknowledged that his life was out of control. Friends and family members had tried stepping in before, but their interventions never took. This time was different. His sons barely knew him, his wife wanted little to do with him, and he occasionally forgot the names of his own team's players. In 1988 after downing several beers during 18 holes of golf with former teammate Jim Davenport in Half Moon Bay, California, Bobby caused yet another alcohol-related car accident. Fearful of jail time, he sped from the scene before the authorities arrived. That night he called Rod Wright, his agent. "I can't do this anymore," he said, crying. "Look at my life. I'm killing myself." Within days, Bobby enrolled in Alcoholics Anonymous, where one of his fellow addicts was Dan Skjerdal, Barry's former Little League teammate. "He was a good man who wanted to help himself," says Skjerdal. "Bobby suffered a lot of pain because of drinking."

By 1993 he had been sober for more than four years, and anxious to return to the game. "Bobby was a completely different person after rehab," says Davenport. "He became much closer as a family man. I'm sure it bothered Barry when Bobby was drinking, and I know it worried Pat to death. When he finally quit, it was like a weight had been lifted."

Sadly for the Bonds family, Bobby was not the only addict among them. Although Barry and Bobby Jr. pursued careers in baseball (Bobby Jr. was an 18th round draft pick of the Padres and spent five years in the minor leagues before becoming a businessman in New Jersey), Ricky—the middle brother—has spent much of his life in and out of rehab, often living at home with his parents and struggling to hold a steady job. One year Barry's junior, Ricky was known for being goofy and unpredictable—a kid "who would drink with you and party with you whenever," recalls Sam Rossi, a schoolmate. "Ricky had two big shadows blocking him out," says Wright. "He was a wonderful kid with a great sense of humor who everyone loved. But he was running from the success of his parents and brother." Unlike Barry, who had always risen up to challenges, Ricky shrunk in the spotlight. He was a solid athlete, but only moderately driven. "Ricky was not as talented as either one of his brothers," says Frank Capovilla, who attended high school with the Bonds brothers. "He was a good guy growing up, but he wasn't gifted like Barry."

Ricky played two seasons as an outfielder at the College of San Mateo, but dropped out. In the ensuing years he bounced around, working as a bus driver and a bartender. "I'd see Ricky's truck at his mom's a lot," says one family friend. "The few times I've seen him, he's in front of the house smoking cigarettes. Every time I'd ask, 'What are you doing now?' it was always something else—a plumber's helper or waiter. It's rough on the family."

Barry showed up at the Giants' spring training facility in Scottsdale, Arizona, on February 21, 1993, three days before the official reporting date. His arrival was the hottest Bay Area baseball story in years. Some two dozen reporters gathered around his locker in anticipation of the big interview. Bonds had nothing to say.

"Not even a comment?" asked C. W. Nevius of the *Chronicle*.

"Nope."

"Not a sentence?"

"Uh-uh."

"Not a word?"

"No, " said Bonds. "Do you want to keep pushing?"

The cold shoulder was the first of many Bonds turned in a long and troubled relationship with San Francisco scribes. "From that first day, you never quite knew where he was coming from," says Nevius. "There was this one time when he spotted me from far away and started walking over just to make small talk. I thought, 'Wow, not a bad guy.' But as he was approaching, a couple of kids were leaning over the railing, begging for his autograph. He looked up and said, 'You little shits, leave me the fuck alone!' Then he turns to me and says, 'So how's everything going in your life? Having a good day?' I was thinking, 'Are you human?' "

What Bonds discovered in San Francisco was a team in need of a makeover. Under former manager Roger Craig, the Giants had won two division titles and reached the 1989 World Series, but after more than seven seasons his unrelenting cheerfulness had grown tiresome, and most players ignored Craig's directives. By the '92 season, his last with the club, Craig was 62 years old and well past his prime. "We were really flat," says Darren Lewis, a Giants outfielder from 1991 to 1995. "Roger Craig was a good man, but he wasn't making an impact anymore. There was lethargy all around. I remember being in the outfield with Barry on one of his first days and him yelling, 'Does anyone talk on this damn team!' That's exactly what we needed."

When a baseball player joins a new club, the unwritten rule is that he should arrive with his head down and his ego checked. Such was not Bonds's style. On his first day, Bonds entered Scottsdale Stadium, dropped his bag by his locker, and strolled over to a corner of the room, where a group of 10 pitchers were holding court. One by one, without even introducing himself, Bonds jabbed his index finger in the chest of each man and said, "I own you. I own you. I own you. I own you."

"He wasn't kidding," says Bryan Hickerson, a Giants pitcher. "I said, 'Whoa, let's wait a minute here. Let's go get some videotapes and see how many of us punched *you* out.'" Bonds, in fact, had gone 0-for-1 with two walks against Hickerson.

As Bonds walked away, the Giants pitchers reached a consensus: Their new teammate was an asshole. The belief was reinforced two afternoons later, when Bonds engaged in the first of his many heated altercations with a teammate. The Giants clubhouse was patrolled by three old-school veterans—third baseman Matt Williams, second baseman Robby Thompson, and first baseman Will Clark—all of whom believed the star on a team deserved no better treatment than the 25th man. On the first morning of full-squad workouts, Bonds exited the dugout wearing black cleats with orange stripes, which did not conform to the team uniform of black cleats with white stripes. Williams, a strong, quiet, no-nonsense man, instructed the newest Giant to change. "Dude, I will do whatever I want, whenever I want!" Bonds barked in front of the entire team. "Now back out of my face!" Williams walked away. He wasn't going to fight Bonds over a pair of shoes. But the damage was done. "It's hard to respect someone who behaves that way," says Dave Burba, a Giants pitcher. "If you're going to mesh as a team, everybody wears the same stuff. It doesn't mean you have to wear your pants down—if you wanna wear 'em high, wear 'em high. But why not do the right thing and put on the correct shoes?"

The next morning Williams made an effort to clear the air. Bonds arrived wearing a black vest with large white splotches, and as he crossed the room Williams called out, "What'd you do, run into a cow on the way to the ballpark?" This was typical clubhouse ribbing. "You old fuck!" Bonds screamed. "What the fuck do you know about fashion?"

"It was," says Nevius, a witness to the exchange, "a psycho-killer moment."

What saved Bonds from being completely reviled by his teammates was the concession that, no matter how grandiose the ego, his bat was what the Giants needed to end two straight losing seasons. Unlike veteran first baseman Clark, who, as usual, reported to camp with the body of a soggy pear, Bonds sported a newly barreled chest, oak tree arms, powerful legs, and 8 percent body fat. He had spent the off season working with Jim Warren, a personal trainer whose main clients were football players. The results were staggering. "Our goal was for him to become a 50–home run, 50–steal player," says Warren. "So we did a ton of sprinting and weights. He was as thin as a whippet when I started working with him. But by the time he reported, he was an athletic freak—Terrell Owens with a baseball bat. We're talking about a 4.4 sprinter who can dunk a basketball, shoot bows and arrows, and throw with either hand."

Confidence oozed from Bonds. He was convinced he could carry the Giants to the promised land. "His approach was 'We're going to beat you and there's nothing you can do about it,'" says shortstop Royce Clayton. "It was much more outward than a lot of the older guys in our organization were used to. But it was contagious." On an early March morning Bonds missed the bus to Tucson for an exhibition game against the Rockies. When he finally arrived via car, it was 12:55. The start time was in 10 minutes. Bonds sprinted into the clubhouse, hopped into his uniform, and, en route to the on-deck circle, told teammate Todd Benzinger, "Watch me hit a home run." First pitch—gone. "Barry was putting his shoes on as he walked to the plate," says Steve Scarsone, a reserve infielder. "That's when we're looking at each other and saying, 'He's different, man. He's just different.'"

On a Sunday in mid-March, Padres outfielder Phil Plantier was hogging a batting cage inside Scottsdale Stadium when Bonds politely asked him to leave. "Fuck off!" shouted Plantier. "I'm in here." Bonds flipped. "You can't talk like that in my house!" he said. "I've been in this league too long to take that shit from a punk-ass like you." Bonds swatted Plantier across the face with the back of his hand. "Pimp slapped him like a little bitch," recalls John Patterson, a Giants second baseman. "Just punked the shit out of Phil Plantier."

The incident was the talk of the Giants clubhouse for the rest of spring training. Not because Plantier was an especially bad guy, but because Bonds's attitude was new, fresh, and audacious. "Nobody else on our team would have had the balls to do that," says Patterson. "But Barry did."

On the ball field, Barry's cockiness and ability brought a new strut to the franchise. On opening night in St. Louis, Bonds's seventh-inning sacrifice fly plated the decisive run in a 2–1 victory. Three days later, Bonds returned to Pittsburgh for the first time as the enemy. Prior to the game, he entered the Pirates clubhouse to greet his former teammates. Sure, there had been some rough patches in the Steel City, but Bonds expected to be received warmly. Instead, not one player or coach so much as glanced in his direction. It brought to mind a quote from several years earlier, when an anonymous Pirate said of Bonds, "I'd rather lose without him than win with him." Bonds exited the room hurt and embarrassed. He responded to the snub—as well as the dizzying outpouring of heckles, boos, and angry signs in the stadium (BARRY, one read, ALL THE MONEY IN THE WORLD CAN'T BUY A THROWING ARM. LOVE, SID BREAM)—by scoring three runs and driving in another in a 6–5 loss.

In the Candlestick opener on April 12, Bonds triumphantly homered in his first at-bat—a sign that things were beginning to turn around for the club. San Francisco was winning, and nobody was more important than the new left fielder and number five hitter, whose stellar April (.431, seven home runs, 25 RBIs) earned him the National League Player of the Month award and carried the Giants to a 15–9 mark.

When *Sports Illustrated* assigned senior writer Richard Hoffer to fly to San Francisco and profile Bonds for a late-May cover story, even the media-loathing Bonds was secretly excited. As soon as Hoffer arrived at Candlestick, however, Bonds went out of his way to behave how he thought an elite athlete should. For seven consecutive days he avoided meeting Hoffer, with one excuse more transparent than the last. Bonds was putting on his own little circus, anxious for those around him to see the way a superstar manhandles the press.

Along with the writer, Bonds made an enemy of well-regarded *SI* baseball photographer Ron Modra, also assigned to the piece. Twice, Modra

Following through on baseball's most perfect swing, Barry Bonds hits his 660th career home run, tying Willie Mays for third on the all-time list. The blast, which came against the Brewers at Pac Bell Stadium on April 12, 2004, created a huge buzz in San Francisco but was largely ignored elsewhere. (BRAD MANGIN)

Bonds arrived at Arizona State in 1982 in a gaudy new Trans Am and with a bull's-eye on his back. Teammates found the freshman to be brash, rude, obtuse—and spectacular.
(ARIZONA STATE UNIVERSITY SPORTS INFO/AP)

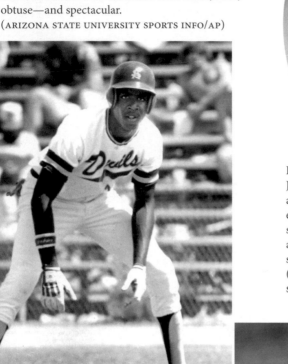

Barry Bonds was all smiles in his 1982 Junipero Serra High yearbook picture, and with good reason. He was the greatest athlete in school history—a three-sport star with all the tools and all the attitude. "Ya know, I'm gonna be a superstar," he told a classmate as a freshman.
(COURTESY OF JUNIPERO SERRA HIGH SCHOOL)

Having been raised by an alcoholic father with little time for his children, Barry longed to become a first-rate parent. Here he cuddles with daughter Aisha at Giants Family Day in 2002.
(BRAD MANGIN)

Bobby and Patricia Bonds and their three sons, Barry, Bobby Jr., and Ricky. All the children were active in youth sports, but only Barry excelled on a higher level, while Ricky drowned in a sea of personal problems. (SAN FRANCISCO GIANTS)

An unrivaled mixture of speed, power, and instincts, Bobby Bonds could not control the substance-abuse problems that shortened his career. With the Yankees, in 1975, Bonds compiled 32 home runs and 85 RBIs, but spent much of his time drinking alone. (MANNY MILLAN)

Though Bobby and Patricia Bonds were less than elated about their son's decision to wed a strip-club bartender, Sun (*far right*) delivered the couple two grandchildren, including five-month-old Nikolai. (SAN FRANCISCO GIANTS)

In his seven years with the Pittsburgh Pirates, Bonds often found himself on the outside looking in. "None of us trusted him," says Logan Easley, a former teammate. "Barry was more concerned about his arm looking bad than winning a game." (RICHARD MACKSON)

In May 1993, *Sports Illustrated* photographer Ron Modra arranged for Bonds to pose with the No. 25 trolley in the city of San Francisco's cable car barn. After being blown off twice, Modra confronted the ballplayer in the Giants clubhouse. "Dude," said Bonds, "you're just gonna have to live with it." Needless to say, Modra was not happy. (RON MODRA)

Though Bonds has often displayed a soft spot for children and those in need, most of his public good deeds have been heavily choreographed photo opportunities arranged by his handlers or by the Giants. (BRAD MANGIN)

With the Pirates earlier in his career, Bonds was much more willing to open himself up to the media. As he came to associate excessive self-promotion with prolonged hitting slumps, the talking stopped. (RICHARD MACKSON)

Though much of the country had by now dismissed the legitimacy of his achievements, when Bonds hit his 700th home run at SBC Park on September 17, 2004, he was greeted with a thunderous ovation. (BRAD MANGIN)

Bonds's three-run homer against St. Louis in the 2002 National League Championship Series helped propel the Giants to their first World Series in thirteen seasons. Bonds celebrated the shot with his typical pizzazz. (ROBERT BECK)

According to leading medical experts, there are two ways for the adult human skull to expand. The first is from acromegaly, a disorder, made famous by wrestler Andre the Giant, that results in abnormal growth of the hands and feet. The second is from injections of human growth hormone. Bonds, whose head was normal in size in 1993 (*left*), now has a cranium the size of a large pumpkin (*right*). He does not suffer from acromegaly.

Greg Anderson, Bonds's childhood friend and longtime trainer, began entering the Giants clubhouse in the spring of 1999, shortly after his client became remarkably more muscular. In February 2004, Anderson was indicted for his part of a steroid-distribution ring. (BEN MARGOT/AP)

BALCO founder Victor Conte, the godfather of the American steroids movement. A former professional musician, Conte counted among his clients Marion Jones, Bill Romanowski, and Barry Bonds. (PAUL SAKUMA)

Barry Bonds leaves a federal courthouse on December 4, 2003, after testifying before a grand jury. Bonds told the jury that he had been misled by Anderson into using steroids—which he allegedly believed to be flaxseed oil. It was hard for the public to swallow. (JUSTIN SULLIVAN/GETTY)

Despite a general belief among fans that Bonds cheated, he continues to be hailed in the Bay Area as a conquering hero. In San Francisco, Bonds can do no wrong. (ROBERT BECK)

arranged for the city to allow *Sports Illustrated* to shoot Bonds in front of San Francisco's cable car barn, where trolley number 25 was waiting. Twice, Bonds blew off the photo. "I offered to send a limo to Candlestick to pick Barry up and bring him there," says Modra. "But he said he knew exactly where to go." Following the snubs an outraged Modra confronted the ballplayer in the Giants clubhouse. "Dude," said Bonds, "you're just gonna have to live with it."

When he finally broke down and spoke, Bonds was charming and insightful. But the damage had been done. On May 24, the *SI* cover read, "I'm Barry Bonds, and You're Not." The inside headline stated, "The Importance of Being Barry: The Giants' Barry Bonds is the best player in the game today—just ask him."

Hoffer's piece was brutal. With scorching honesty, he painted Bonds as talented, enigmatic, and breathtakingly self-absorbed. "As far as anyone can remember, nobody who has really wanted to interview Bonds has failed to get his man," wrote Hoffer. "But negotiations for his time are not for the fainthearted or deadline-driven. A writer might spend the first three days just trying to establish the possibility of an interview. Bonds might fail to look up or register any recognition during conversations with the would-be interviewer, might pick at imaginary scabs on his arm and repeat 'Whatever, dude' over and over. The next phase might be a series of decreasingly vague promises by Bonds as he warms to the idea of the interview. This part of the process also includes actual recognition of the interviewer."

Throughout his years in Pittsburgh, Bonds had been angry over an article here or there, but he'd never felt abused like this. He complained loudly to the local media, insisting that he'd been caricatured by a writer looking to make a name for himself.

Bonds also admitted that he had never actually read the story.

Midway through the season, it was clear Bonds's $43 million salary was money well spent. Less than a year after finishing as fifth-place laughingstocks, the Giants were now ruling the National League West. The main reason was Bonds. "If you ask me, he's a bargain," said Giants pitcher Jeff Brantley. "I know they paid him a lot of money, and everyone expects wonders. But he can pretty much do it all. His baseball instincts are unbeliev-able. And he's not just trying to get a hit, he's trying to crush the ball. If you make a bad pitch, he'll hit a home run and he'll embarrass you."

In mid-April, Bonds missed two starts with a strained right hamstring, returned and had three hits (including a three-run homer off Greg Maddux in the first inning) and five RBIs in a 6–1 rout of Atlanta. Two weeks later, his 408-foot home run into Candlestick's upper deck led the Giants to a 10–5 victory over the Mets. Wrote *Chronicle* columnist Scott Ostler on May 3: "People ask me what Barry Bonds is really like. I tell them the answer changes from day to day. This morning the answer is .425." Ostler's assess-ment came after Expos manager Felipe Alou made the inexcusable decision to pitch to Bonds in the 11th inning with a runner on base and the score tied. Left-hander Jeff Fassero threw a fastball, which Bonds roped into left field for the game winner. "This is Barry Bonds," wrote Ostler, reacting to Alou's gaffe. "Pitch him the resin bag. And for God's sake, don't get it up."

Bonds was unlike anything San Francisco had seen since Mays's prime 30 years earlier. He was athletic, graceful, powerful, intimidating, and a showman to boot. When Bonds hit a towering home run, he flipped his bat, lifted his chin, and admired the flight, his diamond-encrusted earring sparkling in the lights. Pitchers seethed. Teammates cringed. In a 17–2 rout of the Rockies, Bonds hit a second-inning grand slam and, as he rounded the bases, told Colorado second baseman Eric Young, "I'll be back here next at-bat." In his next at-bat, he doubled. "Next time I'll walk," he told Young. Naturally, he walked. "I knew right then and there," says Young, "that this is the baddest damn player in the game." Bonds was routinely roasted in the media for his surliness, but the paying customers wanted more, more, more. He was the first Giant to ever top fan voting for the All-Star Game, his 3,074,603 nods the most one player had received since 1980. (Bonds's re-sponse to the news: "Well, I earned it.") In an NBC News/Wall Street Journal Poll asking Americans "Who has been the biggest success of the summer?" Bonds ranked second to Steven Spielberg, director of the Academy Award winner for best picture, *Schindler's List*. Placing behind Bonds? Supreme Court Justice Ruth Bader Ginsburg, Bill Clinton, and Tom Cruise.

At the All-Star break, the Giants were 59–30, a 15-game improvement from the previous season. Especially noteworthy was that the team's surge occurred without a significant contribution from Will Clark. Playing more like Cap Clark than a five-time All-Star, Clark was hitting just .281, with seven home runs and 46 RBIs. Not that this shocked some Giants players. As soon as Bonds signed with the club, those close to Clark knew he would be roadkill. "Barry was the better player, the better athlete, and Will was the type of dude where it had to be his team," says Patterson. "His ego was that big."

The New Orleans–raised Clark had perfected the art of rubbing teammates the wrong way, what with his irritatingly high-pitched cackle, his gunslingerlike saunters through the clubhouse, and, most notably, his bigoted mindset. "Just an old-fashioned redneck," says Nevius. "He'd say stupid stuff around anyone." The team's African Americans knew to keep their distance from Clark, who early in his career lost his temper with Giants third baseman Chris Brown and called him "nigger." The incident tarnished Clark's reputation—not that he especially cared. Even after apologizing, Clark continued to wear a Hank Williams Jr. T-shirt that read, "If the South Woulda Won We'd a Had It Made."

Like many who share Clark's mindset, he seemed to have a problem with flamboyant black teammates. With his dangling earring and his bright, trendy clothing and his cocky strut, Bonds clearly qualified. Yet the real problem with Bonds was that, for the first time in his professional career, Clark felt intimidated. Bonds was the better player, the flashier player, the more beloved player. On top of that, Barry's insults were loud, piercing, and endless, and Clark could not fight back. "Barry," says Giants first baseman Mark Carreon, "took the wind out of Will's sail."

As the summer wore on, a number of Giants quietly questioned Dusty Baker's approach to handling Bonds. A 19-year major league veteran, Baker was regarded as the consummate player's manager. He wore wristbands like a player; talked trash like a player; hung out in the back of the plane like a player; understood the ups and downs of a 162-game season like a player. He was an African-American man who related wonderfully with blacks and earned the trust and respect of whites and Latinos as well. "Dusty was almost like a football coach, in that he had a spirited, rally-the-troops mentality," says Jim Deshaies, a Giants pitcher in 1993. "Not a lot of base-ball managers have that. It made you want to win for him." Baker's glaring managerial flaw, however, was an undying adherence to the star system. In his eight years as an outfielder with the Dodgers, Baker saw perennial All-Stars like Steve Garvey and Davey Lopes receive better treatment than the other players, and he understood. "Different needs," says Baker, "for different people."

With Bonds, things were more complex. This was the son of Baker's child-hood idol; a man who now served on the coaching staff. There was Barry, and there were the 24 other players. Whereas his teammates rode together from airport to hotel on one bus, Bonds always sat on the *other* bus—the one reserved for team executives. Whereas 10 or 12 Giants would often dine together on the road, Bonds refused to even provide teammates with his room number. "None of your business," he'd snap when asked. From the start of spring training, Bonds made a point of not participating in pregame stretching drills, a seemingly insignificant act that grew more irksome with each passing day. "I remember we were at Shea Stadium early in the season, and I was talking to [catcher] Jeff Reed when I should have been stretching," says first baseman Todd Benzinger. "And Dusty came over to me and said, 'Hey, you better be stretching!' I looked over at Barry, who was sitting 10 feet away from me in the dugout talking to reporters."

Even as Baker created a monster, it was hard to fault him. The revived Giants led the National League West for much of the season, slipping into a dogfight with Atlanta only after the Braves pulled off a July blockbuster that landed slugging first baseman Fred McGriff from the Padres. For the first time in years, San Francisco displayed a prizefighter's intensity. Williams played brilliantly at third and, batting in front of Bonds, added 38 homers and 110 RBIs. Thompson's 19 home runs, 65 RBIs, and .312 average made him the National League's top second baseman. Starters Billy Swift and John Burkett won more than 20 games apiece, and closer Rod Beck saved 48. In a July 22 game against Philadelphia, Phillies starter Terry Mulholland aimed the first pitch of the second inning at Bonds's head. Bonds glared, scowled, stepped back in, and—on the very next offering—hit his 27th home run over Candlestick's right-field wall. He was greeted in the dugout as a conquering hero, especially after he pointed at Mulholland and laughed. On August 15 against the Cubs, Bonds and Williams hit back-to-back home runs—twice. "We were pretty much the same team as a year earlier, except for Barry," says Clayton. "But now we had swagger."

Bonds's runaway season came to a screeching halt on September 4, 1993, when the *San Francisco Chronicle* ran the following article under the head-line, POLICE PROBING 'DISPUTE' AT BONDS' HOME:

> Atherton police are investigating a family dispute that occurred at the residence of San Francisco Giants left fielder Barry Bonds last week.
>
> According to a police log, two officers were dispatched to the home at 12:01 A.M. August 25 to a "family dispute . . . settled on scene."
>
> "I don't know nothing about it; I wasn't even home," Bonds said last night in St. Louis.
>
> "Anytime you got money, people want to mess with you," he said. "My mom called yesterday and said somebody was in my house two days ago, and I'm not even around. My agent called to tell me about the [August 25 incident], so how could I know what it was when I'm not even there?"
>
> Atherton Police Chief Kip Rolle declined to discuss details of the case, saying it is under investigation.
>
> Rolle said he expects that the results of the investigation will be forwarded next week to the San Mateo County district attorney's office for review.

Bonds was, in fact, home that night, as was his wife, Sun. The couple had recently purchased a $2.5 million, 6,100-square foot house in Atherton, California. After five and a half years, their marriage had disintegrated into a series of arguments, too often in the presence of their two young children (Bonds's second child, a daughter named Shikari, had been born in 1991). Although prosecutors cited a lack of evidence as the reason they decided not to file charges against Bonds, the details were ugly. Sun had told police that following a dispute about birth control pills and the quality of the family housekeeper's work, Barry grabbed her around the neck, kicked her, and threw her partially down the stairs. Barry countered that Sun had ripped at his shirt and that he spun around and "kicked her in the buttocks." Somewhere during the melee, Sun called 911, and when police arrived she was standing outside the house, crying and holding her neck. When she was told the altercation would likely find its way into the newspapers, she begged the authorities to leave.

Although friends close to Bonds speak admiringly of his ability to block out distractions, the upheaval took a toll. "It's a nightmare," Bonds told Marc Topkin of the *St. Petersburg Times*. "That's all I've got to say. It's a nightmare." Through the first 19 days of September, Bonds drove in two runs, and the Giants fell from seven and a half games ahead of Atlanta to three behind. San Francisco went 55 innings without scoring more than one run in an inning, 24 games without scoring more than three runs in a single inning, and 17 games without a three-run home run or grand slam. As Bonds went, so went the Giants. And Bonds was going nowhere.

Yet Baker's team was resilient and clawed its way back into the race. On the morning of October 3, the last day of the regular season, the Braves and Giants were tied at 103–58. Unless one team won and the other lost, there would be a one-game playoff. That afternoon Atlanta was hosting the expansion Rockies, who were 0–12 against the Braves. The Giants, meanwhile, were in Los Angeles to face the hated Dodgers.

After great debate, Baker bypassed his veterans to start right-hander Salomon Torres, a hard-throwing 21-year-old who had pitched in just eight games that season. It was a mistake. The petrified Torres allowed three runs on five hits and five walks in three and a third innings, and the Dodgers gleefully pounded San Francisco, 12–1. When Torres approached Thompson before the game seeking advice on his mechanics, most Giants knew it would be a rough afternoon. "The kid had a lot of hype, but he wasn't ready for it," says outfielder Darren Lewis. "I don't blame him for that. He was just a baby."

Torres would catch a lot of grief from teammates and the media for leaving the clubhouse before the game was over. Yet it wasn't his own performance that drove him away; it was the way Bonds reacted. The veteran (who went 0-for-4 with two strikeouts in the loss) tore into the rookie, calling him a "pussy" and a "failure" and wondering aloud whether he had the guts to ever pitch on the major league level. "Soft," Bonds snarled dismissively. "You're just soft."

"What he said to me," says Torres, "comes from a person with no heart."

Shortly after berating Torres, Bonds again revealed his paradoxical nature by handing Clayton a wad of money. "At the start of the season he bet me $500 that I wouldn't hit .280 for the year," says Clayton, who batted .282. "That loss to the Dodgers was crushing, and the last thing on my mind was the money. But Barry didn't wait a week or a month to pay. He came up to me and said, 'You did a good job.' It was a very classy move."

By beating the Rockies 5–3, the Braves advanced to the playoffs and left the Giants licking the wounds of a 103-win season that fell *just* short. Still, Bonds had earned his salary, both in production and at the ticket window. For the first time in years, San Francisco baseball mattered again.

TEN

YOU CAN'T LIVE WITH 'EM. . .

ONE WEEK BEFORE THE Giants were scheduled to report to spring training in February 1994, shortstop Royce Clayton and center fielder Darren Lewis were standing in Clayton's driveway outside his Bay Area home, hitting baseballs off a tee into a net. Strolling down the sidewalk came Barry Bonds, in town and out for a walk on a sunny weekend afternoon. "Hey," he said, "what are you dudes doing?"

"What's it look like," said Clayton, a longtime acquaintance of Bonds. "We're hitting. Only a few more days till spring training."

Bonds was unmoved. *"Pffft,"* he said. "I don't need none of that." Bonds picked up a rock and threw it across the street. Picked up another rock and threw it, too. He swung the bat one time, an imaginary baseball hanging in the air. *Thwack!* "Yup," he said, "I'm ready."

Bonds walked away without saying another word.

"We're sweating bullets, doing all we can to prepare for another grueling season, and he's Barry," says Clayton, laughing. "That's all it took. He really was ready to go."

In fact, Barry Bonds was not ready for what awaited him. Not by a long shot. Yes, Bonds was prepared for the physical rigors of the game, but the 1994 major league season would be like no other. It would test Bonds's patience, decency, and resiliency, and call into question his ability to become an ambassador for the sport.

The season began auspiciously enough. The Giants opened at home by sweeping Pittsburgh. After losing two of three to St. Louis, the team then hit the road for a three-game series against the Braves. Meeting the Giants in Atlanta was a general assignment sports reporter in her early 20s, asked by the editors of her mid-size newspaper to produce 1,500 words on San Francisco's return to baseball glory. For the scribe, this was the assignment of a lifetime. "You're young and naive," says the writer, who requests anonymity to protect her ongoing journalism career. "You think being around pro athletes is like a trip to heaven."

While standing alone in the visitors' clubhouse of Atlanta–Fulton County Stadium, the writer was surprised to see Bonds motioning for her to approach. "Me?" she asked.

"Yeah," said Bonds. "You."

Could this be? Two years out of journalism school, and she was being granted an exclusive one-on-one interview with the great Barry Bonds? Maybe he wasn't so bad after all.

"Hey," said Bonds. "Have you ever seen anything like this?" He whipped out a copy of the most recent *Playboy*, where Becky Delos Santos, Playmate of the Month, revealed all in a risqué centerfold spread. Page by page Bonds flipped through the magazine's photographs, all but shoving them in the scribe's face. "I'd never said two words to him before," says the writer. "Clearly, something was off with him."

For Bonds, this sort of rudeness toward women was nothing new. Once, while walking onto the stage for an appearance on *The Arsenio Hall Show*, the athlete sniffed the chair an attractive female guest had just vacated. Years later he allowed a *San Francisco Chronicle* photographer named Deanne Fitzmaurice to follow him around for a photo essay. She was struck by Bonds's large muscles, his beautiful house, his friendly children—and his jarring inappropriateness. "He's really weird and complex with women," says Fitzmaurice, who otherwise found Bonds likable. "He'd come up and tell me really personal things about his wife and family and his sex life.

Personal stuff that was really off. It was just . . . *weird*."

Throughout a '94 season that began with hopes of a World Series and ended after 115 games with a players' strike, Bonds was dragged down by his complicated, often clumsy dealings with the opposite sex. For several years now, trouble had been brewing at home. Sun had grown tired of Barry—tired of his attitude, his mediocre parenting, his womanizing. Though she had done her best to become what Barry wanted in a spouse and mother, it was never enough. For his part, Bonds wasn't cut out to be an exemplary husband. To him, women seemed to be a convenience, useful mainly for cooking dinner, decorating the house, watching the kids, and having sex. When Rod Wright was Bonds's agent, Sun would routinely call to ask about her husband's finances. She certainly wasn't getting any information out of Barry.

The apparent breaking point in an already tenuous marriage came in early 1994, when Bonds was introduced to Jennifer Peace, a 23-year-old pornographic film star from Pinelawn, Kentucky. Brown-haired, brown-eyed, and large-breasted, Peace had starred in more than 100 films under the moniker "Devon Shire," including such classics as *Buttsizer: King of Rears* and *Switch Hitters 6*. According to a lawsuit filed by Peace in Los Angeles Superior Court, Bonds not only slept with her, he impregnated her. "She's carrying a child, a baby boy, and she believes the father is Barry Bonds," said Peace's attorney, Elliot Abelson. "When offered the opportunity to terminate the pregnancy, she refused because she wants to have the baby since she knows who the father is." In a statement Bonds's attorney admitted, "Barry had sex with her," and—fearing embarrassing headlines—Bonds settled out of court for an undisclosed sum.

Although Peace's paternity claim was ultimately proved false, the damage was already done. On May 27, 1994, after more than six years of marriage, Barry filed for divorce.

Even under normal conditions, the split would have been messy. But Barry and Sun's breakup took place in the heat of the spotlight. In what S. L. Wykes of the *San Jose Mercury News* would call "the biggest, nastiest publicly fought celebrity spat since Jose Canseco rammed his Porsche into wife Esther's BMW," Bonds's ensuing summer, fall, and winter were spent drowning in a sea in which the vessels of the *National Enquirer* and the *New York Times* collided. Interest in the scandal became so intense that, according to Jim Warren, Bonds's trainer at the time, *People* offered him $50,000 to write a Sun-Barry tell-all piece.

The divorce involved heated debate on a myriad issues: Sun requested custody of the couple's two children, four-year-old Nikolai and three-year-old Shikari, and sought child and spousal support, attorney fees, and a determination of property rights. Bonds countered by insisting he and Sun had agreed that his earnings were his and her earnings (which were nil) were hers. Sun said she understood little English when the two married, and that she pretended to grasp what her husband was saying in order to please him. Barry said Sun comprehended his words just fine. Sun said the premarital agreement was shoved in her face at the last minute, a sign-or-get-lost gesture. Barry said it has been discussed long in advance. Sun said her soon-to-be ex-husband would not allow Shikari to bring Silkey, her comfort toy, on visits to his house. Barry said Silkey was welcomed with open arms. Bonds's attorneys seemed determined to portray Sun as a gold-digging opportunist, more concerned with her wealth and status than being a good wife and mother. The court was unmoved—in the first of many judgments to come, Sun was awarded $15,000 per month, plus near-unlimited access to a family credit card account.

In a career filled with dramatic moments, Bonds's play with the Giants that summer stands as one of his greatest achievements. As his private life became daily *Chronicle* fodder, Bonds batted .312, with 37 home runs and 81 RBIs in 112 games. "Most guys, when they're getting a divorce, it affects them," says Lewis, the center fielder. "Their numbers go down, their minds are somewhere else. Not Barry. That wasn't going to stop him. Nothing was going to stop him." During their first two years together in San Francisco, Bonds and Lewis spent their mornings working out with a trainer at Menlo College in nearby Atherton, California. Several times that summer, Lewis would arrive at the scheduled 9 A.M. start time, only to find Barry already gone. "He would have these 9 A.M. court dates," says Lewis. "So he'd get there at 6 A.M. and run in the dark. Barry refused to let his divorce beat him."

But Bonds wasn't merely dealing with a bitter breakup. The year was marked by a number of ugly incidents that made him an even more inviting target. At a January 23 Baseball Writers Association of America dinner in New York City, Bonds failed to attend to receive his MVP trophy. He was ripped by—of all people—his godfather. "We gave him $47 million," said Willie Mays. "He can pick up his award." Then, in late February, he was blasted for missing a day of spring training to attend the ESPY awards. His response? "It's only because I'm a black man." The following month he was criticized for a *GQ* interview in which he was asked what sort of advice he received from Mays and Dusty Baker. "All you get is crud in your ear all day," he said. "From all of them."

In late April Bonds was slapped with a lawsuit, and although the case was ultimately dismissed, the episode generated an inordinate amount of media attention. In the suit, the owner of Creative Expressions, a Riverside, California, beauty salon, filed a restraining order against Bonds. "Barry Bonds came to my business and made threats on my son's life," said Shirley Lewis, who sued Bonds for $25 million. Lewis said Bonds "terrorized me like the Gestapo," and that she suffered from headaches, nausea, insomnia, nightmares, frequent anxiety attacks, and other symptoms as a result. What Lewis failed to mention was her son had allegedly been harassing Bonds's young cousin. "I didn't threaten nobody's life," said Bonds. "I just said he'd get his butt kicked."

In July, a poll of Major League players rated Seattle's Ken Griffey Jr. and Frank Thomas of the White Sox as baseball's top performers—a slap in the face to a three-time MVP. "It's like Michael Bolton at the Grammys," responded Bonds. "Do you want to see him win every year? I'm just letting these other guys have their year." That same month, Bonds was booed at the All-Star Game in Pittsburgh and blamed it on racism, prompting widespread criticism. "Those boos Barry Bonds received . . . were well deserved," wrote John Steigerwald of the *Pittsburgh Post-Gazette*.

Late in the season, Giants coach Bob Brenly left the team to cope with the death of a relative. In his absence, Bonds's close friend, a Hollywood casting agent named Tony Shepherd, slipped into Brenly's locker, put on his uniform, and took the field during batting practice at Dodger Stadium. "It was so distasteful," says Mark Gonzalez, who covered the team for the *San*

Jose Mercury News. "I think a lot of the players viewed it as a guy crossing the line. And Tony was Barry's guy."

To teammates Bonds often appeared emotionless and unmoved, but privately he was a mess. Bonds wept frequently during the '94 season, including a little-known breakdown in a Candlestick Park hallway that stunned a handful of onlookers. Here was the great Barry Bonds, head in hands, sobbing uncontrollably. "He had a lot of pain in his life," recalls a teammate. "We all let our guards down sometimes. But to see a man like Barry—who never showed his feelings—crying was very strange."

With few exceptions, Bonds blocked out teammates, coaches, reporters, and fans, surrounding himself with paid employees and glory-seekers instead. There was Shepherd, the great grandson of movie mogul Louis B. Mayer, who was regarded by beat writers as the ultimate jock sniffer. There was "Dennis the limousine owner," who throughout spring training drove Bonds to and from Scottsdale Stadium via black stretch. Both were men Bonds knew he could denigrate without risking a loss of loyalty. Dennis was handed the nickname "Shuddup Dennis" after Bonds humiliated him in front of a pack of reporters, yet he would come back time and time again. That was the type of person Bonds liked—someone willing to barter pride in exchange for a famous friend.

But with his marriage and reputation crumbling, there were few people willing to offer Bonds comfort. "He had this entourage of people he surrounded himself with in the clubhouse, but I think he was a truly lonely person," says pitcher Billy Swift. "You never saw him by himself leaving the ballpark, but it wasn't like he had friends around to joke with. You might as well have put caution tape around his locker, because nobody wanted to go near him anyway."

Throughout his first season in the Bay Area, Bonds was a conquering hero, beloved for his return home. By now, however, the lovefest had waned, and things were about to get worse. On August 12, 1994, the Players Association went on strike over the league's plan for a salary cap. For 233 days, there was no baseball, wiping out the entire postseason. With each passing day, fan antagonism grew. *How could the players, many of whom earned millions of dollars, strike over money?*

Bonds was indifferent to the spectators, dismissively noting, "They'll be back." Pleading hardship, he petitioned a judge to cut in half his spousal and child support payments. "Mr. Bonds has tightened his belt remarkably," said Robert Nachshin, his attorney. "Mr. Bonds is like someone who is unemployed or someone who was fired." With those words hanging in the air, the monthly expenses of Sun and Barry were released by the court—$1,500 cell phone charges, $2,242 for clothing. The Bay Area resounded with disbelief. *Tightened his belt? On San Francisco streets, the homeless are digging through garbage cans for half-eaten sandwiches, and Barry Bonds needs financial help?* Nevertheless, Judge George Taylor ordered that Sun temporarily receive a reduced $7,500 a month. Barry would continue to pay the mortgage, taxes, and insurance on the couple's Atherton, California, estate where she lived with the children.

Then, after his pro-Barry ruling, the judge leaned across the bench and asked the ballplayer for his autograph.

Despite Bonds's temporary victory, the divorce proceedings provided the public with ugly details about the marriage. In a late-1995 hearing to determine permanent spousal support, Sun testified that Barry had abused her on a regular basis. According to Sun, Barry kicked her when she was eight months pregnant, choked her, dragged her around the house by her hair, and locked her outside naked. When Barry turned especially angry, Sun said she would lock herself in the closet. Sun maintained the agreement she signed with her husband was illegal, because she had no representation and spoke minimal English. In August 2000, the California Supreme Court sided with Barry. "In a majority of dissolution cases in California," wrote Chief Justice Ronald George, "at least one of the two parties apparently is not represented by counsel." Barry and Sun would spend six years in and out of courtrooms, arguing over money, custody, and the legal limits of a prenuptial agreement.

As the saga of Bonds's failed marriage continued to play out in San Mateo County Court, the baseball strike went unresolved. Meanwhile, the Giants reported to Scottsdale for spring training on February 22, but without Barry Bonds or Matt Williams. Replacing them were Barry Miller and Keith Williams—the result of a brainchild by owners to break the strike by paying fill-ins to look like, walk like, and talk like (but not play like) the stars. "It'll never be a major-league camp to me," said a frustrated Dusty Baker. "Not until Barry Bonds, Matt Williams and Robby Thompson show up."

Nobody was hit harder than Bonds, who lost nearly $1.4 million during the '94 strike and would lose $42,350 per day were it to continue into '95. The strike failed to offer Bonds even the thin silver lining he'd hoped for—a few months out of the spotlight. Looking to put in a quick workout, one day Bonds drove to Murrieta Valley High School, located 10 minutes from his home, and headed to the football field for some sprints. Soon a swarm of students were leaving the building to watch a superstar in the flesh. The administration did not take to this kindly. Doug Highlen, a Murrietta Valley High teacher, wrote an angry letter to Bonds and sent a copy to the local *North County Times*. "You parked your flashy car in a no-parking zone in front of the office [then] headed to the football field and proceeded to do windsprints," Highlen wrote. "Mr. Bonds, the taxpayers of this community did not spend $38.5 million to build you a personal training facility."

School district officials spoke with Bonds and told him he was welcome to use the facilities—after school hours.

The battering of Bonds's image was brutal, but it did not last. On April 2, 1995, the strike officially ended, and San Francisco fans seemed willing to embrace their star anew. Like all franchises, the team struggled to lure people back to the park. Only 1,241,500 came to Candlestick, making the Giants 12th of 14 National League teams in attendance. But it was anything but an indictment of Bonds. Heck, he was the only reason people *did* come.

"Over the years we have seen Barry play hurt, play every day at the highest level," says Ann Killion, a columnist with the *San Jose Mercury News*. "He'll literally get one pitch to hit each game and he'll hit it. And that's what people are looking for in Barry—not a wonderful person, but a wonderful baseball player."

When the team finally arrived in Scottsdale for an abbreviated spring training, Bonds was relieved. He dismissed any questions concerning Sun Bonds and Jennifer Peace, and blasted media reports that he had considered crossing the picket line. "You guys could just put a big 'wrong' on your forehead," he said. "But one day you'll be right: I will go into the Hall of Fame."

The return to baseball meant the return of Bonds to the Giants clubhouse, hardly a thrilling proposition for the rest of the San Francisco roster. By the start of 1995, most team holdovers had grown accustomed to Bonds's caustic sense of humor and raw-nerve ribbing, but they hardly enjoyed it. Of all his devices, however, the one Bonds liked best was the silent treatment. After talking gregariously with someone one minute, Bonds would ignore him the next. At first, members of the media were primary recipients of the freeze. Then it spread to teammates. And coaches. He loved to see the hurt in people's faces. For Bonds, the gesture was sending a message. *Get close to me, but not too close.* On a lazy afternoon in St. Louis, Bonds spotted rookie pitcher Shawn Estes and treated him to lunch. "He talked to me like a person," says Estes. "And the next day I didn't exist."

"I was a total team player, so I'd talk to anyone about anything," says John Patterson, the Giant infielder. "I'd be talking to Barry, having a great conversation. Then maybe I'd get up, grab a bat, and come back two seconds later to continue the conversation. He'd look at me like I was a piece of shit. I'd be like, 'Dude, I was *just* talking to you five minutes ago!'"

When Bonds chose to speak to teammates, it usually concerned one topic—Barry Bonds. Behind his back, Williams and Thompson nicknamed Bonds "I-I-Me-Me." If Bonds wasn't discussing his fabulous talents, he was discussing his fat wallet, his new car, his amazing house, his beautiful women. Mark Dewey, a Giants pitcher who lockered near Bonds, could not stand it. Every minute there seemed to be a new boast. "I was going crazy," says Dewey. "So one day I began reading to Barry from the Bible." Dewey encouraged Bonds to make God and his children the priority, and focus less on money. "That was my way of rebuking him," says Dewey.

Did it work?

"Well," says Dewey, "no."

Rebuke or no rebuke, one thing remained clear: Within the white lines of the baseball diamond, Barry Bonds was brilliant. During spring training

Bonds sported a new style of Nike cleats—ones with a hideous black-and-white swirl. As Bonds approached the plate for his first at-bat in a game at Scottsdale Stadium, Cubs catcher Rick Wilkins chortled and said, "What are you, a zebra in those shoes?"

"This zebra," Bonds coolly replied, "is going deep."

The first pitch from Frank Castillo was a split-finger fastball down the heart of the plate. *Pow!* Bonds sent it over the right-field wall. "That was one of the first games I'd played as a Giant, and I'll always remember it," says Dewey. "The zebra was phenomenal."

Bonds would develop greater power as he aged, and his speed and acceleration probably peaked in the late 1980s. But in 1995 Bonds was as at his defensive zenith. Though he committed a career-high six errors, what casual observers forget is that San Francisco's right fielder that season was the lumbering Glenallen Hill, a sumo wrestler in cleats. To compensate for Hill's substandard positioning and reflexes, center fielder Darren Lewis spent much of his time covering right-center, leaving Bonds alone with 10 football fields of terrain in baseball's windiest ballpark.

With its swirling gusts and unpredictable gales, Candlestick—freezing one minute, warm the next—was legendary for turning good outfielders into characters from a Three Stooges routine. As David Montero of the *Ventura County Star* wrote in a 1999 ode to the stadium, "Even when the fog doesn't roll up and cascade over the upper lip, it lurks nearby—ready to pounce, engulf and make a mockery. The coldest park in both the American and National leagues shatters the notion that baseball is to be enjoyed basking under a warm sun while wearing shorts and devouring stadium-steamed hot dogs. It is one of the few places where the fans at a midsummer game look like they should be watching football in winter and the sensible drink choice in August is not soda, but rather, cocoa." Willie Mays, the premier defensive center fielder of his generation, knew the ballpark's vicissitudes better than anyone, and wowed peers with his ability to read the wind. Three decades later his godson possessed similar gifts. "Candlestick was bad—really, really bad," says David McCarty, a Giants utility player. "Then the fog would start coming in like fingers over the stadium. How Barry did what he did out there, I'll never know."

"He got to every ball," adds Hill appreciatively. "What Barry Bonds has is the ability to hyper-focus beyond what people ever truly know. When a baseball was headed toward the outfield, all Barry focused on was getting it. The crowd, the noise—he paid 'em no mind. That's why he was so great."

Gone were the days where Bonds only played shallow, allowing balls to land beyond his reach. Now he was rarely caught out of position, and whether it was San Diego star Tony Gwynn or Reds reserve Eric Anthony, Bonds knew the tendencies of every National League hitter. Did he study tapes and scouting reports? Rarely. His skill came from memory and gut feel. Where once Bonds considered defense an afterthought, it was now a source of great pride—yet another area where he could not be criticized. "He was *always* in the right place," says pitcher Dave Burba. "Always. When you had that sort of person playing behind you, it took a huge load off."

Unfortunately for the San Francisco faithful, Bonds was a one-man show. Featuring one of the National League's worst starting rotations and an even worse bullpen, the '95 Giants posted a nightmarish 5.39 team ERA. Their most successful pitcher, starter Mark Leiter, won 10 games. Nobody else on the staff exceeded six. "You can't win if you can't pitch," says Hill. "Even with Barry, we didn't have much of a chance."

By the end of June, Dusty Baker's club was in last place and going nowhere fast. Were there ever a team in need of a spark to revive a morbid season, it was the '95 Giants. Which is why general manager Bob Quinn eagerly pulled off an eight-player trade with the Cincinnati Reds that landed the one person Barry Bonds absolutely *did not* want to play with.

Not that Deion Luwynn Sanders particularly cared what Bonds thought. Known throughout the sporting world as "Neon Deion" and "Prime Time," the 27-year-old Sanders arrived in San Francisco wearing the sort of halo that Bonds could only covet. As an All-Pro NFL defensive back and a speedy, exciting major league outfielder, Sanders had emerged from the two-sport shadow of Bo Jackson to capture the imagination of a nation. He was a one-man merchandising machine—a ubiquitous corporate pitchman with a megawatt smile and a nose for attention. Though hardly a great baseball player (he brought to the Giants a .240 average and 10 RBIs in 33 games), Sanders stole bases, legged out triples, and lured bodies through the turnstiles. Everyone on the Giants was thrilled to experience the aura of Sanders up close—everyone, that is, except Bonds.

Several years earlier, Bonds and Sanders had engaged in a heated, ego-driven off-the-field confrontation, and while the new guy in town was willing to let bygones be bygones, Barry was not. As soon as Sanders joined the club in Miami, he and Bonds were called into Dusty Baker's office for a 25-minute sit-down. Despite Baker's attempt to foster détente, Bonds never warmed to Sanders.

The snub wasn't solely due to their troubled history. Over the previous weeks, Bonds's aura of invincibility had begun to crack. In a home game against the Mets on June 5, Bonds stood in place as a fly ball off the bat of New York's Kelly Stinnett soared over his head and back, back, back—off the wall. The left fielder had struck this arrogant "Why bother?" pose countless times, only now the baseball was rolling around the grass. Bonds was loudly booed, and his comments after the game only inflamed matters. "I don't care what [the fans] think," he said. "They ain't out there. They don't know what's really going on. If they can do better, bring their ass out there and do it better than me. Put my uniform on and do it." Bonds didn't help the situation by blaming the lapse on his divorce, telling ESPN's Chris Myers that while the ball was in flight he was pondering the impact his split was having on his two children.

In the July 1 *San Francisco Chronicle*, C. W. Nevius penned a scathing column with the headline TRADE BONDS AND BRING BACK THE FANS. "Whether he has meant to or not," Nevius wrote, "Bonds has turned into the poster boy for everything the angry baseball fan dislikes about the modern player. He is seen as overpaid, uncooperative, egotistical and underproductive. . . . While baseball in general and the Giants in particular are desperately trying to regain the fans' affections, Bonds refuses to budge. He is one of the few players in the game who can consistently take a bad situation and turn it into a full-blown disaster."

Try as he might to appear indifferent, Bonds could be deeply wounded by criticism. His defense mechanisms—a stoic face, crossed arms, quick retorts—only worked so well. Throughout two and a half seasons he had been the king of the Giants. *And now I'm no longer wanted?* Shortly after the column ran, one of Bonds's representatives approached *Chronicle* sports-writer Gwen Knapp and offered her $2,000 to spin out a puff piece on his client. "At first I thought he was joking," says Knapp. "But I'm pretty sure that if I said, 'Make it $3,000,' he would have pulled out his checkbook. The thing that struck me is that most agents say, 'If I get you a one-on-one with my guy, you're going to love him, you're gonna see he's a great guy and you're gonna wanna write about him.' So what does it say that Bonds's people had to offer money? It says that Bonds was taking a major beating."

As Bonds brooded over his bad press, along came "Prime Time." Bonds bad-mouthed Sanders repeatedly, ripping him for his mediocre play and for not arriving by team bus because "that ain't Prime Time's style"—even as Bonds had limousines and hotel suites written into his contract. (In fact, Sanders gave the Giants a boost, hitting .285 and tying a career high with a .346 on-base percentage) Bonds went so far as to stack folding chairs in a circle around his locker to keep the reporters waiting for Sanders out of his turf. "The great Barry Bonds," wrote Dan Le Batard of the *Miami Herald*, "reduced to a child."

If Bonds was troubled by Sanders's image, he was equally disturbed by his real-life persona. *Why don't teammates admire me the way they do Prime Time?* "Deion was awesome," says catcher Tom Lampkin, who recalls Sanders's kind gestures when Lampkin was going through marital troubles. "He came in and signed footballs for people, and it was almost like his pleasure to do so. Until that time, the only mega-star I'd been around was Barry, and he wouldn't let you get to know him. But Deion was a burst of sunshine."

As the season drew to a close, Thompson and Williams—the two senior Giants—pulled Sanders aside and urged him to return to the Giants the following season. Sanders was flattered, but eventually decided to take the year off to dedicate to football. "That was an eye-opener for everybody, because nobody would have ever asked Barry to stay," says Ted Robinson, the team's former announcer. "He just didn't have that kind of bond with his teammates. And in two months, Deion Sanders did."

On the night of September 6, the reticent Bonds let his guard down. Relaxing in the Candlestick clubhouse before a game against the Expos, he spotted Michael Duca, a local media member, and invited him to sit. A nearby TV was flashing live images of Cal Ripken Jr., the Baltimore Orioles iron man, bounding around Camden Yards. Ripken had just played in his 2,131st consecutive game, snapping Lou Gehrig's supposedly unbreakable record, and he was shaking hands with every fan within reach. "I could never reach out like that," Bonds told Duca. "I'd be too scared. If you could hear the things people say to me from 50 yards away—I'll never get that close to people. Never."

Bonds put up his usual dizzying numbers (.294, 33 home runs, 104 RBIs) in 1995, but without much satisfaction. The Giants finished last in the division with a 67–77 mark. The season had been pocked by negativity, from his ongoing public divorce and a less-than-enamored fan base to Sanders's arrival. A week before the final game, Bonds announced he was considering retirement. "Happiness is more important to me," he said. "I'd rather do something else. I'm tired of headaches every day and wondering what's going to happen next."

In the Giants clubhouse, Bonds's words were greeted with universal diffidence. Not one coach, teammate, equipment staffer, or reporter believed him. From their vantage point, it was more nonsense.

A week later Bonds put his 11,000-square foot house in Southern California on the market. He moved closer to San Francisco so that he could work out at the ballpark year-round.

After all, spring training was less than six months away.

ELEVEN

ARRIVAL OF AN ENEMY

ON THE NIGHT OF September 22, 1995, Giants second baseman John Patterson was sitting in the dugout at Candlestick Park, watching Colorado Rockies closer Curtis Leskanic throw his late-game warm-up pitches. Leskanic's stuff was nasty—a fastball that blistered the hands of right-handed hitters, a slider as slick as an oil spill. The entire San Francisco bench was in awe, as pitch after pitch whooshed its way toward the catcher. "Man," Patterson said after striking out, "how does anyone hit this guy?"

Though Bonds was not one for in-game chatter, he maintained something of a soft spot for Patterson, a grinder with mediocre talent who fought for every day in the majors. "Here's the thing," Bonds told Patterson. "When Leskanic turns his glove he's throwing a slider, and when he comes in straight it's a fastball." Patterson spent the rest of the inning studying Leskanic. As did Matt Williams. And Glenallen Hill. And Royce Clayton. And Dusty Baker. Every Giants player and coach tried to pick up what Bonds saw, but nobody could. "Barry," said Baker, "you're shitting us. There's nothing there."

"OK," said Bonds. "Fastball."

Leskanic threw a fastball.

"Another fastball."

Another fastball.

"Slider."

Slider.

"Another fastball."

Another fastball.

Bonds correctly predicted every pitch throughout Leskanic's two-inning relief appearance, relishing the stunned silence that provided a soundtrack to a grim 6–1 Giants setback. For Bonds, this was bliss. He was the center of attention and the envy of all. Teammates were looking at Bonds through jealous eyes, wondering, "How the hell does he do that?"

Yet Bonds's foresight on that wind-swept September night did not go over well. In the past, when Bonds had barked that he would never share his secrets, it was dismissed as bluster. But Bonds, apparently, *did* possess valuable knowledge. He knew how to read pitchers. He knew when certain plays were about to unfold. In a spring training intrasquad game in February 1996, pitcher Jeff Juden was standing near Bonds as he prepared to walk to the on-deck circle. "This guy's gonna start me with a little doo-doo fastball inside to try and back me off the plate," Bonds told Juden. "Then he's gonna throw a little changeup down and away. I'm gonna sit on both those pitches and then he's gonna try and sneak a fastball by me. I'll take him out on that pitch to left field."

Pitcher Steve Mintz's first pitch: inside fastball.

Second pitch: changeup away.

Third pitch: a 440-foot home run—to left.

"One of the most amazing things I'd ever seen," says Juden. "But he didn't say how he knew what was coming."

That was Bonds—a mercurial mixture of the astounding and the frustrating. As he explained to a writer during a 2000 interview, "I don't feel comfortable telling teammates my secrets, because one day they'll be playing for another team trying to beat me. So why clue them in on the way my mind works?" From a purely logistical and historical standpoint, the thought process made sense. Back when Willie Mays and Bobby Bonds were with the Giants, they never, *ever* shared secrets. Barry was witness to this. "The mindset of that generation was survival," says Mike Krukow, a longtime Giants pitcher and broadcaster. "That was the era when players worked 12 months per year because they weren't making enough money. So you never showed your hand, because you never wanted to risk your place in the game. If you found out your teammate had a weakness, the last thing you'd do is tell him. You kept it locked up for future information."

Still, his clandestine attitude conflicted with Bonds's stated "one and only true goal" of winning a World Series. His selfishness might have been tolerable during the '93 and '94 seasons, when the Giants were serious playoff contenders. But in 1995 the team was awful, and '96 wasn't looking much better. The Giants were thin in the starting rotation and the bullpen and woefully inexperienced on the bench. Fans knew it was destined to be a long year when 35-year-old Mel Hall—straight off a terrible .236 season with the Chunichi Dragons of Japan's Central League—was signed to pinch-hit. If the team was destined to stink, what was the benefit of paying Bonds more than $7 million to hit 40 home runs but help not a soul?

This was the question running through the minds of owner Peter Magowan and chief operating officer Larry Baer, who agreed to explore all trade possibilities. "We were a last-place team having a very difficult time recovering from the strike in terms of attendance and losing a lot of money," says Magowan. "And if we were going to keep Barry around, he would be a long-term expensive commitment. We had to decide whether he was truly worth holding on to."

There were pros and cons to consider. On the field, Bonds was as good as ever. He had begun training in the offseason with 49ers star Jerry Rice, whose workout routine was legendary. The morning segment consisted of a five-mile trail run near San Carlos on a tortuous course called, simply, The Hill. On the steepest sections, Rice and Bonds would pause to do a series of ten 40-meter uphill sprints. In the evenings, Rice and Bonds would alternate between upper-body and lower-body days, doing three sets of 10 reps of 21 different exercises. "I've trained a couple of hundred NFL players and probably 50 Major League Baseball players and a ton of world-class sprinters and triathletes, but in 25 years I've never found anyone who took training as seriously with as much passion and commitment as Barry," says Jim Warren, Bonds's personal trainer. "I've never had anyone show up early, work hard, stay on task, do the shit nobody wants to do and stick with it every single day."

Bonds also focused on a hitting program designed by his father, during which he took batting practice against miniature baseballs. "The idea," Bobby said, "is that the regular ball then looks much bigger." Bonds arrived at 1996 spring training bench-pressing 315 pounds, resembling an NFL defensive back. and crushing everything in sight.

Off the field, however, Bonds's behavior was as troubling as ever. During a spring lunch date with Hall he made inappropriate comments about Donna Carreon, the wife of Giants first baseman Mark Carreon. While driving Carreon to the stadium the following morning, Hall repeated Bonds's words. Upon arriving at the clubhouse, Carreon went straight to Bonds. "Keep talking about my wife," Carreon said, "and I'll fuck you up good."

"Dude," countered Bonds, "get out of my face."

Carreon threw a punch that landed on Bonds's right ear. Bonds responded by grabbing Carreon and wrestling him to the floor. "Everybody respected Mark after that," says Jay Canizaro, a Giants infielder. "We were all hoping he'd kick Barry's ass." The altercation was broken up, and when Baker called the two into his office Carreon was shocked by Bonds's words. "Look, I'm sorry," he said. "I was being stupid. You're one of my best friends on the team. I didn't mean to hurt you."

Carreon was speechless. *Best friends on the team?* "I didn't even like Barry," he says. "And he thought we were good friends. Man, is he bizarre."

Magowan was willing to overlook the semiregular confrontations between his star outfielder and the other Giants. The encounters were mostly kept under wraps, and Bonds continued to produce at an elite level. (He tied a major league record with 11 home runs in April, and in an April 27 game against the Marlins he became the fourth player to accumulate 300 home runs and 300 stolen bases.) Magowan was even able to ignore some of Bonds's stunningly cruel comments, such as when he draped his arm around the two-year-old son of first baseman Dan Peltier and asked, "Hey Colton, who's your favorite baseball player?" When Colton replied, "My dad!" Bonds said dryly, "Why? He never plays."

"What a jackass thing to say," says Peltier.

No, what seemed to set off an alarm in the Giants executive offices was an incident that took place on May 9, when Bonds shoved *USA Today* baseball writer Rod Beaton in the visitors' clubhouse at Busch Stadium in St. Louis. A respected veteran of the newspaper world, Beaton was standing in the middle of the room, waiting patiently for Robby Thompson as the second baseman wrapped up a conversation with a couple of visiting NHL players. "Don't be hanging out in my house!" Bonds yelled at Beaton as he walked toward the trainer's room. Two minutes later Bonds again passed, demanding Beaton either conduct an interview or leave.

"Barry," snapped Beaton, "you're not my social director."

Bonds (6-foot-2, 220 pounds) cursed Beaton (5-foot-10, 235 pounds) and reached to push him in the chest. When the scribe swatted his hand away, Bonds shoved again—"an open-palmed forearm right in my sternum," recalls Beaton, a soft-spoken man with glasses and a brown beard. "It was pretty hard, but not as hard as it could have been. But it did stagger me backward." Beaton declined Major League Baseball's offer to have the matter investigated, but he did accept the Giants' assurance that Bonds would apologize after the game. "It was weak," says Beaton. "Barry danced around it, but he never actually said anything."

Throughout the season, the Giants let it be known that Bonds was available, but that he would cost a king's ransom. San Francisco wanted a young starting pitcher, a young corner outfielder, a first baseman, and a power arm for the bullpen. In July, the Detroit Tigers showed hefty contracts could be moved, sending Cecil Fielder and his $6.25 million allowance to the Yankees for two players. Fielder, though, was a teddy bear of a man—warm and affable with the media, helpful in the clubhouse. A handful of teams called the Giants new general manager, Brian Sabean, during the year, but none was willing to exchange multiple prospects and surrender millions of dollars for a talented problem child.

Bonds's 1996 run was statistically the best of his life. He set National League records with 151 walks and 30 intentional walks, drove in a career-high 129 runs (coupled with 42 homers), won his sixth Gold Glove in seven years, and snagged the Home Run Derby at the All-Star Game in Philadelphia. On August 6 Reds pitcher Jeff Brantley even took the unprecedented step of intentionally walking Bonds to lead off the ninth inning with a 3–2 Cincinnati lead.

But with San Francisco headed for 94 losses and another last-place finish, those following the Giants witnessed statistical fraud in motion. OK, maybe "fraud" is too strong. Statistical *indecency*. Bonds desperately wanted to join Oakland's Jose Canseco as the only players to hit 40 home runs and steal 40 bases in the same season, and as the defeats mounted, so did the selfishness. Bonds would attempt to steal bases when the margin between the teams was more than five runs. He would attempt to steal with two outs and the winning run on third, or even when a strong-armed catcher like Florida's Charles Johnson or Pittsburgh's Jason Kendall was behind the plate. In a September game against the Padres, Bonds ripped Glenallen Hill for fouling off a pitch when Bonds had a base stolen. "I could have stood on the base," he said snidely. "But what can you do?"

"I don't think anyone would argue that Barry goes out there playing for himself," says Shawn Estes, a Giants pitcher. "But I think he believes that if he plays for himself, it'll still help the team win. Like no matter when he's stealing a base, he's still stealing a base—which he would say is a good thing."

Bonds wound up with 42 homers and 40 stolen bases, but when he clinched the record in the last game of the 1996 season at Colorado, teammates scoffed as he tore the historic base from its moorings and ran it to the dugout. "I wouldn't recommend anyone trying it," Bonds boasted of his feat. "My back has been hurting me. My hamstrings are getting a lot tighter. It's hard." Especially if you steal 15 meaningless bases in a month, as Bonds did in September. "Bonds is turning into the Carl Lewis of baseball," wrote *Chronicle* columnist C. W. Nevius. "All the numbers and none of the respect."

When the season ended, the Giants pushed even harder to move the star, actively calling other franchises. There was talk of a deal with Atlanta for pitchers Steve Avery and Greg McMichael and outfielder Ryan Klesko; with the Marlins for first baseman Greg Colbrunn, second baseman Ralph Milliard, and outfield prospect Billy McMillon; the Mets for first baseman Rico Brogna, outfielders Alex Ochoa or Carl Everett, and pitchers Mark

Clark or Bobby Jones. San Francisco would have likely pulled the trigger, but concerns over Bonds blocked the path toward fruition.

In October, the Giants demoted Bobby Bonds to part-time scout after enough players complained that as a hitting coach he was unapproachable and only worked with the best hitters. Barry reacted by demanding a trade—laughable in that the Giants would struggle to peddle their $8.6 million man for four Diet Sprites and a bag of Skittles, let alone top major league talent. He wasn't worth the migraine.

When it became clear that Bonds would stay put, Sabean had to turn elsewhere to trim the Giants' $35 million payroll. On November 13, 1996, he reached an agreement on a trade that sent third baseman Matt Williams and a player to be named later (outfielder Trenidad Hubbard) to the Cleveland Indians for three apparent nobodies—pitcher Julian Tavarez, shortstop Jose Vizcaino and second baseman Jeff Kent, as well as a player to be named later (pitcher Joe Roa).

Dozens of angry letters to the *Chronicle* demonstrated that the exile of a four-time All-Star and beloved member of the community did not play well. "Was Brian Sabean possessed by the spirit of Spec Richardson?" asked Marty Gaetjens of Berkeley. "Did he believe that he was getting a couple of 'untouchables' in Jeff Kent and Jose Vizcaino since the Mets and Indians had each dumped both of these players in less than four months?" Pacifica resident Marilyn Polacci wondered, "Is there some mind-altering substance in the water lately? The Giants pull the blunder of the year in trading Matt Williams, the heart and soul of the ballclub, for a handful of scrubs. Hey, Magowan, with these kind of bonehead moves, If You Build It, They STILL Won't Come." The media were no more sympathetic. Buster Olney of the *Baltimore Sun* wrote that Kent "just isn't a good major-league player." *Newsday*'s Jon Heyman noted, "The No. 1 question on everybody's mind after the Giants traded Matt Williams, who on a bad day is 10 times the player that Jeff Kent or Jose Vizcaino is, was: 'What the heck were the Giants thinking about?'"

On the job for less than a year, Sabean was flabbergasted by the negativity. The Concord, New Hampshire, native had dedicated his life to baseball.

Though he had coached at St. Leo College and the University of Tampa, and then served as director of scouting and vice president of player development for the New York Yankees, this was the first time he'd been publicly attacked. Sabean understood Williams was beloved, and that fans were still prickly over the '94 strike. But *this* was too much. Dusty Baker hated the trade. The members of his coaching staff hated the trade. The Giants' phone lines were jammed for two days. A couple of the calls were death threats. Most were from angry fans venting or promising to never attend another Giants game as long as—well, for at least a week or two.

Two days after the trade Sabean took the unprecedented step of holding a news conference to defend himself. "I'm not an idiot," he declared. "We had two players [Williams and Bonds] at the high end of the salary structure. That was drag on our payroll. . . . We are so far behind L.A. and San Diego in the terms of talent on the roster."

With his status as the team's leader and number one star firmly established, the Giants were certain Bonds would be accepting of the deal. They were mistaken. Now who would hit behind him? Vizcaino? Kent? "When Matt Williams got traded, that was devastating," Bonds told the *Oakland Tribune*. "I didn't come here to go backward. They looked me dead in the face and told me they were going to put a contending team in here." Bonds upheld his demand for a trade, and accused Sabean and Magowan of lying to him about being baseball's highest-paid player. During the winter, the Giants offered to extend Bonds's contract (which was set to expire after 1998) with a deal in the $10 million-a-year range. Weeks later Albert Belle signed with the White Sox for $11 million, and San Francisco didn't budge. Was this lying? Not really.

For the Giants star, it was a matter of disrespect. His father had been fired. His All-Star teammate was traded. The Giants looked like 90-game losers again. And he was underpaid and underappreciated. "If we don't work this out," he said, "I'll play out my two years and then I'm leaving."

On February 20, 1997, the Giants announced that Bonds had been signed to an extension. He would receive $22.9 million over two years, followed by either a third year for $10.3 million or a club buyout for $2.5 million. In the most drastic personality switcheroo this side of George Foreman, Bonds was suddenly Mr. Optimistic. "I want to stay in San Francisco," he giddily told a throng of reporters. "Everything I love is there. San Francisco is my home, I love playing there and I love being there." Was this suddenly upbeat Bonds legitimate? It was hard to tell: A clause in his new contract with the Giants called for a greater effort in the field of public decency.

Within the first few days of spring training, it was clear Bonds and Jeff Kent would not be sharing baking tips or arranging off-season vacation plans. Bonds arrived sporting a new necklace, from which dangled a sparkling gold "40/40" pendant. Behind Bonds's back, teammates snickered at the arrogance and audacity. Not only was Bonds bragging about a flawed accomplishment, the necklace was downright *ugly*. Kent, meanwhile, reported for his first day wearing a plaid shirt, jeans, and a battered pair of Nike tennis shoes. His wardrobe was classic Sears; his light brown hair cut by a hometown barber. He was a practicing Mormon. "Jeff wanted to be left alone," says Chris Jones, a Giants outfielder in 1998 who had lockered next to Kent with the Mets two years earlier. "He'd have his *Field & Stream* magazine, and he would be very happy to read, take some infield, hit some balls, and go about his life."

Kent was 28 years old when he was sent to San Francisco; a five-year major league veteran who knew something about being swapped for a superstar. In 1992 he and an outfielder named Ryan Thompson were traded by the Blue Jays to the Mets for All-Star pitcher David Cone. Four years later, just three and a half months before the Williams deal, he was shipped to Cleveland by the Mets as part of a package for second baseman Carlos Baerga, another All-Star. "I felt a lot of pressure when I was traded for David Cone because that was the first time," says Kent. "But by the time I came to San Francisco, I no longer worried about those things. I was confident enough to believe people wouldn't be booing me for long."

Lost in the brouhaha over Williams's departure was that, in Kent, the Giants were adding someone *Sports Illustrated* characterized as "a tightly coiled spring—intense, huffy, unapproachable." Raised in Huntington Beach, California, Kent was a surfer who aspired to be a cowboy. He paid little to no attention to the major leagues. "Never cared," says Kent. "Baseball wasn't my thing." When he was acquired by the Mets, Kent quickly earned a reputation as a humorless, self-centered jerk. He bashed New York fans and teammates alike, openly rooting for fellow second baseman Fernando Vina to fail in his 1994 bid to make the club. When he was sent to Cleveland, few in the Mets clubhouse mourned the departure. The reaction was similar in Cleveland when he left.

Part of Kent's problem was that, unlike Bonds, he refused to adhere to the longstanding (and mostly mindless) rituals of baseball. He didn't speak in jock clichés or live in an isolated world measured only by statistics and headlines. Kent spent his offseasons fishing and hunting deer. "If you want to get to know me," he once told *ESPN the Magazine*'s Jeff Bradley, "you have to get off the baseball field."

As soon as he reported to camp, Kent could tell Bonds was not his type. Even those who detested the second baseman acknowledged he was a man unafraid to dirty a uniform. "Jeff put his helmet on, he brought his lunch pail, and he played hard," says Shawon Dunston, a Giants utility player. Kent felt there was a right way and a wrong way to approach the game. Skipping stretching, loafing after fly balls, not running hard to first? Wrong ways. "Those are the things Barry and I had confrontations over from the beginning," says Kent. "I had pitchers and players on the team telling me, 'What the fuck is going on out there? What is he doing?' Because at times Barry was so great, and at other times he didn't want to play. We all expected the most out of him every single time, and he didn't provide that."

Kent was the first prime-time Giant to refuse to cower in Bonds's presence. Whereas Will Clark meekly surrendered to the left fielder, Kent stood tall. When Bonds tried the silent treatment, Kent fired back in kind. Kent called out Bonds for not stretching, and cried foul when he stood and admired his own home runs. The two traded across-the-clubhouse barbs with increasing frequency—Kent enraged by Bonds's arrogance, Bonds enraged by Kent's audacity. "Jeff was an ornery Texan who really didn't give a shit what you thought," says catcher Brian Johnson. "He obviously didn't like Barry at all, and he didn't take Barry's shit."

"They've hated each other since the day Kent came to town," *Chronicle* columnist Ray Ratto once wrote. "They hate each other today and they'll hate each other when they both join the feathered choir. The one who lives longer will attend the other's funeral, just to make sure he's dead."

Normally, Dusty Baker would have called Kent into his office and urged the second baseman to ignore Bonds. Yet through spring training and into the early months of the season, a stunning thought entered the minds of Baker and his players: *Matt who?* Kent was a sure-handed second baseman with a limitless supply of thunder in his bat. Hitting directly behind Bonds in the Giants lineup, Kent drove in 26 runs in April, and followed that up with a team-best 20 more in May. Williams was enjoying an equally successful season in Cleveland, but few in San Francisco took notice. The Giants surged to a 15–5 start, and at the All-Star break were 51–36 and leading the National League West. Though nobody offered Sabean an apology, he deserved one.

Here was the strange thing about the Bonds-Kent pairing. As teammates came to know the new second baseman, they saw that he was, in many ways, Bonds's mirror image. Both were talented, sheltered, moody—*and* immensely productive. "They're sort of like Tony Curtis and Sidney Poitier in *The Defiant Ones*," says Baker "It's not that they have similar personalities, because they don't. But you're talking about two guys with similar attributes and attitudes toward the game."

The most peculiar by-product of Kent's arrival was the off-the-field impact it had on Bonds. Taken aback by the attention afforded his new teammate, and equally struck by Kent's surliness, which rivaled his own, Bonds decided that it was time to be friendly. He granted more interviews, said hello on occasion, and graciously praised the franchise for piecing together an improved cast. Throughout his career, Bonds had been extremely hands-off when it came to charitable endeavors. Sure, he would lend his name to the Baseball Tomorrow Fund or make an appearance at a new youth field in Marin City. But these were almost always projects that one of his advisors had pushed for as "good publicity."

Even this temporarily changed. Speaking before the United Way board of directors in mid-February, he voiced his concerns for the plight of African Americans who require bone marrow transplants. Bonds then befriended a 13-year-old leukemia patient named Anthony Lee Franklin. Those who witnessed Bonds with young Anthony recall a compassionate man struck by the boy's condition. When it was determined Anthony might need a bone marrow transplant, Bonds registered as a donor. "He's making a conscious effort to give more of himself," Baker said that April. "A lot of what Barry does is under the radar of the cameras, because getting applauded for his work is not his goal," added Eric McDonald, a senior vice president of the United Way of the Bay Area. "I have often heard about the side of Barry as portrayed by the media, but we have never seen it here. All we have seen is the side that absolutely loves kids and will devote time and money to help them."

The press praised Bonds for his new warmth and leadership—the *Cleveland Plain Dealer* proclaimed A GIANT STEP TOWARD MATURITY in an April 13 headline, and Tim Keown of the *Chronicle* noted on May 28 that "For the first time since he joined the Giants, Bonds is well-liked by his teammates." Privately, however, his fellow players scoffed at what they saw as a calculated attempt to create goodwill. "Anyone who believed Barry had a capacity to be a great guy was just falling for his act," says one teammate. "Yeah, maybe Barry was talking to the media a little. Maybe he gave a little more time. But I could never get past the way he wouldn't say 'Thank you' or hold a door open for someone—simple kindness that anyone with decency should have. I want to see everything good in a person. I'm looking for that good. But Barry never, ever looked to put an arm around a guy to see how he was doing. He never offered to pay for a meal. He was all about Barry."

Away from the spotlight, teammates agreed little had changed. At one point during the season the Giants were visiting Colorado when Bonds was tapped on the shoulder by a Rockies clubhouse employee. "I'm friends with Brian Fisher," he said. "Remember? He was a pitcher with you on the Pirates." Bonds sighed dismissively, but continued to listen. Fisher's son Kyle had been diagnosed with cystic fibrosis (he died the following year), and Brian held an annual pool tournament fund-raiser to fight the disease. Bonds was well aware of the boy's condition. "Brian was wondering if you'd sign a couple of posters and balls that they could raffle off," the clubhouse staffer asked. "A lot of guys have contributed—Larry Walker, Randy Johnson, Steve Reed . . ."

Bonds scowled. "Fuck you," he said. "And fuck Brian Fisher."

•••●

Bonds was not having his typical season. He struggled to hit .250 for the first two months and routinely fell short in big spots. In a June 2 game at Florida, the Giants were trailing 4–2 in the top of the ninth inning with two outs, runners on first and second, and Bonds at the plate. Normally a manager might order an intentional walk, loading the bases but taking the outcome out of Bonds's hands. Not this time. Bonds meekly grounded out to second, and San Francisco lost. "I shouldn't be allowed to wear a uniform," he said afterward. "It's a disgrace."

Bonds blamed his lack of production on his efforts to make nice with the media. He immediately stopped talking, insisting anyone requiring an interview submit questions to his management team. Dating back to high school, Bonds had believed the more he discussed hitting, the less he would actually hit. Was it mental? Sure. But as Kevin Costner's Crash Davis famously notes in *Bull Durham*, "If you believe you're playing well because you're getting laid, or because you're not getting laid, or because you wear women's underwear, then you are." On June 6 Bonds walked twice and drove in a run against Atlanta. After the game, he refused to talk about it. Two days later, prior to a game against the visiting Braves, Bonds ran into Atlanta starter John Smoltz in the outfield of 3Com Park (as Candlestick was renamed in 1995). "You ain't going to pitch to me," Bonds yelled, laughing. "You're afraid to pitch to me."

"No way," Smoltz replied. "I'm coming right at you, Barry. Right at you."

BAM! BAM! Bonds homered twice in a 5–3 win.

At 3:30 the next afternoon—a full three and a half hours before game time—two out-of-town writers who had scheduled interviews with Bonds approached, wearing broad smiles. "Can't you see I'm busy!" Bonds barked in the midst of picking a scab from his elbow or watching a *Growing Pains* rerun or fondling his cell phone. That night he singled, stole a base, and drove in a run.

Indeed, the muzzled Bonds was back to his old self, hitting 11 home runs in June and another eight in July. When he struggled through a 1-for-28 slump in August, it was because pitchers no longer offered him anything within the strike zone. Kent, batting fourth, was seeing fastball after fastball. Bonds, batting third, was not. "Jeff was an excellent player," says Brian Johnson. "But nobody was pitching to Barry instead of Jeff. You'd have to be crazy to do so."

As the Giants and the Dodgers came down the stretch fighting for first place, Bonds was San Francisco's savior. He batted .303 in September, with a team-best nine home runs and 19 RBIs. Against Los Angeles he had seven home runs and 13 RBIs in 12 games. "Clutch," says pitcher Julian Taverez. "The man was clutch almost all the time." On September 17, Bonds's 426-foot two-run homer off Dodgers starter Chan Ho Park gave San Francisco a 2–1 win, and pulled the team within one game of Los Angeles. The next day the Giants won again, with Bonds hitting another home run and a triple. He attributed the surge to his father, who had noticed an unintentional uppercut in his swing. "We talked, we walked with his dog, and I got a broomstick and started talking about hitting and telling him what I saw," Bobby explained. "The reason he didn't hit was because of his swing."

When the Giants clinched the National League West with a 6–1 victory over San Diego at 3Com Park, those who had ripped Bonds as a selfish SOB were shocked by the man in the number 25 Giants uniform. He hugged fans, danced across the dugout roof, sprayed everyone in sight with champagne. His eyes were moist and his smile was wide, and even the media that swarmed him after the game couldn't spoil the moment. "I'm so happy," he said. "This . . ." He stopped talking, but the words could easily be inserted. *This means a lot.*

The good news for Bonds was that he was returning to the playoffs for the first time in five years. The bad news was that he would be facing the Florida Marlins, whose manager was Jim Leyland.

Though overtly loyal to Bonds, Leyland understood his former protégé was not, in fact, a clutch performer. The reason was simple. Bonds's determination to be the greatest baseball player who ever lived heightened several degrees in the postseason. He knew everybody was watching, and he wanted to meet the world's expectations. So Bonds thought and thought about the playoffs until he was nearly paralyzed by fear. That's why Leyland instructed his pitchers to go right after Bonds. Don't worship him; don't even respect him. Pitch him hard and inside, and never cower.

Leyland didn't have to offer such guidance to game one starter Kevin Brown, an ornery 32-year-old right-hander with a killer's intensity and three nasty pitches. Bonds flied out in the first and struck out in the fourth, appearing progressively feeble. But in the top of the seventh inning, Brown made a rare mistake, throwing a fastball over the heart of the plate. Bonds cocked, swung, and launched a fly ball that sailed higher and higher until it hit the wall in left-center field and rolled back toward the infield. Convinced that he had flown out, Bonds stood still as outfielders Devon White and Moises Alou dashed backward. By the time Bonds began to move, a sure-bet triple had become a double. Instead of having a man on third and none out, the Giants had a man on second. Huge difference. The next three batters failed to produce, and San Francisco possessed only a 1–0 lead. When the Marlins came back to win 2–1, it was clear Bonds's poor judgment was partially to blame. Not that he took responsibility. "This is not a baseball field," he said of the Marlins Pro Player Stadium (which was, in fact, designed for football's Miami Dolphins). "The lights are crappy. It has to get dark before you can see, or you need to play day games."

With Bonds held to a .250 average and no home runs, the Marlins swept the series in three games. San Francisco's star was a playoff choker yet again. "We all just ran out of gas," says pitcher Roberto Hernandez. "The Marlins got so hot that I don't think the '27 Yankees would have beaten them. We had to bring our perfect game and we weren't even close to perfect. Not even Barry."

Especially Barry.

TWELVE

EXPANSION

THREE AND A HALF years after he filed for divorce from Sun, Barry Bonds remarried in an opulent black-tie ceremony in the ballroom of the San Francisco Ritz-Carlton Hotel. Held on the evening of January 10, 1998, the gala affair featured a lemon-leaf-and-rose-covered pergola; open-face ravioli with lobster, prawns and scallops in a tomato-lobster broth served on platinum-beaded chargers; silver Tiffany harmonicas for all the groomsmen; and more than 25,000 roses flown in from Ecuador. Even the father of the groom rose to the evening's festive atmosphere, leading the guests in a rousing rendition of "My Girl."

Barry and his new wife, Elizabeth Watson, took to the dance floor as the band played Babyface's "Every Time I Close My Eyes." Two years earlier, Elizabeth and one of her bridesmaids, Anna Hymel, had wagered whether Barry would shed a tear during the ceremony. "When he started crying," said Elizabeth, "I looked at Anna. She was smiling."

At the conclusion of the event, Barry and Liz retreated to their suite, stocked with 240 tea candles—one for each guest. It had been a perfect evening. Guests left the reception with the postwedding glow that consumes us all from time to time. *Love, sweet love.* Barry and Liz were meant to be together. You just knew it in your heart.

And yet, there were a couple of things about Elizabeth Watson most guests were unaware of. Raised in Montreal, the 28-year-old former track star at Marymount Academy was a one-time exotic dancer. This was her brief career choice in the early- to mid-1990s, when she moved to Toronto to make more money. "In Canada, being an exotic dancer isn't the stigmatized profession it is in the United States," says Kristian Gravenor, a columnist for the *Montreal Mirror* and coauthor of *Montreal: The Unknown City*. "There's very little money in Montreal, especially if you're English, black, or an immigrant. Many of the jobs are kept for the French. So in parts of Canada you'll find strip clubs filled with pretty black girls. Bonds's wife was no exception."

Through it all, Watson remained steadfast in the belief that she was destined to marry famous. Some could find contentment being the wife of a doctor or lawyer. But Watson, according to a longtime friend, needed more. She wanted to be taken care of in grandiose fashion. Her first famous boyfriend was Tommy Kane, the former Seattle Seahawks and Toronto Argonauts wide receiver who, in 2004 (long after his relationship with Watson had ended), pleaded guilty in Montreal to manslaughter in the death of his wife. In the 1990s she also had a tryst with Michael Jordan, the married Chicago Bulls superstar. Watson took great pleasure in playing for friends a message Jordan had left on her answering machine. "One time she was on TV in the background when he was competing in a celebrity golf tournament," says Watson's friend. "I thought she was definitely getting caught." Though Jordan sent Watson bouquets of flowers, as well as plane tickets to meet him on the road, she was never busted. "She was one of those girls who would go to a basketball game and wait afterward to meet the guys," says the friend. "She was addicted to the idea of fame."

For a sports celebrity junkie, there were few intoxicants more enticing than Barry Bonds. Watson met the star athlete when the Pirates were visiting Montreal in 1987—the same year he met Sun. The two first hooked up at an after-work hot spot called the Sir Winston Churchill Pub. Among a crowd of mostly 20-something Montrealers dancing to pulsating music, Bonds homed in on Watson, a breathtaking woman of West Indian, French, Spanish, and Chinese ancestry. The two began an on-and-off relationship that cooled when Barry married Sun, but never entirely died. "Elizabeth and I were always friends," Bonds told *In Style* in 1998. Apparently the friendship was intimate enough that when Sun found out about it, she confronted Watson directly. "Liz said it was awkward," says her friend. "But I don't think it bothered her. I think she always believed that she and Barry would wind up together."

As with Sun, what Barry liked about the woman he called "my little princess" was her apparent indifference to the real world. She didn't fret over politics or financial news, and never pried into her husband's on-the-road activities. Though she eventually became aware of Barry's infidelities, in the weeks following the dream wedding Watson was positively blissful about being the new Mrs. Barry Bonds.

Her husband, meanwhile, wasted little time returning to his old ways. Four years earlier, while the Giants were home in San Francisco, Barry had met a 24-year-old part-time model named Kimberly Bell. Brown-haired and petite, Bell wasn't a typical baseball groupie. She had a good job at a leading Silicon Valley–based software firm and never cared much for hobnobbing with the rich and powerful. Bell simply fell for Bonds, whom she found charming and interesting. Immersed in his own divorce, Bonds told Bell he had no interest in remarrying. Bell said that was fine with her. She told the *San Francisco Chronicle* that over the ensuing years they spent two or three nights per week at Bonds's condominium or at her apartment, and that Barry even took her to meet his parents. "He told me what a great girlfriend I was," she said, "because I didn't complain a lot, and I did what he told me to do."

Bell said that when Bonds married for the second time, she feared their relationship would end. Instead, immediately after Bonds and Watson returned from their Caribbean honeymoon, Bell received a phone call from Barry. The newlywed made it clear that when Watson wasn't around during spring training, Bell was welcome to join him. The same went for the regular season. Bonds paid for her to come along on road trips, and even had the Giants traveling secretary book her rooms (in order to receive the team discount on hotels). He promised to buy her a house in Scottsdale, not far from the team's training facility, and financed part of her college tuition. There was speculation that Bonds wed Watson not so much out of love but so that his first wife, Sun, would not get sole custody of their children, and because he would face less negative public scrutiny with a non-white spouse. Says one former Bonds teammate: "A lot of us assumed Barry and Liz was a business deal, not a marriage." From Bonds's vantage point, the arrangement was perfect. At home, he had a beautiful wife to raise his children and provide domestic bliss. On the road, he would rarely spend a lonely night in a hotel room.

No wonder Bonds was bragging to the media that he had recently found God.

With a new wife who liked to go shoe shopping and a hefty wedding tab, Bonds was in no mood to spend money in the early months of 1998. This was nothing new for a man described by teammates as "a penny-pinching cheapskate" and "a cheap bastard." Members of the Giants remained dumbfounded by an incident that took place midway through the 1997 season, when at Bonds's urging the team bus stopped at a McDonald's on its way from the airport to the hotel. Without the slightest sense of irony, Bonds went from seat to seat, collecting $5 a teammate for Big Macs, fries, and medium Cokes. "A billion dollars in the bank and you gather money for hamburgers?" says one former Giant. "People were going, 'Is this really happening?'"

Now, in the wake of the wedding, Bonds was at his stingiest. He offered to defer some of the $31.4 million remaining on his contract to help the Giants acquire a power-hitting right fielder, but only if the team would repay the loan at a ludicrous 10.75 percent interest rate (an offer the Giants turned down). After complaining to Mike Murphy, the team's veteran equipment manager, that the food in the clubhouse was inedible, Bonds announced during a team meeting that $25 per week would be collected from each player to improve the cuisine. "Maybe that wasn't a lot of money for Barry," says Jacob Cruz, a Giants outfielder, "but there were Latin kids sending money back home who were more than happy with peanut butter or bananas or whatever we ate. Twenty-five bucks was the world to them."

Midway through the announcement Bonds was interrupted by Orel

Hershiser, the longtime Dodgers ace who was in his first spring with San Francisco. "Guys, don't worry about it," he said. "Barry and I will split the cost so no one else has to."

Bonds shot to his feet. "I ain't paying for nobody!" he said. "I've got a family to feed." Hershiser took a deep sigh and said, "OK, if that's the way you feel, I'll pay for it myself. No big deal."

"Barry always wanted stuff done," says pitcher Steve Soderstrom, "but he never wanted to take care of it."

That same spring, Hershiser obtained an OrbiTrek elliptical machine and had it placed in the complex's weight room. Anyone was welcome to hop on. "That's the way Orel was," says Cruz. "A total class, team-first guy." Inspired by Hershiser's purchase, Bonds bought a Bowflex Home Gym and also had it installed in the weight room. When Cruz wanted to do a shoulder workout, trainer Stan Conte rebuffed him. "Barry says this is his machine," he said. "Only his machine. He paid for it."

To be a Giant meant learning to tolerate Bonds's selfishness, but it didn't take much to set some players off. In an April 22 game at Pittsburgh, Giants pitcher Danny Darwin became incensed when Bonds lazily jogged after a line drive off the bat of Pirates catcher Jason Kendall. Instead of catching the ball, Bonds allowed it to fall in for a single. Darwin was pulled from the game one batter later, trailing 3–0. When Bonds returned to the dugout, Darwin expressed his displeasure. "I'm out there busting my butt for the team, and I feel like I deserve the same from other players when I pitch," says Darwin. "That particular play he didn't give it 110 percent." Darwin screamed that Bonds should have been embarrassed, and questioned aloud whether he deserved a paycheck. The two took the argument into the tunnel leading to the clubhouse, where Bonds swung at Darwin and Darwin ripped out Bonds's dangling cross earring. "I didn't hate Barry," says Darwin. "But he wasn't my favorite person."

Later in the season, Darwin felt vindicated when his 10-year-old cousin waited patiently for Bonds to sign a baseball card before a game at Atlanta's Turner Field. "I warned my cousin that Barry's not very approachable, so the best bet is to stand by the railing and hope he feels like signing that day," says Darwin. "This was a kid who just loved Barry Bonds, so he stood there for a long time." Darwin watched as Bonds told his nephew that he didn't like kids, then tore the card up and walked away. "Talk about an easy way to lose total respect for someone," says Darwin.

One of the most confusing elements of Bonds's personality is his Jekyll and Hyde approach to those in need of special attention. "People ask me if Barry's a jerk, if Barry's a good guy, if Barry's gregarious, if Barry's aloof," says Dan Brown, who covered the Giants for the *San Jose Mercury News*. "He's all of those things. It just depends on the way the wind is blowing." There is no greater illustration of this than the way his dismissal of autograph seekers contrasts with his treatment of Marge Wallace—known to Giants fans and employees as "Ballpark Marge."

Born developmentally disabled, Wallace was raised in the Sonoma State Hospital, where she remained until her 31st birthday. Although details of her life are sketchy, in 1958—the same year the Giants left New York— Wallace, too, moved to San Francisco. She immediately became a regular at games, arriving hours early in order to greet each player. Before long, Wallace was a fixture of Bay Area baseball. The Giants began leaving a chair outside the clubhouse door, reserved strictly for good ol' Marge. "Every player who ever donned a Giants uniform or who played in the National League knows Marge," said Jack Bair, the Giants VP and general counsel.

On the day of his introductory press conference in December 1992, Bonds gazed into the audience and excitedly exclaimed, "Hey, there's Marge!" Each day without fail, Bonds would bend down to hug Wallace before entering the clubhouse—ask how she was doing, gently touch her arm or shoulder. "Never when the TV cameras were on," says C. W. Nevius, the *Chronicle* columnist. "It wasn't a formality with Barry. He was genuinely concerned for the woman's well-being."

On June 22, 2003, Marge Wallace died of pneumonia at age 77. According to the *San Francisco Chronicle*, Wallace's favorite Giant was J. T. Snow. She thought he was a cutie.

Her second favorite was Barry Bonds.

During the 1998 season, the Giants star did everything possible to cement his status as baseball's reigning king. He hit for average (.303) and for power

(37 home runs, 122 RBIs, .609 slugging percentage). He stole 28 bases, no easy feat at age 34. His 44 doubles were a career high, and he was selected to his eighth All-Star Game. He also drew 29 intentional walks, leading the league for the seventh straight season.

A remarkable moment came against the Diamondbacks on May 28. With his team leading 8–6, Arizona manager Buck Showalter had Bonds walked with the bases loaded and two outs in the bottom of the ninth inning. Even Bonds looked stunned. You're walking *me? Now?* "I know it was a little unorthodox, but I just felt it was the best chance for us to win a baseball game," Showalter said. "It was the choice between one of the great players in the game or a very good player." The move was a wise one—Giants catcher Brent Mayne followed Bonds by lining out to right field. Arizona held on.

Just how feared was Bonds? The last player intentionally walked with the bases loaded was a Cubs outfielder named Bill "Swish" Nicholson, who in 1944 was granted the honor by the Giants after having already hit four home runs in that day's doubleheader. Many superstars had approached the plate with the bags full in the ensuing years, but none had been walked intentionally. Until Bonds.

It didn't matter. None of it mattered. In his greatest and lowest moments of 1998, Barry Bonds was as significant as a flea in a Costco warehouse. He could have hit 20 home runs in an inning, set his hair aflame, run nude through the streets of San Francisco screaming, "I am a hamster named Biff! I am a hamster named Biff!"—nobody was watching. This was the year baseball saved *itself* from *itself*, when Big Mac and Slammin' Sammy woke America up from its poststrike doldrums and returned the goodness of the national pastime to us all. Who had time for snarling Barry Bonds when there was a love train going 'round? Roger Maris's treasured 37-year-old single-season home run record was about to fall, and each day there seemed to be a different leader of the pack. Would it be Mark McGwire, the lovable St. Louis Cardinals hulk with the bulging muscles and the schoolteacher's sensibility? Or would it be Sammy Sosa of the Chicago Cubs, who would smile like a child and say, "Baseball's been very, very good to me" in that endearing Dominican accent?

On August 23, Bonds crushed a fastball from Marlins left-hander Kirt

Ojala into the bleachers of Miami's Pro Player Stadium, becoming the first man in major league history to compile 400 home runs and 400 stolen bases. On the scoreboard "400/400" flashed in bright yellow letters, and most of the 36,701 fans in attendance rose in appreciation. Outside the stadium, however, few people cared. Bonds's achievement found its way into every sports section across America, but on the second, third, or fourth pages (the *Miami Herald* placed it on page 6D). David O'Brien of the *Sun-Sentinel* wrote, "There were no live network cut-ins, no throngs of national media chronicling his every at-bat. But Barry Bonds did something Sunday at Pro Player Stadium that Mark McGwire could only dream of doing, something Sammy Sosa could only accomplish if he doesn't slow down for another six or seven years."

For Bonds himself, the ultimate statistics scavenger, reaching 400/400 was momentous. He had gone beyond his father, beyond Willie Mays. Even beyond Babe Ruth and Hank Aaron. In the sort of aw-shucks false modesty he put on from time to time, Bonds told the small number of assembled reporters that he was nothing compared to McGwire and Sosa. "I have nine writers standing here," he said. "McGwire had 200 writers back when he had 30 home runs. What they're doing is huge. Phenomenal. Two guys might break [Maris's] record. I mean, what's the chance of that ever happening again?"

Though Bonds delivered this contrived sentiment with a broad smile, in fact he was feeling frustrated, grumpy, and terribly jealous. Despite his protestations that he only wanted "to be left alone," Bonds cared immensely about his status. He was the best, and he knew it. Why didn't everybody else? "Barry yearned to be the Michael Jordan of baseball," says one teammate. "The icon of the game. He knew he was better than McGwire and Sosa, and at that point he was, factually, better. But everyone loved Mac and Sammy, and nobody loved Barry."

The drama of McGwire and Sosa's back-and-forth chase so captivated the American media, no one thought to look behind the curtain. At the start of his career in 1986, McGwire was a muscular, well-proportioned man who packed 210 pounds onto a 6-foot, 5-inch frame. By the home run chase, he was 250 pounds, and sported bulging muscles, no neck, and odd fleshy patches beneath his ears. Sosa's transformation was equally remarkable. As a rookie with Texas in 1989, he weighed 165 pounds and had the physique of a young Tito Jackson. Through 1992, his power numbers were laughable—four home runs his first year, 15 the next, then 10 and eight. Then, without warning, Sosa super-sized into Lawrence Taylor. In 1998, he weighed 225 pounds, attributable, he said straight-faced, to "hard work."

In his 1999 book, *Ruth, Maris, McGwire and Sosa: Baseball's Single Season Home Run Champions*, William F. McNeil perfectly exemplifies the media's gullibility. Under the heading "Physical Size and Conditioning of the Home Run Champions," McNeil explains Sosa's production by noting, "Like Maris, he was dedicated to the game, and he worked out religiously during the season lifting weights, running and doing various aerobic exercises. He, like many major leaguers, also took a number of legal dietary supplements." Of McGwire, McNeil added, "He added 20 pounds of muscle over the winter of '91–'92, arriving in spring training at a muscular 235 pounds on a big 6'5" frame. He added another 15 pounds over the next six years, bringing his weight up to a full 250 pounds." McNeil's tone offers not a trace of disbelief or suspicion.

Not until 2002, when former National League MVP Ken Caminiti told *Sports Illustrated* about his steroid abuse, did those outside Major League Baseball's tight fraternity seem to suspect performance-enhancing drugs were responsible for the boom in power. Yet the men who wore major league uniforms knew. Not every player, perhaps, but most. Steroids had been creeping their way into baseball clubhouses for the past decade, and by 1998, anyone with professional experience had been offered a chance to partake. "You'd have to have been blind not to know," says one major league catcher. "When home runs go that far, and they're hit by dudes that big, it's obvious. I tried telling some writers it was worth looking into, but nobody did."

Certainly Barry Bonds was aware of the abuse—he was, after all, its greatest victim. During one of his best seasons, Bonds was overshadowed by players who many suspected had cheated to become great. "I think watching America fall in love with McGwire and Sosa just killed Barry," says Jim Watson, his former trainer. "Knowing that those guys were juiced out of their minds. And I'm sure he said, 'I want the love. I want to hit 70 bombs, too.'"

"Barry told me how mad he was," says Bob Nightengale, a writer for *USA Today Sports Weekly* who enjoys a close relationship with Bonds. "The people are all saying, 'OK, here are our two biggest stars,' and Barry is thinking, 'That's bullshit. Yeah, they hit a bunch of home runs. But can they do what I do?' Everybody in baseball knew those two guys were juiced up. It was no secret. It really pissed Barry off."

Charlie Hayes, the Giants third baseman and one of a few teammates with the guts to confront the star, would openly taunt Bonds. "I've got Sammy Sosa's autograph, and it's worth a helluva lot more than yours!" he'd yell. "Hell, you won't even sign a baseball for me! But fuck, I don't care! You see how far Sammy hits that ball! See how far! He's the best!" Bonds had always been prone to jealous fits, but now his rage seemed justified. Becoming the first 400/400 player was a milestone that warranted front-page headlines or confetti or—something. Certainly not silence.

"When he accomplished great feats, Barry knew that he worked hard to get it," says Hayes. "I remember one day showing up at the stadium at 7 A.M. because I had to pick something up. And there was Barry, doing yoga for the past one and a half hours. While most of us were getting out of bed, Barry was up pumping iron and running laps. He was aware that being great meant busting your ass. Even he couldn't just show up at game time and play."

When Associated Press reporter Steve Wilstein spotted a bottle of androstenedione in McGwire's locker, the news became a national story. Was McGwire cheating? Andro is an over-the-counter steroid compound that was legal in the major leagues but banned by the NFL and International Olympic Committee. Many athletes believe that the pills, which raise levels of the male hormone, build lean muscle mass and speed recovery from injuries. Many critics say it's no different than shooting up a banned steroid. When the McGwire-andro report first hit newspapers on August 22, the Giants were in Miami for a three-game series with the Marlins. Bonds found the news comical. "Shit," he told teammates, "I use that stuff, too. The difference is Mac's doing stuff I wouldn't think of."

Bonds's invisibility came at an enormous price. As McGwire and Sosa were playing Top This, he was shedding his image as a fader come crunch time. With the Giants, Cubs, and Mets battling for the wild card spot in the playoffs, Bonds carried San Francisco. He hit .340 with 10 home runs and 29 RBIs in August, then .389 with another seven homers and 22 RBIs in September. With six walks, five singles, two doubles, and two home runs in a three-game stretch in early September, Bonds broke a National League record by reaching base safely 15 consecutive times. "Nobody could get him out," says Giants infielder Ramon Martinez. "Here's a guy who would get three walks, then in his fourth at-bat he'd get one pitch and lace a double, or hit it off the wall, or take it out of the stadium."

While Bonds's feats would have once led the sports news, now he was barely a footnote. On September 8, the same day the Giants beat the Padres to pull within a game of the wild card lead, McGwire broke Maris's record with a fourth-inning blast over Busch Stadium's left-field wall. As 43,688 fans erupted into euphoria, McGwire approached first base, pumped his fist, and exuberantly ran the bases. After embracing his son Matthew, McGwire made his way to the Maris family, sitting in the front row, and engulfed them in a hug. Earlier in the day the Baseball Hall of Fame had introduced him to the Louisville Slugger Maris had used to hit number 61. "When I touched his bat tonight before the game, I knew tonight was going to be the night," McGwire said. "And I can honestly now say I can rest my bat alongside Roger Maris's bat in the Hall of Fame, and I'm damned proud of it."

The moment was 100 percent baseball schmaltz. Everybody swallowed it.

"McGwire is a hero because he works hard," wrote Bob Hunter of the *Columbus Dispatch*. "He is a hero because he loves his son. He is a hero because he has sincerely embraced the family of the man who owned the record for 37 years."

John P. Lopez of the *Houston Chronicle* waxed even more poetic: "We knew his son, Matthew, the cute little guy with the giddy eyes, would be there waiting for him as he crossed the plate. He would hug the kid and lift him high in the air like a proud father does. We knew he would kiss his fingertips and touch the sky. He would raise his arms high and wide, as if hugging the entire world. And we knew we would hug back . . . he was a hero. A real one. And sometimes, it's still all right to be a sucker for it all."

Had he watched McGwire's postgame tear fest, Bonds would have taken issue with Lopez. *No, it's not OK to be a sucker for it all. Not when I'm busting my ass. Not when you're celebrating mediocrity and missing the real show.*

Before the season slipped away, Bonds was presented one last chance to seize the spotlight. With a late-season surge, the Giants caught the Cubs from behind to force a one-game playoff at Wrigley Field on September 28. It was the sweetest of opportunities for San Francisco's underappreciated slugger, who would square off against Sosa in the national spotlight before 39,556 rabid fans.

But while Sosa put a bow on his MVP-worthy season with a 2-for-4 night, Bonds and the Giants played miserably. Starting pitcher Mark Gardner surrendered six hits and four runs in five and a third innings and Jeff Kent went 0-for-4. When Bonds was hitting everything in sight—bashing balls into the San Francisco fog—the cameras were nowhere to be found. But now, in yet another playoff disappointment, the nation was watching. In the seventh inning, with the bases loaded and the Cubs leading 4–0, Bonds meekly grounded out against reliever Felix Heredia, he of the 5.09 ERA. Bonds fired his helmet into the dirt, a gesture that summed up the afternoon.

In the ninth, Bonds had one final chance. Again with the bases loaded and the score 5–1, Bonds stepped in against Terry Mulholland, who had thrown 121 pitches one day earlier against Houston. With a ferocious swing, Bonds hit a ball high, hard, and short—a sacrifice fly to Sosa in right field that scored one run. San Francisco's pulse was gone. They lost 5–3.

"I've gone 0-for-4 before," Bonds said afterward. "It's not going to be the last time. If you want to trash me, just write whatever you want. You don't need me for that. We win as a team and lose as a team. But if you have to make this a trash Barry Bonds story, go right ahead."

No invitation was necessary. The next morning, the *Chicago Tribune* headline read BONDS AGAIN FAILS TO MAKE PLAYOFF DENT. The *Chronicle* contributed BONDS LETS CHANCE TO BE GAME'S HERO SLIP THROUGH HANDS.

THIRTEEN

BIG

THE HIGH CONCENTRATION OF sports and entertainment superstars living in the 800-acre Windermere, Florida, enclave known as Isleworth can make an afternoon stroll down one of its sidewalks seem like a rehearsal for the red carpet at the ESPYs. Shaquille O'Neal, Tiger Woods, Orel Hershiser—name a legend, any legend, and odds are fairly good he'll own an Isleworth pad. Of all the community's multimillion-dollar abodes, though, few match the splendor of the 13,000-square-foot residence owned by Ken Griffey Jr. Decorated in serene linen white and creams, the home features floors of marbled Macedonian stone and a mini movie theater. Video games line the walls of an entertainment center, and outside a large in-ground swimming pool begs for balmy days. "I wanted a place that would be our home all of our lives," Griffey said. "So I wanted it right for us."

Griffey's friendship with Barry Bonds dates back to 1987, when he was a 17-year-old Seattle Mariners prospect playing in the Arizona Instructional League. Bonds, a young Pirate at the time, was living near Phoenix, and he took the future star under his wing. "Barry would come by and pick me up in his white Acura Legend," Griffey recalls. "He probably treated me to four or five dinners." The two bonded over baseball and the identity crisis that comes with having a renowned parent. (Griffey's dad was a three-time

All-Star who played 19 seasons in the big leagues.) Neither man was especially comfortable with the trappings of fame or the relationships they had with their fathers. Like Bobby Bonds, Ken Griffey Sr. was hardly the most reliable role model. "Now whenever I go to San Francisco Barry takes me out to dinner," Griffey says, "and when he comes to Cincinnati I'll take him out. I fly my mom in because Barry loves the way she cooks macaroni and cheese and fried chicken. That's the kind of relationship we have. It's not just about baseball."

In the winter of following the 1998 season, drawn by Isleworth's proximity to Disney World, Barry Bonds brought his family on a four-day vacation to Orlando and to visit his longtime buddy. After spending a day toting his two children around the Magic Kingdom, Bonds came to Griffey's house for dinner. On an otherwise ordinary night over an otherwise ordinary meal, Griffey, Bonds, a representative from an athletic apparel company, and two other associates chatted informally about the upcoming season. With Griffey's framed memorabilia as a backdrop, Bonds spoke up as he never had before. He was neither angry nor agitated. Simply frustrated. "You know what," he said. "I had a helluva season last year, and nobody gave a crap. Nobody. As much as I've complained about McGwire and Canseco and all of the bullshit with steroids, I'm tired of fighting it. I turn 35 this year. I've got three or four good seasons left, and I wanna get paid. I'm just gonna start using some hard-core stuff and hopefully it won't hurt my body. Then I'll get out of the game and be done with it."

Silence.

Griffey was uncertain how to react. At age 29, he was at the top of his game, fresh off a season in which he compiled 56 home runs and 146 RBIs. As the pressure to indulge in performance-enhancing drugs mounted, the man known as "The Kid" stayed clean. Sure, he, too, could see the physical differences in many players, including some on his own team. But baseball wasn't *that* important to him. "If I can't do it myself then I'm not going to do it," Griffey says. "When I'm retired I want them to at least be able to say, 'There's no question in our minds that he did it the right way.' I have kids. I don't want them to think their dad's a cheater." Nevertheless, Griffey surely understood Bonds's feelings. For most of the past decade they were the sport's two top players. Now men with significantly less talent were abusing drugs to reach the elite level. Where was the fairness? The integrity? Griffey didn't agree with Bonds's position, but he empathized.

By the time Bonds arrived at Scottsdale Stadium on February 26, 1999, he had a new daughter—Aisha Lynn, born February 5—and a new body. Everything seemed to have blown up—his arms, his chest, his shoulders, his legs, his neck. When asked by Rick Hurd of the *Contra Costa Times* to explain his physique, Bonds blew the question off. "It's the same thing I've always done," he said. "It's just that I started so early."

Within the San Francisco clubhouse, Bonds's transformation was met with skepticism. His face was bloated. His forehead and jaw were substantially larger. "And the zits," says Jay Canizaro, a Giants second baseman. "Hell, he took off his shirt the first day and his back just looked like a mountain of acne. Anybody who had any kind of intelligence or street smarts about them knew Barry was using some serious stuff."

If there was one Giant who could relate, it was Canizaro. Long before he was an obscure middle infielder fighting to make a big league roster, Canizaro starred at West Orange High School, located 23 miles to the east of Beaumont, Texas. During his senior year, after accepting an athletic scholarship to play baseball at Oklahoma State University, Canizaro injured his right arm. "I was a small guy who spent a lot of time in the weight room," he says. "But in recovering from the injury I lost a lot of weight. I felt like I needed to start at Oklahoma State as a freshman, but that summer I was having so much trouble putting the pounds back on. I was helpless."

At the gym one day, some fellow fitness buffs suggested Canizaro try steroids. "I started messing around with them," he says. "I just blew up." Upon arriving at Oklahoma State, Canizaro was shocked by the size of his new teammates. "I was like, 'Holy shit! They're a lot bigger than the high school players I played with. I need to keep using." Canizaro says he was warned by an Oklahoma State trainer to be careful, and also informed that he would be tested every few weeks. "I thought, 'Well, this can't be too bad if everyone knows about it,'" Canizaro says. "They never told me not to use steroids. They just wanted to make sure I wouldn't test positive."

Following a season in which he hit .282 with nine home runs and 36

RBIs (and during which he was removed from the roster for academic reasons), Canizaro went to Texas to play for the Amarillo Texans of the highly competitive Jayhawk summer league. While there, Canizaro continued to use performance-enhancing drugs. "One day I'm injecting the steroids into my rear, and everything goes black," he says. "My mouth felt as if I had swallowed a lemon. I blacked out. I kept thinking, 'God, let me live. God, let me live. God . . .'"

Canizaro lived, and learned. Although the temptation lingered for years, it was the last time he ever took steroids. "People who say steroids make no difference are completely full of shit," he says. "It doesn't help you make contact, but the power you have is enhanced tremendously. On steroids, at the end of the year you're still playing like it's spring training. And you just feel so alive. I can remember running three or four miles after going out, or running and working out at 4 in the morning, then getting up and playing a doubleheader and going out again that night. You're just a maniac. And you know that the steroids are giving you that surge, and you're that much more confident. When it all comes together it's like you can't do anything wrong."

Observing from a nearby locker throughout spring training, Canizaro was almost 100 percent certain Bonds was using steroids and human growth hormones. *Almost.* After all, there's always an exception to the rule. Maybe Bonds did lift weights 10 times a day. Maybe the acne was a result of a new chocolate-and-KFC diet. All doubts were eradicated, however, when Canizaro approached Greg Anderson, Bonds's trainer, and asked a simple question: "What's he on?"

Anderson didn't hesitate. "He was calling out Deca-Durabolin and testosterone and all these different things that were steroids and hormones," recalls Canizaro. "Then he told me he could easily put a cocktail together for me, too."

Canizaro was tempted. He was fighting for a job against scores of other players who were clearly using. *Why not take another shot? Surely I won't have another bad reaction. This Anderson guy is a pro.* Then he recalled the side effects. "I had bad acne when I used," he says. "My tits were swollen. My face was bloated. And your testicles get really small."

"Thanks," he told Anderson, "but no thanks."

Bonds wasn't the only Giant using performance-enhancing drugs. "The Giants that year were really out of control," says Canizaro. "It started in the minor league system, where a lot of guys are getting steroids when they play winter ball in Latin America. You're in Triple A and you think you need that extra boost to make the majors. So you give in and cheat."

What was the motivation *not* to? Sure, the possession of steroids for non-medical reasons is a crime under United States law. But who was busting athletes? Plus, Major League Baseball had no steroid policy or testing program in place for big leaguers. (Baseball did test minor leaguers, but violators were neither penalized nor required to undergo counseling.) It might be against the law, but it sure wasn't against the *baseball* law.

Bonds was the best player in the game, making more than $8 million a year. In that regard, he was the least likely drug abuser baseball would ever see. With or without another five or six great years, Bonds was guaranteed enshrinement in Cooperstown. He didn't *need* the help.

But he wanted more.

On the second day of spring training, Barry Bonds approached the Giants new utility man, F. P. Santangelo, and demanded that he hand over some of his chewing tobacco. "Dude, give it to me," Bonds said. "Now." Though he was a baseball vagabond with a .250 career average, Santangelo had pride, coupled with a sense of humor. "Bitch," Santangelo replied, "say please first."

Bonds was stunned. "Do you know who I am?" he shouted. "I'm Barry Bonds."

"I know exactly who you are," said Santangelo. "And frankly, I don't give a fuck."

In the ensuing years, Santangelo has retold this story countless times—not to brag, but to make a point. "Too many people shy away from a superstar like Barry," he says. "I liked Barry, but I was never intimidated. I'd give him as much shit as he gave me. I don't know why everyone else wasn't the same way."

Had the occupants of the Giants front office followed Santangelo's lead by not allowing Bonds free rein, one wonders how things would have played out. Instead, having grown accustomed to tiptoeing around their star left fielder, nobody—not Peter Magowan, not Larry Baer, not Brian Sabean, not Dusty Baker—bothered to check the credentials of Greg Anderson, Bonds's new personal trainer and a man spending a significant amount of time around San Francisco's players. His background was disturbing. Three times in his life Anderson had been in trouble with the law: once after shoplifting a bottle of cologne from Macy's, twice after road rage incidents that ended in physical altercations between Anderson and other motorists. With any other professional sports franchise, Anderson would almost certainly have been denied access.

Yet Magowan and Baer agreed that whatever Barry wanted, Barry got. Even one year later, when a private investigator informed the Giants that Anderson was rumored to deal steroids, Magowan and Company refused to act. They were not merely scared of Bonds's wrath. They were petrified. Born in Millbrae, California, and raised in the hills of San Carlos, Anderson had ties to Bonds that dated back to childhood. The two had participated alongside each other in youth baseball—Bonds an all-world merging of skills, Anderson a stocky little grinder with minimal talent but ferocious desire. "They played San Carlos Little League together and Police Athletic League, he and Barry and Barry's brother Rick," said Darlene Alioto, Anderson's grandmother. "Baseball was always in Greg's mind—he loved it."

At Nevada Union High, Anderson was a good-field, weak-hit second baseman—a "short, squatty, roly-poly" player with the range of a stone, recalled one teammate—who went on to play two years at Butte College in Oroville, California, and another two at Fort Hays State University in Kansas. Not much is remembered of his unremarkable collegiate career, except he spent up to four hours per day in the weight room, sometimes urging a night janitor to unlock the door for 8 P.M. lifting sessions. "He got too big to play shortstop," recalled Fort Hays teammate Joe Blandino. "He was more of a weight room guy than a baseball player."

When his college career ended, the Fort Hays coaching staff told Anderson he had no chance of a professional career. So Anderson started his own personal training business, Get Big Productions, near his home on the

Peninsula. His clients were primarily high school jocks and the wannabe muscleheads who frequented nearby gyms. For a short time he lived with Bob McKercher, Bonds's closest friend and a former Serra teammate.

Midway through 1998, Anderson reconnected with his old buddy. By the end of the year, they were working together. "All of a sudden this guy named Greg was hanging around the clubhouse," says Canizaro. "He'd be walking around with his black bag. I think most of us had an idea what was inside. Especially when Barry started blowing up. It was totally obvious."

"Guys like Greg Anderson are very convincing to athletes who'll do any-thing to get better," says *Chronicle* columnist Scott Ostler. "'You take this right away and you won't really hurt yourself. The side effects have been exaggerated. It's like any other drug—taken in doses, it's fine. Do you wanna be the best?' You wonder whose interest a guy like that has—Barry Bonds's or his own?"

When questioned about performance-enhancing drugs, the Giants front office always pleaded ignorance. *How could we have known? Steroids? What steroids? Our guys just work really, really hard.* "We don't administer tests," says Magowan. "So it's not like teams can ban their own players based on suspicion." They can, however, ban trainers. Perhaps Magowan, Baer, Sa-bean, and Baker didn't know for sure that something was amiss, but they had to have at least noticed the miraculous new muscles sprouting throughout the clubhouse. The team's philosophy—baseball's philosophy—has always been the same: *Put butts in the seats, sell lots of gear, hit homers—and we're happy.* "You're a product," says Brian Johnson, the former catcher. "Teams say they care about their players, but it's only true until you stop producing. So it's hard to see a motivation for having your players stop using steroids if it's working for them."

In Bonds's case, it was working. The first steroid Anderson had Bonds on was Stanozolol, best known as the drug used by Canadian sprinter Ben Johnson in the 1988 Olympic Games. Though Stanozolol has myriad side effects, from baldness to mood swings to a risk of prostate cancer, it can be remarkably potent. Bonds's newfound physical stature and offensive power were instantly noteworthy. A study conducted by the Society for Ameri-can Baseball Research found that the peak age for players with at least 200 career home runs was 27. After age 30, a noticeable decline began. At age 35, the decline became a steep hill. Yet here in 1999, at age 35, Bonds was hitting the ball harder and farther than ever. He started the regular season on a tear, leading the Giants with an April average of .366 and, after going 0-for-3 in the opener, collecting nine hits in his next 16 at-bats. "One of the things I noticed was how fast he was able to put the bat on the ball," says Russ Ortiz, a Giants pitcher. "He could recognize the pitch well before he had to swing, and then Barry would get around so fast, so hard." Equally amazing was Bonds's indifference to fatigue. He could lift weights, play, lift more weights, then arrive early the next morning to pump more iron.

"To be honest, I never really looked at Barry and thought about steroids," says Giants outfielder Stan Javier. "Maybe I was naive. But what strikes me now is how I used to get hurt a lot, and I could never recuperate. Then there were these bigger guys like Barry who'd be in the weight room before the game, be in the weight room after the game, be in the weight room all the time, day after day. I was in the training room with five bags of ice covering my body, and these guys just bounced right back. It does make you wonder."

According to Canizaro, such are the recuperative powers of steroids, which cause one to crave nonstop workouts. But there are also side effects, one of which is the body's inability to handle rapid muscle growth. "Certain injury patterns just don't occur with normal people," says Craig Levitz, the cochief of sports medicine at New York's South Nassau Hospital. "For example, tendon ruptures without significant trauma are a telltale sign of steroid use. It shows that the muscle is getting overloaded, and while the steroids are helping the muscles get bigger, the tendon doesn't get the help it needs." In a mid-April series against Houston, Bonds began to feel pain in his left elbow. He tried playing and sleeping with a protective rubberized sleeve, but to no avail. The pain only worsened, and at one point became so bad that Bonds needed someone to rub his arm to dull the sensation before at-bats. On April 19, the Giants placed Bonds on the 15-day disabled list. He underwent surgery the next day for, of all things, a damaged triceps tendon.

Was this coincidence? Or was Bonds's injury—the kind specifically tied to steroid use—attributable to Greg Anderson and a new drug regimen? In his first six years with the Giants, Bonds missed a total of 19 games, and in 12 seasons overall he spent only one stint on the disabled list. Now he was breaking down like a used Daewoo. "Only air is invincible," Bonds meekly explained. "Last time I checked, we're not."

During Bonds's tenure on the sideline, he returned home and spent time with his family. He worked out with Anderson, desperate to make a quick return. He read some books and watched a lot of television. And he entered the breakfast cereal business.

This had long been a dream of Bonds—not to become a cereal mogul, per se, but to boost his red carpet status. How else to explain opening day of the 1993 season, when Bonds asked—of all people—pop singer Michael Bolton to present him with his National League MVP trophy? "He's always wanted to do the Hollywood thing, and that means acting and endorsements," says James Mims, Bonds's friend and former business associate. "I've seen him out with Eddie Murphy, Sugar Ray Leonard, Arsenio Hall—he craves the life and the attention they've been given. But he can't get it. He doesn't generate the interest they do."

Bonds, notes Mims, is perplexed by the lack of buzz generated by his name. "I like Barry a lot," says Mims. "But he doesn't get that if you treat people like dog shit, they don't keep calling." Many believe Bonds's most glaring weakness is his smile—he never seems to have one. On the field, after the game, at public appearances, Bonds wears the expression of a man pondering teen suicide rates. "In private his smile lights up a room," says Ted Robinson, a Giants announcer for nine seasons. "But he doesn't use it enough. I used to tell him, 'Here's Ken Griffey, hardly the warmest guy around. But Griffey will stroll onto the field and smile and laugh. That's why he ends up on every magazine cover and SportsCenter highlight.'" Bonds was especially irked in 1996, when Nike ran a nationwide KEN GRIFFEY JR. FOR PRESIDENT! advertising campaign (with the Mariner Moose as VP and George Clinton as campaign manager). To Bonds, it was inexplicable. Who wouldn't want his face on a package of bubble gum or crackers or ice pops? At the very least, one of San Francisco's 500 bail bonds agencies would call, right? *Hi, I'm Barry. And when I need bonds, heh-heh, I use Red Dragon Bail Bonds*! "We knocked on every single door. It just wasn't there for him," said Jeff Borris, one of Bonds's agents with the Beverly Hills Sports Council. "Barry is everything to baseball that Michael Jordan is to basketball and Tiger Woods is to golf. I feel sorry for him in that sense."

So when a company named Famous Fixins called in 1999 with the intent of creating a new cereal, Barry Bonds MVP Crunch, the injured superstar was elated. The outfit was responsible for Olympia Dukakis' Greek Salad Dressings, as well as cereals like Slammin' Sammy's Frosted Flakes (Sammy Sosa) and A-Rod's 40–40 Crunch (Alex Rodriguez). "Most athletes jumped at the opportunity," says Michael Simon, the cofounder of Famous Fixins. "They were excited, because they all knew the Wheaties thing, and this was their own product."

As part of the agreement with Famous Fixins, the athletes were asked to choose a charity to donate a percentage of the cereal's sales. Sosa put money into his Sammy Sosa Foundation. "Cal Ripken gave 100 percent of Cal's Classic O's to causes," says Simon. "So did Derek Jeter. They all did."

When Bonds learned that a charitable endeavor was part of the package, he flipped. "Why should I hand away my own money?" he complained to Simon. "I've got bills to pay." Eventually Bonds gave in. Although the side panel of Barry Bonds MVP Crunch reads, "Fifty percent of the net proceeds will . . . be donated to 'The Barry Bonds Family Foundation,'" Simon says the final total was actually 1 percent. "Here's a guy making millions and millions of dollars, and he would rather have the money go into his pocket," says Simon. "I'd never met anyone like him."

Later in the season, after Bonds returned from the disabled list, Simon and photographer Albert Ferreira went to Shea Stadium on a prearranged visit to have Bonds pose for the box-cover portrait. For three hours, Simon and Ferreira waited in the oppressive 90-degree heat for Bonds, who finally emerged from the Giants clubhouse complaining of a stomachache. "Let's do this next time I'm in town," he said, turning to walk away.

"But Barry," said Simon, "the cereal comes out in three weeks."

The ailing Bonds kept walking, although he later managed to take batting practice and go 1-for-3 with two runs. Famous Fixins wound up paying

$4,000 for an image of Bonds in action. "Money," notes Simon, "that went against his profit and hurt the charity even more." Weeks later, with the cereal set to hit the supermarkets, Simon called Bonds with a final idea. As a reward for those stores that order the most boxes of Barry Bonds MVP Crunch, would he be willing to sign some memorabilia to present to the managers?

"Who the fuck do you think I am?" Bonds responded. "Do you think that when Bill Cosby has a book come out the publisher asks him to take the shirt off his back? I don't fuckin' think so. You have no idea what I've fuckin' been through. Don't ever fuckin' ask me . . ."

"Barry," Simon blurted out, "you're such a dick." Then he hung up.

Ten athletes had their own cereals produced by Famous Fixins, and Barry Bonds MVP Crunch was the only one not to sell. "He put no effort into it," says Simon. "But the one thing we didn't realize was how unpopular Barry was, even in his own area. The day Sammy Sosa's cereal went on sale, they were lined up around the block. The day Barry Bonds's cereal went on sale, they continued to buy Kellogg's."

Anyone who questioned Bonds's baseball resolve was surprised when the outfielder returned to the San Francisco lineup on June 9, three weeks earlier than expected. Bonds did not play especially well in his first game back, going 0-for-4 in a loss to the Angels, but the mere fact that he stood in the batter's box was impressive. "The man could be very tough," says Javier. "When you didn't think he could do something, he'd usually do it."

The key to the early comeback was Stan Conte, the Giants trainer and resident physical therapist. At the time of the tendon injury, some thought that Bonds might need season-ending surgery to remove the scar tissue. Conte didn't believe it. He took Bonds into the training room and manipulated his elbow so severely that the scar tissue cracked. Bonds screamed in agony, but the tactic worked. "It's not something one human being should do to another human being," Conte said. "I pushed it to where he couldn't take it any longer, and then I pushed it some more."

Because of the missed time, Bonds was not voted by fans to the All-Star team—a minor indignity compared to the other roster he failed to make.

Before game two of the World Series between the Braves and Yankees at Atlanta's Turner Field, Major League Baseball introduced the members of the MasterCard MLB All-Century team in a Vegas-style on-field ceremony. From July through mid-September, fans were given a ballot of 100 players and asked to vote for a 25-man roster. That Bonds did not make the list was hardly shocking—the nine outfielders selected were Babe Ruth, Hank Aaron, Ted Williams, Willie Mays, Joe DiMaggio, Mickey Mantle, Ty Cobb, Griffey Jr. and Pete Rose. What irked Bonds, however, was that of the 34 outfielders listed on the ballot, he ranked 18th in total votes, placing six spots behind Joe Jackson—a man dead for nearly 48 years. Bonds considered the entire process a sham, privately ripping the fans for their ignorance and the majors for allowing such a ludicrous contest to occur. "How does Junior make it," he asked confidants, "and I don't?"

The 1999 season was that kind of year for Bonds, who played a career-low 102 games and batted just .262 for a team that finished 11 games out of the playoff race. Steroids made him big and strong, as evidenced by the 14 home runs he hit in a late-season 16-game stretch. But they didn't make him happy.

FOURTEEN

ACROMEGALY

S THE 14TH PITCH of his new baseball life approached the plate, Barry Bonds swung ferociously with a pronounced uppercut. Bat met ball, and the noise, an echoed *thwack!* beckoned everyone—his teammates, the security guards, the reporters—to stop and watch. The baseball cut through the crisp, thick San Francisco winter air. Going, going, going—splash! Over the right field wall and into the China Basin.

Splash! Had there ever been a sweeter sound?

Into the arctic water dove Marty Jansen, fully clothed, boots still on. A caulker hired to help put the finishing touches on the area behind the right-field wall, Jansen just couldn't help himself. He was moved by the spirit of baseball—by the spirit of Barry. It was an omen of things to come.

The date was January 21, 2000, and Bonds had just hit the first home run in brand-new Pacific Bell Park, the Giants' long-awaited downtown sta-dium. Surrounding him at the batting cage were teammates J. T. Snow, Bill Mueller, Rich Aurilia, and Jeff Kent—all braving the chill to take the debut cuts in a ballpark that wouldn't open for another four months.

Throughout the previous years, several state-of-the-art stadiums had been introduced to America: Baltimore's ground-breaking Camden Yards, Jacobs Field in Cleveland, Atlanta's Turner Field, and the Ballpark at Arlington in Texas, among others. All were beautiful, all necessary. Yet no team was in greater need of new digs than the San Francisco Giants. By the end of the 1999 season, Candlestick Park was more than just a cold, wet, dreary place to play and watch baseball—it was a paint-peeling, wood-rotting, metal-rusting, mildew-coated dump. "That was the most miserable place I've ever played," says Doug Creek, a former Giants relief pitcher. "I had to thaw myself out in the shower after every game, it got so cold. In June, in July, in August—it was always uncomfortable. Horrible weather, not much life. Just misery."

When Peter Magowan purchased the team back in January 1993, a key component of his plan was to build a stadium that would serve as its own draw. Bob Lurie, the Giants owner from 1976 to 1993, repeatedly tried and failed to convince voters to pay for the new facility out of their own pockets. In the liberal bastion of San Francisco, voters would willingly agree to finance a new library, open a museum, save the endangered Ohlone tiger beetle. But provide money to construct a baseball stadium? No way.

Magowan initially announced his intentions in December 1995. His plan was a stroke of genius. Of the $357 million needed to build the stadium just south of Market Street in downtown San Francisco, Magowan pledged to pay $170 million directly from the team (in annual $20 million chunks). Furthermore, he promised to raise the remaining funds from several sources—including seat licenses, concession contracts, and merchandising. According to Magowan, this would amount to another $187 million. On March 26, 1996, the voters of San Francisco approved the plan, 66 percent to 34 percent. "One of the greatest moments of my life," Magowan says. "It was like we were really ready to take San Francisco baseball in a whole new direction."

When asked to list the factors contributing to the ballpark's construction, Magowan and Larry Baer refuse to give Bonds any of the credit—and they are sadly mistaken. Had the Giants remained a floundering franchise with, say, Kevin Bass in left field, voters would have once again rejected the stadium, even with the lure of private money. Under Lurie, Giants fans suffered from a bad case of the blahs. Why waste valuable downtown real estate on a pulseless franchise featuring Jose Uribe and Scott Garrelts? For better or worse, Bonds's arrival changed everything, adding a presence the team had lacked since Willie McCovey's final years. People might not want to watch the Giants as a whole, but they would always pay to see Bonds.

Designed by HOK Sports Facilities Group, the same company that built Camden Yards, the 40,800-seat Pacific Bell Park was an instant classic. Unlike Candlestick, where even the closest spectator felt like he was watching from Zimbabwe, Pac Bell features a home plate just 48 feet from the first row of seats. Outside the entry plaza is a 9-foot bronze statue of Willie Mays swinging a bat. Behind the left field wall is a play area for kids, featuring an enormous slide within an equally enormous glowing Coca-Cola bottle. Much of the stadium is constructed of old-fashioned brick, and throughout the park food stations offer every conceivable delicacy. Unlike Candlestick, which smelled like a soggy sneaker, Pac Bell boasts the distinct odor of garlic fries.

From a player's vantage point, the ballpark's most distinct element is its unique dimensions. While Pac Bell's outfield wall was a respectable 335 feet away down the third base line and 404 feet to dead center, many were shocked to learn of a right-field foul pole just 307 feet from home (by comparison, Candlestick was 328 feet). Surely the left handed hitting Bonds would have a bonanza. Fifty home runs in a season? Try 150. It would be too easy.

"Everyone seemed to look at that and assume we wanted Barry to hit all these home runs to right," says Baer. "That's not true. Our dimensions are our dimensions because when you build up to water, you're limited by your environment. You can't build a stadium on top of water, so you build up to it. Physically it'd be impossible to have a 400-foot fence at the right-field pole. You'd be swimming."

Bonds and the Giants quickly learned that Pac Bell was, in fact, a horrible place for left-handed hitters. Instead of sailing down the lines, most home runs travel straightaway or into the power alleys. In those areas, the stadium is excessively deep. "It turned out to work to our advantage," says Baer. "You have one guy who can defy normal dimensions because he's so much a cut above the others. And he happened to be our guy."

In the shadow of the injury-ravaged '99 season, Bonds rejoined the Giants in 2000 looking happy, healthy, and even larger than he did a year earlier. The bulging muscles of the previous spring remained enormous, but what stood out this time was Bonds's head, which had expanded to the size of a large Halloween pumpkin. Back in his first few years with the Giants, Bonds's skull was no visually different in size than Will Clark's or Darren Lewis's or any normal *Homo sapiens*. Now it rivaled Gheorghe Muresan's. Once upon a time Bonds cut a dashing figure, handsome enough to be included among *People* magazine's Most Beautiful list for 1992 ("Bonds's most appealing attribute is that stadium-illuminating smile he flashes in moments of triumph.") Now he looked bizarre, almost freakish.

Although Bonds maintains that the dimensions of his head are unchanged, seeing is believing. Two side-by-side photographs, one from 1993, the other from 2000, provide a revealing juxtaposition: small head, huge head. According to a longtime Giants employee, at least twice in the late 1990s and early 2000s the team had to increase the hat size ordered for Bonds. When Bonds played with Pittsburgh, he had a substantial amount of hair on his head. Now he shaves his scalp bald. If his head had not grown, surely he would presently require a *smaller* cap.

After one's teenage years, there are only two ways an adult human head can expand. The first is from acromegaly, a disorder in which the pituitary gland produces excess growth hormone. Diagnosed in approximately 60 out of every million people, acromegaly derives its name from the Greek words for "extremities" (*acro*) and "great" (*megaly*). One of the most common symptoms of the disorder is abnormal growth of the hands and feet. Although Bonds often dismisses questions about breaking baseball's records by noting, "Anything is possible," it is *not* possible that he suffers from acromegaly. Unlike the late wrestling star André Roussimoff (aka "Andre the Giant"), the most famous bearer of the disorder, Bonds's extremities are normal. He does not suffer from any of the symptoms, which include enlarged sinuses, visual problems, bone overgrowth, and thick skin.

The second way an adult human's head can grow—and the only available explanation of Bonds's cranial expansion—is with the use of human growth hormones (HGH), a dangerous, illegal polypeptide that regulates multiple metabolic and growth functions. Used by a mounting number of professional athletes to gain an edge, HGH is highly effective, obtainable, and—best of all for cheating ballplayers—not listed among the banned substances Major League Baseball screens for. (Besides, tests for HGH are expensive and inconsistent.) "There is good scientific data showing that HGH increases muscle size, bulk, strength, and performance," says Peter Sonksen, a professor of endocrinology at St. Thomas Hospital in London and one of the world's leading HGH experts. "Potentially it's more anabolic than testosterone. But the problems are the side effects. With enough usage you can get enlargement of the jaw and the separation of the teeth. The sinuses above the eyes also grow. It's not a good thing."

Among baseball's advance scouts, an unofficial system emerged to spot athletes who likely abused HGHs. Nearly all players fit comfortably into batting helmets, which are designed to smoothly slide over a capped skull with room to spare. Every so often, however, someone would stand in the dugout frustratingly trying to hammer on his helmet before advancing toward the on-deck circle. Among others, Bonds partook in this ritual.

Prior to the season, Bonds had gone to Cashman Field in Las Vegas to partake in a charity home run derby. Tampa Bay Devil Rays slugger Jose Canseco wowed Bonds with a staggering 28 homers and the body of a Greek God. "Dude," Bonds asked, "where did you get all that muscle?" Shortly thereafter, an inspired Bonds began using another steroid, Deca-Durabolin, as well as large doses of growth hormones. Though Bonds was by no means the only Giant taking performance-enhancing drugs, he was one of the few using HGH. First, it's expensive. A sufficient dose of HGH can cost nearly $200 per day on the underground market. Second, it wasn't as available as your run-of-the-mill anabolic steroids, which could be had in any Gold's Gym or Dominican pharmacy. Third, the side effects were relatively unknown but potentially frightening. Though baseball players weren't thrilled by acne-covered backs or marble-size testicles, an expanding skull was in a different league.

"HGH's biggest benefit is it makes you ridiculously able to train," says Jim Warren, Bonds's former personal trainer. "You can get up in the morning, run, lift, go home and have a sandwich, take a nap, and hit 300 balls. Then go back and hit later. You're never sore. You have the body of an 18-year-old, and tomorrow it's a 17-year-old. You're essentially getting younger every day. And you feel wonderful. It's not like steroids, when you feel like you want to rape, maim, and pillage. You're on an even keel."

Bonds has denied ever using HGH. However, in 2003 federal investigators raided the home of Greg Anderson, Bonds's personal trainer, and found—among other things—vials containing what are believed to be human growth hormones and containers labeled Serostim, a human growth hormone. Warren, who trained Bonds from 1993 to 1994, defends his former client by noting, "When I worked with him, Barry took everything I told him to without asking or questioning. He wasn't that curious about it all. So could he have taken things from Greg Anderson without knowing? It's possible." But, he is asked, can head growth occur without an individual's knowledge? Warren laughs. "Well," he says. "That's a lot harder for me to believe. When you jump from 7¼ to 7½ to 8 to 8½ to 8¾ in hat size, you might be curious as to why nothing fits on your head anymore. At least I'd be."

Although the Giant superstar's swelling head became a running joke in the clubhouse and press box, neither Magowan, Baer, Sabean, nor Baker found it alarming enough to confront Bonds about whether he was abusing illegal drugs. These were the leaders of baseball's most civic-minded organization. Pick a cause—any cause—and the Giants were benefactors. AIDS awareness. Youth smoking. Breast cancer. Say No to Drugs. San Francisco led the league in pregame ceremonies to bring attention to world problems. Yet when one of their own appeared to be breaking the law, nobody found it necessary to investigate.

The Giants officially opened Pacific Bell Park on April 11, losing 6–5 to Los Angeles as Dodgers shortstop Kevin Elster hit three home runs. The game inaugurated a new era in Giants baseball, and apart from the defeat, everything seemed perfect. A sellout crowd of 40,930 fans soaked in all the goodies a $357 million facility had to offer. It was a beautiful day by the Bay, with the sun shining and not a trace of the old Candlestick wind.

And yet, something about the new joint didn't feel quite right. The Giants had always been a blue-collar team with blue-collar fans, and the passion and grittiness of the Candlestick crowd reflected a genuine love affair with the game. With a new stadium, the aura shifted radically. Pac Bell's stands were an ocean of silk ties and cell phones. The vehement booing that routinely greeted the Dodgers was replaced by relative silence. Spectators came to see the ballpark, eat the garlic fries, buy a $30 T-shirt, and watch the team—in that order. "Pac Bell was a testament to dotcom opulence," says Michael Silver, a *Sports Illustrated* senior writer and Bay Area native. "It was built during the technology gold rush, when all the instant millionaire assholes in their Beamers were clustering at Pac Bell."

This impersonal feel trickled its way into the clubhouse, where Dusty Baker's talented team was detached and unemotional. As part of the new setup, Bonds was gifted with a major league–topping four wood-paneled locker stalls on his own wall. He purchased a $3,000 Sharper Image black leather massage recliner and placed a large television set at the base. The chair was not a necessity (as Bonds has claimed, citing back problems), but yet another status symbol. Bonds's region became known as "The Kingdom."

Once by one, Giants players were asked by reporters whether they minded Bonds's special privileges, which included three personal trainers, his own media relations specialist (childhood pal Stevie Hoskins, who once denied famed scribe George Will an interview because he had never heard of him), and his own stretching schedule. One after another, Giants players said, "No." Every man was an island, and Bonds could do whatever he wanted. "It was so quiet in that clubhouse, like everyone was afraid to speak up," says Doug Mirabelli, a Giants catcher. "We were teammates without too many deep friendships." By exiling stand-up veterans like Charlie Hayes, Darryl Hamilton, Kirt Manwaring, and Matt Williams, the Giants had created a dull collection of men unwilling to confront Bonds. "We had a lot of very good players," notes Mirabelli, "but we were never a team."

Nevertheless, the Giants would make their new stadium a venue worth attending in 2000. Regular sellout crowds were able to witness closer Robb Nen slamming the door on 41 saves, ace Livan Hernandez confounding hitters while winning 17 games, and Bonds sending six balls over the right-field wall and—plunk—into McCovey Cove, where a slew of boats waited.

The Giants would win the National League West with 97 victories, their first title in three years.

For Bonds, however, team success did not bring happiness. Though he hit a career-high 49 home runs to go with 106 RBIs and a .306 average, for one of the first times in his life he was not the best player on the field. The honor instead went to second baseman Jeff Kent, whose hot bat and steely determination gave teammates someone else to lean on. Hitting behind Bonds in the lineup, Kent always seemed to deliver when the team needed him most. His .334 average and 33 home runs were career highs, but it was his penchant for playing hard that separated Kent from Bonds. In the fifth inning of a May 28 game against the Cubs, Bonds batted with the bases loaded and one out and hit a towering popup in front of home plate. As the ball went up, up, up, and then down, Bonds stood and watched its flight, never thinking to sprint toward first. When the ball hit the infield, catcher Joe Girardi scooped it up, stepped on home, and threw to first for the double play. Bonds's excuse for not running was understandable (he was confused by the infield fly rule) but indicative of his philosophy: *Why hustle unless I truly must?* Kent was the polar opposite. His uniform was always dirty, his brow always coated in sweat. "Not everyone liked Jeff, but you always knew what you were getting," says outfielder Calvin Murray. "His effort was never questioned."

As the season rolled on and the Giants separated themselves from the rest of the National League West, the talk of the clubhouse was the two-man MVP race. Pitting the low-key white cowboy versus the cocky black showboat provided a fascinating sociological study. In baseball, as a general (and unfortunate) rule, blacks stick with blacks, whites stick with whites, and Latinos stick with Latinos. "Look out for your own," says Dock Ellis, the former Pirates pitcher. That's how it was and had always been with the Giants. This season, however, a strange movement was afoot. One by one, members of the club—black, white, Latino—concurred that the team's MVP was clearly Kent. Many of the black players didn't like or trust Kent, who gave off a strong air of redneck narrow-mindedness. But, man, could he play.

The bitter relationship between Bonds and Kent made the rivalry even more intriguing. As the team's player representative with the union, Kent held clubhouse meetings to announce the latest news from the labor front. "Jeff would say something that was supposed to be a rule for the team, and Barry would always—*always*—say real loud, 'Nah, that's not gonna happen. This is my clubhouse,'" recalls outfielder Armando Rios. "Jeff would tell Barry that he had no choice, and that would set off some big argument. To them it was very serious. To the rest of us it was funny." Kent and Bonds both desperately wanted the MVP trophy—each for his own glory, but also to deny it to the other. Things turned especially awkward late in the season, when Baker made his support of Kent known. "That really angered Barry," says Nick Peters, the veteran *Sacramento Bee* baseball writer. "Because he thought he was the MVP of the team, and he couldn't believe someone else thought differently."

"What do I care?" Bonds told those close to him, feigning indifference. "Dusty's opinion don't mean shit."

Of course, the opinion of the team manager mattered a lot. Through eight trying years, Baker and Bonds's relationship remained awkward. Because of their long-standing family ties, fans assumed the two enjoyed a father-son bond. In fact, Baker saw Bonds for what he was—an arrogant, petulant, pretty-boy egomaniac. He tolerated Bonds because of his talent and spoke kindly of him to the media. But when tape recorders were turned off, Baker often made it clear that managing Bonds was about as much fun as swapping honey with a gang of killer bees. If Bonds wasn't whining about his spot in the order or a lack of respect, his teammates were whining about him. Baker spent an inordinate amount of time sitting behind the desk, convincing his other players that Bonds was more bluster than bite. "Don't listen to the dude," he'd say. "Barry's crazy."

"Dusty was extremely frustrated with Barry a lot of the time," says Josh Suchon, who covered the Giants for the *Oakland Tribune*. "I think for the most part Barry felt like he was the superstar and he didn't need the help of his manager. So Dusty did what he could to keep him happy, because he needed Barry to produce. But I certainly don't think he did things out of love for Barry."

"Dusty admired Barry's ability," says Roy Firestone, the former ESPN host and one of Baker's closer media acquaintances, "but he also thinks he's one of the biggest pricks of all time."

Despite any lingering hostility, Baker rarely hesitated to stand up for Bonds. Heading into a series against the Dodgers in July 1998, Baker told the press that "a couple of sources" within the Los Angeles organization had told him Bonds would be drilled in retaliation for past showboating, including a spin move after a particularly dramatic homer. "What's amazing to me," Baker said, "is the way they clowned on us in '93, and they get mad about a pirouette. Why is it good for one and not good for the other? We don't start anything, but we don't take anything either. I hope it's nothing more than a rumor and it's not true . . . I don't like threats, and I don't respond well to them." This was a skipper standing up for his guy, in the way that made Baker beloved by nearly all his players.

When the manager's words were repeated to Bonds, the ballplayer inexplicably went on the offensive. "You can tell Dusty to kiss my ass," Bonds said. "What does Dusty plan to do about it? What did Dusty do when [Dodgers pitcher Antonio] Osuna hit me in my leg last year?" Upon learning of Bonds's reaction, Baker smiled and told nearby reporters, "Well, that's how it goes." Inside, though, Baker's blood boiled. As much as he had abhorred Tommy Lasorda, his manager for eight years with the Dodgers, Baker believed in respecting those in charge. Bonds had crossed the line.

Baker was a professional, however, and his backing of Kent for MVP had nothing to do with personal feelings. It came down to the production. Who would Baker rather have at the plate late in the game, down by three with the bases loaded? Who was the guy who hit .366 in August, the month the Giants pulled away from the rest of the division? The guy who hit .343 with runners in scoring position? (Bonds, by comparison, hit .290) "Jeff went up there to hit," says Rios. "Barry had a lot of chances to swing at pitches that were close to the plate, but he was always OK with the walk. We needed him to swing at those pitches to make big things happen, and he didn't. Guys on the team—from the coaches on down—would get upset and wonder what Barry was trying to do, pad his statistics or help us win. With Jeff, you never wondered about that. He was a winner."

When San Francisco clinched the National League West title with an

8–7 victory over the Diamondbacks at Pac Bell, Bonds was euphoric. In the midst of the clubhouse champagne celebration, he led everybody back onto the field for a thank-you nod to the fans. Over the stadium PA system, he was asked what he'd like to tell the team's supporters.

"You're beyoooootiful!" he bellowed, the crowd roaring with approval.

For days, Bonds's rare display of spontaneous glee softened feelings toward him. "He's taken an active interest in being a better teammate," raved Jon Miller, the club's famed announcer. Only later was it learned that outfielder Ellis Burks urged him to take the team onto the field, all but pushing Bonds out the door. Later that evening Bonds was tossed the softball question of whether the postseason served as his baseball motivation. "I got bills to pay," he said. "I got three kids! I play baseball to support my kids! I don't need motivation."

The heavily favored Giants would face off against the Mets in the National League Division Series. Despite running a team short on dominant pitching (or, for that matter, overwhelming top-to-bottom talent) New York manager Bobby Valentine refused to cower at the sight of Bonds twirling a bat. After all, San Francisco's star had gone 16-for-80 with one home run and five RBIs in four postseason series. "It's hard for the really great players," explained Giants pitching coach Dave Righetti, "because so much of the other team's game plan is focused on shutting down that one guy." Not this time. Pitching around Bonds was not an option for Mets hurlers, so they went after him with the same ferocity they applied to Kent, J. T. Snow, and the rest of San Francisco's lineup. The strategy worked beautifully.

Bonds opened the series by going 2-for-3 with a key third-inning triple in a 5–1 San Francisco win at Pac Bell, and it seemed that maybe he was at last prepared to produce when it counted. Yet if game one was a revelation, game two was a reaffirmation of his ineptitude under pressure. With two outs in the bottom of the 10th and the Mets leading 5–4, Bonds faced John Franco, New York's 40-year-old left-handed reliever. Once one of the league's dominant firemen, Franco now had a fastball that rarely peaked into the 90s, and his changeup—masterful five years earlier—was hit or miss. At this point in his career, Franco relied on guile and trickery.

Bonds and Franco battled back and forth, until the count was full. The Pac Bell crowd was on it feet. On first base, Bill Mueller, the tying run, pumped his fists at Bonds. Franco threw an 87-mph fastball that appeared to be high and inside. Bonds stood still, expecting a walk. Instead he was punched out. Strike three. Game over. As Franco bellowed with glee, Bonds slammed his bat to the ground. After the game he stormed off. He was the only Giant to refuse to speak to the media.

The series moved to Shea Stadium. Though the Mets' mediocre pitching staff was hardly stocked with Tom Glavines and Randy Johnsons, it made no difference. Playoff pressure was what mattered. In a 13-inning 3–2 game three loss, Bonds went 0-for-5 against the mighty foursome of Rick Reed, Dennis Cook, Franco, and Rick White. In the ninth, with the score tied 2–2, two outs, and a runner on first, Bonds swung through a shoulder-high Franco fastball for strike three. Afterward he whined about home plate umpire Jerry Crawford. The following morning's *New York Post* ran an appropriate headline: SAN FRAN'S JUNK BONDS.

One night later, Bonds's postseason misery came to a close. He swung at the first pitch he saw from Mets right-hander Bobby Jones in the ninth inning, flying out to left to close New York's 4–0 win and series triumph. For the third night in a row, Bonds made the final out for the Giants—symbolic, haunting, and to some minds perfect. As he drifted off the field, Bonds was nearly run over by a cameraman rushing to film the Mets celebration. He could only shrug.

"What is there really for me to be upset about?" Bonds said afterward. "God has given me the ability to play baseball and given my family gifts that I've never even dreamed of. What do I have to worry about?"

The answer came one month later, when Kent received 22 of 32 first-place votes and 392 total points to be named the National League MVP. Bonds placed second with 279 points, but it was no consolation. Two days before the announcement, he had one of his representatives call the commissioner's office to try to learn the victor's identity. "It's important," said the man. "Barry's planning a vacation, and if he's not gonna win he doesn't want to bother sticking around."

FIFTEEN

THIS GRACELESS SEASON

O**N JANUARY 19, 2001,** a story by Giants beat writer Joe Roderick appeared in the *Contra Costa Times* under the headline LACK OF LOYALTY BUGS BONDS. Noting that Bonds was about to enter the final year a contract that would pay him $10.3 million, Roderick posed an important question: Why did San Francisco seem blasé about extending its star's deal?

He turned first to Giants GM Brian Sabean, whose response was strikingly casual. "If Barry's a free agent at the end of next year and he doesn't re-sign with us and we don't get a player for him [via trade] that's not going to concern me," Sabean said. "I don't apply to that logic. If he helps us win, we do what we need to do."

Approaching Bonds in a mostly empty clubhouse, Roderick relayed Sabean's words—and watched the sparks fly. "I don't know what to think," Bonds said. "I mean, if I get an answer like what you're saying, 'We'll see how things go during the course of the season,' I guess that kind of hurts my feelings a little bit and makes me feel not wanted, if you have to wait and see. How long have I been here, eight years, and I have to wait and see?

"I'm just going to play. That's what I've always done. It hurts my feelings, from what you've said their statement was. That hurts, to think I'm not wanted."

As soon as the newspaper hit the racks, the Bay Area went ablaze. Were the Giants really not interested in keeping their favorite son? Would Bonds truly consider playing elsewhere? Sabean was furious at Roderick, who he believed took a quote out of context and ran with it. Bonds, too, thought he had been blindsided by a writer anxious to create news.

On KNBR, the Giants' flagship station, fans jammed the phone lines, bashing Bonds one second, praising him the next. Finally host Bob Fitzgerald took a call from "a Barry in San Francisco."

It was not *a* Barry. It was *the* Barry.

"[Roderick] should be sued," Bonds fumed to a stunned Fitzgerald. "I have never once, ever, made negative comments about the Giants organization. Nor did I make any inquiries toward the Giants, like, if they don't sign me I'm upset. I'm not upset about anything. The only thing I want to do is win a World Series ring. OK? That's it."

The call turned into a 22-minute tirade. "Every question toward me is always, 'Well, you're getting older,'" Bonds said. "Well, I'm playing like I'm 25, OK? I don't play like I'm 36. I dedicate myself to this game. And I love this game. And I can't force anybody to do anything. And I'm not going to force [the Giants]. And I'm not going to beg anybody. I want to play the game. Whether it's here in San Francisco, that would be my ideal choice. But if it's not here in San Francisco those are not my choices, [so] don't sit there and make quotes and statements like I'm upset."

Near the end of the conversation, Bonds cooled down enough to apologize for having to "get on the phone like this." Indeed, it was remarkable— akin to George W. Bush randomly dropping in on the *The McLaughlin Group* for a sit-down.

One thing was clear: The eight regular Giants writers who showed up at spring training a month later were in for some turbulence. In what had become an annual ritual, Bonds met the media for his "State of Barry" give-and-take, but this one had a much edgier tone. "I've been here my whole life," he said. "I came back home. I'm pretty lucky. But I look at it this way: Why should I be any different than the way my godfather was sent out, the way Matt Williams was sent out, the way the rest of them were sent out?" At one point Bonds insisted he did not hold grudges, pointing to Roderick and saying, "If I did I would punch you," then turning to Henry Schulman of the *Chronicle* and adding, "and I'd have punched you a long time ago."

It was going to be a memorable summer.

Although the 2001 season didn't officially begin for the Giants until the April 2 opener against San Diego, for Bonds the action kicked off on January 11. That was the day Sabean made what seemed to be one of the *least* significant transactions of his tenure, signing 16-year veteran Eric Davis to serve as a part-time outfielder. Back in the mid-1980s, Davis was considered a sure-shot future superstar. In 1987, his second full season, he compiled 37 home runs, 100 RBIs, and 50 steals for the Cincinnati Reds, numbers so dazzling that a young Pirates outfielder named Bonds approached him and said, "You're the measuring stick for me." But just when it looked like Davis would dominate the sport, his body broke down. In the 1990 World Series against the A's, Davis lacerated his kidney while diving for a ball, an injury that, he says, "set me back at least two years." With Detroit four years later Davis suffered a herniated disk in his neck, and in 1997—as a member of the Baltimore Orioles—he was diagnosed with colon cancer. All told, he lost nearly six years' worth of games to injuries and illnesses. "Any disappointment in my career has to do with health," says Davis. "Had I stayed healthy, I know I'd be a Hall of Famer."

Instead, at age 38 and with rapidly declining skills, Davis arrived in San Francisco with the primary purpose of being Barry Bonds's "guy." In his eight previous seasons in the Bay Area, the Giants made sure to supply Bonds with a teammate he could relate with. To Magowan, Baer, and Sabean, this meant the person had to be black, hip, and talented—at least a solid major league veteran. Past "Bonds's guys" included Mel Hall, Charlie Hayes, Darryl Hamilton, and Ellis Burks, but all four were gone. "Barry was the whole reason I came," Davis says. "I think they wanted us together."

Bonds was thrilled by the addition, as well as by the return of Shawon Dunston, another veteran African American who had played with the team in 1996 and '98. In Bonds's mind, the Giants had added two men who could empathize with what it was like to be Barry. Yet within the first couple of days of spring training, it became clear that, in Davis and Dunston, Sabean had found quite the opposite: a pair of veterans determined *not* to take Bonds's shit. "His fame didn't matter to me, because I was making money before him," says Davis. "Barry doesn't respect everybody—he's one of those guys who demands your respect. And if you come at him like a man, he'll give it to you. If you don't, he'll try chewing you up."

With ordinary teammates, Bonds would bark orders and they'd immediately be followed. Or he'd rip someone for a boneheaded play and watch the man slink away with his tail between his legs. Davis and Dunston were unwilling to comply. One time, after suffering a mild injury in a game against Colorado, Davis was lying on a training table when Bonds entered the room. "Hey Eric," Bonds said, "how many years you got in the major leagues?" Davis answered 16, to which Bonds snapped, "Yeah bitch, and you've been in here for, like, six of them." Bonds continued. "So Eric, how many home runs do you have, anyway?" Bonds knew the answer (280), but he enjoyed putting teammates in their place. Standing nearby, Dunston had heard enough. He walked to Davis's locker and removed his 1990 World Series ring. "Hey faggot!" he yelled toward Bonds. "How many of these you got?" Davis cackled with delight. "Both Eric and Shawon kept Barry in line," says outfielder Armando Rios. "It was a beautiful thing."

If Bonds stopped to watch a home run, Dunston—a former Cardinals teammate of Mark McGwire—greeted him in the clubhouse with a pointed "Bitch, Mac woulda hit that ball 200 feet further." If Bonds ran halfheartedly after a ball, Davis cursed him out. Upon returning from the weight room, Bonds would often find Dunston sprawled out in his recliner, flipping the channels on his personal television. "Get the fuck out of my chair!" Bonds would yell, prompting Dunston to pick up a bat and say, "One step closer and I take out the knees." On team flights, Bonds occasionally dominated in poker games against his teammates. Dunston put an end to that. "He was used to winning, but he never got me," Dunston says. "I took $1,000 from him once, no problem."

Bonds benefited most from Davis and Dunston in the area of race relations. For much of his life, Bonds struggled to cope with his blackness. As a rich suburban kid with all white friends, he was often intimidated by other blacks. He didn't talk the talk, didn't walk the walk, certainly didn't live the lifestyle. In Pittsburgh, outfielder R. J. Reynolds used to plead with his white teammates not to tell Bonds where he and the other African-American Pirates were going that night. "We didn't want him with us," says Reynolds. "Dude didn't fit in." Bonds speaks in an effeminate, high-pitched manner, reminiscent of the voice Eddie Murphy would use to imitate an uncool white guy on *Saturday Night Live*. Whereas black players filled the San Francisco clubhouse with the beats of Tupac, Nas, Missy Elliott, and Jay-Z, Bonds's four favorite performers are Barbra Streisand, Kenny G., Michael Bolton, and Celine Dion. He also backed Republican candidates, going so far as to actively campaign for conservative Pete Wilson, an outspoken opponent of affirmative action, in his 1994 race for California governor.

"He didn't know what it meant to struggle, and to some degree that meant he couldn't understand what it was to be prototypically black," says former teammate Darryl Hamilton. When *Sports Illustrated* columnist Rick Reilly was researching a piece on African Americans being stopped by the police because of their skin color, he approached Bonds. "Barry," asked Reilly, "I was just wondering if you've ever been pulled over for DWB?"

"Get the fuck out of my face!" screamed Bonds. "What the fuck? What kind of fucking question is that?"

Only after teammate Ellis Burks explained that DWB stood for "driving while black" did Bonds cool off. "He was the only African-American athlete who didn't know what it was," says Reilly. "And I interviewed a lot of people."

Sometimes Bonds would speak out and accuse the media or baseball officials of not "understanding" the plight of the black man. This was laughable. Bonds *himself* didn't understand the plight of the black man. "He hasn't been to the ghetto in his life," says Dunston, a Brooklyn native. "He'd say, 'Yeah, man, I'm from the 'hood,' and Eric and I would say, 'San Carlos is *not* the hood, Barry!' I mean, the guy didn't know how to use slang, but he wanted to look cool. We wouldn't let him get away with that." Bonds fell into the habit of telling fellow African Americans that he was from Los Angeles, thinking it sounded tougher and more urban. "If I were a black guy who grew up in the streets of Compton, I would kick Barry's ass," says Jim

Warren, Bonds's former trainer. "I'd be like, 'Bro, you have no idea what it is to be black.'"

By repeatedly calling his bluff, Davis and Dunston were actually accepting Bonds for who he was. He no longer had to pretend to be Barry X once everyone knew it was ludicrous. The two veterans talked trash to Bonds from season's beginning to season's end, and it created a comfort zone the star had never before enjoyed. "I like to think we brought something out in Barry that made him feel more relaxed," says Dunston. "I was like, 'Just be yourself, man. Don't worry about putting up this front.' We made it fun for him."

As a result, Bonds developed a softer outlook toward the media. If one thing can be said of the men and women who cover Major League Baseball on a daily basis, it's that they're searching for something positive to write about. For every journalist who trashes ballplayers as "overpaid jerks," there are 10 others eager to witness brilliant athleticism and off-the-field respectability. This was particularly true in San Francisco, where a forgiving press corps longed to be embraced by the city's grandest star. There was a feeling—a hope, perhaps—that behind the snarl hid a decent, loving man.

With his new agent, the omnipotent Scott Boras, pleading with Bonds to behave, there did in fact seem to be a cuddlier ballplayer wearing the number 25 Giants uniform. One of the reasons Bonds had left the Beverly Hills Sports Council a year earlier was that, in Boras, he saw an agent who had mastered the art of image swabbing. When Major League Baseball chose Ken Griffey Jr. as its player of the 1990s, Bonds blamed the Sports Council for not sufficiently burnishing his persona. Boras, he believed, was the right person for job.

San Francisco opened the season with a riveting 3–2 home victory over the Padres, during which Bonds homered and made a terrific throw to nail a sliding Tony Gwynn at the plate. Afterward he took a few questions, then politely excused himself, saying, "Sorry guys, my son has a game tonight at 5:30 and I don't wanna miss it."

Sorry guys? My son has a game tonight?

That wasn't "Get outta my face!" or "I ain't talkin' to none of you!" It was gentle. Decent. Things turned even stranger when Bonds spent much of

April submerged in the second-worst slump of his career, an 0-for-21 slide that left his batting average at .103 on April 10. Bonds went four straight games without a hit, but never ducked out without facing the press. On April 15 at Milwaukee's Miller Park, Bonds dropped a routine line drive in the Brewers' 7–3 win, then stood and fielded question after question. The only topic he refused to discuss was the one that could have offered solace—his 499th career home run, hit that night off David Weathers. Instead, he took the heat. "I straight fucked it up," he said about the error. "That's the best way I can put it. I just, wow. That's all I can say. I saw it. I just took my eye off it at the last minute. I took it for granted that I had it and made a beeline for the dugout."

Dunston was impressed. In his two previous tenures with the Giants, he had pegged Bonds as a selfish, me-first player with the backbone of a snail. "I didn't care for him," Dunston says. "All he ever wanted to do was talk about himself. But in 2001, he started helping us look for pitches and think more aggressively. I'll be honest—I used to root for him to mess up, even when we were teammates. But it was different this time." Bonds even took a rookie outfielder named Jalal Leach under his wing. Whenever he spotted Leach in the cage, Bonds would adjust his hands or lift his elbow or explain the thoughts of an opposing pitcher. "One time we were facing the Rockies, and they had a starter who owned me with fastballs," says Leach. "Well, I'm walking up to the plate and Barry says, 'Just go up there and sit on the slider.'" Leach ignored the wisdom and nubbed a slider to third for an easy out. "See, I told you," said Bonds. "You have to look at the situation. Look at who's coming up behind you. What the score is. Where the runners are on base. Situational hitting."

More remarkable than the words emerging from Bonds's mouth was the thunder suddenly exploding from his bat. Baseball lore suggests that slumps are snapped by little things—a bunt, a Texas Leaguer, a strange hop. Gradually, the hitter regains his composure and starts swinging with authority. With Bonds, this did not apply. On the day after an 0-for-5 game against the Padres extended his slump to 20 straight at-bats without a hit, Bonds homered. Then he homered the next day. And the next day. And the next day. And the next day. And the next day. With home runs in six consecutive games, including back-to-back three-RBI days against Mil-waukee, Bonds announced that, even at age 36, he was far from through. Writers had speculated that his bat had slowed, that his muscles weren't as quick—and they were wrong. Bonds was as good as ever.

To some teammates, though, it was hard to believe that Bonds's improved behavior was not another act. Those who looked hard enough saw the old Barry lurking. "Bonds spent the season zigzagging from charming to rude," wrote David E. Early of the *San Jose Mercury News*. "One day, he would light up the media with a million-watt smile, the next, his glare would chop them into bloodless bits." When 6-foot, 205-pound pitcher Ryan Jensen was called up in May, Bonds took one look at his hefty frame and nicknamed him "Jenny Craig." When fellow rookie Cody Ransom struggled after his September debut, Bonds would only call him "Corey."

"Uhm, my name's Cody," Ransom nervously said.

"I know," Bonds replied. "but I won't call you that until you get a fuckin' hit."

Ransom began his career 0-for-7.

On April 17, Bonds's teammates returned the favor. The San Francisco night was beautiful—a bit cool, but with clear skies and a slight wind blow-ing into the Bay. Entering the game against the visiting Dodgers, Bonds needed one blast to join the exclusive 500 home run club. In baseball his-tory, no player who reached the magic number had been denied access to the Hall of Fame. It was the reason that Harmon Killebrew, with a .256 average and 573 homers, got in, and why Fred McGriff (493 homers) likely never will.

Though he spoke modestly of 500 throughout the start of the season, to Bonds it was a meaningful feat. That afternoon, there was a feeling his-tory was about to be made. Baker sat among the writers in his office and said, "The best setting would be tonight, game-winning home run in the ninth. We'd all be extremely happy." He wasn't far off. With his team trailing 2–1 in the bottom of the eighth inning, Bonds turned on a 2–0 slider from journeyman reliever Terry Adams and mashed it. The baseball sailed 417 feet into the night, out of the stadium, over the portwalk, and into the Bay.

A Pac Bell–record 41,059 fans rose to their feet, and as the ball carried the noise evolved from a hopeful "Ohhhhh" to a thunderous, ear-popping roar. Flashbulbs lit the sky as Bonds jogged the base paths, a wide smile across his face.

When Bonds reached the end of his memorable trot, he was greeted by fireworks, water shooting from the right-field cannons, family members escorted onto the field—and one teammate. Rich Aurilia, who had been on third base with a triple, gave Bonds a hug and retreated. Not one other Giant player or coach sprinted from the dugout to congratulate Bonds. This wasn't an orchestrated plot, but a humiliating snapshot of how Bonds's teammates felt. When McGwire became the 16th member of the 500 Club two seasons earlier, he was swarmed by his fellow Cardinals, who surrounded home plate and exchanged high fives and signature gut punches with their beloved first baseman. This was a long way from St. Louis.

"There was nothing malicious about it," says Snow, the San Francisco first baseman. "He hit it, we were watching it, and by the time he rounded the bases it was too late. It happened too fast. It was only after the fact that guys were like, 'Wow, nobody went out there.'"

What Snow fails to mention is that joy is an emotional—not ceremonial—reaction. Joy inspires someone to run out of the dugout and bear-hug a teammate.

A lack of joy prevents it.

Though Bonds's achievement made the front page of most sports sections, it failed to truly resonate outside the Bay Area. "The home run record is the old gray mare of sports," wrote Dan O'Neill of the *St. Louis Post-Dispatch*. "She ain't what she used to be." When McGwire and Sammy Sosa chased Roger Maris three seasons earlier, even a *near* home run carried the import of a presidential election. Since then, the home run had dropped in emotional value. In the entire decade of the 1970s, one man (Cincinnati's George Foster) cleared 50 home runs in a season. In the 1980s, nobody did. But beginning in 1996, when an unexceptional leadoff hitter named Brady Anderson bulked up and hit 50 home runs for the Baltimore Orioles, attitudes changed. If Anderson, whose previous career-high for homers had been 21, could send *that* many balls out of the yard, was the home run such a grand achievement? Over the ensuing four seasons, 50 or more home runs were hit nine times, often by once-average-looking men who now boasted anvil muscles and Herculean lumber.

The single-season record still intrigued fans, though. By the end of April Bonds had 11 home runs, and there was already chatter about the fall of McGwire's three-year-old mark. Meanwhile Kent, the reigning National League MVP, was stuck on four homers. That he was on pace for a respectable 24 home runs was lost amid Barry Mania in the Bay Area. *How are you hitting with such power? Are you in better shape than ever? What's your secret, Barry?*

Kent was no dummy. He worked as hard as any player in the majors, and he knew that even nonstop weight training couldn't turn someone into the Incredible Hulk, as Bonds had become. Though in public he gave Bonds his due as an offensive machine, privately he seethed. "He knew that Barry was cheating, or at least he strongly suspected it," says Nick Peters, the veteran *Sacramento Bee* baseball writer. "That bothered Jeff immensely. He worked his ass off for 30 homers, and Barry did it the wrong way. I think the two of them pushed each other, but there was a big difference. Jeff didn't cheat. Barry did."

Kent was not alone in his furor. Opposing pitchers, led by Curt Schilling of the archrival Diamondbacks, began to openly question the development of some of the game's best—and biggest—players. "When you see a guy hit home runs that travel 340 feet start hitting every ball 420 feet, it's sort of obvious," says one longtime National League scout. "Barry was on a chase to break 70 home runs, and he never even hit 50. C'mon now."

Bill Jenkinson, the noted baseball historian, was growing suspicious. At his home in Willow Grove, Pennsylvania, Jenkinson compiles what he calls "power performance curves" for anyone with more than 300 major league home runs. The curve measures power versus age, taking into account both the frequency and distances of home runs. "Henry Aaron is my favorite example," says Jenkinson of the all-time home run leader. "He was so extraordinary because as he aged he got smarter, and that helped him hit more home runs. But he never hit the ball farther as an older man than he did as a young one. Every single slugger I've ever evaluated peaked for distance in their mid-to-late 20s." Jenkinson considers this a point worth emphasizing. "Every . . . single . . . one," he says.

Except Barry Bonds. "In 2000, Bonds turned 36 in the middle of the season, and his power performance curve just completely whacked out," says Jenkinson. "It's ridiculous. From age 36 on he starts hitting the ball farther and farther." According to Jenkinson, over the first 14 years of his career, Bonds hit three baseballs beyond 450 feet. "I've got the Department of Weather records for those three balls," he says, "and all three had powerful tailwinds." Beginning in 2000, however, 450-plus foot home runs became commonplace. "His optimum power used to be in the 435–440-feet range," Jenkinson says. "At age 36 it went up to 480. That is not humanly possible. It cannot be done by even the most amazing athletic specimen of all time."

Jenkinson pauses. "Unless," he says, "that specimen is cheating."

Bonds, of course, *was* cheating, but before it was fact—before names like Greg Anderson and Victor Conte were known across the nation—there was the chase to smash McGwire's record. And though it would never become the national phenomenon that was Sosa McGwire '98, Bonds's performance itself was breathtaking.

In baseball's long history, there has never been a better hitter than Barry Bonds in 2001. Babe Ruth in 1927? Awfully good. Joe DiMaggio in 1941? Stunning. Mickey Mantle in 1956? Unbelievable. But performance-enhancing drugs be damned, some things are too remarkable to ignore. In 2001, Barry Bonds would see one good pitch per game and—more often than not—hit it very far. He did not venture outside the strike zone, and rarely was fooled by anything over the plate. Along with the home run mark, Bonds set four other all-time single-season records—walks (177), slugging percentage (.863), home run percentage (15.34) and home run ratio (one homer every 6.52 at-bats). Twice Bonds homered in six straight games, and he established a career-high 15-game hitting streak from mid- to late-May.

What truly dazzled those who played with and against Bonds was the climate that accompanied his accomplishments. It's one thing to hit home runs when you're seeing meaty fastball after meaty fastball. But in 2001 nobody pitched to Bonds. "Why would you?" asks Ryan Dempster, a Florida Marlins starting pitcher. "You knew you didn't stand much of a chance." On 35 occasions Bonds was intentionally walked, which weighs on a man's patience and his feet. A typical day was akin to the afternoon of May 1, when Bonds put on a dynamic batting practice display at Pittsburgh's new PNC Park (six times he hit balls into the Allegheny River, some 456 feet away), then was walked in each of his first four plate appearances. "He might have hit 90 home runs were he not so disciplined at the plate," says Alan Embree, a Giants pitcher. "He had a selectiveness that I'd never seen before. The reason why he hit the ball so well is that he waited and waited for what he wanted. Then when he got it, he hit it to the moon."

When Bonds smashed his 14th home run at Philadelphia on May 4, he tied Arizona's Luis Gonzalez for the league lead and initiated a most unexpected power duel. Like Bonds, Gonzalez spent most of his career as a thin, quick outfielder with great ability but less-than-otherworldly power. Through his first seven big league seasons, he never surpassed 15 home runs or 75 RBIs. In 1999 things changed. Gonzalez began pounding the ball—hitting it farther than ever before, with greater frequency. He compiled 26 homers and 111 RBIs in '99, and those totals increased the next season. Now, at age 33, he was lethal. "Gonzalez was the last guy you'd expect to hit so many home runs," says Jeff Bradley, a baseball writer for *ESPN the Magazine*. "And here he was, fighting with Barry for the home run lead."

The younger brother of former Seattle Mariners catcher Scott Bradley, Jeff Bradley could barely contain his suspicions. At the end of his career, Scott was advised that steroids would help keep his struggling game afloat by adding pop to a moribund bat. He declined. "I was always the steroid buzz-kill during the summer of 2001 at our magazine," says Jeff Bradley. "In meetings they'd be talking about writing on all the power and I'd be saying, 'This is a complete and total joke! Why aren't we looking into it?'"

The answer, Bradley knew, was a sad one: Nobody cared. Like McGwire versus Sosa, Gonzalez versus Bonds was terrific theater—the smiling, happy-go-lucky Diamondback versus the villainous Giant. For San Francisco fans, Bonds supplied one jaw-dropping moment after another. At 12:38 on the morning of May 20 in Atlanta, Bonds hit his third solo home run of the

night—this one coming after a pair of rain delays totaling 2 hours, 51 minutes. Though the power display dazzled, it was the reaction of those remaining in Turner Field that shocked the system: As he trotted the bases
after homer number three, Bonds was saluted with a standing ovation—by
Braves fans, whose team was losing at home, *in Atlanta.* "I'll always remember [Braves manager] Bobby Cox throwing his hat in disgust," says Giants
reliever Chad Zerbe. "He was completely helpless against Barry."

One day later, Bonds hit two more homers, giving him 22 in 40 games.
That suggested an 83-home run season, which the Giant star laughed off.
He was asked by Josh Suchon of the *Oakland Tribune* to explain this kind of
pop. "Ask God," he said. "There's some things I can't understand right now.
The balls that used to line off the wall just go out (of the park). I can't answer that question. It's like women. Do you understand why they do some
things?"

Suchon, along with the other beat writers, nodded his head and laughed.
A deft wordsmith with barely a year on the beat, the 27-year-old Suchon
was seduced by Bonds's bursts of apparent kindness. When Suchon first
introduced himself during spring training in 2000, Bonds's reply was "Yeah,
so?" Over time, however, Bonds seemed to give the friendly Suchon the
benefit of the doubt. He answered most of his questions without being crass,
and when Suchon told Bonds he was planning on penning a book about
the 2001 season, the ballplayer didn't discourage him. Although Suchon's
account, *This Gracious Season: Barry Bonds & the Greatest Year in Baseball*, was written without Bonds's help, Suchon let his subject review the
entire text before submitting it for print. Such a move speaks volumes about
Bonds's power over the press. Ignoring logic, Suchon used his book to defend Bonds against drug allegations. "Looking back, that was incorrect,"
says Suchon. "Part of it was naiveté. And part of it might have been that I
wanted to believe this guy I was writing a book about had reached his accomplishments legally."

In his defense, Suchon wasn't alone. Though Jeff Bradley strongly suspected Bonds was cheating, he never asked the question—"Have you taken
illegal performance-enhancing drugs?"—during a lengthy sit-down interview. This, even after a scout told Bradley, "His body's been transformed.

His back looks twice as wide as it used to be. He's got a barrel chest, a tight end's neck. He also looks a lot heavier in the face."

"I should have asked," says Bradley, "and I regret it." But nobody asked. Not Henry Schulman of the *Chronicle*, Joe Roderick of the *Contra Costa Times*, Mark Purdy of the *Mercury News*, or any of the other beat writers or local columnists. Jay Mariotti, the *Chicago Sun Times* star columnist, went so far as to shush anyone with the audacity to question Bonds's authenticity. "The whispers have been out there about Bonds, as they've been about any hitter who flirts with history," he wrote. "But any innuendo should stop at once."

It would be two more years before reporters discovered that in the months before the 2001 season, Bonds met for the first time with a fitness guru named Victor Conte. A former professional bass guitarist who had collaborated on 15 albums with musicians like Herbie Hancock, Conte had retired from music in 1984 to try his hand at a different sort of business. He invested in a preventive medicine center, as well as a machine that traced 40 minerals in the blood. "I couldn't pronounce the name of the thing," recalled Conte, laughing at his own naiveté. "But I figured if it cost me $25 to do a test, and I could charge $100 to give one, maybe I could make a business out of it."

Thus the Bay Area Laboratory Co-Operative (BALCO) was born. With a detailed knowledge of music but minimal fitness background, Conte spent his days at Stanford's medical library, photocopying articles about minerals. One day in 1985 Conte attended a medical conference, where he was approached by a swim coach from Cal-Berkeley. "How would you like to help the world's fastest swimmer?" Conte was asked. "A kid named Matt Biondi."

Using a battery of tests, Conte determined that a magnesium depletion was causing Biondi to flounder after 120 meters. With the help of Conte-supplied supplements, Biondi shattered the American 200-meter record just six weeks later. Two stars emerged that day—the swimmer, and the supplier. (When Biondi's name arose during the BALCO scandal, the swimmer wrote in an e-mail to the *Chronicle*, "I have no clue what work this company does or how I might have been previously associated with them.")

"One thing led to another," said Conte, "and I started to work with athletes who were heading to the 1988 Olympics in Seoul. I prepared 15 Americans—in track, in swimming and judo—who brought back medals."

Several years later it occurred to Conte that honesty didn't necessarily bring success. In preparation for the 1992 U.S. Olympic Trials, he was working with a young shot putter named Gregg Tafralis who tested positive for steroids. Conte swears he never supplied Tafralis with illegal drugs, but recalls being astonished when the United States Olympic Committee allegedly covered up his client's flunked test. "That's when I learned there are two sets of rules," Conte said. "The ones in the book and the ones everybody plays by."

Over the next seven years, Conte became a millionaire by designing ZMA, a supplement marketed to football players as a zinc and magnesium replacement. But the Olympic Committee's reaction to Tafralis's failed test never left his mind. *Why should I abide by the rules*, he thought, *if nobody else does?* Appearing at a bodybuilding exhibition in Southern California, Conte was given norbolethone, a steroid invented in the 1960s that had never been marketed, and which later led to the development of tetrahydrogestrinone (THG), the preferred designer drug for most cheating athletes. Conte said he first gave THG (aka "The Clear") to Bill Romanowski, an NFL linebacker. Then he began distributing to Olympians—sprinters like Chryste Gaines and brothers Alvin and Calvin Harrison. His most famous Olympic athlete was Marion Jones, who went on to win three gold medals in the 2000 Olympics. Soon, Conte staked out the world of Major League Baseball.

With Anderson serving as his connection, Conte agreed to take Bonds on as a client. Within months of working with Conte, the Giant added nearly 20 pounds of muscle to a frame that was already puffed up thanks to steroids provided by Greg Anderson. According to the book *Game of Shadows*, Conte had his star client on a cornucopia of drugs, including growth hormones, testosterone, insulin, and Mexican beans, the fast-acting steroids that quickly cleared the system. Bonds also used a steroid known to improve the muscle quality of cattle. So hooked was Bonds that when Anderson warned his friend that it wasn't yet time to inject, Bonds would insist, "Fuck off. I'll do it myself."

On July 3, 2001, Kyle Tucker, a summer intern at the *Macon Telegraph*, became one of the first newspaper writers to directly question Bonds's assault on the record book. In a piece entitled, "Someone Needs to Take Baseball Off All the Juice," he wrote: "Everything in baseball is on 'roids. Take a look at the physical makeup of the one major sport that doesn't regulate the use of steroids. These guys aren't Mickey Mantle and Willie Mays. They're Lou Ferrigno and Arnold Schwarzenegger . . . Baseball players once could be confused with golfers. Now it's hard to tell if you're looking at a right-fielder or a middle linebacker. So when some people say it's not the ball, just better athletes, I can't totally disagree. How they got to be better athletes, that's the problem. Guys don't blow up overnight just by hitting the weights a little harder."

Nobody outside of Macon reads the *Telegraph*.

Nobody followed Tucker's lead.

By the beginning of June, The Chase of 2001 was a one-man show. Bonds had 28 home runs, eight more than Gonzalez and six games ahead of McGwire's '98 pace. Even with a rare 44-at-bat homerless stretch near midseason, Bonds could not be stopped. The spectacular became commonplace. The dazzling mundane.

Boom!

On June 7, Bonds launched a 451-foot shot to dead center in Pac Bell Park, the longest home run in the stadium's short history. It was his 32nd homer, nine games ahead of McGwire's pace. "We'd have these Saturday morning games, and a lot of the time Barry wouldn't take any BP or even hit in the cage," says Aaron Fultz, a Giants reliever. "But it seemed like every time he stepped in for that first at-bat in the game, he'd hit a home run. That's like running a marathon without warming up."

Boom!

On July 12, in his first post–All-Star Game at-bat, Bonds became the fastest to ever hit 40 homers with a line shot over the center-field wall at Seattle's Safeco Field.

Boom!

On August 4, Phillies starter Nelson Figueroa was untouchable, befuddling the Giants with an awesome mixture of fastball-curveball-slider. Calvin Murray led off the sixth by feebly striking out, and shortstop Ramon Martinez followed with an accidental single. Then Figueroa threw Bonds a 95-mph inside fastball, which he pounded into the waters of McCovey Cove for homer number 47.

Boom!

On August 7, the Reds and Giants entered the 11th inning tied at 3. Before leading off against Cincinnati closer Danny Graves, Bonds made an announcement. "You know what? I'm tired," he told his teammates. "I'm gonna end this right now!" Bonds hit the ball 425 feet over the Cinergy Field center-field wall. The Giants not only won, but moved half a game ahead of Houston and Arizona in the wild card hunt.

Boom!

No, really. Boom.

The death threat came in early September, at a time when almost everything in Bonds's life was going beautifully. The Giants were visiting the Astros in Houston when Baker and an FBI agent arrived at Bonds's suite at the Westin Galleria. The information they gave Bonds was chilling: Someone had called a Houston television station vowing to shoot him. This wasn't Hank Aaron, hated for the idea of a black man surpassing the legendary Babe Ruth as the all-time home run king. This was Barry Bonds, simply hated. He immediately called his wife, telling her the details but urging her not to worry. But how could she not worry? And how could *he* not worry? In these new ballparks, like Pac Bell and Enron, fans sat a mere 20 feet away. For even a halfway decent marksman, the shot would be an easy one. *Boom!*

This was on September 10. The next day was September 11, 2001.

Bonds was woken up by a ringing telephone. "Turn on CNN." A first plane had hit the World Trade Center. A second plane had hit the World Trade Center. Home run chase? What home run chase? That evening, thousands of fans were prepared to file into Houston's Enron Field to watch Bonds try to hit home run number 64. Instead, they stayed inside and faced the horror.

"I just want to be home," Bonds told the media on September 12, as the

stranded Giants held an informal team workout at Enron. "The people want
to know what their leaders are thinking, not us. People want to hear more
what [President Bush] is thinking. I hurt a lot for those people, I hurt a lot.
We are caring people just like you guys. We care about people, too."

Bonds's reaction was mature and thoughtful, and—from the vantage
point of many past and present teammates—phony. When he had voted in
past elections, it was always with his wallet, not his conscience. Civil rights
never seemed to interested him. Neither did human suffering. So when play
resumed a week later, and Bonds stood along the third base line waving
a miniature American flag, wiping tears from his eyes, it was difficult for
some to digest. Equally hard to credit was the $10,000 Bonds pledged to
donate to the United Way's 9/11 Disaster Relief Fund for every home run
he hit—an idea hatched not by the ballplayer, but by his team of handlers.
"Barry must have a level of sensitivity in private, because all human beings
do," says one former teammate. "But whenever he does anything nice in
front of the media, you know it's bullshit. Because he would never reveal
himself like that, and he's not that nice to begin with."

Still, the Bonds-obsessed media had a field day, transforming the baseball star into a national hero and his home run chase into a symbolic ode to
American steadfastness. "It's impossible to root against Barry Bonds now,"
wrote Jason Whitlock of the *Kansas City Star*. "For those of us who follow
sports because it's our passion, Bonds is a symbol, a sign of American resilience to quickly restore order and get back to the business of being the best."

On September 18, the Giants returned to action, hosting the Astros at
Pac Bell. Everything was different in the world, and in baseball. When closer
Robb Nen made an appearance, the song "Smoke on the Water"—with its
disquieting reference to "fire in the sky"—was replaced by Led Zeppelin's
"Kashmir." Jeff Kent's stroll toward the plate was no longer accompanied by
AC/DC's "TNT." Fans cheered loudly, but not too loudly. It was a matter of
respect—with bodies still undiscovered at the bottom of the World Trade
Center rubble, it didn't seem right to rejoice in a game.

And then Bonds hit home run number 64.

The shot came on September 20, in the bottom of the fifth inning
with the Giants trailing Houston, 4–2. Astros starter Wade Miller threw

a changeup that hovered over the plate, and as Bonds whipped the bat around, the entire attendance of Pac Bell—40,470 fans—unleashed a sound as loud and powerful as a space shuttle launch. The drive into the center-field bleachers was what everyone in San Francisco had been waiting for. They were allowed to celebrate again. To release. As Bonds circled the bases, the noise refused to let up. That the Giants lost 5–4 in 10 innings mattered, but not really. The night was about Bonds.

"For months Bonds has dismissed the home run totals," wrote Ann Killion of the *San Jose Mercury News*. "But not now. Now he has found meaning in his ability to crush a baseball over the fence. He knows he will be watched through a veil of tears. He knows the ability to go back to work is a fragile, precious thing."

Behind the scenes there are moments in Bonds's life, however fleeting, that reveal a touch of humanity. When Bonds hit his 61st home run in Denver, a Giants clubhouse attendant dove 8 feet into a frigid, rocky waterfall-fountain beyond the center-field wall to retrieve the ball. Bonds was so touched he later bought the man a motorcycle. Years earlier, when Bonds was still with Pittsburgh, the son of hitting coach Milt May nearly died in an automobile accident in Bradenton, Florida. As soon as he heard, Bonds made the two-hour drive from Orlando to sit at Scott May's bedside at Blake Memorial Hospital. "It wasn't anything we asked him to do and he didn't make any announcements to get attention from the media," says Milt May. "Barry very quietly showed up because he wanted to help my son. I'll never forget the depth of that goodness."

In the midst of the hottest stretch of the home run chase, Bonds again showed that—when nobody was looking—he could be more than just a baseball player. On September 27 Franklin Bradley, Bonds's friend and part-time bodyguard, died after complications from gastric-bypass surgery. The procedure was Bradley's idea—a way for the 37-year-old (and 400-pound) Oakland resident to look good for his upcoming wedding. When Bonds received the 9 A.M. call that Bradley was having complications, he threw on some clothes and drove to the hospital. En route the phone rang again— Bradley was dead.

Upon arriving at the hospital, Bonds saw Bradley's lifeless body and broke down. This was one of the few people he had trusted, both as a body-guard and as a friend. Bradley was a roly-poly man with a barroom scowl but a soft heart. Not once did Bradley ask Bonds to autograph a bat or ball. "Franklin meant everything to me," Bonds told *Baseball Weekly*'s Bob Night-engale. "He's been around me before my kids were born. And the one time he wants to do something for himself, something fatal happens." Bradley's passing had a much greater impact on Bonds than did September 11. This was someone he had personally embraced, and now he was gone. Bonds paid for Bradley's funeral expenses and told nobody.

When Bonds arrived at Pac Bell on the following afternoon, he sat down for his pregame press conference expecting to mindlessly handle the usual questions about home runs, Mark McGwire, and the visiting San Diego Padres. "Barry," a reporter asked, "what are you doing to maintain your tremendous focus?"

That was all it took.

"Right now, I'm trying to just relax," Bonds said. His eyes watered. "One of my friends, I lost yesterday," he added, his gaze aimed downward. "So it kind of added a little bit . . . right now, I just have a lot of emotions right now about everything that's going on for me off the field, and there's been distractions for all of us. I've got a lot of things on my mind right now, and I'm just trying to stay as calm as I can."

Few in the media ever felt genuine sympathy for Bonds. But here it was—sympathy. The man was clearly hurting. Though the Giants were but two games behind Arizona, a free pass was available. Were Bonds to sit out or go 0-for-5, nobody would complain. That, however, wasn't his way. Bonds thrived off emotional moments. The aftermath of Bradley's death clearly qualified.

In the first inning, Bonds faced Padres starter Jason Middlebrook and was walked on five pitches. The sold-out Pac Bell crowd booed lustily—it was Bonds's 163rd free pass of the season, a National League record. Yet the pitcher's actions were understandable. Middlebrook had already allowed Bonds's 65th and 66th homers. Enough was enough. The next inning, the Giants surged to a 3–0 lead, and Bonds came up again. This time, Middlebrook threw three straight balls, each one met with boos. In a momentary lapse of basic good sense, Middlebrook reared back and tossed his next pitch across the plate, letter-high.

Bonds crushed the ball, sending it 438 feet into the center-field bleachers. When he reached home, Bonds pointed to the sky, a routine part of his ritual. This time, though, his ritual was prolonged. The home run was for Bradley. Upon returning to the bench, Bonds sat alone and cried.

After the 10–5 Giant victory, Bonds proceeded to an interview room and recapped the night. "It was hard to hold back [the emotions]," he said. "I just said, you know, let God handle it. I've got to play the game. Let God handle all of the emotions."

Bonds now had 68 home runs, with an improbable 69th on the horizon. One day after he watched the brutalization of Middlebrook, Padres manager Bruce Bochy wasn't taking any chances. In the sixth inning of a 1–1 tie, he called upon left-handed reliever Chuck McElroy, aka "The Bonds Stopper."

A mediocre journeyman who pitched for nine franchises in 13 years, McElroy possessed one gift—an ownership of Barry Bonds. In 32 career at bats, Bonds had compiled two hits against McElroy. Three years earlier, after lining out, Bonds went so far as to call the at-bat a success. "I don't get discouraged about the balls that I hit off him," Bonds said at the time. "Because if I hit the ball hard and they make the play, that's not an unsuccessful at-bat. I did my job." It was a startling admission of self-doubt.

McElroy was as loved as Bonds was detested. Nicknamed "Urkel" after the geeky character from the 1990s sitcom *Family Matters*, the Port Arthur, Texas, native was a bighearted softie who liked to arrive at the stadium in crazy wigs and draw pictures in the bullpen dirt with a stick. After he was traded by the Reds to the Angels in 1996, McElroy left thank-you phone messages for Cincinnati's beat writers.

Now, with the Pac Bell crowd once again on its feet, McElroy toyed with Bonds. He threw two outside fastballs for balls, then a breaking ball for strike one. His fourth pitch was a fastball, this one finally within reach. The ball exploded off the bat and sailed over the right-field wall and into McCovey Cove. Providing San Francisco with a 2–1 lead, the homer gave

Bonds his 69th of the season and tied Reggie Jackson—his distant cousin—
for seventh on the all-time home run list with 563. He was now one away
from tying the record. There were seven games remaining.

On October 2, ESPN's Roy Firestone was standing near the batting cage at
Enron Field for the start of a three-game series between the Astros and Giants. Though famous for his status as longtime host of the interview show
Up Close, Firestone blended in well with the 249 other journalists in attendance.

"Hey Roy! Come on over!"

It was Barry Bonds.

"How ya doing, man?" asked Bonds, engulfing the reporter in a lengthy
hug. "Talk to me—how's it going? How's life at ESPN? What are you up to?"

Firestone was pleasantly shocked. "I'm OK, Barry," he replied. "How are
the kids?"

"Oh man! My kids are great," said Bonds. "I'll tell you, the thing about
kids is they really keep you busy. Sometimes I feel like I have time for nothing. You know what I mean?"

For 15 minutes the two engaged in a friendly conversation, Bonds's arm
draped around Firestone's shoulders. Finally, Bonds coolly said, "OK, see
ya. Thanks for that."

Firestone was confused. *Thanks?* "Yeah, thanks for keeping the cameras
away from me," Bonds said. "They might all be here to take my picture, but
they're not gonna take my picture hanging out with *you*."

Moments later, a weird situation turned weirder. Firestone was tapped on
the shoulder by Magowan. "You're friends with Barry?" the Giants owner
said. "Wow! Do you think you could talk to him on our behalf about his
contract for next year?"

"I can't do that," countered Firestone. "I have a job."

"Oh, I understand," said Magowan. "It's just that I can't even have dinner
with Barry. He doesn't talk to us."

In American history, October 4 is destined to go down as a significant date.
On October 4, 1777, the Battle of Germantown was fought. On October 4,

1970, Janis Joplin died. And on October 4, 2001, Shawon Dunston had an unshakable premonition: He was destined to receive a new car.

Although this wasn't Dunston's first thought the moment Bonds crushed a fastball from Houston reliever Wilfredo Rodriguez, surely it entered his mind. With 70 down and three games to go, there was no way Bonds wouldn't break the record. "It was as good as gold," says Dunston. "He wasn't going to just stop at 70."

Way back on May 18, with the Giants stretching before a game at Atlanta, Dunston issued a challenge designed to embarrass his teammate. "Barry, you're gonna break Mac's record!" he yelled. "I've got no doubt about that! You're breaking the record! Nobody's stopping our Barry!" Each word was louder than the previous, each syllable drawn out. *Ow-weeeer Baaaaaaaa-reeeeee!*

"Aw, that's horseshit!" Bonds snapped back. "You're not supposed to be humiliating me like that!"

"Fuck you!" countered Dunston. "I think you can break the record, you little faggot! You little punk! In fact, how 'bout if you break the record, you buy me a new [Mercedes-Benz] CL 500?"

Bonds jumped atop Dunston and placed him in a playful sleeper hold. "OK," he said. "I'll be happy to buy you a new CL 500."

"Say that again," said Dunston, "so everyone here can hear it."

Bonds stood up and cupped his hands to his mouth. "If I break the home run record," he yelled, "I will buy this asshole a Mercedes!"

Now, as his teammates were streaming out of the Enron Field dugout to congratulate Bonds, Dunston smiled. "A CL 500," he thought. "Cool."

Then, one more thought. "Knowing Barry, he'll buy used."

For the first time all season, the pressure was gone. The Giants had three games remaining, all at home against the rival Dodgers. At worst, Bonds and McGwire would go down as coholders of the single-season home run record. "That," Bonds said, "is good enough for me."

Besides, there were other things to consider. Entering the series with Los Angeles, the Giants were two games behind Arizona in the National League West and two games behind Houston for the wild card. Lost in the hype surrounding the home run chase was the fact that the Giants were compiling a heck of a season. Other than Bonds, Kent, and shortstop Rich Aurilia, the lineup was mediocre at best. Nonetheless, San Francisco was 89–70. It was Baker's greatest managerial success, especially considering the maddening chunk of time he devoted every afternoon to enlightening the media on the Zen of the home run.

On the night of October 5, a record 41,730 people crammed into Pac Bell to witness two events—Bonds surpassing McGwire and the Giants inching closer toward the promised land. That afternoon, Bonds and his wife had attended Franklin Bradley's funeral, not the best way to prepare for an important game. Bonds arrived at the stadium at 2:45 P.M., facing the media for yet another exhausting session. He was asked how he would respond to surpassing McGwire.

"What's there to celebrate?" he said. "I'm going to be happy, but I'm not going to have a party or anything like that. I'm going to move on and hopefully we are in the playoffs. And if we aren't, I'm going to give my body a bit of rest. I'm going to go back into the training room and try to give myself another chance to go to the playoffs."

Asked to offer advice to the hundreds of fans stationed in boats, kayaks, and canoes beyond the right-field wall in McCovey Cove, Bonds grinned ever so slightly. "Don't drown yourselves, man," he said. "It isn't worth it."

Bonds looked at ease. Either he knew the record was about to be broken, or he was simply giddy after only three hours of sleep. As the Giants jogged out to the field for the start of the first inning, the fans began a raucous chant of *"U-S-A! U-S-A!"* which morphed into the familiar taunt of *"Beat L.A.! Beat L.A.!"* Something special was about to happen. One could feel it. Bonds and the Giants would pummel Los Angeles and reach the playoffs. What better way to cap off the most amazing season in franchise history?

Poof.

Giants starter Shawn Estes, once one of the league's most promising young pitchers, was shelled from the get-go, allowing five earned runs in two-thirds of an inning. By the time Baker mercifully pulled the plug, the energy of the stadium had been sucked away. It was a stunning mood swing, as if the Dodgers had stolen into Pac Bell and kidnapped the garlic fries.

When, in the bottom of the first, Bonds approached the plate to face Dodgers starter Chan Ho Park, the crowd rose to its feet, but not with the vigor of fans witnessing history. In a sense, Estes's failure was to Bonds's advantage. With two outs, nobody on, and a 5–0 lead, Park could afford to challenge Bonds.

The Los Angeles right-hander also happened to be the right man for the moment. Unlike the myriad other hurlers who dreaded being known as "the guy who gave up *the* homer," Park was unmoved. Not only had Park allowed a dramatic home run to Cal Ripken Jr. in the 2001 All-Star Game (Ripken's final appearance in the midsummer classic before retiring), he also was the only pitcher in the 20th century to surrender two grand slams in one inning—both by Fernando Tatis of the St. Louis Cardinals, on April 23, 1999. Were there a Nobel Prize for Big Moment Ineptitude, Park would have been a multiple-time victor.

Park started Bonds off with a low fastball for ball one. Catcher Chad Kreuter flashed the follow-up sign—fastball, away. Pitching from the stretch to protect his injured back, Park let the ball go. It was hard (93 mph on the radar) and straight. Too straight. With flashbulbs clicking, with the bathrooms empty, with time momentarily frozen, Bonds whipped back his bat and lunged forward. Jon Miller of FOX Sports Net made the call.

"There's a high drive . . . deep into right-center field . . . to the big part of the ballpark . . . Number 71! And what a shot! Over the 421-foot marker! The deepest part of any ballpark in the National League! Barry Bonds is now the home-run king! Number 71! And it was impressive!"

"I think he was saving himself," says pitcher Ryan Jensen. "He could have done it earlier, but he wanted to give something to the home fans."

Bonds reached home plate and squeezed his son, Nikolai. To the left of the scoreboard, a large banner reading BONDS unfurled. Liz Bonds walked onto the field and kissed her husband. Some fireworks went off. Bonds waved to the crowd.

Ho-hum. Compared to McGwire's moment of three years earlier, this was a day at the library. The Giants trailed, 5–1.

More noteworthy than the spectacle was the absence of commissioner Bud Selig, who despite having attended many McGwire-Sosa moments during the 1998 run, was nowhere to be found. (Neither, for that matter, was Bobby Bonds, who was in Bridgeport, Connecticut, for his annual charity golf tournament; this didn't bother Barry, who knew well in advance that October 5 was booked.) The Selig no-show was a slap in the face. Instead of witnessing what Bonds considered a defining sports moment, the commissioner opted to go to San Diego, where he honored Rickey Henderson's all-time record for runs scored, as well as the impending retirement of Tony Gwynn. The two Padres were touched. Bonds was not.

Though the game was largely anticlimactic, it had its moments. In the bottom of the second, Eric Davis hit a three-run double to close the gap to 6–4, Dodgers. Los Angeles battled back with a two-run homer by Marquis Grissom. When Bonds led off the third inning, he was greeted by an even longer ovation than last time. Showing both courage and stupidity, Park refused to issue a walk. With the count 1–1, he hung a meaty breaking ball over the plate, and watched it soar over the center-field wall. Homer number 72.

"This begins to leave the realm of reality!" shouted ESPN's Gary Thorne, and finally—after a season of Bonds Mania—someone was speaking the truth. This was not reality. Baseball is a game of failure. Hit the ball three times, miss it seven—that's the ratio the best players hope for. With age, it becomes even harder. Think Babe Ruth with the Boston Braves, Willie Mays with the New York Mets. But here was Bonds, ballooned up, toying with the most challenging of sports.

The realm of reality? Reality was dead.

The Giants wound up losing, but not without a fight. In a back-and-forth game that lasted 4 hours and 27 minutes (a major league record for nine innings), Bonds nearly homered again. But he was out of steam and so—in the end—was his team. With the 11–10 defeat, San Francisco was eliminated from the playoffs. There was a very strange vibe in Pac Bell afterward. With approximately 60 percent of the crowd remaining, the Giants rolled a stage onto the infield and held a ceremony. Devastated by the loss, Baker retreated to the clubhouse. His players were ordered onto the field, where they lined up behind Bonds. A handful—Dunston, Davis, Aurilia—

appeared happy to be there. Others would have preferred extensive nasal hair extractions.

Aurilia spoke briefly, followed by Magowan. Finally, at 12:30 in the morning, Willie Mays stepped to the stage and babbled away. "You gotta shut up now," he told the crowd, then spent five minutes rambling about Barry and Bobby and the need for Magowan to lock his godson up with a long-term contract. "I think that if Barry looks around and sees all the guys behind him, that should tell him they all appreciate what he's done," Mays said. It was awkward and uncomfortable. The players, many of whom liked Mays no more than Bonds, stood and shrugged. Did they have to stay here all night? Wasn't a *Seinfeld* rerun on?

When Bonds wrapped up the event with a brief speech, it was no better. "I know some of you took cheap shots on me," he said of his teammates. "I know who you are." Then he became somber. "I love you very much," he said. "I'll play with you any time, any day, any hour, any year." Tears welled his eyes. The moment meant something to him.

On the last day of the season, when there was nothing to play for *but* statistics, Bonds hit his 73rd and final home run, a blow against knuckleballer Dennis Springer. As it sailed away, Bonds laughed. Fastball. Curveball. Changeup. Slider. Knuckler. In a year during which he'd seen it all, Bonds had now sent every type of pitch out of the park.

On October 26, 2001, Bonds called Dunston at his home outside San Francisco. "Next week you'll have to go down to the Mercedes dealership," Bonds said. "They'll have something for you."

Dunston remained skeptical. "You playin' me?" he said.

"Boy, just go down there," countered Bonds. "You'll have your car."

The next week Dunston drove away in a sleek black CL 500, brand new and fully loaded. "I really appreciate that car," says Dunston. "He didn't have to do that. The challenge—I was just clowning on him. I didn't truly think he'd give me a new ride. But it says something about Barry. Inside, he's a softie."

Thanks to Bonds's achievement, new attention was afforded to one of the most obscure baseball legends of the 20th century. In 1954, a left-handed first baseman named Joe Bauman hit 72 home runs (in 138 games) for the Roswell (New Mexico) Rockets of Class C Longhorn League. At age 79, Bauman still lived in Roswell, where he was retired after years of owning a gas station. When Bonds initially broke the record, Bauman was thrilled. But as time passed, he soured on the accomplishment.

"Home runs are cheaper than ever," he said in early 2005. "The stadiums are tiny, the pitching stinks. It's not what it used to be." Bauman paused, measuring his words. "What bothers me is the cheating. Did Bonds honestly break my record? I don't think so. I worked very hard to hit 72. I wasn't the best ballplayer around, but I got the most out of my ability. Can he say the same?"

On May 20, 2005, Bauman died of pneumonia. He was 83.

SIXTEEN

A WINNER AT LAST

THE BOOK WAS BLACK, 36 pages, and hardbound. In anticipation of his client's impending free agency, Scott Boras—the proud author—shipped a copy to every major league general manager. Page by page, Bonds's greatness was spelled out in statistical detail, including a comparison between several Hall of Famers at age 37 and Bonds at age 37. According to Boras's calculations, not only was Bonds the greatest "old" ballplayer in history, but by 2006 he would break Hank Aaron's career home run mark of 755 and conclude that season with 802.

Of course, who really needed Boras's book? After decisively winning his unprecedented fourth MVP trophy in 2001, Bonds was inarguably the most accomplished free agent of all time. There were 104 players testing the market in the winter of 2001–02, and none—not Jason Giambi, not Juan Gonzalez, not Moises Alou—came close to matching Bonds's numbers.

That's what makes what happened next so fascinating.

Despite Boras's claims to the media that he had received "a slew" of messages from teams and that "several" would offer a five-year deal, Bonds was once again being ignored in free agency. This time the indifference had less to do with attitude than age. Throughout history, by their 38th birthday (which Bonds would be celebrating in July) the greatest sluggers were either retired or in serious decline. Frank Robinson batted .245 with 22 home runs at age 38; Harmon Killebrew hit .222 with 13 dingers. In San Francisco, a heavy, slow-swinging 38-year-old Willie Mays put up career lows in nearly all categories. Sure, there were exceptions—Babe Ruth mashed 34 home runs in 1933, second in the league to Philadelphia's Jimmie Foxx. But Ruth was a rarity.

Bonds was an old man in a young man's game, and when it was learned late in the 2001 season that a degenerative disk in his back was causing pain, the damage to a potential bidding war was irreparable. There was nothing Boras could write that would convince the Yankees, Mets, Dodgers, or any other club with a fat wallet to submit to his demand of a five-year, $100 million contract. What if Bonds's drop-off was about to begin now? Or even in a year or two? Just recently, 38-year-old Mark McGwire had retired due to declining health. Was Bonds next? Nobody knew for sure.

Then there was the question of bottom-line value. Rich men purchase major league franchises to accrue profit. Was Bonds—even at his best— profitable? In a December study of American sports interests produced by the search engine Lycos, Bonds's 2001 season was shown to captivate, well, no one. According to Aaron Schatz, who headed the research, Bonds generated fewer Internet searches than, among others, Roger Maris, Susan Sarandon, and the Liverpool Football Club. He even trailed Sir Francis Drake, a 16th-century explorer who had died 405 years earlier. This was not a good sign for marketability.

When it became painfully clear that he would not be presented with a lucrative long-term deal, Bonds tucked his tail between his legs and gave in. On December 19, just hours before the midnight deadline, he accepted San Francisco's offer of salary arbitration. In an effort to save face, Boras told the Associated Press that prior to committing to the Giants, "Barry had many things to consider." What things? There were no other offers and no other potential offers.

Despite this, the Giants continued their inexplicable pattern of allowing Bonds & Co. to manipulate the team's decisions. With no pressure to do so, owner Peter Magowan handed his left fielder a five-year, $90 million contract with a $10 million signing bonus. The deal also included a post-retirement 10-year, $10 million personal services contract. (Which essentially would require Bonds to smile and pose for photos.) "You can make the argument that we could have signed Barry Bonds for less money," says Magowan. "But he's the MVP who'd just hit 73 home runs. We wanted to do something that wasn't going to look to Barry as if we were slapping him in the face."

From the time Bonds signed with San Francisco nearly a decade earlier, this had been an obsession of Magowan's—*how will my decisions look to Barry?* In other cities, owners and general managers considered the opinions of their superstars. Mike Piazza was occasionally consulted by Mets general manager Steve Phillips before a big trade. The same went for Frank Thomas with the White Sox and Carlos Delgado with the Blue Jays. But often it seemed as if Bonds ran the Giants. How else to explain the presence of Rachael Vizcarra? The former director of publicity and marketing at the Beverly Hills Sports Council, Vizcarra had been hired by Bonds to meet his PR needs. This was done without consulting the Giants, who employed their own public relations experts. But Magowan never stepped in, allowing Bonds's handler to enter the clubhouse as she pleased. Vizcarra and her assistant, a former Chapman University volleyball player named Lisa Nitta, were attractive, impeccably dressed, and staggeringly useless when it came to acting as Bonds's press liaisons. The local media mockingly referred to the pair as "Barry's Angels."

"They basically get paid to tell people no and to be Barry's friends," says Josh Suchon, the *Oakland Tribune* beat writer. "They exist so Barry can have an entourage. So he can have 'his people.'" When called upon to defend her client's charitable instincts, Vizcarra would note that she was a single Mormon mother with two children—"one of them hearing impaired." The insinuation: How could Bonds be a bad guy if he was respected by someone like *her*?

Over time, the size of Bonds's clubhouse crew rivaled Vanilla Ice's early-1990s hip-hop posse. Along with his Angels, there were Greg Anderson and Harvey Shields (the trainers), Anthony Phills (the photographer/creative director), Greg Oliver (the videographer/assistant trainer), and Barry Bloom (the writer). "Barry is similar to Ted Williams and Joe DiMaggio, in that he likes to surround himself with guys who are no threat to him physi-cally in any way," says Roy Firestone, the former host of ESPN's *Up Close*. "If you look at his entourage, they're mostly little clubhouse guys or docile girls."

Behind Bonds's back, his sidekicks were assigned nicknames by the media. Shields, Phills, and Oliver—black men with shaved scalps—were tagged "The Coneheads." Bloom, once a hard-hitting *San Diego Union Tri-bune* baseball scribe, was dubbed Bonds's "sycophant." (A staff writer for Major League Baseball's website, Bloom began ghostwriting Bonds's per-sonal diary on barrybonds.com) The entire clan came to be known as "Barry's Foofs."

When Major League Baseball ruled in 2004 that the personal trainers, friends, and agents of players were banned from "all playing fields, dugouts, clubhouses and related facilities," Magowan placed Shields and Oliver on the Giants payroll as team trainers, even though they worked almost ex-clusively with Bonds. "The Giants caved because Barry pouted and sulked," says Henry Schulman, the *Chronicle* beat writer. "The team probably would never admit this publicly, but I think the medical staff isn't too happy about that. The organization has career trainers in the minor leagues who can't move up because they've got two trainers here on the payroll for Barry."

Magowan and Baer weren't making sure that Pedro Feliz's locker space was comfortable or that J. T. Snow had fluffed pillows. "Barry says jump," says Glenn Dickey, a longtime *Chronicle* scribe, "and the Giants say, 'How high?'"

"I know there's a perception that we let Barry do whatever he wants, and I think it's unfair," counters Baer. "Yes, he's chosen to go with outside media relations people. Is it so wrong that Lisa and Rachael are around the club-house? And then you have his workout regimen, which is a special situation. We had to make the judgment whether Harvey Shields has the credentials to be a team employee, and he does.

"You hear different things from different people. But the view that's been taken throughout the organization is that if a guy has 700 home runs and all those MVPs, an extra locker, a TV, and all that other stuff is warranted, and the other players don't begrudge him that."

Really?

"There's no excuse for one person being treated better than the rest of the team," says Steve Reed, a Giants pitcher in 1992 and '98.

"I never understood why they let him get away with so much," says Dave Burba, a Giants pitcher from 1992 to 1995 and 2004.

"I like Barry, but how couldn't he get a big head with the way they treated him?" says Shawon Dunston.

"How does it make a guy feel to see the team's best player sleeping when everyone else has to stretch?" asks Jeff Kent.

"Clearly, there are different rules on this team," says J. T. Snow. "One set for Barry, one for everyone else. I'm not saying it bothers me. But I don't love it."

In his time off after the 2001 season Bonds continued to make choices that left people scratching their heads. On January 27 he arrived at the Sheraton Hotel and Towers in Manhattan for the annual New York Baseball Writers Dinner, where he would receive his fourth MVP trophy. Trailing Bonds was a burly bodyguard, dressed entirely in black and broadcasting intimidation. Even for those in attendance—many of whom were familiar with Bonds's eccentricities—the hired protection seemed excessively weird. Among the other guests were baseball luminaries like Mike Piazza, Yogi Berra, Randy Johnson, and Roger Clemens. All went unguarded.

"There's a VIP reception before the dinner starts for special guests," says T. J. Quinn, a *New York Daily News* writer and chairman of the event. "There are no working writers, no one's asking questions, no autograph hounds, no fans. You have Yogi Berra chatting with Joe Torre, and Ralph Branca with Bobby Valentine, and Roger Clemens is pushing his mother around in a wheelchair. But you've also got Barry Bonds, standing behind his bodyguard just in case Yogi's gonna rush him with a butter knife.

"It was," says Quinn, "incredibly awkward."

Yet around the same time, Bonds went out of his way to do something extraordinarily kind. A couple of weeks before the start of spring training, he flew from San Francisco to Ottawa, where he made an appearance on behalf of Sam Holman, a sandy-haired carpenter and president of The Original Maple Bat Company (also known as Sam Bats).

Impressed by their firmness and durability, Bonds had started using Holman's maple bats in 1999, and before the 2001 season the company developed its very own model for the Giants star, the 2K1. "You know the iron ring they put over bats?" says Holman. "With the 2K1, you can't put a ring on because the handle is bigger than the hole for the doughnut. All great hitters do something contrary to the conventions of hitting. Barry uses one of the thickest handles in baseball. So we looked out for his needs."

Bonds was uncommonly appreciative of Holman's handiwork. During the entire 73-home run season, Bonds broke only one bat, and in that instance the ball still left the yard. So when he came to Ottawa to publicly thank Holman, it was done with heartfelt sincerity. Bonds toured the mill where the maple was cut, signed autographs until his hand ached, and held a press conference at the Mayflower Pub. His speech brought tears to Holman's eyes. "Sam wants to give me credit because I'm out there playing baseball, but it takes two to tango," Bonds said. "You know, it's my record, but it's still [Holman's] bat." For the 150 in attendance, it was clear all this Barry Bonds-is-a-jerk talk coming out of the States was malarkey. How could anyone *this kind*, *this loyal* to a humble craftsman like Sam Holman be a bad person? Surely, the press was wrong about Bonds. Had to be.

Not long after Bonds received the praise for his Canadian warmth, however, he turned around and did something truly heinous. On the morning of April 7, 2002, Joseph Lang and Paul Scott, a pair of groundskeepers at Pittsburgh's PNC Park, were driving to the stadium when their car was broadsided by an SUV. Both men died. In the accident's aftermath, Pirates team photographers Dave Arrigo and Pete Diana organized a picture auction, with the proceeds to go to the victims' families. "Neither of the guys who died had insurance," says Arrigo. "One of them had three little girls, the other had a son."

Whenever a new team came to town, the Pirates would explain the tragedy and ask if the opposing club's star players could sign some photographs. "We had guys say, 'Bring as many as you want—we'll sign them all,'" says Arrigo. "Sammy Sosa sent us a bat and four pictures. Craig Biggio, Jeff Bagwell, Curt Schilling, Randy Johnson—all were more than happy to help." When the Giants arrived, Arrigo approached Bonds, whom he'd known from his days with the Pirates.

"I ain't signing shit," Bonds told Arrigo. Then he walked away.

"The sad thing is, I knew he probably wouldn't sign," says Diana. "But we just thought, 'Why not ask him, since he played here and knew these guys.' Look, I understand everybody wants something from Bonds. That's why we were like, 'These guys are dead. We're not making this up.' But why should he take time out to help a couple of families that lost their father and husband? Why should Barry give a fuck about anybody?"

Rachael Vizcarra, Mormon mother of two children—"one of them hearing impaired"—had no comment.

At the start of spring training, Bonds reported to camp looking significantly smaller than he had toward the end of the 2001 season, when he weighed a reported 228 pounds. To many teammates and writers, it was obvious—a transparent post–73 home run return to non-Godzilla-size clothing. Yet when confronted about his girth by Nick Peters of the *Sacramento Bee*, a straight-faced Bonds said, "I weigh the same as I did when I finished the season. I reduced my body fat by building muscle. My workouts stayed the same, but I watched my diet more carefully, eating a lot more protein."

Peters had to refrain from laughing.

With more medical experts openly questioning the size and strength of modern athletes, journalists stopped attributing baseball's power surge to a juiced ball and started suspecting juiced players. Around this time, Dave Newhouse of the *Oakland Tribune* sat down with Bonds and asked the type of questions a reporter should have posed long ago.

QUESTION: "Your home runs carried greater distances more consistently last year than in previous seasons. More powerlifting last winter?"

QUESTION: "Did those rumors last year about you using steroids affect you?"

QUESTION: "Did you do something differently in your off-season workouts last year to quicken your swing?"

Although Bonds answered with typical evasiveness—"[The rumors] don't affect me because I know who I am"—the interview was a clue the media were beginning to cast a skeptical eye on late-career statistical and muscular gains. A defining moment came on June 3, when *Sports Illustrated* published a 5,069-word cover story by Tom Verducci on baseball's growing steroid crisis. Entitled "Totally Juiced," the article included an admission from three-time All-Star Ken Caminiti that he had abused steroids regularly during his 1996 National League MVP season with the Padres. Caminiti was a groundbreaker—the first major leaguer to 'fess up in detail to using performance-enhancing drugs.

"It's no secret what's going on in baseball," Caminiti told Verducci. "At least half the guys are using steroids. They talk about it. They joke about it with each other. The guys who want to protect themselves or their image by lying have that right. Me? I'm at the point in my career where I've done just about every bad thing you can do. I try to walk with my head up. I don't have to hold my tongue. I don't want to hurt a teammate or friends. But I've got nothing to hide.

"If a young player were to ask me what to do I'm not going to tell him it's bad. Look at all the money in the game: You have a chance to set your family up, to get your daughter into a better school. So I can't say, 'Don't do it,' not when the guy next to you is as big as a house and he's going to take your job and make the money."

Not long after the *Sports Illustrated* piece, Bonds told FOX's Lisa Guerrero that he never used steroids—only legal supplements. "I have taken creatine, those little protein pills and amino acids," he said. "I go to GNC like everyone else."

The floodgates had opened. In May, former Oakland A's slugger Jose Canseco announced his intention to name names in an upcoming steroids book, prompting Bonds to express concern for the world's children. "I get upset," Bonds said, "because you're putting false statements in a lot of these kids' minds." Throughout the season, whenever he would arrive in a new city, Bonds would inevitably be asked about steroids in sports. Most reporters lacked the guts to directly say, "Are you using?" but there was no denying the implication. Why were journalists asking Bonds and not, say, Jeff Kent or Reggie Sanders or J. T. Snow?

Ten sports journalists were invited to the White House on June 27, 2002, to talk physical fitness with George W. Bush. Among the contingent was *Sports Illustrated* columnist Steve Rushin, whom Bush nicknamed "Mr. Sports Illustrated."

Upon concluding the meeting, the president shook Rushin's hand. "Let me ask you a question," he said. "Do you think Bonds is using steroids?"

Rushin shook his head. "Not sure."

"Yeah," said Bush, patting his belly. "As we get older many of us tend to get heavier."

By this point, Bonds himself had stopped talking to the national media. As always, his play went unaffected. "He's like Michael Jordan," says Eric Young, a veteran major league infielder. "Blocking out all the noise is one of the hardest things about playing professional sports. We've all struggled with it. But Barry's impenetrable."

Beyond the nagging steroids charges, Bonds faced many other potential distractions throughout 2002. He was skewered by the national media for refusing to acknowledge an invitation from the Negro Leagues Baseball Museum to be honored at its second annual Legacy Awards. He engaged in a silly public spat with the Cubs' Sammy Sosa about the home run record. When he accused the Giant pitching staff of not protecting him, one teammate shot back to the press, "Who cares what he says?"

Most devastating was the news from home. After years of abusing his body with alcohol and cigarettes, Bobby Bonds was in declining health. His deterioration began in the early months of the season, when severe back pain left him crying for help. The diagnosis was a tumor in his kidney, which Bobby had removed on July 11 at Stanford Hospital. "The doctors right now are taking care of him," Barry told the inquiring media throng. "God is keeping him alive."

What maintained Bonds's sanity during these crises was the chase for a World Series ring. For one of the few times in his 10 years in San Francisco, the Giants were rugged, resilient, talented, and—best of all—deep. In the break between the 2001 and 2002 campaigns, Brian Sabean did his niftiest work as a general manager. He acquired a pair of players who combined for 48 home runs in 2001—former Mariners third baseman David Bell and

Diamondbacks right fielder Reggie Sanders. Midway through the season he also brought in center fielder Kenny Lofton from the White Sox, adding speed atop the order. With an upgraded cast surrounding him, Bonds actually bettered his 2001 season. Although he hit "only" 46 home runs, Bonds won the first batting title of his career with a .370 average, and set major league records with 198 walks and a .582 on-base percentage (the old mark of .553, set by Boston's Ted Williams, had stood for 61 years).

"I played with a lot of guys who'll be in the Hall of Fame one day, but Barry was a freak of nature," says Lofton. "Most of us see a pitch and plan on hopefully hitting it. Barry would see a pitch and know for certain what would happen. He knew he was about to hit a home run before he even knew what pitch was coming. It's like he read the way the game would go before it even started. He was the master."

Among Bonds's masterful moments, two stand out.

The first came on June 5 at Qualcomm Stadium in San Diego. On the mound for the Padres was a pretzel-thin rookie right-hander named Dennis Tankersley. A 38th round draft choice out of St. Charles High School in St. Charles, Missouri, Tankersley was 23 years old and making his sixth big league start. Needless to say, he was nervous. After retiring the sides through the first two innings (and the first eight batters overall), Tankersley found trouble, loading the bases with two outs and Bonds stepping up to the plate. San Diego catcher Tom Lampkin signaled for a fastball and spotted his glove on the outside corner. Tankersley threw a sinker with Cy Young intentions—and Keith Garagozzo placement. "Right down the middle of the dish," Tankersley sighs. "With a lot of guys, you figure if you make a mistake they *might* hit it out. But with Bonds, there's no doubt it's gone." This time, the ball was not simply gone. It was G-O-N-E—a missile as high and as far as any home run many could recall seeing. The ball hit the bottom left side of the scoreboard 29 rows beyond Qualcomm's right-center-field wall. Even in San Diego, where Bonds was the enemy, the homer was greeted with a long moment of awestruck silence. Nobody could recall witnessing a more brutal exhibition of power. When the press box announced the ball had traveled 482 feet, few believed it. The measurement was surely too short.

"Guys still give me a hard time about it," says Tankersley, who has gone on to a career toiling the minor leagues. "But the way I see it, if you're pitching to Barry Bonds it means you're in the big leagues. Plus, I was part of history." The blast was the 587th homer of Bonds's career, pushing him past Frank Robinson to number four on the all-time list.

Twenty days later, Bonds was involved in a second incident, again in San Diego. In the bottom of the second inning, Bell fielded a ground ball at third base and immediately threw to second for the force-out. Expecting Bell to throw to first, second baseman Jeff Kent was standing off the bag when the ball arrived, and the runner was ruled safe. San Diego went on to score four runs, and as the Giants jogged off the field at inning's end, Kent lit into the mild-mannered Bell, ripping what he perceived to be a bone-headed decision. Bell fired back with a fusillade of expletives.

"I was the leadoff hitter the next inning, so I really didn't have much of a chance to respond or argue," says Bell. "I was walking out to the on-deck circle when I heard some noise coming from the dugout. That's when I turned around."

What Bell saw—what many in the stadium saw—was Bonds wrapping his hands around the second baseman's neck. This wasn't the first heated confrontation between the two rivals, but this time Bonds was righteously coming to a teammate's defense.

"Barry did the correct thing and I was appreciative," says Bell. "The way I saw it was that Barry stuck up for what he thought was right in that situation. It didn't matter that it was me. It was the circumstance that mattered."

Dusty Baker—feeling less philosophical—lit into Kent. Kent lit into Dusty Baker. *San Jose Mercury News* columnist Skip Bayless called for Kent to be traded. The team was in chaos, and with that day's 10–7 loss to the last-place Padres, San Francisco fell to 42–33, four and a half games behind the Dodgers and in third place in the National League West. But the dustup had repercussions few could have predicted. One month later the Giants were 12 games over .500 and alone in second. Many on San Francisco's roster pointed to the fight as a defining moment. Yes, the team still went through streaks. But a new cohesion existed. "We could have fallen apart, or we could have rallied together," says Shawon Dunston. "We rallied. It was like this big weight had been lifted from our shoulders. Everyone knew Jeff and Barry hated each other, and it was just a matter of time before they mixed it up. Well, they mixed it up. And we survived."

Although Bonds and Kent will never be friends, those paying attention noticed a subtle change in their relationship. Kent no longer scowled at the mere mention of Bonds's name. Bonds seemed to acknowledge Kent's talents more willingly. If it was all just a show, it sure was a convincing one. "When Barry and I scuffled, it was a turning point," Kent later said. "It showed the guys on the team, the front office, and the fans how much we really cared. That cleared the air. It showed we were serious about getting something done this season." Before a mid-July game at Los Angeles, Dunston looked out onto the field to see the two standing next to each other at second base—laughing. Dunston immediately grabbed a photographer's camera and began snapping pictures. "Look at this!" he yelled. "Dumb and Dumber talking to each other! Call a press conference!"

With Bonds nearing his 600th career home run, *Chronicle* photographer Deanne Fitzmaurice asked the superstar whether he would allow her to shoot his off-the-field life for a special package. Surprisingly, Bonds agreed. Over the course of a week, one moment stood out in Fitzmaurice's mind. On a lazy afternoon, Barry and Liz attended daughter Aisha Lynn's gymnastics class. "He's just loving it," recalls Fitzmaurice. "He's smiling, laughing, relaxed." In the middle of an exercise, a young boy asked Bonds for an autograph. "Sorry," Bonds said. "I'm watching my daughter." When the child began to cry, Bonds said, "OK, OK. Come on over."

Chaos ensued. Everyone in attendance—children, teenagers, adults—swarmed the baseball star with markers and scraps of paper.

"That's it!" Bonds said. "I'm out of here."

"It was just sad," Fitzmaurice says. "All he wanted to do was watch his daughter."

Throughout the 2002 season, baseball's biggest story was not Bonds, but the looming inevitability of another work stoppage. The collective bargaining agreement between the Major League Players Association and Major

League Baseball had expired, and as in 1994, the two entities were dead-locked. As it looked increasingly likely that there would once again be no playoffs or World Series, fans fought back. Signs with messages like NO BALLS, ONE STRIKE—YOU'RE OUT and STRIKE AND WE'RE FINISHED popped up in stadiums throughout the country. On sports talk shows enraged call-ers threatened to permanently abandon the national pastime.

Bonds seemed not to care. When asked by the *Washington Post* whether his sport could handle its ninth work stoppage in 30 years, he provided a flip, misguided answer. "It's entertainment," said Bonds. "It will come back. A lot of companies go on strike, not just baseball. And people still ride the bus." So did he expect fans to empathize with players making an average salary of $2.4 million? "It's not my fault," Bonds replied, "that you don't play baseball."

Fortunately for the major leagues, the two sides reached an agreement. And on the afternoon of August 9, Bonds began to think about what would become one of the most meaningful hits of his career. Seven hours before game time, Bonds stood in his kitchen and turned to Fitzmaurice, with whom he had grown friendly in her week as a shadow. "Who's pitching [for the Pirates] tonight?" Bonds asked.

"Kip Wells," she said.

"Oh, I can hit a home run off of him," Bonds said. "No problem."

That night, Bonds kept his word and took Wells deep for the 600th home run of his career. As always, the fireworks exploded into a clear night on the Bay.

Wrote Schulman in the *Chronicle*: "Bonds took five backward steps to-ward first base, and when the ball cleared the wall he raised his left arm and began a trot only three other men have known. . . . The fans beckoned Bonds for a curtain call. He emerged from the steps closest to home plate, waved and ducked back down. That wouldn't do. As Bonds paced across the dugout the fans wanted more, and he gave them more, popping up from the other set of dugout stairs."

Bonds knew what 600 meant: nearly unrivaled greatness. The critics could say he was moody and occasionally indifferent, but of the thousands of men who had worn major league uniforms, only three others—Hank

Aaron, Babe Ruth, and Willie Mays—were members of the 600 Club. His ego surely swelled with the idea of a nation of fans worshipping him as a baseball deity.

Ironically, by hitting so many home runs, Bonds was making his own craft obsolete. When Babe Ruth hit his 60 homers in 1927, it was eye-popping because, with the exception of teammate Lou Gehrig's 47 homers, nobody else in the American League hit more than 18. The home run was special, like spotting a comet as it zooms across the sky. Now it had become as hackneyed as the ballpark wave. Yes, Bonds finished with 46. But how did Cubs second baseman Mark Bellhorn hit 27? How did Devil Rays shortstop Chris Gomez hit 10? "Have we lost our sense of wonder because we have grown to expect the outrageous?" mused John Romano in the *St. Petersburg Times*. "Is this the price we pay for the excesses of recent seasons?"

Because of the unnatural surge in power throughout the game, Bonds's 600th homer does not go down as his most impressive feat of 2002. What instead stands out is that, for the first time in his career, he carried a team not only to the playoffs, but *through* them. On the day Bonds hit number 600, the Giants were 63–52, seven and a half games behind first-place Arizona and one and a half games behind the Dodgers in the wild card race. From that point on, San Francisco went 32–14, with their superstar posting a .393 average, 13 home runs, and 37 RBIs.

"Back when I was first with the Giants in 1996, Barry used to put down all of us," says Dunston. "He'd say things like, 'How can you make the big leagues?' and 'You're a terrible fuckin' hitter.' He made other guys nervous, and that's a hard way to play. It causes a team to lose games they should win. But in 2002, he was awesome. When we were in the batting cages taking BP, he'd walk up to anyone and say, 'You need to look for this. You need to think about that. You need to slow down.' For the first time in our years together, I got the sense that Barry wanted it bad."

Bonds was well versed in the saga of Ernie Banks, the legendary Cub who went his entire 19-year career without reaching the postseason. Banks was a two-time MVP and 11-time All-Star with 512 home runs and a first-ballot ticket to the Hall of Fame. But what always accompanied his name? *Ernie Banks—who never played in a World Series.* If Bonds had to serve as a guru to reach postseason glory, so be it. He was 38 years old. Time was short. "It was beautiful," says Dunston. "He knew he couldn't get to the World Series by himself, and that was the one thing in his career he never accomplished."

After falling 8–5 to the division-leading Diamondbacks on September 5, the Giants found themselves a full three games behind the Dodgers in the wild card race (and an insurmountable eight and a half games behind Arizona). The next afternoon in the Pac Bell clubhouse, Bonds loudly urged his teammates to get it together. "We've got 22 games left," he said. "Make them count!" He was no Jim Valvano, but when a baseball legend speaks, people listen. "You could see it in him," says first baseman J. T. Snow. "He had real drive to win." San Francisco took the next three from the Diamondbacks, and entered a three-game series against the Dodgers (who had dropped two of three to Houston) trailing by one game in the wild card.

In past years, this would be the time Bonds fell off, hitting long outs to the warning track or swinging at outside pitches he usually ignored. But there was something different about 2002. Maybe it was the outward support of teammates that had been absent in the past. Maybe it was the confidence that comes with big muscles and a bigger head. Maybe it was age and experience. Whatever the case, Bonds and his Giants crushed the Dodgers, taking two of the games to pull even.

Bonds's performance made the difference. In the series-opening 6–5 win, his second-inning homer off Odalis Perez set the tone and gave the Giants the early 1–0 lead. A day later, Bonds again struck early, singling in two first-inning runs in a 5–2 victory. "Every time we needed a big hit, Barry was there," says Dunston. "Literally every single time."

Bonds had never been part of a more confident, more determined operation. "We didn't have great chemistry," says Bell. "But there was no phony bullshit, either. It was a bunch of tough older individuals who stuck to themselves away from the field but came together and worked their asses off." With the pesky Dodgers hanging on for dear life, San Francisco went into hyper-drive. Baker's club won 10 of its last 11 games, including the final eight of the season. Bonds even extended a most improbable olive branch, urging the franchise to re-sign free-agent-to-be Kent. "If he's not back next year, I will be one pissed-off player on this team, period, and I'm not afraid to say it," Bonds said. "Jeff has done his job, so they need to put up or shut up.

"Michael Jordan had Scottie Pippen," he added. "Magic Johnson had Kareem. There's always going to be somebody to help that other person become a better player or challenge themselves, and Jeff Kent challenges me a lot."

On September 28, the team clinched the wild card slot with a 5–2 triumph over the Astros at Pac Bell. The game was tied 2–2 in the fifth when Bonds unloaded on a 2–0 pitch from left-hander Jeriome Robertson and sent it splashing into McCovey Cove, his 613th career homer. The Giants would never relinquish the lead. In the clubhouse afterward, mayhem reigned. The interpreter for Japanese outfielder Tsuyoshi Shinjo dumped an entire bottle of champagne on his client. Bonds was spritzed by his son, Nikolai. When the bubbly ran dry, a rainbow of Gatorade splashed across the room.

"I'll be excited when we win a World Series," said Bonds, who remained relatively low-key during the bash. "We have to win a lot more than this."

The Atlanta Braves loomed—for the Giants, and especially for Bonds. In 50 playoff at-bats against Atlanta, Bonds had 10 hits, one home run, two RBIs, and eight strikeouts. Those were Johnnie LeMaster numbers. But here was a different Barry—one who had been intentionally walked a record 68 times and terrified opposing pitchers with his mere presence.

"This isn't the Bonds who got nudged from the playoffs three straight Octobers in the early '90s as a Pirate," wrote John Shea of the *San Francisco Chronicle*. "Or the Bonds who bowed out in 1997 and 2000 as a Giant. Pitchers pitched to that Bonds. Pitchers don't pitch to this Bonds. Bonds has reached such a high level that opponents fear him like never before. They don't want him to swing. They won't allow him to swing, at least not when the game is in doubt. His eyes, his stroke, his power, his knowledge, his anticipation. Nobody ranks with him."

Just like the Atlanta clubs that shut Bonds down in the 1991 and '92 NLCS, these Braves were all about starting pitching. Their rotation of Greg

Maddux, Tom Glavine, Kevin Millwood, and Damian Moss led the majors with a sterling 3.13 ERA. "Barry didn't care about that stuff," says Dunston. "Was he intimidated when he was a younger player? Maybe. But in 2002 he was so locked in that nobody could stop him. I guarantee you he wasn't thinking about what the Braves had done to him. He was thinking about what he was about to do to the Braves."

In San Francisco's five-game series triumph, Bonds played to eradicate past postseason failures. He batted .294 with three home runs and four RBIs, and saved his best for the decisive game five in Atlanta. Leading off the fourth inning against Millwood, Bonds powered a fastball into the left-center-field stands and also scored the first two runs of the evening. The Giants won easily, 3–1.

Afterward, a surprisingly forthright Bonds admitted that the specter of another playoff failure had weighed heavily on him. "I'm kind of in shock," he said dryly. "I've never been past the first round."

The Giants would face St. Louis in the NLCS, and anyone who thought the emotional Cardinals would somehow grind their way past San Francisco was badly mistaken. With the recent deaths of pitcher Darryl Kile and longtime announcer Jack Buck, manager Tony La Russa's club had temporarily become America's team, trudging on in the face of tragedy. But sentiment alone does not assure victory. The Giants battered St. Louis, easily winning the best-of-seven series in five games.

La Russa was convinced the way to beat San Francisco was to pitch to anyone but Bonds. In the eighth inning of game four, Bonds stepped to the plate with two outs, the bases empty, and the score tied, 2–2. Following the mindset of every other major league manager, La Russa had right-handed reliever Rick White intentionally walk Bonds and instead pitch to catcher Benito Santiago. With the count full, Santiago walloped a deep fly to left field, where it drifted, drifted, drifted—gone. For those who assumed Bonds's ego demanded he be the hero, it was a sight to see him pumping his fist as Santiago's shot left the park. Bonds batted .273 with one homer and a team-high six RBIs against St. Louis, and he was thrilled with the win.

"A lot of times strategy is judged on whether it works," La Russa explained after his team's 4–3 defeat. "Bonds is the most dangerous hitter in the league right now. It's tough to walk in the clubhouse after giving him a chance to get the hit to beat you."

One day later, it was official—Barry Bonds would no longer be haunted by the ghosts of playoffs past. Although he went 0-for-2 with a walk in San Francisco's 2–1 game five victory, the statistics no longer mattered. When Lofton's single in the bottom of the ninth drove in Bell with the decisive run, Bonds was beside himself. He smiled widely and grabbed his son and pulled him tight.

After 17 seasons, Barry Bonds was heading to the World Series.

SEVENTEEN

MR. NOCTOBER NO MORE

WITH THE GIANTS ADVANCING to face the Anaheim Angels in the 98th Fall Classic, many Bay Area denizens believed the outcome was a foregone conclusion. San Francisco was a 95-win juggernaut, featuring a legitimate ace (13-game winner Jason Schmidt), a dominant bullpen duo (right-hander Felix Rodriguez and closer Robb Nen) and—in Kent and Bonds—back-to-back MVPs in the heart of the lineup. Dusty Baker's club had sailed through the first two rounds with relative ease, leading *Sports Illustrated*'s Stephen Cannella to predict a four-game Series romp.

The Angels, on the other hand, were a team steeped in tragedy and failure. Since the organization's debut in 1961, a black cat had followed the club from city to city. In 1978, star outfielder Lyman Bostock was shot to death in Gary, Indiana. Eight years later the Angels came within one strike of reaching the World Series before reliever Donnie Moore surrendered a home run to Dave Henderson of the Red Sox. Moore eventually committed suicide. "We had the bus accident in '92," said former Angels shortstop Gary DiSarcina, alluding to the crash that sidelined manager Buck Rodgers for three months. In '95 the Angels led the Mariners by 11 games with 48 to play, only to miss the postseason by losing a one-game playoff with Seattle. "We also had the death of Rod Carew's daughter [from leukemia] in 1996,"

DiSarcina said, "and [three years] before that, our [former] bench coach, Deron Johnson, died too."

In Anaheim, however, there was reason to believe the dark cloud had finally dissipated. Unlike the Giants, the Angels were a close-knit, excitable lot of ballplayers, easily embraceable and beloved in the community. Whereas San Francisco used Bonds to bludgeon opposing teams, manager Mike Scioscia's Angels relied on speed, defense, and a refreshing never-say-die outlook. Were Anaheim asked to provide a signature player, it would have been shortstop David Eckstein, a 5-foot-6, 170-pound Muppet whose uniform was always dirty and whose energy level seemed stuck on high.

Anaheim had begun the season by dropping 14 of its first 20 games, and most fans expected they would finish as they had the year before: 41 games out of first. Instead, the Angels went on to capture the wild card with a franchise-record 99 victories, then upset the Yankees in the ALDS and thump the Twins in the ALCS. They were for real. When the series opened in Anaheim, 44,603 fans packed Edison Field sporting Angel-red outfits and armed with Thunderstix, the inflatable plastic tubes that, when banged together, numb the eardrums with a sound akin to a chorus of drunken frogs. The Angels had never played in a World Series, and the hype was overwhelming.

Bonds didn't care. There is a now-famous video clip of him before one of the World Series games, standing next to Giants announcer Mike Krukow during batting practice. When Krukow asks Bonds if he's ever faced that day's pitcher, the star coldly responds, "I don't care who pitches. If it comes there [he points chest high], I'll hit it out." Bonds was determined to show he could shine under the brightest lights. As the Giants took BP before game one, Bonds stood alone in a stairwell alongside the visiting dugout, quietly soaking in the goings-on. No man in baseball history had ever played in more games (2,439) before appearing in his first World Series. He was ready. Anaheim pitching coach Bud Black assured him, "You'll get some pitches to hit. We're not planning on avoiding you," and although Bonds was internally gleeful, he remained outwardly stoic. "He was indifferent," said Black. "You know Barry. He didn't give a shit. He didn't respond. All I did was infer he wasn't going to get walked 20 times this series."

Upon taking the field, Anaheim starter Jarrod Washburn was visibly nervous, easily getting through the first inning but not without the twitches of a young man in the center of a storm. Bonds walked up to lead off the top of the second, and Washburn fired three pitches. Then he threw a belt-high fastball over the heart of the plate.

Tick, tick, tick . . .

As soon as Bonds swung, he knew it was gone. He flipped his bat in the air, tilted his head to the left, smirked, and began to stroll up the first base line. In the dugout, Giants hitting coach Gene Clines screamed aloud, "Oh! My! God!" Washburn smiled and shrugged his shoulders. The 418-foot shot was not the longest home run ever hit, but it was quick, high, and deadly. It smacked off a hospital billboard and floated gently down into the stands. A loud stadium remained loud, but now the noise was generated by shock, not enthusiasm. *Did he do that? Did he really just do that?* It was Bonds's only hit of the night, but it set a lasting tone. Two batters later, Reggie Sanders added a homer of his own, and behind five and two-thirds solid innings from Schmidt, San Francisco won 4–3, taking the Series lead.

"After that game, all the talk in our locker room was that we were participating in a baseball game and the Giants had a guy playing Wiffle ball," says Eckstein, the Angels shortstop. "I saw that first home run and I immediately knew, 'This man will hit it out of the park whenever he wants. He was unlike anyone or anything we'd seen all season.'"

The following evening's game two would support Eckstein's take. In one of the most memorable (and—at 3 hours, 57 minutes—longest) back-and-forth contests in World Series history, the Angels jumped on Giants starter Russ Ortiz for five runs in the first inning, only to watch San Francisco come back in the top of the second with four runs of its own off veteran right-hander Kevin Appier. The offensive outburst had much to do with Bonds, who led off the inning and was walked on a full count. Smart and savvy after 14 years in the league, Appier wanted nothing to do with Bonds. But this time it backfired, as Reggie Sanders and David Bell followed with homers. Anaheim, however, tacked on two more runs in the bottom of the inning, and with the Angels pitchers now determined not to give Bonds anything hittable, 7–4 seemed relatively secure. It wasn't.

Kent's solo homer in the third cut the lead to 7–5, and in the fifth the Angels again played it safe, intentionally walking Bonds with one out and shortstop Rich Aurilia on second. In the San Francisco dugout, Baker was not happy. He understood the fear of Bonds, but he was also a firm believer in confronting challenges. *Trying to strike out the game's best player*—that's what World Series drama was all about. If he beats you, at least you took a shot. To walk Bonds deliberately was soft.

Anaheim's strategy didn't work. Mocked by fans and the media throughout the season for providing Bonds with squirt gun–like protection, catcher Benito Santiago followed with a hard single to left, and when J. T. Snow lined a single to right, Aurilia and Bonds scored to tie the game. Two more runs courtesy of RBI singles from Bell and Dunston gave San Francisco a 9–7 lead, as well as a potentially suffocating two-games-to-none Series lead without having yet played at home. Yet the Angels were remarkably resilient, scoring two runs to tie the game at nine.

That's when the chimp arrived.

Whenever the Angels needed a late-inning surge, a mystical white-haired capuchin monkey named Katie (aka the "Rally Monkey") would jump up and down on the video scoreboard. Did it work? The Angels posted a staggering 43 come-from-behind triumphs during the regular season. On this evening Katie appeared in the sixth inning, waving her arms in the air, desperate for a rally. The fans responded, furiously banging their Thunderstix and stomping their feet. "We fed off that stuff," says Eckstein. "It actually does make a difference."

With two outs and Eckstein on first in the bottom of the eighth, Giants reliever Felix Rodriguez threw slugger Tim Salmon a 97-mph fastball. It was Rodriguez's 37th pitch of the inning, and the exhausted right-hander's usual pinpoint control was off. The pitch was fat and flat—his worst of the night. As the ball was blasted into the Anaheim bullpen for an 11–9 lead, Edison Field erupted in glee. The haunted Angels were finally turning their luck around. With flame-throwing Troy Percival, one of the game's most fearsome closers, taking the mound for the ninth, San Francisco was surely dead. Nobody rallied on Percival.

The first two Giants to face Percival were Aurilia and Kent, and both went down meekly. Now, with every fan in the stadium standing and most of them screaming, Bonds approached the plate. He looked out at Percival, took a couple of practice cuts, adjusted his balance, and dug in. "With a two-run lead and nobody on, I didn't really have to have an approach besides 'Don't walk him,'" Percival said. "No matter what, I'm gonna try throwing a strike."

His first pitch was a 97-mph fastball, as nasty as any thrown that night. Bonds leaned back, cocked his bat, and swung. The baseball was crushed with a brute force usually reserved for football and boxing. Back. Back. Back. The ball continued to fly, and fly, until it landed in a tunnel halfway within the right-center-field bleachers, some 485 feet away. As Bonds circled the bases, a FOX TV camera panned the Angels dugout, where Salmon's lips could be easily read: "That's the farthest ball I've ever seen."

"It's a good thing that federal officials rejected the request by baseball officials to restrict airspace over the ballpark," wrote Thom Loverro of the *Washington Times*. "They might have shot Bonds' home run down."

Santiago ended the evening one batter later with a harmless pop fly to second, giving the Angels a breathtaking 11–10 triumph. But one of the great games in postseason history would be obscured by a single, awe-inspiring at-bat.

On the night of October 22, the World Series returned to San Francisco, bringing back memories of the last time it had come to town. The year was 1989, and the neighboring Giants and Oakland A's squared off in what promised to be an emotional Fall Classic. Yet all thoughts of baseball were quickly forgotten when a magnitude 7.1 earthquake struck just before game three at Candlestick Park. The tremor collapsed a section of the San Francisco–Oakland Bay Bridge, killed 63 people, and resulted in more than $6 billion of damage to the city. When the Series was resumed and the A's swept the Giants in four straight, few seemed to care. What did a sporting event matter in the midst of disaster?

Now the energy and passion for the game were striking. A capacity crowd of 42,707 squeezed its way through the turnstiles, and hometown favorite Tony Bennett sent chills through the stadium with a rousing version of "America the Beautiful." Moments later, Willie Mays walked out to the mound and threw the first pitch to Bonds, who crouched behind the plate. As the ball reached Bonds's glove, fans rose to their feet. This was how a World Series should feel.

The euphoria soon crumbled. Though Bonds again homered, this one a fifth-inning blast that traveled 437 feet, it wasn't enough. With the Angels lighting up San Francisco starter Livan Hernandez for five runs in three and two-thirds innings, then pounding reliever Jay Witasick for two more runs in a third of an inning, the Giants never had a shot. They lost 10–4, another Bonds moment wasted.

Afterward, Bonds was cornered by a gang of reporters. He was in no mood to talk.

QUESTION ONE: "You've walked 20 times in the postseason thus far. Does that bother you?"

BONDS: "Can you talk about something else besides all my fucking walks?"

QUESTION TWO: "Does the postseason mean as much as the 73 home runs?"

BONDS: "I just want to win a World Series ring. That's it."

QUESTION THREE: "How do you feel about being in the first Bay Area World Series in 13 years?"

BONDS: "It's a dream. It's everything I've ever dreamed of. But I don't feel like talking all fucking day. So why don't you guys find something else to do."

Interview over.

Although nobody was conceding the Series, Anaheim clearly boasted a talent base the Giants lacked. Two men carried San Francisco, and when Bonds and Kent didn't produce, the team usually failed. Equally apparent was the fact that while the Giants were a fine group of players in matching uniforms—"We had nice guys on the team," says Bell, "but after the game we went our own way"—the Angels were a family. Anaheim's bench sparkled with nonstop chatter, from superstars like Salmon and Darin Erstad to grinders like Eckstein and second baseman Adam Kennedy. The players bonded over the franchise's past misfortunes, and together battled the perception of the team as a perennial sad-sack organization.

Immediately prior to the following night's game four, Pac Bell played host to a terribly misguided promotion. Sponsored by MasterCard, Major League Baseball announced the 10 greatest moments in the history of the sport, as voted by fans. With Billy Crystal narrating and stirring music blaring and fireworks blasting, one by one the "moments" were introduced—even though honored achievements such as Joe DiMaggio's 56-game hitting streak (number eight on the list), and Ted Williams batting .406 (number seven) were not, technically, "moments." The number one spot went to Cal Ripken breaking Lou Gehrig's record for consecutive games played. Again, not truly a "moment."

The most peculiar honoree placed fourth—the 1998 home run derby between Mark McGwire and Sammy Sosa. Had baseball's fan base forgotten that McGwire's record of 70 homers had been broken just last season? That Barry Bonds—who did not make the list—was now the single-season home run king?

Or did they just not care?

Down two games to one, San Francisco called upon veteran left-hander Kirk Rueter to start game four. Known affectionately as "Woody" for his physical resemblance to a character from the animated film *Toy Story*, the 31-year-old Rueter was the perfect candidate to put a stop to the Angels. Reared in rural Hoyleton, Illinois (population: 200), he was a dim-yet-lovable sort, naively oblivious to the pressure of a must-win World Series game.

If the Angels weren't overly concerned with the less-than-ferocious Rueter, they did fear Bonds. After watching their nemesis set a World Series record by homering in three straight games, Scioscia decided that, unless Anaheim was leading 262–0, Bonds was to be avoided.

"Imagine how it was to be Barry," says Bell. "Your art is hitting a baseball, but they keep taking the brush out of your hand." In yet another tight game, Bonds was intentionally walked three times. In the first inning, with runners on the corners and one out, Angels pitcher John Lackey granted Bonds first base, then forced Santiago into a rally-squashing double play. In the third, with one out and runners on second and third, Bonds was again walked, and Santiago hit into another double play. The plan failed in the fifth, when Bonds was walked with Aurilia on second. This time Santiago laced a single to center, driving in a run to tie the game at three.

Finally, on Bell's eighth-inning RBI single, San Francisco prevailed 4–3, and the frustration Bonds felt throughout the game turned into giddiness. A win was a win.

The next night, the Angels inexplicably began pitching to Bonds again, and the results were disastrous. In a 16–4 rout that placed the Giants one game away from their first World Championship in 48 years, Bonds went 3-for-4 with two runs, an RBI, and a walk. The fault lies with Washburn. The Anaheim starter's 18–6 regular season record and 3.15 ERA belied an assortment of ordinary pitches (a low-90s fastball, a decent slider). Washburn, however, was not one to duck from a challenge. With runners on first and second and one out in the first, he stared down Bonds before throwing a Little League changeup that crossed the heart of the plate. Baseball's best player slashed a double to right, driving in Kenny Lofton with the first of many San Francisco runs.

In a potentially classic World Series, the game was mostly forgettable—save for one moment. In the bottom of the seventh inning, Baker's three-year-old son, Giants batboy Darren Baker, toddled toward home during play to pick up a bat. Little Darren failed to notice that Snow, San Francisco's 6-foot-2, 202-pound first baseman, was charging down the third base line (with David Bell not far behind, also scoring). In one spectacular motion, Snow stepped on the plate, reached out his arms, and lifted Darren by the collar of his jacket. The image is destined to be replayed for generations. "First call I got when I got back to the clubhouse was my mom to tell me, 'I know you listen to me sometimes; just listen to me this time,'" a chastened Dusty Baker said with a chuckle.

In victory, the laughs come easier.

Despite sitting one win away from his first World Championship, Bonds was behaving like his old self. At the start of the Series, he seemed genuinely giddy to be appearing on the game's biggest stage. Slowly, surely, that façade was crumbling. In the post–game five press conference Bonds answered

lengthy questions with one- and two-word answers, shooing off those queries he found to be beneath him.

QUESTION: "Can you talk about the double off Washburn?"

BONDS: "Threw a changeup."

QUESTION: "And?"

BONDS: "Double."

Several reporters left the conference room before Bonds was finished.
Who needed to be treated this way? In the October 26 *Contra Costa Times*,
columnist Gary Peterson teed off: "When Bonds jerks reporters around,
he's jerking the public around as well. . . . Bonds said Thursday night he
would rather let his actions on the playing field do his talking for him. Then
he would be well advised to go the Steve Carlton route. Decline all interview requests, all the time. But don't indulge us one day, then rain conde-
scension on our heads for the next 19. Bonds is a staggeringly gifted athlete,
pure magic on a ballfield. There's no debate there. But life, ultimately, comes
down to how you treat people. Bonds treats people as if they were put on
this planet specifically to annoy him."

For those who detest Barry Bonds, there is no sweeter date than October
26, 2002, at Anaheim's Edison Field, when baseball's greatest player fell flat
on his face.

Through six and a half innings of game six of the World Series, all indi-
cators pointed toward Bonds experiencing his crowning moment. While
stretching before the game, Bonds approached Dunston—who would serve
as that night's designated hitter—and mockingly asked, "You scared, Peanut? You scared of playing on the big stage?"

When Dunston told Bonds to bug off, the star made a bold prediction.
"You're gonna hit a home run tonight," he said. "I just feel it." With one on
and one out in the fifth, Dunston broke a scoreless tie by depositing a junky
Appier fastball in the left-field stands. Upon returning to the dugout, Dunston repeatedly shoved Bonds, yelling, "How'd you know that? *How did you
know that?*" In 147 regular-season at bats, Dunston had homered one time.

The Giants ended the inning with a 3–0 lead, and after starter Russ Ortiz
shut down the Angels in the bottom of the fifth, Bonds led off the ensuing

frame. On the mound for Anaheim was 20-year-old phenom Francisco Rodriguez, a lightning-armed right-hander who had spent much of the year
anonymously tucked away with the Double A Arkansas Travelers. Called
up on September 15, K-Rod (as an overzealous media had begun to call
him) struck out 13 batters in just five regular-season innings and tied a
major league record with five postseason victories.

If ever a moment evoked *The Natural*, this was it: Rodriguez, the hotshot
kid from the impoverished streets of Caracas; Bonds, the aging star near the
end of the line. "Here is the great home run slugger, Barry Bonds," said Jon
Miller, the night's TV commentator, "versus the great phenom, Rodriguez."

Rodriguez's first offering was a this-should-get-your-attention 99-mph
fastball. Bonds was not impressed. His swing was as pure and smooth as
fresh whipped cream, identical to the one he used to hit number 70 against
Houston's Wilfredo Rodriguez one year earlier. Bonds did not take to pitchers kindly, especially those who were *supposed* to strike him out. The baseball
followed a similar path to others Bonds had hit—deep into the right-field
stands and through the tunnel marked Section 355–354. As Bonds tossed
his bat and began to trot, Rodriquez changed before 44,506 pairs of eyes.
K-Rod was Francisco again, a lost 20-year-old boy overmatched by man-
hood.

By the middle of the seventh, the game was over. The Giants were leading
5–0, and not even Reggie Jackson, Thurman Munson, and the '78 Yankees
could have overcome such a gulf. In the bullpen, San Francisco relievers
Chad Zerbe and Jay Witasick were debating where to tuck their possessions
when they made the inevitable sprint onto the field to celebrate. "I couldn't
believe I was about to win the World Series," says Zerbe. "I just couldn't
believe it."

"I felt the ring on my finger," says Lofton. "I felt the damn ring."

Sparked by a breathtaking display of poor judgment, everything changed.
With one out in the bottom of the seventh, Anaheim's Troy Glaus and Brad
Fullmer reached base on consecutive singles, prompting Baker to stroll to
the mound and remove his starter. Russ Ortiz had thrown 98 pitches, a
gutsy effort that deserved kind words, hearty applause, and a firm pat on
the buttocks. What it did not warrant was a baseball in his hand.

That, however, is exactly what Baker gave Ortiz as he left the mound—the game ball. Later on, Baker would explain that he was simply attempting to present Ortiz with a keepsake from a defining life moment. But as far as etiquette went, it was a major no-no. On their bench, members of the Angels could not believe what they were witnessing—bush league garbage, and a glaring lack of respect for a team that had returned from the dead time and time again. (Little did they know that in the Giants clubhouse, stadium employees were wheeling in the Commissioner's Trophy, setting up a platform and loading the room with champagne bottles featuring the Giants' logo and "World Champions" inscribed on the labels.)

Into the game came reliever Felix Rodriguez, and on his eighth pitch Angels first baseman Scott Spiezio belted a three-run home run, cutting the lead to 5–3. Thunderstix banged. Feet stomped. Music blared. Baker cursed himself. Russ Ortiz could barely watch. *Take that!*

"When Spiezio hit that home run, you got the feeling maybe we could turn it around," said Appier. "Just maybe."

Rarely had momentum shifted with such speed and drama. The Giants failed to score in the top of the eighth, but in the bottom of the inning the Angels continued their roll. Encouraged by the gyrating Rally Monkey peering down from the scoreboard, Erstad led off with a homer off Tim Worrell, then Salmon followed with a single. Next up was Garret Anderson, Anaheim's powerful left fielder, who lifted a seemingly impotent blooper toward left field.

Here, for Bonds's haters, was *the* moment.

Charging too fast, Bonds overran the ball, bobbled it twice, then reached out with his left hand and awkwardly tumbled to the ground—a gargantuan blunder, allowing Chone Figgins (running for Salmon) to reach third and Anderson second. Baker called on closer Robb Nen to face what was surely the most daunting save opportunity of his career. The Angels would not be denied. Glaus greeted Nen by ripping a double to the wall, handing Anaheim a stunning 6–5 lead. The score would hold up.

"And the Anaheim Angels," said Jon Miller, the announcer, "are still breathing."

••••●

In sports, few teams collapse as profoundly as the Giants did in game six and then proceed to win the following day in a do-or-die situation. It takes character and togetherness, a refuse-to-lose outlook that, frankly, San Francisco didn't possess. When his teammates from years past reflect upon their time with Bonds, they often note his inability to raise the level of play in those around him. Statistics alone do not assure a legacy. Michael Jordan scored and scored, but what made his teams win was his talent to make mediocre players like Dickey Simpkins, Scott Williams, and Bill Wennington shine. "When you're selfish, guarded, angry, and only interested in your own performance," says former outfielder Armando Rios, "it doesn't help the team too much."

In game seven, San Francisco actually jumped out to a 1–0 lead on Reggie Sanders's second-inning sacrifice fly off Angels starter John Lackey. But when Anaheim roasted Livan Hernandez for three third-inning runs, a noose had been placed around the Giants' neck. There was no more fight.

Upon retiring Lofton on a fly ball to center for the final out of the 4–1 victory, Percival pumped his fists and howled. As he was stampeded by a herd of teammates, Edison Field erupted one final time. In the visitors' dugout, Bonds (who went 1-for-3 with a walk) could only sit and watch, a blank expression masking his inner thoughts. He had dominated the Angels with an offensive barrage worthy of Babe Ruth's praise and it wasn't enough. He had carried an unspectacular collection of ballplayers to the verge of glory, and it wasn't enough. He had played his heart out, and it wasn't enough. If the 2002 Giants could not win it all, would Bonds ever be a World Series champion?

He had to wonder.

Just 35 minutes after the conclusion of game seven of the 2002 World Series, Bonds was standing in his cramped locker space at Anaheim's Edison Field, surrounded by hundreds of reporters pushing and elbowing for position. For the past eight days, he had posted unprecendented World Series numbers. A .471 average, four home runs, 13 walks, seven intentional walks, and a .700 on-base percentage. "Any talk about Barry being a playoff choker was dead," says Shawon Dunston. "D-E-A-D, dead. It could never be said again."

In the clubhouse, every reporter desired Bonds's take. There were questions to be asked. How disappointed are you? Was this your last chance? Did the better team win? What about the play where you fell? Are you proud of the Giants? Did this meet your expectations?

With the mob inching closer and closer, Bonds was trapped.

"You guys need to go," he said. "Go, go, go, go. Bye. Go. Thank you. Go."

The mob retreated several steps, allowing Bonds to dress. When the writers and TV cameras returned, and somebody accidentally stepped on his tote bag, Bonds was even angrier. The five words tumbled out in a tone as venomous as any he had ever uttered: "Back off or I'll snap!"

Silence.

They backed off.

A reporter respectfully asked if Bonds would take comfort in his amazing performance. "What are you going to write," he snarled, "that I had a good postseason and we still lost?" Another scribe wondered if he would be haunted by game six. "Why would it haunt me?" he grumbled. "What does that have to do with me?"

After three or four more short retorts, Bonds departed.

Alone.

EIGHTEEN

DEATH OF THE FATHER

ON THE NIGHT OF November 9, 2002, a photographer from *Friday*, a daily Japanese tabloid magazine, tailed Barry Bonds's taxi as he rode from the Tokyo Dome to Kabuki-Cho, Tokyo's infamous red-light district. Along with 24 of his fellow major leaguers, Bonds was visiting the Far East to take part in an exhibition series against Japanese players. According to reports attributed to *Friday*, Bonds left the stadium after a 8–1 American victory over the Yomiuri Giants and entered a so-called Soapland parlor. Once there, he allegedly paid $600 for a 100-minute "massage." Wrote *Friday*'s editors: "The people were thinking, 'This can't be true.' He was playing a doubleheader!"

The photographs accompanying the story were damning—a man who appears to be Barry Bonds exiting a Kabuki-Cho sex club.

Remarkably, the item sank with barely a trace. With the exception of a column in the *New York Daily News* by Filip Bondy, who happened to be covering the series, nobody jumped on another opportunity to slam San Francisco's star. Perhaps after an intensive few years of steroid scandals and attacks on Bonds's character, editors simply deemed the matter trivial enough to let pass. They were giving Bonds a break.

Though he was temporarily stung by the World Series defeat, Bonds had reason to be happy. He had just enjoyed one of the best seasons of his career, capped off by a fifth MVP trophy. His swing was as potent as ever. His three children were healthy. And his favorite sports team—the Sacramento Kings—was dominating the NBA's Pacific Division. Although Jeff Kent had gone to the Houston Astros as a free agent, the Giants upgraded at manager, replacing Dusty Baker with the savvy and eternally optimistic Felipe Alou. Upon his return to spring training, Bonds was even glib with the media, recounting a conversation he had with his wife on the flight back from Anaheim after game seven of the World Series. "She said, 'You asked God your whole life to be in the World Series, and you got your wish,'" Bonds said. "I said, 'You're right, I did. Why didn't I wish to win? That was really dumb.'"

The headline in the next day's *Sacramento Bee*—BEAMING BONDS ARRIVES—was on the money. Bonds was beaming.

Even the latest news on the steroids front gave Bonds an excuse to smile. Near the end of the 2002 season Major League Baseball announced its first-ever drug testing policy—intended to once and for all put the issue to rest. Bonds, along with every other suspected cheater in the game, publicly supported the standards, and why not? Under the new guidelines, baseball would test for steroids in 2003, but the results would serve only for informal "survey" purposes. Were a player to test positive, he would be punished with—well, nothing. For survey purposes, all players would be tested twice. Though the players would *not* be told in advance of the date of the first test, they were informed that the second would always come within a week. If more than 5 percent of the tests returned positive (remarkably, they did), testing would continue in 2004 under a program in which offenders would be placed in a treatment program and face penalties for future usage.

Because the policy called for no off-season testing, players could easily circumvent the cycle. Also, there were no provisions for human growth hormones—a mounting problem within the game. "What's the point of having a policy where there's no penalty?" an anonymous American League source told the *Boston Herald*. "How can you test positive the way it's set up now? This is all to make it look like something is being done. But it's not. Nothing is going to change." Bonds praised the new rules, encouraging those who asked to "let the system work." The news was too good to be true—baseball had instituted a useless testing policy.

Yet beneath the grin and good tidings, Barry Bonds was falling apart. In mid-December, just five months after he had a cancerous tumor removed from his kidney, Bobby was diagnosed with lung cancer. Though Barry had long maintained a complicated love-hate relationship with his dad, the ice truly thawed once Bobby sought treatment for alcohol dependency. After joining the Giants in 1993, Barry gradually came to view Bobby as a trusted friend. His father knew the pressures and the anxieties of being a superstar in the big leagues, and he never judged his son.

Giants first baseman J. T. Snow remembers sitting in the lobby of the Ritz-Carlton in Atlanta one day, watching Barry try to cross the street. "He was waiting for the light to turn, and every single person who walked by either immediately realized who he was and said something or eventually realized who he was and turned around to say something," recalls Snow. "And I looked at a friend and said, 'Man, what is that like?'" Bobby knew. He was often the lone voice urging Barry to keep his cool, to turn the other cheek and accept the responsibility that comes with fame. "Like it or not," he'd tell Barry, "it goes with the territory."

Now, at the relatively young age of 57, Bobby Bonds was slipping away. The once-strapping athlete grew increasingly frail. Despite the illness, he continued to dig into his pocket and pull out cigarettes, smoking one after another. When neighbors in San Carlos saw Bobby sitting outside the family house, he was feebly puffing away. "Saddest thing you'll ever see," recalls Marlene Rossi, a longtime neighbor. "Poor Bobby was nothing like he used to be."

In the midst of Bobby's decline, the most scathing profile ever written about Barry hit newsstands: A 2,158-word opus in the March 30 *Boston Herald* by Howard Bryant, entitled "Beauty and the Beast: Bonds' Achievements Overshadowed by Belligerence." In light of the agony the son was going through, Bryant's denunciation is a painful read.

"[Barry Bonds] feels no compelling reason to explain his lies and contradictions, or his almost pathological desire to belittle people," wrote Bryant. "Yet he will curiously and disastrously engage in periodic campaigns to be liked . . . while treating many of the people who do see him when the game is over—his teammates, the employees of his teams and the reporters who cover him—with churlish and inexplicable disdain. This is why his talent is awe-inspiring, but Bonds the man is hated.

"For someone of magnificent accomplishment," the author went on, "he is the most insecure man in baseball, contemptuous of people, yet confused and embittered when they aren't enamored by his hollow image burnishing."

Bryant's take was dead-on, with one essential omission. What the scribe failed to perceive was Bonds's vulnerability. This was not Bryant's fault, because Bonds had spent a lifetime concealing all traces of humanity. Beneath the childish machismo, however, Bonds suffered from a deep yearning to be embraced and an almost savage inability to act on that need. Many found it strange that Bonds could be so rude and degrading—until the day, that is, a teammate was traded or sent down, when suddenly, in Bonds's eyes, the ex-Giant became the greatest guy in the world. In 1995 a right-handed reliever named Chris Hook was demoted for 10 days even though he sported a 5–0 record. "Chris, you'll be back," Bonds told Hook. "I don't know what the fuck this team is thinking, sending a guy like you to Triple A. You mean a lot to this team." When outfielder Darryl Hamilton was shipped to Colorado midway through the 1998 season, Bonds whispered, "I love you, man," and wrapped Hamilton in his arms. "That was the first time we'd ever had a conversation like that," says Hamilton. "I was shocked." Four years later Calvin Murray, another outfielder ignored by Bonds for much of his two full seasons in San Francisco, was dealt to Texas. Bonds was the only Giant to call his hotel room. "We're gonna miss you around here," he said. "If you need anything, let me know."

"It's hard to explain," says Hamilton. "I think Barry is a very emotionally confused man, afraid to open up to people who might see what's going on inside. So when I was traded, it was much safer for him to be himself. If you look closely at Barry, you can see past the machine."

Throughout Bonds's career, journalists have trumpeted his ability to play through adversity. Nothing prepared him, however, for the daily rawness of alternating the joy of baseball with the excruciating sadness of a father's looming death. In the April 13 edition of the *Chronicle*, Henry Schulman, the Giants beat writer, dryly noted, "Eleven games into the 2003 season, Bonds has shown himself to be quite human. His batting average of .273 is ordinary. His seven strikeouts in 33 at-bats is not bad, but very un-Bonds-like. Four home runs? He had that by Day 2 last year." Schulman forgot to note (and he was not alone in this) that Bonds was a .273 hitter *struggling to keep his mind out of the operating room.* After years of presenting himself as some sort of baseball cyborg, Bonds was expected to be mechanical and emotionless.

On April 17, Bobby underwent surgery at Stanford University Medical Center to have a brain tumor removed. As soon as he was able to speak, he was on the telephone with his oldest son, more interested in the Giants' upcoming series with the Dodgers than in recounting his most recent ordeal. The following night Barry went 0-for-3 in a win against Los Angeles, but nobody complained. Within the clubhouse, even those who disliked Bonds understood what he was playing through. "I'm just not here right now," Bonds said at the time. "I try to concentrate, but I just can't. My father has been a huge part of my life. Baseball right now, I can't even think about it. The desire isn't the same right now.

"All of that is meaningless," he continued. "How we lost the World Series, how many homers I hit, it's irrelevant. I'm sure one day I'll get over it and be excited about baseball again, but right now it's like therapy for me. I'm doing the best I can. It takes my mind off those other things."

In late April, when Vicki Schmidt, the mother of pitcher Jason Schmidt, died of brain cancer, Bonds displayed genuine empathy for his teammate— a first for Barry, as far as many Giants could remember. He pulled Schmidt aside and offered not just support, but understanding. "I got to see a different side of him than what people usually witnessed," says Schmidt. "When you're going through something like that, it's nice to talk to people who have been in similar situations. We were there for each other."

Though the Giants qualified for the playoffs again in 2003, winning 100 games and their first National League West title in three years, the team's finest—and most emotional—moment came in a seemingly insignificant game on the final day of April. Making his first start since his mother's passing, Schmidt pitched a complete-game three-hitter, striking out 12 Cubs in a 5–0 San Francisco triumph. After each of his starts, Schmidt had made a point of calling home to recap the evening for Vicki. "I said a little prayer before the game," he said afterward. "I said, 'It's Your will, just give me this game tonight.'"

Schmidt's fortitude had an especially strong impact on Bonds, whose father had mustered the strength one night earlier to attend his first game in weeks. As Barry took batting practice, Bobby leaned against the cage next to Alou, shouting tips and encouragement at his son. It was hard to say who benefited more from the experience: Barry, seeing his father with a smile on his face, or Bobby, out in the fresh air surrounded by the environment he loved. Though Bonds went 1-for-2 with an intentional walk and two hit-by-pitches, it hardly mattered—his father was on the rebound.

The reprieve didn't last. Too often, it doesn't. Medicine can prop a human being up, even make him feel like his old self. But when it comes to metastasizing cancer, hope is frequently optimism displacing logic.

Bobby Bonds was dying.

As her husband's strength and resistance deteriorated, Pat Bonds's strength and resistance deteriorated, too. Marlene Rossi, her longtime neighbor, bumped into Pat one day and offered a wide-armed embrace. "Marlene," Pat said, "I'm sorry to say this, but I just wish he'd die at this point. I'm tired of reading about it, tired of him being sick. It's too much."

Barry did not share his mother's feelings. He wanted to utter some magic words and have his dad reappear in uniform, dashing down the first base line with the speed of a rocket. "I've never played baseball without my dad," Bonds said. "Now I play alone. I could take a bad swing on the field, and my dad could make a phone call in five seconds and tell me what's wrong. There's no more phone calls." After most home games, Barry could be seen bolting out of the clubhouse to race to Bobby's bedside. But the man in the hospital, with the IVs stringing from his arms—this wasn't the Bobby Bonds he knew.

With few close friends to turn to, Bonds treated the media as his personal grief journal. Bonds seemed to take comfort in baring his soul to Schulman, Suchon, and the other beat writers. After years of obsessing over Bonds on a daily basis, the scribes knew what they were witnessing was genuine. This wasn't Bonds pining for a restructured contract or suggesting a trade or ripping Kent. This was a man in crisis.

When the Giants visited Kansas City for an interleague series against the Royals, he made a visit to the Negro Leagues Baseball Museum, the same institution he had shunned four months earlier. "My hands are shaking a little bit, because I'm overwhelmed by what I've seen," he said afterward. "It touches a very emotional part of my heart." If this was a case of Bonds peddling rubbish to the masses, it sure didn't appear that way. "The whole visit seemed to be something of a revelation for him," says Chuck Johnson, the veteran *USA Today* baseball writer. "That's when he really started talking about race and how Babe Ruth is exalted to a certain level a black player may never reach."

At a certain point, Bonds's honesty became too much. At the 2003 All-Star Game, held at Chicago's U.S. Cellular Field, Bonds used a session with the press to expound on his climb up the all-time home run chart. At the time Bonds was 17 shy of tying Willie Mays's 660. "Willie's number is always the one that I've strived for," Bonds said. "And if it does happen, the only number I care about is Babe Ruth's. Because as a left-handed hitter, I wiped him out. That's it. And in the baseball world, Babe Ruth's everything, right? I got his slugging percentage and I'll take his home runs and that's it. Don't talk about him no more."

Not long after the sentences left his lips, Bonds privately acknowledged he might have gone too far. Ruth was an icon—beloved even 55 years after his death. There was no point in unnecessarily degrading the man. Bonds tried backing off, but it was too late. "Our prince of petulance has discovered his latest new low," wrote Greg Cote of the *Miami Herald*. "Bonds bashing Babe Ruth during the All-Star break is sort of like a cardinal choosing Easter at the Vatican to knock the Pope. You don't disrespect the Bambino; deference to him is baseball law. If America's Pastime has a deity, it's Babe Ruth."

When the Babe Ruth Birthplace and Museum issued a statement condemning Bonds's comments as a "complete disregard for the history and tradition of our national game," it seemed as if a controversy had been sparked that would go on for weeks. Instead, Bonds wisely apologized and it disappeared.

On June 23, Bonds entered the record books again by stealing his 500th career base, becoming the first member of baseball's 500-steal, 500-home run club. Among the 42,474 watching the Giants play the Dodgers at Pac Bell that night was Bobby Bonds, but he left well before the 11th inning, when his son reached the milestone. Over the next month, Bobby's condition would slip from bad to worse.

On the night of July 24, Barry hit a game-winning home run to complete a four-game sweep of the Diamondbacks and increase San Francisco's divisional lead to 11 games. It was Barry's 39th birthday, but instead of relishing the moment, he headed straight for the hospital. The next morning, Bobby was scheduled to undergo open-heart surgery. The operation had nothing to do with his cancer, but because of it Bobby was unable to continue with chemotherapy. Barry missed the day's game against San Diego to be with his family. "When Bobby first started the treatment, his attitude was, 'I'm gonna beat cancer!'" recalls Jim Davenport, the former Giants star and one of Bobby's close friends. "But there was just one thing after another—a blood clot in his leg, a tumor in the back of his head, open-heart surgery. It was a crying shame to see a big, strong man reduced to nothing."

In a poignant piece in that Friday's *Contra Costa Times*, columnist Gary Peterson surmised what Barry Bonds was going through:

> If you've ever ushered a parent through a long, debilitating illness, you know. And if you haven't, take it first-hand: It's the omnipresent downer on every day of your life. It's unrelenting sadness, a sickening feeling of powerlessness, hope sacrificed at the altar of nature's way.
>
> There are days when you have to leave work early, days when you'd rather not be at work, days when you were on the job but might as well not have been. This is what Bonds has been enduring this season, and for all the talk about a silly game providing a distraction from real life, that's all it is—talk.
>
> He has plenty of time to think while he's standing sentry in

left field, or while he watches ball one, followed by ball eight, followed by ball 17 at the plate. His head may be in the game, but his heart is with his father.

When he returned to the stadium the next afternoon, Barry was flabbergasted by what awaited him. Scattered around his locker were cards and bouquets of flowers—from colleagues, from teammates, from fans. A few weeks later, Bonds took a four-game bereavement leave from the club to spend what were likely to be final moments with his father. "My dad wants everybody to know that he thanks them all for their support," Bonds told a reporter before his comeback game against the Braves on August 19. "With God willing, he's going to try and come out to the game tomorrow. Unfortunately he's in a real fight with this cancer right now. He wishes he could be here on a regular basis." This was no act. Bonds was preparing to lose his dad. That night at Pac Bell, he led off the 10th inning of a 4–4 game by turning on a slider from reliever Ray King and sending it 457 feet into McCovey Cove. Four steps into his trot, Bonds raised his arms and index fingers to the sky.

On the evening of August 20, after the media retreated from the Giants clubhouse, Bobby Bonds entered. He was in a wheelchair, fragile and taciturn, but happy to be home "It was very difficult to watch," says Eric Young, the second baseman acquired by San Francisco a day earlier. "You could see it was just a matter of time for Bobby. He couldn't do nothing." Because he had been escorted into the clubhouse under the media's radar, few knew Bobby was in the stadium. Then, immediately before the bottom of the first inning, a message flashed on the scoreboard: A GIANT WELCOME TO BOBBY BONDS. 3-TIME ALL STAR.

There were 41,974 spectators in attendance that night, and each one rose to offer a prolonged standing ovation and—though it went unspoken—farewell to a Bay Area baseball deity.

Three days later, Bobby Bonds died.

The funeral was held on a Thursday at the Glad Tidings Church of God in Christ in Hayward, 20 miles outside San Carlos. Among the luminaries to attend were Willie Mays, Willie McCovey, Joe Morgan, and Reggie Jackson, as well as actor Danny Glover and former NBA standout Reggie Theus. Gospel artist DeLeon Sheffield, the wife of Braves outfielder Gary Sheffield, sang. Outside the church a sign read, "Today's memorial services are private. The Bonds family extends their appreciation to the general public for their cooperation. Your thoughts and prayers are greatly appreciated." A dozen security guards in red blazers kept uninvited curiosity seekers away. The press turnout was surprisingly small.

Barry sat in the front row, next to his wife and near his mother and grandmother. This was the second child 87-year-old Elizabeth "Momma" Bonds was forced to bury, and the pain was palpable. "Mother Bonds understands everything about life and death," said the Reverend Jerry Louder, a family friend and pastor of Riverside's New Jerusalem Christian Center. "But this is her baby boy." A handful of mourners gave eulogies, including Barry and his two brothers, Ricky and Bobby Jr., as well as Rosie Bonds, Bobby's sister. As with all funerals, the good was remembered and the bad ignored. "Bobby was a great community guy and a good family man," said Olden Henson, a Hayward council member who attended the service. "He also had a strong affiliation to the church."

None of those in attendance who were interviewed for this book recall a great deal about Barry's speech, except that it was heartfelt and relatively brief. The most poignant moment came when Jim Davenport rose to offer a few words. With his voice cracking, Bobby's longtime teammate remembered a fun-loving guy who was loyal to the end. Close with Bobby at a time when much of society was uncomfortable with whites and blacks maintaining friendships, Davenport considered the deceased to be his brother. "Toughest thing I've ever done in my life," Davenport says. "When you love someone the way I loved Bobby, it hurts."

Barry returned to the team on Saturday, August 30, walking quietly through the visiting clubhouse doors of Arizona's Bank One Ballpark and sidling over to his locker. On one of the shelves Barry placed an old RC Cola can with his father's picture on it. Around his neck he wore a metal necklace, also featuring Bobby's picture on a pendant. One week had passed since his father had died, and Barry decided it was time to get back to baseball.

Bonds spoke in hushed tones to a few teammates, receiving hugs from Marquis Grissom and Andres Galarraga before spending 10 minutes on the couch in Alou's office. After a handful of swings at the indoor batting cage, Bonds walked onto the field and received, of all things, cheers from the Diamondbacks fans.

Bonds was drained and overwhelmed. His mind surely wasn't on hitting a 100-mph fastball. That night, Arizona's starting pitcher was Randy Johnson, a 6-foot-10 intimidator with five Cy Young Awards. "Nobody wants to face Randy," says Eric Young. "Not after just coming back from a tragedy, not in the middle of a hot streak, never." In the top of the first Bonds singled, and at inning's end he spoke briefly with Sidney Ponson, a Giants pitcher. For the first time in weeks, there was a spark in Bonds's eyes. "If he throws me inside one more time," he told Ponson, "I'm taking him deep." Bonds strode to the plate to lead off the fourth, the Giants leading, 1–0. His heart was beating unusually fast, and his mind wandered back and forth between baseball and his father. After starting Bonds off with a ball outside, Johnson fired a heater that caught the inside of the plate.

"Oh boy," thought Ponson. "Big mistake."

Bonds ripped the ball 403 feet into the right-field bleachers for his 40th home run. As the baseball flew, Bonds eschewed his standard show of cockiness. He neither flipped the bat nor offered a superior glare. Instead, he simply put his head down and began to run, eyes watering with thoughts of the man who would no longer call with advice or criticism; who would never call again. After an emotional Bonds crossed the plate and returned to the dugout, Stan Conte, the Giants team trainer, took his pulse. The 150–160 beats-per-minute reading was dangerously high. "You have to come out," Conte told Bonds. "This isn't safe."

Bonds refused. This was for his father. He went 2-for-2 with an intentional walk before finally calling it a night in the eighth inning. Earlier in the year, Bonds had accomplished some amazing feats. His first spring training home run traveled 400 feet and hit the roof of a passing car. During a batting practice session at Coors Field in Colorado, he hit another baseball nearly 600 feet. (Says Giants outfielder Jose Cruz Jr.: "That's when

I knew what The Barry Bonds Show was like.") But what he did in Arizona belongs in its own category. "How can you not pick up a bat for a week and then come back and face Randy Johnson?" says Young. "That's beyond incredible."

"It was spectacular in every sense of the word," says Scott Eyre, a Giants reliever. "Human beings are not supposed to do what Barry did. Not normal human beings."

This is the point where everything changes. Not with the swing of a bat or a fire-breathing fastball or even a managerial call to the bullpen. No, with the publication of a simple newspaper article. The story ran on September 4, 2003, on the front page of the *San Mateo Daily Journal.* Beneath the headline STAR ATHLETE LAB RAIDED, staff writer Dana Yates wrote 331 words that would forever alter professional sports.

> A Burlingame lab that specializes in nutritional supplements and serves athletes including Barry Bonds, Marion Jones and 250 professional football players was raided yesterday afternoon by the IRS and the San Mateo County Narcotics Team.
>
> Agents from the IRS Criminal Investigations Unit and San Mateo County Narcotic Task Force raided Bay Area Laboratory Cooperative, also known as BALCO, located at 1520 Gilbreth Road. Arriving in unmarked cars, agents slipped into the low-profile building with tinted windows at 12:30 P.M. Computer technicians were seen entering the building and boxes of unknown items were removed.
>
> "We're limited on what can be said. All the court documents are sealed at this point," said IRS spokesman Mark Lessler, adding that more information will be revealed today. . . .
>
> BALCO's founder and nutritionist Victor Conte's name is familiar in athletic doping circles. Conte worked with American shot-putter C. J. Hunter at the 2000 Olympics when Hunter tested positive for the steroid nandrolone. Hunter was banned from Olympic competition. . . .

Unknown at the time was that what had transpired was no mere drug raid. A team of more than two dozen FBI agents barged into BALCO's offices armed with guns and the knowledge that Victor Conte was the man who provided steroids to the great Barry Bonds. A pair of agents escorted Conte into a back room, then sat and listened as BALCO's CEO offered a meticulous account of his business operations. According to the book *Game of Shadows*, Conte implicated 27 athletes—15 from track and field, 7 from the NFL, and 5 from Major League Baseball—including Bonds. Conte said he made a deal with Bonds: you promote my legal supplement, ZMA, I hook you up with undetectable steroids, the Cream and the Clear.

Conte then took the agents to the storage locker where he kept his products. For the FBI, it was too good to be true: Boxes upon boxes of performance-enhancing drugs. James Valente, BALCO's vice president, told the agents his company had directly provided Bonds with the Cream and the Clear on a couple of occasions. It was a breathtaking confession.

On the day the *Daily Journal* piece ran, *San Francisco Chronicle* reporter Mark Fainaru-Wada was in his office when Glenn Schwarz, the newspaper's sports editor, approached him. Three weeks earlier, Fainaru-Wada had transferred from sports to news. "I wanted a change," says Fainaru-Wada. "So they had me doing campaign finance reform stories, which were surprisingly boring." Although Fainaru-Wada was no longer in his department, Schwarz needed a reporter to check out this BALCO thing. "No one was terribly excited, because we had no idea what we were looking into," says Fainaru-Wada. "Truthfully, the *Daily Journal* beat us on a story and we were just trying to catch up. It wasn't like the office was beside itself, thinking we were about to embark on some steroid blockbuster. It was just another story."

The next morning Yates wrote a follow-up piece, entitled SPORTS LAB PROBE DEEPENS.

> Sports insiders speculate that Wednesday's raid of a popular sports nutrition center in Burlingame is just the tip of the iceberg in what could put dozens of professional athlete's [sic] jobs in danger.

What started as a raid of one business spread to a nearby gym
yesterday where witnesses report seeing law enforcement agents
questioning Greg Anderson, personal trainer for San Francisco
Giants slugger Barry Bonds. . . .

Bonds offered no immediate reaction to the news, blowing off the irksome media as he'd done countless times before. As usual, the scribes covering the Giants assumed that Bonds's play would go unaffected by the
looming threat of another controversy. For the first time, they were wrong.

On the afternoon of Yates's second story, Arizona came to town for a
three-game series. There was no reason to think San Francisco's left fielder
might feel any pressure. Two days before, Bonds went 2-for-4 with a walk
and a run in a win against the Rockies at Pac Bell, giving him hits in 17 of
the previous 18 games.

At 85–53, the Giants were 13 games ahead in the National League West.
Bonds was once again the MVP frontrunner. Yet in those three games, with
the clouds of a scandal looming, Bonds compiled no hits or RBIs in five at-
bats. It was his longest consecutive-game dry spell all season, the worst one
since July 2001. The Diamondbacks took two of three. Was Bonds's mind
elsewhere? It appeared so.

At the *Chronicle*, Fainaru-Wada first grasped the magnitude of the
BALCO story when he visited the company's website and scanned its roster
of clients. Although Bonds was the biggest name on the list, he was hardly
alone. Conte's services had helped track-and-field stars Marion Jones and
Tim Montgomery, and Oakland Raiders linebacker Bill Romanowski. "It
was eye-opening," Fainaru-Wada says. "These weren't nobodies."

Two weeks after the FBI raids, Fainaru-Wada received an anonymous
telephone call from a man who would become the sporting world's Deep
Throat. The person possessed detailed information about the raids—too detailed for him to be a mere crank caller. "He basically said that this whole
thing is about steroids," says Fainaru-Wada. "That all these athletes will be
implicated and that Bonds will be implicated. The information was clearly
credible. The more we talked, the more I knew he was legitimate."

Though Bonds continued to fend off reporters asking about BALCO, his camp feared that something was about to explode. When approached by reporter Matthai Chakko Kuruvila of the *San Jose Mercury News*, Harvey Shields, one of Bonds's trainers, practically leaped from his jogging suit. "I train Barry Bonds on fitness, stretching and running," he said. "That's all I do. I don't know anything about BALCO. I know nothing about Greg Anderson." The denial might have been believable were Shields and Anderson not veritable coworkers on Team Bonds.

As Fainaru-Wada and fellow *Chronicle* reporter Lance Williams probed further into BALCO's background, they reviewed a fascinating article entitled, "What Fuels Baseball Superhitter Barry Bonds?" that had run three months earlier in *Muscle & Fitness* magazine. In the piece, writer Jim Schmaltz painted a glowing portrait of Bonds and his training regimen. Wrote Schmaltz: "At 6'2", 230 pounds, [Bonds is] in the best shape of his life, which sounds like a hoary cliché until he peels off his shirt to expose sledgehammer biceps and thick, contoured delts worthy of Michelangelo's craftsmanship. It's the physique of a man who works at it." Bonds attributed much of his success to Conte, who he said measured nutrient levels in his blood and prescribed supplements to correct imbalances. The word *steroid* does not appear once in Schmaltz's piece.

"I'm just shocked by what they've been able to do for me," Bonds told the magazine. "Before I didn't understand how important these nutrient levels were, because I was just listening to old standard nutritionists who tell you to just eat 4,000 calories a day. Everyone's body changes over time, and every individual is different. To have your blood drawn and analyzed can tell you what your body produces more of, what it lacks. You're able to create a program that fits for you as an individual."

Alongside the story, the magazine ran a chart of Bonds's day-by-day training sessions. The workouts consisted of an array of exercises, and were in context unrealistic. A 25-year-old man can do a load of crunches and sit-ups and weight work and *maybe* turn into Hercules. A 39-year-old man cannot. When interviewed by the *New York Post*, Sal Marinello, a strength and conditioning specialist from the Millburn–Short Hills Athletic Club in New Jersey, reviewed Bonds's workout and scoffed. "[It] is not and cannot be responsible for the development and maintenance of the Bonds' physique," he said. "To train any athlete in the manner of a bodybuilder is counter-productive and potentially injurious."

Logic dictates that a ballplayer accused of using steroids would face intense resentment from the fans. Why would anyone spend upward of $50 per ticket to witness deception? Yet as the Giants cruised into the playoffs behind Bonds's potent bat, San Francisco fans hailed their star not only as a hero, but as a martyr. "You have to consider who the Giants fans are these days," says Nick Peters, the longtime *Sacramento Bee* baseball writer. "The team plays in a yuppie ballpark, and these are people who have to justify paying their big money to watch a baseball game. What do they come for? They come to see Bonds hit homers."

"The feeling here is that he might be an asshole drug user, but he's *our* asshole drug user," says Michael Silver, a San Francisco–based *Sports Illustrated* senior writer. "It's like your asshole brother. You can talk about what a shit-head he is, but as soon as someone else does it, 'Fuck you.' Barry has brought a lot of fame and glory to San Francisco. As long as he hits home runs, he's OK with them."

Much of the media went along for the ride, too. In a September 14 story in the *Marin Independent Journal*, writer Dave Albee painted the portrait of Bonds picking up a baseball and playing catch with 10-year-old Spencer Vergara in the stands. "We should all understand, even appreciate, what Bonds is going through," wrote Albee. "We're seeing a softer, more compassionate, playful side of Bonds." Dan Le Batard's interview with Bonds in *ESPN the Magazine* concluded with the author writing, "[Bonds] has never been more immortal. Or more human."

As rumors swirled, Bonds basked in the glow of an adoring city still dazzled by his long blasts, and still sympathetic over the loss of his father. On September 15, his first-inning homer off Padres starter Brian Lawrence gave Bonds 655 for his career, leaving him 100 behind Hank Aaron's all-time mark. When the information was posted on the scoreboard, Pac Bell's spectators erupted.

Two days later, San Francisco clinched the division title by beating San Diego, 8–3. As Bonds jogged off the field, the fans cheered until they could cheer no more. Even when the Giants were manhandled by Florida in the first round of the playoffs (during which Bonds batted .222 and was pitched around constantly), Bonds could do no wrong in San Francisco. He was hailed as the inevitable National League MVP (indeed, he won the award after batting .341 with 45 homers, 90 RBIs, and a league-leading .749 slugging percentage). On the streets, fans would stop and offer their unyielding support. "You're the best thing to happen to this city," they'd say. "Keep it up."

In late September, Bonds was subpoenaed by a federal grand jury. The prosecutor had a few questions for the slugger.

About steroids.

NINETEEN

A TARNISHED LEGACY?

No lie ever reaches old age.
—SOPHOCLES

THE LOW POINT OF the steroids scandal may have come on a warm October night in Miami, when Barry Bonds turned the honorable Hank Aaron into a sucker. Before game four of the 2003 World Series between the New York Yankees and the Florida Marlins, Aaron, in town to throw out the first pitch, was asked by reporters to comment on the mounting BALCO furor. Aaron was predictably graceful. "I have complete and utmost confidence that Barry is as clean as a whistle," he said. "I don't have any doubt in my mind. What he's done these past few years has strictly been because he's very talented and is capable of doing it. I don't think there's anybody who can take that away from him."

Nearly three decades earlier, Aaron had experienced a wretchedness only Jackie Robinson could fully comprehend. As he approached Babe Ruth's all-time home run mark of 714, the Atlanta Braves superstar was the subject of repeated racial taunts and death threats. Hundreds of venomous letters found their way into his hands, including one that read, "Daddy, please think about us," attached to a newspaper photo of his 11-year-old daughter,

Dorinda. A student at Fisk University in Nashville, Aaron's oldest daughter, Gaile, received suspicious phone calls; FBI agents advised her to cooperate with her abductors should she be kidnapped. "During my last two years chasing Babe Ruth's record, I felt very isolated," Aaron said. "I stayed at different hotels on the road. My children had to change schools. During her last two years at Fisk my daughter couldn't leave campus. It should have been the best time of my career. Instead, it was a tough time."

By surpassing Ruth's record against the resistance, Aaron elevated a remarkable feat of power and endurance into something far more meaningful. With Aaron atop the leader board, baseball fans were forced to recall the struggle African Americans endured. Aaron was no different from Rosa Parks or James Meredith or Robinson—pioneers who stared down hatred with confidence, pride, determination, and principle.

By 1999, Bonds's first season using performance-enhancing drugs, Aaron had come to know and even like the San Francisco slugger. The two performed together in a humorous commercial for a brokerage firm, and appeared simultaneously at a handful of events. As Bonds inched closer and closer to 755, goodwill oozed from both men. Aaron praised Bonds as a worthy successor. Bonds called the home run king his "idol" and "mentor," glowingly recalling for USA Today's Chuck Johnson a conversation he had with Aaron and Willie Mays. "Both said, 'You represent African-American ballplayers.'" Bonds said. "They talked about how they had to deal with discrimination when they played. They said I have a chance to make it more interesting and more fun for the fans. They told me to ease up and maybe give a little bit more because even though you're trying to accomplish something, the fans also enjoy watching you."

As it became increasingly clear Bonds was cheating his way to hallowed ground, critics began to reckon with the ultimate baseball sin: the illegitimate assault on Aaron's record. How could Bonds profess to idolizing Aaron one minute and illegally pursue his record the next? How could he humbly speak of the nightmares Aaron endured and also attempt to erase his name from the history books? How could he listen to Aaron say, "I believe Barry is clean," and maintain a straight face? "We lie loudest when we lie to ourselves," Eric Hoffer, a noted U.S. philosopher, once said. But in lying to himself, Bonds was also lying to the most beloved of baseball greats, a man who, thanks to his courage and sacrifice, paved the way for Bonds and other African-American ballplayers. "In the twisted world of Barry's head," says Nick Peters, the veteran baseball writer, "that's one thing I don't understand."

With the arrival of the winter of 2003, Bonds was sucked into a whirlwind of accusations from which it seemed he might never escape. When he won his record 11th Silver Slugger award, few noticed. When he was named National League MVP for the sixth time, the news was met by dozens of columns questioning the legitimacy of the trophy. His press conference, ordinarily an occasion for cream-puff queries, was one big drug probe. Bonds dedicated the honor to his late father, and nobody took the bait. The grace period following Bobby Bonds's death had long passed. "Bonds' historic honor didn't come wrapped in organ music and peanut shells and blissful innocence," wrote Ann Killion of the *Mercury News*. "It came with questions about steroid use . . . and tarnished legacies. His unbelievable accomplishment arrived with a large dose of disbelief."

With each passing day the *Chronicle* printed more and more damning articles linking Bonds to performance-enhancing drugs.

October 18, 2003: BONDS SUBPOENAED IN PROBE OF LAB

October 19, 2003: RAID UNCOVERED SUSPECTED STEROIDS

October 21, 2003: MONEY AT HEART OF LAB PROBE; ATHLETES' PAYMENTS TO SUPPLEMENT MAKER SCRUTINIZED

October 29, 2003: STATE TOLD BALCO TO STOP TESTING ATHLETES; REGULATORS HAD THICK FILE ON EMBATTLED LAB

October 31, 2003: GRAND JURY HEARS FROM 5 ATHLETES

The most damaging piece ran on November 23, under the headline DETAILS EMERGE IN RAID ON BONDS' TRAINER:

> Federal investigators seized suspected anabolic steroids in a
> Sept. 5 raid on the home of the personal trainer to San Francisco
> Giants superstar Barry Bonds, according to two sources familiar
> with the results of the search. Investigators who searched the
> Burlingame condominium of Greg Anderson, who supervises

Bonds' weight-lifting program, also found information they
suspect detailed the use of performance-enhancing drugs by
some athletes, the sources said. . . . The information seized from
Anderson's home—some in computer files, the rest in a manila
envelope—contained names of athletes, along with types of
drugs and the schedule on which they were allegedly admin-
istered. . . . Bonds, in the past, has consistently denied using
steroids. He said Tuesday that on the advice of his attorney he
could not comment on the investigation. His attorney, Michael
Rains, said he wasn't concerned by the report about Anderson. "I'm aware that Greg trained a number of other athletes
other than Barry, a lot of nonathletes and bodybuilder types, as
well," Rains said. "Whatever they found, if they did find steroids,
doesn't worry me so far as any relation to my client."

For investigators, the contents of Anderson's abode were a gold mine:
Containers labeled Serostim (a human growth hormone), Depotestosterone
and Andriol (anabolic steroids). Ziploc bags with pills labeled Dyazide and
Aldactone (diuretics banned by many sports organizations). More than 100
syringes, needles, and alcohol pads. Envelopes stuffed with cash ($60,000 in
total) with the first names of famous athletes scribbled on them.

As long as Victor Conte remained the focus of the investigation and the
media, Bonds could maintain he barely knew the man. But Anderson was
different—a lifelong friend whom Bonds personally brought into the Giants clubhouse. There were no more than five people within Bonds's inner
circle, and Anderson was one of them. So when Bonds would later insist
that he was shocked—*shocked!*—that Anderson allegedly distributed drugs,
it was thoroughly unconvincing. "I can't answer any questions about Greg
Anderson," he said during his MVP press conference, "because I don't know
what a person does after they leave me. . . . All I know is Greg Anderson
and I are good friends. . . . But I'm associated with a lot of people. It doesn't
mean I'm involved in anything."

On December 4, Bonds became the highest-profile athlete to appear
before the San Francisco federal grand jury investigating BALCO. Nattily

dressed in a gray suit and tie and accompanied by his attorney, Bonds spent five and a half hours testifying at the Phillip Burton Federal Building. With the media locked outside (and lurking in the hallways), Bonds was assured his testimony would remain private.

Given the nature of the case, that seemed most unlikely.

Clearly, the time had come for Peter Magowan, the Giants managing general partner, to step in. Were one of his lesser players suspected of abusing crack or heroin, surely Magowan would have investigated the situation, and most likely cut the culprit loose. In February 1994, outfielder Darryl Strawberry had tested positive for cocaine (resulting in a 60-day suspension from Major League Baseball for violating his aftercare program). He was immediately released.

With Bonds, however, Magowan continued to behave like a wide-eyed fan. His passive response to the scandal is a black mark on an otherwise successful franchise turnaround. Did Magowan see Bonds's head growing larger? Certainly. Did he see the muscles rippling from a once-thin frame? Of course. Did he hear the rumors? Read the newspapers? Talk to reporters? Have his suspicions? Without question. Magowan, though, never took the simple step of asking Bonds whether he was achieving immortality legally. At November's general manager meetings, Magowan even pushed for a rule change that would award two bases for a second intentional walk and three bases for a third. The gesture was a clear nod toward Bonds, and it was greeted with ridicule. "Memo to Magowan," wrote Carl Steward of the *Alameda Times-Star*. "Just get your cronies to pony up for a real hitter to protect the man. It's that simple."

In Magowan's defense, he behaved no differently from owners and managers of other teams with stars accused to using steroids. When Jose Canseco was tearing the cover off the ball as an Oakland Athletic in the late 1980s and early 1990s, nearly everyone—from manager Tony La Russa on down—suspected he was cheating. Instead of reporting Canseco to the league office, however, the team defended him, challenging anyone who dared question the morality of a Bash Brother. The same went for Ken Caminti in San Diego, Mark McGwire in St. Louis, Sammy Sosa in Chicago,

Jason Giambi with the Yankees. Power meant money, and money trumped integrity. But there was something about Magowan—a genuine decency—that led many in the Bay Area to believe he was better than the others; that he wouldn't stand for less that 100 percent honesty. They were wrong.

In January 2004, President George W. Bush used a portion of his State of the Union address to urge athletes to stop abusing performance-enhancing drugs and challenge professional leagues to vigilantly monitor their players. In February, Conte and Anderson were two of four people indicted by a grand jury for their part in the steroid-distribution ring. "I am saddened by the news of the indictment against my trainer and friend," Bonds said in a statement. "I don't know the matter of the evidence and it would be inappropriate for me to comment on this matter."

Bonds arrived in Scottsdale on February 23, and immediately held his annual spring training press conference. Speaking publicly for the first time since the indictments of Conte and Anderson, Bonds dared his detractors. "They can test me every day," he said. "I don't think we're going to have to talk about it much when all the testing comes out. It's going to come out. You'll be able to see it, and there won't be any questions after that point." Though well aware of baseball's toothless drug policy (as well as the many masking agents that render testing useless), none of the writers in attendance challenged Bonds's statement.

"If I wasn't going for these records it would be a nullified situation right now," Bonds added. "But because of the records, because of what I've been accomplishing in my career, it's just more magnified. Like I tell everybody, 'You want to be on top, you have to have broad shoulders.'"

When asked whether it was fair for his name to be associated with steroids, Bonds shrugged and responded, "Is life fair?"

On March 2, Fainaru-Wada and Williams jointly bylined a front-page *Chronicle* story that, for the first time, bluntly accused Bonds of using steroids. According to the piece, federal investigators confirmed that Bonds, Giambi, Yankees outfielder Gary Sheffield, and three other major leaguers received steroids from BALCO. Wrote Fainaru-Wada and Williams: "Anderson allegedly obtained a so-called designer steroid known as 'the clear' and a testosterone-based steroid known as 'the cream' from BALCO and supplied the substance to all six baseball players, the government was told. In addition, Bonds was said to have received human growth hormone, a powerful substance that cannot be distributed without a prescription, investigators were told."

The news hit like a cluster bomb. Former Giants pitcher Jeff Brantley, now an ESPN commentator, said, "Do I think he had [used steroids]? Yes, I do." Cardinals outfielder Reggie Sanders, a Giant during the 2002 World Series run, noted, "If, in fact, it's proven, baseball should take action. It tarnishes the record." Richard Pound, the chairman of the World Anti-Doping Agency, greeted the news with a weary sigh. "Look at before and after photos of Barry Bonds," he said. "I mean, *hello*?"

Former Pirates teammate Andy Van Slyke said Bonds "unequivocally has taken" steroids. "I never saw Barry as a 50-home-run hitter," he said. "He was too thin and too light. It's like he went from being a Marlboro Light to a Camel unfiltered." Even Reggie Jackson, a special assistant with the Yankees and Bonds's distant cousin, jumped in. "There is a reason why the greatest players of all time have 500 [homers]," he said. "Now, all of a sudden you're hitting 50 [homers] when you're 40 [years old]."

The words were strong, and nothing Bonds could do made them go away. Magowan and Giants manager Felipe Alou remained defensive, and teammates followed the game's unwritten code of loyalty by speaking up on behalf of their embattled star. But more than anything, people around the game seemed to feel that they had been hoodwinked. Maybe Bonds's 2001 pursuit of the single-season home run mark didn't supply the magic of Maris-Mantle or McGwire-Sosa. But for those covering the day-by-day chase, it was the chance to witness history. "You think you're watching a great moment of human achievement only to find out it's enhanced," says Dan Brown, who covered the Giants for the *San Jose Mercury News*. "What if you learned that the Miracle on Ice was set up? That someone had paid off the Soviet goalie? It's just not the same anymore."

On the day after the *Chronicle* report, the Giants positioned Blake Rhodes, the team's director of media relations, in front of Bonds's locker to serve as a Plexiglas shield. When reporter Paul Giblin of the *New York Times* attempted to fire a question at the ballplayer, Rhodes testily barked, "Dude, don't even try it!" When Giblin asked Bonds from afar whether he agreed with Rhodes, Bonds shouted, "Get out of my locker!" The next day a female reporter requested that Bonds address the allegations. "We're not discussing that, sweetheart," he said. As he walked away, Bonds called himself "the most wanted man in America," raised a fist, and hollered, "Black power!"

He thought the scandal would go away. The steroids, the human growth hormones—all of it would surely evaporate into thin air once baseballs again left the ballpark. On opening day of the 2004 regular season, Bonds's eighth-inning three-run homer helped lift the Giants to a 5–4 victory in Houston. One week later, as the sellout crowd at SBC Park (the new name of the Giants' stadium) showered him with standing ovations, Bonds hit his 660th home run against Milwaukee's Matt Kinney, tying Mays for third on the all-time list. Bonds clapped his hands, bounded around the bases, and, upon reaching home, pointed upward in homage to his father. Chants of "*Bar-ry! Bar-ry! Bar-ry!*" filled the air, and Mays immediately limped out of the San Francisco dugout and handed an Olympic torch to his godson.

In other parts of the country, the milestone was greeted with an indifferent yawn—*cheater continues to cheat*. But in the Bay Area, Bonds remained king. Cruising the stands, *Washington Post* writer Steve Fainaru tracked down a myriad of Giants fans. Each one stood in Bonds's corner. Gayle Turner, a kindergarten teacher, hugged her eight-year-old son, Zachary, as her idol circled the bases. "I've seen him," she said of Bonds. "The man is a saint." Even with the regional loyalty, though, Bonds would never again enjoy the sheer pleasure of unquestioned success. At the postgame news conference, Rhodes had to cut off another reporter who tried asking Bonds about drug abuse. The controversy was not going away.

Against the Dodgers on April 16, Bonds hit one of the most awe-inspiring home runs of his career. With his club leading 3–0 in the bottom of the ninth, Los Angeles manager Jim Tracy allowed his closer, reigning National League Cy Young Award winner Eric Gagne, to pitch to Bonds with one out and a runner on first. Gagne knew Bonds was geared up to hit the fastball. Bonds knew Gagne would bring the heat. Gagne got ahead 1–2 with a series of fastballs that were clocked 99–101 mph on the radar. He followed with a 72-mph curveball that Bonds took for a ball, then two 100-mph fastballs that were fouled off. ("One of which Barry was early on," says Giants pitcher Jim Brower. "What human being is early on a 100-mph fastball?") With players on both benches standing, Gagne unleashed a 101-mph zinger that crossed the inside black of the plate. "Gagne has different stuff," says Dustan Mohr, a Giants outfielder. "Nasty, nasty, unhittable stuff that nobody can touch."

Bonds cocked his bat, stepped toward the mound, and launched a base-ball beyond the center-field wall. The Giants were dumbfounded. The Dodgers were dumbfounded, too. "I saw that and thought, 'I'll never be able to do that,'" says Mohr. "Never, ever, ever. It was a home run only the most gifted among us could hit."

Such moments served only as Band-Aids on a broken leg. On the road, Bonds was booed. In newspapers, he was degraded and ridiculed. When a series of KFC commercials he had filmed with former *Seinfeld* costar Jason Alexander produced no appreciable boost in sales, the fast food restaurant allowed Bonds's contract to expire. In late April Bonds homered in five straight games, but the nation reacted with skepticism. When asked about handling the Giants star from a broadcasting perspective, FOX play-by-play commentator Joe Buck shrugged his shoulders. "It's embarrassing when you roll a highlight of Bonds when he was with Pittsburgh," he said. "It's a different human being. How can you not say something about the dif-ference in size?"

In an effort to rehabilitate his image, Bonds hired a team to design and produce www.barrybonds.com, a website dedicated to all things Barry. In-stead of helping to humanize the athlete, though, it served as a reminder that Bonds wasn't especially likable. The site's links section guided readers to the home pages of various corporate sponsors. Even more appalling was the store section, which peddled Bonds merchandise for prices only Don-ald Trump could afford. ($60 for a Microfleece pullover; $214 for a road jersey) "I've been answering e-mails for the past few days," Bonds wrote breezily in his website introduction. "I notice that everyone wants to know when the 660 memorabilia items will be available. I've been looking over the items with my production team. We have some great stuff!"

There was a diary section that was intended to let the world into Bonds's head, yet the largely superficial passages were ghostwritten by others. When the site's creative director bragged to the *New York Times* that Bonds answers at least three e-mail messages a day from places as far away as Iraq, it only made Bonds look more foolish. Aren't you *supposed* to write people back?

It was almost as if Bonds was trying to damage himself. On the field he was as dominant as ever, leading the majors in home runs (10), batting average (.463), and on-base percentage (.704) through early May. Off the field, he remained antagonistic and defensive, often using race as a sledgehammer. Bonds told Gordon Edes of the *Boston Globe* that Boston's racist ways would prevent him from ever wanting to play in the city, then went on a lengthy rant. "All I want you to do when you write your story is list all the white athletes that they say things about, and then list the black athletes that are talked about in a positive way," he said. "Ted Williams will always be positive. Babe Ruth will always be positive. They had a ceremony here at the World Series [the MasterCard-sponsored "most memorable moments," as chosen in fan balloting] and Willie Mays wasn't even in it. How can you not have one of the best baseball players to walk on the planet not there? He was downstairs here, with me.

"How can 70 home runs [McGwire's total] outdo 73?"

In his hands, Barry Bonds held a bat.

"See, we're like baseball bats," he said. "We're equipment. When this breaks, they get another one to replace it. In any sport, you try to do the best you can and don't break, so they don't replace you. That's all I do."

This came not long after Bonds had argued that Houston ace Roger Clemens received special treatment because of his race. (The Astros allowed Clemens to miss games to spend time with his family.) "I ain't white," Bonds said before a game against the Mets at Shea Stadium. "What world you living in? I live in reality. They'll never let a black man get away with that."

Those with an intimate understanding of Bonds watched with increasing horror. He was a man who spoke without forethought, especially when the emotions were running high. "People don't grasp that Barry is not a good communicator," says Michael Tucker, a Giants outfielder. "He doesn't have it in him to sit and talk to you like most people. He'll say five words to you, and all five words will really piss you off. It's just the way he's wired."

For a moment, the frenzy came to a halt. On June 4, Bonds was devastated to learn that Carol Armanino, the mother of his longtime San Carlos pal, Bobby McKercher, had died after a lengthy battle with bone cancer. She was 60 years old.

To Bonds, this was a death in the family. How many afternoons had Barry spent at Bobby's house, having "Ma McKercher" fix him a plate of pasta and talk baseball or girls or school or whatever was on his mind? "She was a mom to all those kids in San Carlos," says Dave Stevens, Bonds's varsity baseball coach at Serra High. "If they got in trouble or had some big news, she was the woman to talk to."

Bonds returned to San Carlos on June 10 to attend a Mass in Carol's honor at St. Charles Church. The building was packed with faces from his youth—Rob Leary and Sam Rossi and Greg McDonald and dozens of others. For a moment, he wasn't Barry Bonds, controversial baseball star, but plain ol' Barry, the kid with the goofy smile and the quick tongue who chugged soda pop and ate like a horse. As he listened to the eulogies, Bonds's eyes welled up. Near the end of the Mass, he spotted a portrait of Carol near the front of the church. He approached the lectern and announced, "You know, before we all go our separate ways maybe we should all take one last picture with Ma McKercher." The old gang gathered around the photograph, Barry just one of the guys.

It felt like home.

The respite was short-lived. Bonds's hope that astonishing baseball would put a rest to talk of steroids was wishful thinking. Not with the *San Francisco Chronicle*'s investigative team breathing down his neck. Not with a mounting army of skeptical fans. Not with more and more opponents scoffing at Bonds's achievements. With each new *Chronicle* piece, the Giants clubhouse was inundated with more journalists looking to add to the scoop. Every day, some unlucky middle reliever or backup infielder would be sitting by his locker, innocently reading the latest issue of *Maxim* or

Baseball America, when a reporter would furtively sidle up and ask if he had a minute to talk.

"I got asked about him more than I was asked about myself," says Jason Christiansen, a reliever. "Most of us became callous to the whole circus. I have my own shit to worry about, so I don't really care about the steroids issue. I certainly didn't want to get asked about it all the time."

Throughout his 11½ seasons in San Francisco, Bonds's looming presence in the Giants clubhouse had always cast a negative shadow. Now the shadow was of Bonds and steroids, and it was larger than ever. As the media came calling—*What's the BALCO investigation been like for you guys? Has the team rallied around Barry? Do you think Barry is using steroids? Is Greg Anderson around Barry a lot?*—any player with common sense spent his free time in the side rooms off limits to the press. It was the only way *not* to discuss Bonds. New to San Francisco after three full seasons in Minnesota, catcher A. J. Pierzynski was shocked by the atmosphere. "I came from a team where everybody did things together, and on the Giants it was like the veterans weren't open to anyone," Pierzynski says. "It wasn't just Barry, but his whole situation certainly wore on people. There was a weight on that team every single day."

On June 24, the *Chronicle* reported that Tim Montgomery, an Olympic track star, told a federal grand jury in 2003 that Bonds had obtained the steroid Winstrol from BALCO founder Victor Conte. Although Bonds angrily replied, "I ain't never met Tim Montgomery" and called him a "son of a bitch," the sprinter's words were corroborated by a statement Conte had made to federal authorities. (Conte maintains he never directly supplied Bonds with steroids.) They also represented a nightmare for Bonds—that the "sealed" testimony of the BALCO investigation would be released to the public. This was more than a possibility—it was inevitable. Every newspaper in the Bay Area was vying for the next day's headline, and somewhere, someone with knowledge had to be willing to talk. Barry Bonds, after all, wasn't Gandhi. He was a man to whom few people felt a personal loyalty.

The shame of the ongoing controversy is that it made another outstanding season difficult for fans to appreciate. The most impressive factor in Bonds's on-field success is an attention to detail that goes unseen. When the Giants are hitting but Bonds is not due up, he often finds a pitching machine and sets it to throw left-handed. "The assumption," says Glenn Dickey of the *Chronicle*, "is that in the late innings the other team will bring in a tough lefty to face him. Say what you want, Barry's mental preparation is terrific." Bonds entered the July All-Star break with 71 intentional walks, surpassing the full-season record of 68 he set in 2002. In a fascinating *Sports Illustrated* breakdown of Bonds's output, writer Tom Verducci noted that of 444 pitches thrown to the Giant through early May, Bonds deemed only 107 good enough to swing at. "He put 59 of those into play, 10 for home runs," wrote Verducci. "An alarming rate of solid, square contact by a rounded bat on a round ball." In Bonds's first 100 at-bats of the season, a pitcher went 0-and-2 against him nine times.

One week after publishing Montgomery's blockbuster testimony, the *Chronicle* ran another damaging report. Former Giants outfielder Armando Rios had confirmed to a federal agent that he had purchased human growth hormone and testosterone from Anderson—Bonds's guy.

Bonds was a man alone in the ocean, desperately trying to stay afloat as the waves grew larger. He would hit a home run and flash his patented "I'm the greatest!" smirk, but outside San Francisco nobody was buying. The glorious moments were coming to an end; the praise waning. Felipe Alou argued that opposing managers should feel obliged to pitch to Bonds if a game was out of reach, but the point fell on deaf ears. *Feel obliged? What for?*

On August 29, with Hank Aaron in attendance, Bonds hit two home runs off former teammate Russ Ortiz in a 9–5 victory at Atlanta. The first ball went 467 feet, the second 462. Afterward, Bonds went out of his way to praise the man he seemed destined to obliterate, without a hint of guilt. "To have Hank there, it's important to all of us," Bonds said. "Hank is always going to be our mentor, just like Jackie Robinson and the black athletes who went through the Negro Leagues and couldn't participate in the major leagues. They're stepping stones for what we are now."

Three weeks later, Bonds became the third man in major league history to hit 700 home runs, when his third-inning shot off Padres starter Jake Peavy traveled three rows beyond the wall in left-center. An announced crowd of 42,526 at SBC Park let out an earsplitting roar, and Bonds received a standing ovation. Before the Giants took the field in the fourth inning, two enormous banners were unfurled from the center-field light towers. Bonds's picture adorned the one to the left, Aaron's and Ruth's the one on the right. A third banner, featuring shots of Mays, Aaron, Ruth, and Bonds and reading, A GIANT AMONG LEGENDS, was displayed along the left-field wall.

In the following day's *Los Angeles Times*, columnist Bill Plaschke condemned fans for prejudging Bonds. "Barry Bonds . . . keeps his eye on the ball," he wrote. "So why can't the rest of us? Why can't America see past the unproven accusations and appreciate the greatest power hitter in baseball history, a man who one day will break the greatest record—755 homers—in sports history?"

Nobody remembers the rest. That the Giants, a strong team for much of the season, finished 91–71 and second in the National League West, two games behind Los Angeles and one game behind Houston in the wild card race. That Bonds ended the year with a .362 average, 45 homers, and 101 RBIs—hands down the best statistics for a 40-year-old in any professional sport, ever. That Bonds was voted his seventh MVP award.

Nobody remembers because, on December 3, the inevitable came to pass. Beneath the headline WHAT BONDS TOLD BALCO GRAND JURY, the *San Francisco Chronicle* ran a 3,265-word story detailing Bonds's supposedly concealed testimony. According to the newspaper, Bonds admitted that he had received and used "clear" and "cream" steroids from Anderson during the 2003 season, but was told they were flaxseed oil and a rubbing balm for arthritis. As if this were not damaging enough, one day earlier the *Chronicle* had reported that Jason Giambi—Yankee slugger and close Bonds confidant—admitted to the grand jury that he used human growth hormone and steroids, and that he was drawn to Anderson because of Bonds's success. He also said that while Anderson did not provide him with the HGH, he was the supplier of most everything else. According to *Chronicle* reports, Jeremy Giambi, Jason's brother and a former major league outfielder, told the grand jury that he had injected banned drugs received from Anderson.

There was more. Two months earlier an anonymous source provided the

Chronicle with a clandestine audio recording of Anderson in which he confided that Bonds was using an "undetectable" performance-enhancing drug during the 2003 season. Anderson also said that he expected to receive advance warning before Bonds had to submit to a drug test under baseball's new steroid-testing program. "Everything that I've been doing at this point, it's all undetectable," Anderson said on the recording. "See the stuff I have, we created it, and you can't buy it anywhere else, can't get it anywhere else, but you can take it the day of [the test], pee, and it comes up perfect."

In the October 4 issue of *Sports Illustrated*, New York Yankees star Gary Sheffield revealed that Bonds had introduced him to BALCO in the winter before the 2002 season. That's when Bonds invited Sheffield (at the time a member of the Atlanta Braves) to stay in his Bay Area house for several weeks so the two could train together. During that time, Sheffield said he was instructed by Bonds's people to use something called "the cream" to heal a surgical scar on the outside of his knee. "I put it on my legs and thought nothing of it," Sheffield said. "I kept it in my locker. The trainer saw my cream." When he learned "the cream" was a steroid, Sheffield said he became incensed. He not only felt angry, but betrayed by a friend.

In the course of his time at Bonds's house, any warm feelings Sheffield had for his host quickly waned. To thank Bonds for taking him in, on February 2, 2002, Sheffield arranged for the two to see the Roy Jones Jr.–Glen Kelly boxing match in Miami. "I was going to pay for the plane, the flight, pay for the limo service, the hotel," Sheffield said. "[Bonds] gets my mail. He looks in my mail and sees he can get better seats, so he gets better seats. He can get a better flight, so he gets a better flight. He can get a better limo service. And he can get a better hotel. So basically my plan, in trying to do something in return, he wound up doing it. And [that type of behavior] just escalated." According to the Yankees slugger, the low point came when Bonds made a covert job offer to Sheffield's personal chef. "That's the kind of person I found out I was dealing with," Sheffield said. "To me, I don't want friends like that. I never will have friends like that."

At last, it had to be over. After Giambi's admission and Anderson's audio recording and Sheffield's accidental use of "the clear" and one *Chronicle* scoop after the other, no longer could anyone logically believe Bonds was a clean baseball player. (Except for the enabling Magowan, who dropped a provision that would have allowed the Giants to free themselves of Bonds's $18 million salary in 2006.) Bonds, who insisted on controlling every detail of his physical well-being, who ate six specially prepared meals per day, each one between 350 and 450 calories, who had his blood and mineral levels tested monthly—he was now maintaining that he'd mistaken steroids for *flaxseed oil*? If Bonds was telling the truth, where was his outrage at Anderson? Why wasn't Bonds screaming murder about his own trainer—a trusted employee—deceptively handing him steroids? Were fans expected to believe that Bonds never once questioned the expansion of his own skull, the acne coating his own back, the muscles that sprouted like fungus on a wet rock?

"I believe Barry Bonds," wrote *Sports Illustrated*'s Rick Reilly. "I believe Bonds never *knowingly* took steroids. I believe Bonds—a man who won't eat buttered popcorn unless he knows its saturated fat content—would put any old thing into his body that his trainer, Greg Anderson, told him to.

"I believe Bonds—a man who has his own nutritionist and won't eat from the postgame spread, a man who studies his own body the way a rabbi studies the Talmud—really thought he was using 'a rubbing balm for arthritis,' as he told the grand jury, not a steroid. . . .

"And I believe reindeer fly, President Clinton did not have sexual relations with that woman, and Rogaine really can re-grow your hair. Now, if you'll kindly move out of the way, I believe I'm about to get sick."

In the midst of a darkening steroid cloud, the seven-time MVP came to New York City on Friday, December 10, to play his part in a bizarre coda to the season. In the Astor Ballroom of the Marriott Marquis Times Square, Bonds and Yankees third baseman Alex Rodriguez spent approximately two hours mingling with 70 fans, each of whom had paid handsomely for the opportunity.

The shindig was billed by promoters as "The Ultimate Event," but this was the grossest of understatements. In exchange for the ticket price, a scant $7,500, not only did wealthy fans spend *at least* five minutes each with Bonds and Rodriguez ("I got 12 minutes out of Barry!" gushed Ari Malatlian, a Sarasota, Florida–based architect), but they dined on a bevy of appetizers that featured shrimp, caviar, and four varieties of cheeses. An end-of-the-evening gift bag included A-Rod/Bonds blue jeans, cranberry cognac, a coupon for a custom-made dress shirt, and a Jim Thome action figure.

Kept at bay by hotel security were five reporters who snuck up to the seventh floor and hid behind a Christmas tree near the elevator bank. Whenever the word "Bonds!" was heard, the journalists would peek out, only to be threatened with expulsion by Jason Barron, the hotel's overzealous acting general manager. At one point Ron Dicker, covering the event for the *Chronicle*, passed a note to a security guard, requesting comment from an event organizer.

"Get lost," was the reply.

If the unease stemmed from Bonds, there was good reason. A couple of days earlier, Rodriguez announced that he would donate his profits from the event to charity. Bonds had no such intention, and he and his handlers were livid with A-Rod for setting the Giant up as Evil Money Grubber.

The crowd inside the ballroom, however, seemed not to care. By all accounts Bonds was charming and chatty. "I just don't think somebody could put on a performance like that and it be fake," said Vince Donahue, a memorabilia collector from Denver. "He was a wonderful person to be around. It changed my opinion. He's a good man."

Fortunately, none of the guests was overly curious: Event planners had agreed beforehand that anyone who questioned Bonds on his use of steroids would be forcibly removed.

Money be damned.

TWENTY

THE PICNIC TABLE MONOLOGUES

IN JANUARY 2005, THE powers that be at ESPN asked Pedro Gomez to attend a meeting at the network's offices in Bristol, Connecticut. A long-time newspaper writer, most recently for the *Arizona Republic*, Gomez had jumped to TV two years earlier, intrigued by a career change and the opportunity to earn substantially more money. In his first full year as a television reporter, Gomez enjoyed the here-today-there-tomorrow nature of the gig. One day he'd be tracking Josh Beckett of the Florida Marlins. The next day it'd be Yankee Stadium and Bernie Williams. The beat was fun, there was no threat of writer's block, and he didn't mind the occasional "Hey, you're the ESPN guy!" airport recognition.

On this afternoon in Bristol, everything changed for Gomez.

"We've decided that the Barry Bonds watch is too big of a story to cover from time to time," said one network executive. "We want somebody to follow him on a daily basis beginning with spring training. We think you're the right guy for the job."

Gomez swallowed hard. Cover Bonds? *Daily?* Wasn't there a blocked toilet to plunge? A water-logged corpse to drag? Anything?

"That," says Rod Beaton, the *USA Today* baseball writer, "might be the worst job in America."

The 42-year-old Gomez became Bonds's shadow, tailing him from the clubhouse to the field, from the field to the batting cage, from the batting cage to the dugout. Fellow reporters felt sympathy for Gomez's plight. Players found the whole scene comical. "Hey Pedro, Barry's not gonna talk to you!" pitcher Kirk Rueter would bark across the clubhouse on a near-daily basis. "He's not here! So now you can leave!"

What kept Gomez afloat was his love of history. A baseball buff since his boyhood in Miami, he often wondered what it would have been like to track Hank Aaron's pursuit of Babe Ruth. "If I could do something like that now," says Gomez, "it would be a dream come true."

He quickly discovered the Barry Bonds beat would not be a buffet of monumental home runs and flabbergasted SBC Park crowds, but one of negativity, innuendo, legal posturing, word play, and hour upon hour of frustration.

Gomez's debut on the Bonds Watch came on the morning of February 22, 2005. It was a day fans, critics, teammates, and opponents alike had been anticipating—the day Bonds reported to spring training and addressed the press for the first time since the steroid reports of two months earlier. More than 120 media representatives attended Bonds's scheduled State of Barry press conference. There was a gunslinger's aura in the air. No more intimidation. No more BS. The evidence of cheating was concrete, and the press was anxious to hammer the issue.

Since Bonds's last sighting, even more incriminating news had been reported. On February 12, Geraldo Rivera of FOX News interviewed Kimberly Bell, Bonds's longtime girlfriend and mistress. Bell supplied the network with ample proof of her status as Bonds's Girl (a horrible pun, and also the working title of Bell's book)—a sheaf of airline tickets, love notes, and photographs. At Rivera's urging, she also confirmed Bonds's steroid use. "He told me between 1999 and 2000 that this is something that he was doing," Bell said. "The way he explained to me was that what he was using was helping him recover quicker from his injuries. And that as a result of that it caused the muscles and then the tendons to grow at a faster rate than the joint could handle."

Two days later a second bomb detonated in the form of the release of

Jose Canseco's autobiography, *Juiced: Wild Times, Rampant 'Roids, Smash Hits and How Baseball Got Big*. Along with admitting his own steroid abuse, Canseco—the former Oakland A's slugger—tattled on such alleged users as Mark McGwire, Rafael Palmeiro, and Ivan Rodriguez. "The simple fact," he wrote, "is that Barry Bonds was definitely using steroids."

So here they were. Bonds and the media, together in one room. Over the ensuing half hour, the world (thanks to well-placed ESPN cameras) would be treated to one of the most entertaining, fascinating, breathtaking, confrontational press conferences in recent memory. Nursing his right knee just weeks after arthroscopic surgery, Bonds hobbled to the lectern, grunted, and leaned into a chair. He wore blue jeans and a black short-sleeve shirt, and his head appeared to be freshly shaved. There was a nakedness to the man; a disconcerting mortality. He was a superhero stripped of the cape and tights.

When Henry Schulman of the *Chronicle* placed his tape recorder on the table, Bonds snapped "You can't have yours on there, Henry." Moments later, he spotted Gomez. "Hey Gomez," he asked, "you still lying?"

Jim Moorehead, the moderator and Giants media relations manager, began by instructing those in attendance that Bonds would answer absolutely anything *but* BALCO-related inquiries. Seconds later, a reporter fired the first shot. . . .

QUESTION: "Barry, can you explain over the last four or five years your amazing production, your expansion in tremendous growth in muscle strength getting stronger as you get older? Can you finally put to rest and point blank say how all this happened?"

BONDS: "Can I?"

QUESTION: "Yes."

BONDS: "Hard work, that's about it. Now it's to rest."

QUESTION: "That's it?"

BONDS: "That's it."

An awkward silence followed. Where was this heading? In spring training sites throughout Florida and Arizona, players stared in disbelief at clubhouse televisions. Though Bonds appeared neither nervous nor contrite, his body language—arms crossed, face rigid—told the story of his emotional state: a wounded animal trapped in a corner. Reporters held up their hands, eager to be *the one* to trip up Bonds.

QUESTION: "Barry, you know, I understand legally you're not allowed to answer a lot of the questions people would like to ask. Do you look forward to the day when maybe you can set things straight and you can come right out and be honest?"

BONDS: "I look for the day for you guys to stop being a rerun show and this thing will blow over and everybody will go about their business as though it has. Baseball, sports, basketball, football will continue on.

"It's just sad that, you know, this is where sports has become a spectacle now. It's not—it's become comical and it's sad, because we're not—we're not trying to make it comical because we're not writing the stories. You know, we're just trying to go out there as human beings and do our job."

QUESTION: "Through all of this controversy, it has to have taken an emo tional toll on you. Have you lost sleep over this?"

BONDS: "You know, the part that I lose sleep over is my family and my kids and what pain—which I say—should I blame you guys for it? There's no facts on Barry Bonds, but should I blame you? Who should I blame? Who should I blame for the things that go on that my kids have to listen to? Who should I blame? You know, I don't. I tell my kids, you know what, just don't be famous. If you don't want it, don't be famous. You know what, let people say whatever they are going to say."

QUESTION: "Who do you blame? Is it the people who are writing stories about the grand jury testimony or the fact that a grand jury was called? What do you see as . . ."

BONDS: "We're not even on grand jury testimony. We just told you that about 15 times, didn't we? We need to move on."

Every so often, someone would interject a question that had nothing to do with drugs, and the mood would lighten. Bonds felt optimistic about the upcoming season. His knee was improving. He was excited to play with new teammate Moises Alou.

Nobody cared. Not one person. This wasn't about baseball. Bonds and Moorehead be damned, this was a steroids press conference. "We were all there for one reason," says Daniel Habib of *Sports Illustrated*. "To hear

Bonds explain himself." Those present recall the air growing thick with tension, almost as if smoke was streaming into the room.

QUESTION: "Right or wrong, true or false, a lot of the allegations and accusations, particularly involving Canseco's book, people are saying it's damaged the game. Do you agree with that? And if so, does it bother you that it's damaged the game that you play for a living?"

BONDS: "I don't—I think a lot of things have damaged sports with a lot of just the whole . . . everything. But there's a lot worse things going on in our world, a lot more worse. You should focus on fixing those first."

QUESTION: "Jason Giambi felt the need to kind of give a blanket apology. Is there anything that you need to apologize for?"

BONDS: "What did I do?"

QUESTION: "Well, he talked about the grand jury testimony."

BONDS: "Yeah, but what did I do? I'm just sorry that we're even going through all this rerun stuff. I'm sorry that, you know, this fictional stuff and maybe some facts, who knows? I'm sorry that, you know—we're all sorry about this. None of us want to go through this. None of us want to deal with this stuff. We want to go out and do our job. But what's your purpose and what you're doing it for—rewriting it, writing it over and over and over and over again. What's your reasoning? What are you going to apologize for when you're wrong?"

Bonds's facial expression had changed. When he first entered the room, there had been a trace of a grin; proof that he was an uncrackable nut. Now he could barely smirk; his eyes went black, his nostrils flared. If reporters were going to make this personal, Bonds would shoot back.

QUESTION: "Guys have asked you about your knees and you mentioned a setback. What we've been told from the beginning since July 31 when you had this operation, was that you would be ready to play in an exhibition game no later than the 15th of March and there . . ."

BONDS: "Where did you hear that from?"

QUESTION: "That was what was in the release, I believe that was . . ."

BONDS: "Why do you guys never give up your source? Who? Name, name, name, please."

QUESTION: "Stan Conte [the Giants head athletic trainer]."

BONDS: "Stan Conte did not say that, that's a lie. I know for a fact Stan could not have said it. See, you guys . . ."

QUESTION: "The official release . . ."

BONDS: "See, you lied. You lied. Next question."

Finally, after more than 20 minutes of meandering back-and-forth exchanges, a reporter swallowed hard and pulled the pin on the grenade. No more beating around the bush.

QUESTION: "Barry, have you ever inadvertently or otherwise used steroids?"

The ballplayer didn't so much as flinch.

BONDS: "Why do you keep asking me the same question? I'm not a child, OK. You repeat those things to children and eventually they tell you. I don't."

QUESTION: "One of the things Bud Selig talked about a month ago at the owners meetings was the integrity of the game and working on that. Do you believe that's been damaged, and if so, how? He called on Jason Giambi to come clean or say 'I'm sorry' or whatever. What's going to be your approach, as such a high-profile person in this game, to repair it from here on out? Do there need to be admissions made, and are you expecting other people to come clean and move forward?"

BONDS: "We just need to go out there and do our jobs, just as you professionals do your job. All you guys lied. All of y'all. In the story or whatever—you have lied. Should you have an asterisk beside your name? All of you lied. All of you have said something wrong. All of you have dirt. All of you. When your closet's clean, then come clean somebody else's. But clean yours first, OK.?

"But I think right now baseball just needs to go forward. You guys need to turn the page and let's move forward. Let us play the game, and we will fix it. I think we all want to, I think we all have a desire to. I think we all are hurting, including myself."

QUESTION: "How can we move forward if we don't know what we're moving forward from? What are we moving forward from?"

BONDS: "OK. Strike one, ball one, one out, cheer, boo, yeah, game over, let's go home. I mean, what else do you want to talk about? You know, there's a sports world—the sports world is as bad as it is because this is the only business that allows you guys in our office to begin with. You can't just go to Bank of America, walk in the office, start interviewing employees. Just the sports world. What for? Well, we don't want to get into the money aspect of it—we'll leave that to the side.

"But now, don't turn it into a spectacle now just because you have the freedom to come into our office and snoop and make up stories if you choose to, because, you know, a lot of it's not true. I mean, baseball players, every baseball player I know of—and I've been around this game since I was a child—all care about this game, all love this game, all have had their own personal problems or nonpersonal problems. But for the most part, no one goes out there and wants to embarrass the game of baseball, no one wants to go out there and embarrass themselves. I don't want to go out there and embarrass myself in front of people. I don't want people looking down on me. No one does.

"You know, unfortunately we have different personalities or different agendas. But if some of us are treated different than others, like I am, I get treated a little bit different than others, but that's kind of like fun for me, though; at times, I like it. It keeps me going. It makes me want to go out there and prove you wrong. That's my driving force to being the player that I am. You know, when you don't talk about me, I kind of get lonely a little bit and figure out something I need to do. But that's me. That's not everybody else, you see what I mean?"

QUESTION: "Barry, you've accused a lot of people here who you don't know of lying . . ."

BONDS: "Wow, wow, did you do it to me? Wow."

QUESTION: "Have you lied about anything?"

BONDS: "Yeah, I lied to my parents when I was growing up. Lied to my friends. Have I lied about baseball? Yeah, I told a couple of stories that I hit a couple of balls a couple of places that I really didn't, yeah. That's about the extent of it."

QUESTION: "Do you view the use of steroids as cheating?"

BONDS: "As cheating? I don't—I don't know what cheating is. I don't know if steroids are going to help you in baseball. I just don't believe it. I don't believe steroids can help you—eye-hand coordination—technically hit a baseball, I just don't believe it and that's just my opinion."

QUESTION: "You talked about protecting your family. When your kids come home and they tell you stories of your reputation under attack, what do you say to them?"

BONDS: "None of your business, because I wouldn't let you in my house."

With that, Bonds rose and limped off. Once the dialogue had been absorbed, many of the journalists were outraged. What had just happened? Was Bonds turning the tables on them? "I was amazed at the whole thing," says Bill Madden, the *New York Daily News* baseball writer. "There are a lot of players like Bonds who think we love writing about this stuff; who think we live to dig up dirt on the game. That infuriates me. I happen to love this game and cherish this game, and if anyone thinks I'm happy watching its downfall, they're crazy."

Throughout spring training camps, most players had a different take. True, many disliked Bonds, but they weren't big fans of the media, either. In Winter Haven, Florida, Cleveland Indians pitcher Chad Zerbe nodded appreciatively. "I thought Barry did a great job," said Zerbe, a former Giant. "Because the press tried to get him again to admit he used steroids. And he won't do it. He's gonna stick to what he said from the beginning."

At Washington Nationals camp in Viera, Florida, outfielder Jeffrey Hammonds—also a former Giant—took it a step further. "Barry is a throwback to the heroes of the past," said Hammonds "He presented himself as another Muhammad Ali—the kind of athlete who doesn't come around so often. Some call it defiant. I call it strong-willed."

If Bonds's ranting press conference was an hors d'oeuvre, the meat and potatoes were soon to follow. Again displaying a surprising naiveté, Bonds genuinely believed his State of Barry address had put the substance abuse controversy behind him. In January, Major League Baseball initiated a new testing policy, stipulating a one-year ban after a fourth positive finding. Shouldn't that have finally shut the damn press up? What more could they possibly want?

Bonds soon found out. On March 9, the U.S. House of Representatives' Committee on Government Reform subpoenaed 11 former and current Major League Baseball players and executives to appear in Washington one week later for a congressional hearing on steroid use in baseball. Among the men called to testify were commissioner Bud Selig and union head Donald Fehr, along with Red Sox pitcher Curt Schilling, Orioles first baseman Rafael Palmeiro, Cubs outfielder Sammy Sosa, and former Cardinals first baseman Mark McGwire. Also on the list was Jose Canseco, whose inflammatory book on steroid abuse had sparked a forest fire of interest and accusations.

Notably absent was Bonds. "We want this hearing to be about baseball and steroids and the health of kids around the country," said David Marin, the committee's deputy staff director. "With Bonds, the hearing becomes about Bonds, as anyone who's heard his recent ramblings about the issue understands." If Bonds took this to be a lucky break, he misread the magnitude of the hearings. Under 11 hours and 15 minutes of intensive questioning from a panel of 44 congressmen, a national viewing public watched Canseco willingly spill his juiced guts, Sosa dodge questions with a sudden outbreak of Me-English-No-Speak-Very-Good-itis, Fehr squirm like a worm on blacktop, and McGwire impugn himself with a persistent refusal to "talk about the past."

"Theatre of the absurd," was how the event was described by California representative Tom Lantos—politicians flexing their muscles, athletes hiding theirs. Those who bemoaned its minimal immediate impact missed the point. No previous congressional hearing had drawn so many TV crews. Baseball was humiliated for the whole world to see. There was no more denying reality—the national pastime had been contaminated by liars and cheats.

Though Bonds was 2,400 miles away in Scottsdale, his presence was felt. Without Bonds, without BALCO, would this all be taking place? Was Congress truly concerned that *Rafael Palmeiro* might be ingesting steroids? No, this was a battle about the history books and the soul of a game that represented America. If Mark McGwire broke Roger Maris's single-season home run record under the influence of drugs, what did it say about the sport we loved? And if Bonds were to surpass Hank Aaron in the same manner, using the same drugs, well, how could anyone take baseball's honor and integrity seriously again?

In nearly all posthearings media reports, Bonds was prominently mentioned. Though he wasn't physically in Washington, his was the face of steroids *in* baseball. The name. The stats. The scowl.

The essence of Bonds's 2005 season was distilled on Tuesday, March 22—at a picnic table. That's where Bonds sat himself outside the Giants spring training facility on a breezy Scottsdale morning, mere minutes after an hour-and-a-half meeting with team trainer Stan Conte.

The news was not good. One week earlier Bonds underwent his third knee operation in five and half months. Hobbling around on a pair of stainless steel crutches, the Giants star feared his career might be over. The optimism from recent BP sessions was dead. If injuries had been all that was weighing on Bonds's mind, perhaps frustration would not have morphed into furor. But the powwow with Conte came less than 48 hours after the *San Francisco Chronicle* had run a front-page story highlighting Bonds's nine-year extramarital affair with Kimberly Bell. The article was painfully precise, providing previously unknown names, dates, and financial data that detailed Bonds's relationship.

As Bonds exited Scottsdale Stadium, the last person he wanted to see was Henry Schulman, the *Chronicle*'s Giants beat writer. "Hey, Barry," said Schulman, "do you have a couple of minutes?"

"Get away," said Bonds. "I will never talk to you again for the rest of my life."

Bonds found his way to a nearby picnic table, where a slew of media representatives gathered. Bonds refused to speak unless Schulman departed. So the reporter left. "I'm just going to try to rehab myself to get back to, I don't know, hopefully next season, hopefully the middle of the season," Bonds said. "I don't know. Right now I'm just going to take things slow."

This was a Barry Bonds few had seen. Beaten down. Defeated. His expression was one of pure resignation, like a downed boxer listening passively to the count. "I really don't have much to say anymore," Bonds said.

"My family's tired. You guys wanted to hurt me bad enough, you finally got there.

"You wanted me to jump off the bridge, I finally have jumped. You wanted to bring me down. You finally brought me and my family down. Finally done it. From everybody, all of you. So now go pick a different person. I'm done. Do the best I can, that's about it."

When asked to elaborate, Bonds muttered away. "Inner hurt, physical, mentally. Done. I'm mentally drained. I'm tired of my kids crying. Tired."

Bonds's raw display did not play well. Here was a man who had taken illegal drugs to enhance his baseball legacy; who had spent most of his two decades in the majors abusing teammates, fans, opponents, clubhouse attendants, and media representatives. Now *Bonds* was suddenly the vulnerable punching bag? "He is America's victim, craning his neck to blame everyone else in the room, looking all around for the loudest slanderers when in reality all he's ever needed to do is look in the mirror and have a glance at his own enormous head," wrote Mike Vaccaro in the following morning's *New York Post*. "Listening to Bonds expound on life really has grown terribly tiresome even before this steroids morass he helped fuel; now it's like listening to Lenny Bruce at the end, reading from his court transcripts on stage and obscuring everything he once had been."

Sitting next to Bonds was his son Nikolai, 15 years old and outfitted in baggy jeans, a Barry Sanders Detroit Lions jersey, and the sullen look of one who'd rather be anywhere but here. On any given day, it was hard enough being the teenage son of a self-aggrandizing father. Now the media were swarming around him.

As photographers and TV cameramen aimed their equipment Bonds's way, the embattled Giant saw an opportunity. "You guys need to get my son in this [shot], too," he wailed, "so you can show the pain you caused my whole family."

To those who knew Bonds—who *really* knew Bonds—using his adolescent son to make a point crumbled a final façade of decency. Even among his critics, there had always been the admission that, despite his many faults, he was at least a loving, involved family man. Nikolai had spent several seasons as one of the Giants batboys, and at the conclusion of each home run

Bonds would stomp on home plate and plant a kiss on his son's lips. The heartwarming gesture was more than enough to conceal that, in truth, he was at best a mediocre role model for his kids.

Away from the spotlight, Bonds was much like his own father—stern, aloof, condescending. When Nikolai was younger, Bonds often berated the boy as he shagged fly balls during Giants BP, wondering aloud, "How do you not catch that?" and "What the fuck are you doing?" Clearly, Nikolai would not continue the family's athletic legacy. (As a sixth grader, he placed 80th out of 131 runners in the Independent School Athletic League Cross Country finals, finishing the 1.95 mile run in 15 minutes, 49 seconds.) This frustrated his father. How could his only son be so *mediocre*?

As Nikolai and Shikari, his two children with ex-wife Sun, grew older, they chose to spend less time with their dad, often passing on planned visits to remain home with their mother. Once regulars in the Giants clubhouse, they now appeared sporadically. Barry complained to his ex-wife that the kids only wanted to see him when it was coupled with a trip to his house in the Caribbean. "I'm never with them anymore," Bonds told a reporter in 2004. "They're old enough to decide who they want to be with, so the ball's in their court."

Against Bonds's wishes, Sun enrolled Nikolai in Valley View School, an expensive North Brookfield, Massachusetts, boarding academy that, according to the facility's website, offers "a year-round therapeutic environment for boys between the ages of eleven and sixteen who are having difficulty coping with their family, the world around them, and themselves." Bonds preferred that Nikolai attend Serra, but he was overruled. The boy needed special attention. Father and son were farther apart than ever.

"Barry's one of those guys who has everything," says Ann Killion, the *San Jose Mercury News* columnist. "All the talent in the world, all the money in the world. But I think he has kind of a shitty life."

Whenever things have gone wrong for Barry Bonds, the Giants slugger has found sanctuary on the diamond. Never was this truer than on the afternoon of April 5, 2005, when the people of San Francisco once again embraced their favorite son. This opening day was the franchise's 47th since relocating from New York and—as always—Bonds spent the pregame hours lounging in his black leather recliner, watching ESPN and chatting on his cell phone.

Despite the trappings of routine, the day was anything but normal for the superstar. Stuck on the 15-day disabled list with his knee problems, Bonds was merely a spectator—a terribly uncomfortable position for a ballplayer who had never missed the season's first game. Even before the injury, there was little for Bonds to say to his teammates, some of whom were young enough to be his sons. Now he felt like a cripple. An old cripple.

When the Giants were introduced in a pregame ceremony, everything changed. Bonds limped onto the field and buried his face in his hat as a roaring ovation rained down. As the Giants retreated to the dugout, Bonds was called back out to receive his seventh MVP trophy as well as the Silver Slugger award. The noise grew more deafening.

"I'm speechless," Bonds told the crowd. "I want to thank my family for being behind me for all these years. I thank God for the blessings he's given me to be able to play this game. Last but not least, I thank the city of San Francisco. I thank these fans. There are no better fans in the world."

Bonds paused for a moment, perfectly setting up the ensuing four words.

"I will be back!"

One more wave of noise filled the stadium and Bonds picked up his hardware, pointed to the sky, and headed into the dugout.

"For one afternoon, one beautiful opening day by the bay, Barry Bonds felt an outpouring of appreciation he may not have known existed—not like this," wrote William C. Rhoden in the *New York Times*. "The afternoon reinforced the cliché: there really is no place like home."

Regrettably for Bonds, opening day proved to be the highlight of an otherwise dreary season. Despite nonstop rumors of his impending return to the lineup, it became increasingly clear that Bonds was a long way from being game-ready. As hope of a resurrection waned and Bonds's status became a subject of mounting curiosity, focus turned to the dysfunctional relationship between the player and the franchise.

To the embarrassment of Peter Magowan, not one Giants executive actually knew what Bonds was up to. As the season progressed, he checked in with the front office with audacious infrequency, rarely showing up for games or training at the ballpark. On April 9, the *San Francisco Chronicle* reported that—to the surprise and dismay of the organization—Bonds was still working out regularly with Greg Anderson, even after the trainer's indictment and after five major leaguers swore under oath that Anderson had supplied them with steroids. "In the conservative world of legal advice, I have told Barry that it was probably better that he not have contact with Greg," said Michael Rains, Bonds's attorney. "But I've had enough discussions with Barry to know what friendship means to him. He values his friendship with Greg and always has, as well as the training regimen Greg has given him."

Those scratching their heads at such poor judgment did not know Bonds's history. Throughout his life, Bonds refused to be held accountable to someone else's standards. If he wanted to play a shallow center field with the Pirates, there was no other way. If the media were bothering him—fuck off. And if he wanted to train with Greg Anderson—his lifelong friend and longtime supplier—well, who the hell were the Giants or Major League Baseball to say otherwise?

The Giants, naturally, knelt, kissed Bonds's hand, and continued to grant their $20 million employee his every wish. Instead of presenting the media with regular updates on the star (as any other team would have), the franchise ordered all personnel to remain silent on matters of Barry. If Bonds wanted to talk, he'd talk. If he didn't want to, oh, well.

With information as rare as the Seattle sunshine, there was only one place left to turn—www.barrybonds.com.

April 23, 2005

Hello fans,

I just wanted to give you an update of what happened Thursday, 4/21. I had some fluid drained out of my right knee because there was a little bit of swelling. By draining the fluid, it alleviates the discomfort. My doctor wants me to use crutches for the next couple of days to make sure the fluid doesn't come right back. This was merely a precautionary measure. My spirits are still high about my recovery as a whole and I can't wait to get back to rehabbing next week.

The media has been requesting daily updates, but I feel it is best for everyone to hear about my status directly from me—without any spin. Day to day, there isn't much change on my knee, but when there is something significant, like Thursday's events, I am able to report to you exactly what's going on.

On Friday, I had a great day at the ballpark. I participated in the "Buses for Baseball" program put on by the Major League Baseball Players Trust. Fifty students from Martin Luther King Middle School came and visited with me in the dugout prior to the game. I spent some time talking with the kids, finding out what sports they play. A funny moment happened when one of the young ladies came to up to shake my hand, but instead jumped up and gave me a giant bear hug. I don't know who was more surprised she did it, me or her! There was nothing like seeing the smiles and energy from those kids—it makes me want to get back out there on the field.

During Spring Training, I attended a press conference at my alma mater, ASU, announcing the re-naming of the stadium to honor coach Jim Brock. After the announcement, I spent some time with the baseball team during their batting practice. I had a great time and was able to give the guys a few hitting pointers. Jeff Evans from ASU sent me this link today. Check it out.

Barry Bonds

This is what it had come to: News of Bonds's recovery was available via one source—his own website, which seemed to take pride in mocking the media's denied access. From Bonds's vantage point, it was perfect. He could say what he wanted sans risk of misquotation or mention of the dreaded S-word.

With or without the aid of the mainstream press, it was obvious that Bonds's spring training prediction of a late-May return was way off. On May 4—after an infection in his right knee—Bonds underwent yet another operation, performed for the third time by Dr. Arthur Ting. Unbeknownst to the Giants, Ting had twice been disciplined by the state medical board and was on probation through 2009 for "unprofessional conduct." Had the Giants, say, insisted that Bonds use the team physician, Ting's status would not have mushroomed into the major Bay Area story it became. "The reality is that he's trying as hard as he can to get back," said Larry Baer, the Giants chief operating officer. "And if you've had an 18-year career and won seven MVPs, you might have an idea or two how you can best get back on the field. We're going to respect his ideas. You have to be open to it."

The Giants were held hostage by Bonds—they would be updated, along with everyone else, only when the spirit moved him to provide information. Was Bonds taking BP off a machine? Was he shooting up in a gym with Anderson? Was he starring in *Die Fledermaus* at the Bayview Opera House? Your guess was as good as Magowan's. One day Bonds was feeling great. The next day he was on intravenous antibiotics. When Baer told *USA Today* that Bonds's relationship with the team was, "outstanding," the local media couldn't help but laugh. *Outstanding?* Baer didn't even have Bonds's current cell phone number.

Finally, Brian Sabean had had enough. After Ting's third try at Bonds's knee, the Giants general manager stepped in and demanded changes. In early July he announced that Bonds was now being looked at by doctors recommended by the Giants, and that a new line of communication would open at once. This was the street-tough Sabean at his best, but it came too late. The PR damage was done. Bonds had played the Giants for fools.

Though there was panic and confusion in the front office, a newfound tranquillity had entered the Giants clubhouse. San Francisco would go on to suffer through a disappointing 75–87 season, but the atmosphere was looser than it had been in years. Without a dark presence hovering above the room; without having to tiptoe around Bonds and his posse, players could be as loud and jovial as they wanted. "When I first arrived in San Francisco, Barry's mannerisms bothered me a bit," says Brett Tomko, a Giant pitcher in 2004 and 2005. "I didn't like the tone it set in the clubhouse—you say hello to someone, that person should say hello back. I mean, I got used to it.

But with him not here, there was a load taken off. It doesn't mean we were a better team, because obviously you want that bat. But the clubhouse was definitely more relaxed."

For Giants players, the best part about Bonds's absence was the silence. In past years, journeymen and stars alike would be chased down by pesky prodders with notepads and microphones. Now, obscure pitchers like Jim Brower and Scott Eyre were left to their magazines and handheld video games. "If you're shy or uninterested in attention, the benefit to being a teammate of Barry is that very few people ask about you," says Jason Schmidt, the veteran pitcher. "But if you mind being asked a lot of Barry Bonds questions, it's probably not the ideal place to play."

While Bonds remained out of sight, spending most of his time at his Beverly Park home and working in Los Angeles with Angels orthopedist Dr. Lewis Yocum and physical therapist Clive Brewster, he was never completely out of the news. On May 31 sports talk radio spent the day addressing Bonds's apparent racism after a thorny passage from the recently released autobiography of former major league outfielder Ron Kittle made the newspapers. In *Ron Kittle's Tales from the White Sox Dugout*, the author recalled once asking Bonds to autograph some items for a charity, to which Bonds replied, "I don't sign for white people."

After being blasted by commentators across the nation, Bonds fired back. "Who is Ron Kittle?" he said. "How long did he play? He played in our league? Ha! Do you guys believe that? Do you guys know my life history a little bit? One, you insult my children, who are half-white. I was married to a woman who was white, so let's get real. Tell [Kittle] he's a fucking idiot. Somebody said he wanted a piece of me. Tell him I'm at 24 Willie Mays Plaza and he can come get me anytime he wants to—with pleasure."

On June 1, Bonds wrote on his website that his knee was progressing, and that he had recently played catch for the first time since the surgery. Nine days later he made a rare on-field appearance, taking part in a 10-minute workout with a team trainer. The Giants expressed hope that Bonds would return as a designated hitter in interleague play by month's end. In early July, however, Bonds admitted to new swelling in his knee. "My outlook is still positive," he said.

Throughout the year, there had been much behind-closed-doors speculation on the true nature of the injury. Was Bonds's knee as bad as he was saying? Or was this some sort of ploy, perhaps to keep himself as far away from the steroid controversy as possible? On baseball's myriad blogs, fans seemed torn on the issue. Some were convinced it was more than coincidence that Bonds was suddenly hurt. Others saw a 41-year-old man's body breaking down and chalked it up to the grim reality of aging.

Truth be told, Bonds *was* hurting, and anyone who came into contact with the superstar saw the agony in his face. He wasn't hiding. He was disabled. On August 1, Bonds conceded for the first time that he would likely not play in 2005. "I don't think you're going to see me out there this year," Bonds told mlb.com. "That's the reality of the situation."

And then, against the odds, Bonds's knee began to improve. In late August he took two days of batting practice at UCLA and experienced only mild pain. A few days later the Giants came to Los Angeles and Bonds worked out with the team. Again, no big problems. "I did pretty well today," Bonds said after an exhausting-yet-productive round of exercises. "When I get back on the field, I want to be playing where I left off."

On September 12, 2005, Barry Bonds was penciled into the Giants lineup for the first time all season. That the team was 64–78 and seven games behind San Diego in the National League West race didn't matter. That the tranquillity of the San Francisco clubhouse was suddenly shattered didn't matter. That Bonds hadn't faced live major league pitching in nearly a year didn't matter. There was a buzz to Bay Area baseball again. For months, swaths of empty seats had been the norm at SBC Park, and vendors and ticket scalpers bemoaned bone-dry sales. "Say what you want about Barry," said Clay Pandorf, who peddled hats near the stadium, "but he brought excitement. Without him, the scene is dead."

Outside SBC Park, 1,142 fans walked up to purchase tickets for the night's game against the visiting Padres. An impressive 39,095 spectators attended overall. It was as if, after a season of seeing Brad Oscar play Max Bialystock in *The Producers*, Nathan Lane was returning for a final-month run. The Barry Bonds Show was must-see.

Inside the stadium, as most of the Giants took the field for 4:20 stretching, Bonds relaxed in the clubhouse in front of his four lockers. His television was turned to CNN, and inches away Harvey Shields, one of Bonds's trainers, was fetching his boss a cup of coffee. "Four-twenty stretch!" yelled relief pitcher Scott Eyre with a smile, knowing that Bonds would join the team for pregame drills as soon as the earth turned pink.

Bonds's debut at-bat came in the second inning, and for the first time in years he appeared slightly apprehensive in the on-deck circle. Bonds had never gone this long between plate appearances. On the mound, Padres starter Adam Eaton had no plans of avoiding a crippled 41-year-old superstar. He threw Bonds 10 pitches before the 11th cruised across the outside portion of the plate. Bonds swung forcefully, driving a ball to the far reaches of the outfield. Could this really be happening? An if-you-wish-upon-a-star *Welcome Back!* home run?

Almost. The ball was soaring toward the top of the outfield wall when a fan reached out and grabbed it. Double. Bonds stood on second base, breathing heavily but elated. Though it was his only hit of the night, it was more than enough to rekindle the fire. The Giants won, 4–3, which was only a footnote to the news.

RETURN OF THE KING, screamed the front page of the *San Francisco Chronicle*.

BACK WITH A BANG, yelled the front page of the *San Jose Mercury News*.

BONDS IS BACK, AND STILL SLUGGING, roared the front page of the *Sacramento Bee*.

The following afternoon at 4:45 Bonds sauntered out of the dugout for BP. Before reaching the field, he was stopped by a group of fans with ALL ACCESS badges dangling from their necks. The winners of a team-sponsored auction, they thrust balls and pens in the star's direction. Head down, mouth shut, Bonds signed.

FAN ONE: "Barry, used to live in Pittsburgh! Loved ya with the Pirates."

BONDS: (Silence)

FAN TWO: "You're my favorite player! Welcome back!"

BONDS: (Silence)

FAN THREE: "Thanks for doing th—"

BONDS: (Jogs off before thought is completed)

Once on the field, Bonds positioned himself next to 38-year-old short-stop Omar Vizquel, one of the few Giants who played in the 1980s.

"Man, I'm sore," said Bonds.

"Man, we're old," replied Vizquel.

In that night's 5–4 win over San Diego, Bonds singled and walked twice, but it wasn't the statistics that stood out. It was the pain. Bonds's feet ached from wearing spikes for the first time in months. His knee throbbed and stiffened from the crisp Bay wind. In between innings, he retreated to the training room to have his legs rubbed. "Everyone thinks great athletes age gracefully," said Ray Durham, the Giants' 33-year-old infielder. "Not true. We hurt as much as anyone."

On September 16 Bonds hit his first home run of the season, a solo shot off Dodgers starter Brad Penny that landed in the center-field bleachers and brought a sellout crowd of 42,962 at SBC Park to its feet. The homer was the 704th of his career, leaving him a mere 10 behind Babe Ruth on the all-time list. As a humongous "704" flashed across the scoreboard in bright lights, Bonds circled the bases quickly and purposefully, with his head down and face expressionless. When Penny later bemoaned what he called "a stupid pitch," Bonds showed old arrogance dies hard. "I've hit a lot of stupid pitches," he said. "What's one more?"

Two days later Bonds was at it again, clubbing a fastball from Dodger reliever Hong-Chih Kuo into the waters of McCovey Cove. That afternoon, in between cheers for Bonds, a reporter roamed the stands of SBC Park, polling random fans on two questions:

A. Do you believe Bonds used performance-enhancing drugs?

B. Do you care if Bonds used performance-enhancing drugs?

The results were eye-opening. Though 92 of 100 respondents were certain Bonds had cheated, only 24 of 100 were interested. "If you look around, every athlete gets bigger as they get older," said Marc Shapiro, 50, who shared a pretzel with his seven-year-old son, Adam. "And even if he was using, so is everyone else. Is that really wrong?"

"Why would Barry cheat?" asked Ryan Reynolds, an 18-year-old student from Oakland. "He has great bat speed, great talent. What would be the point? Anyhow, I don't think the Giants would let someone do that. They're a great organization."

As Reynolds spoke, a man in a neighboring seat held a miniature TV. Across the screen flashed a FOX Sports commercial that featured only two words: HE'S BACK! Surrounding Reynolds, a packed house gorged themselves on garlic fries and sushi and hamburgers. Reynolds was wearing a Bonds Giants jersey, as were hundreds of other spectators. The place was hopping. The cash registers were humming.

Perhaps most noteworthy to those who covered the Giants was the reception Bonds received away from the Bay Area. When the team traveled to Washington, D.C., to face the Nationals, most assumed Bonds would be lustily booed in the home city of the recent steroids hearings. Instead, Bonds hit an upper-deck home run at RFK Stadium and was saluted with a standing ovation. "It's my conclusion that no matter what people feel about Barry, they want him to hit home runs," says Schulman. "They feel like it's something special to see."

The Giants won 11 of their final 20 games, pulling within three games of the first-place Padres before finishing third. Bonds's return was a resounding success—his five home runs and 10 RBIs came in only 14 games, and not once did he pull, tweak, or bruise his tender muscles. Throughout the Bay Area, Bonds brought excitement and pride back to town. Once again, there was anticipation for 2006. Bonds would enter the season with 708 home runs. Maybe, just, maybe he could muster the 48 needed to overtake Hank Aaron. At the least, he would storm past Ruth. "You wonder what more he can do," said Giants outfielder Todd Linden. "Seeing Barry up close, you realize anything is possible. If you can think it up, he can accomplish it."

Near season's end, Bonds began talking a bit more. Though his words were mostly dull and clichéd—the sort of blather athletes feel comfortable surrendering to the writers—there was one moment, in an interview with Barry Bloom of mlb.com and Janie McCauley of the Associated Press, when Bonds let his guard down. Asked about his playing weight, which was reported at 228 pounds, Bonds did not hedge. "I'm going to be skinny [next year]," he said, pledging to drop to 200 pounds. "I want to get my legs strong again. Hopefully I'll train hard all winter. I can hit it, but I don't feel like I feel when I'm strong. I can tell out there. I'm older now. It's harder." In baseball's lengthy history, Bonds was arguably the first fit player who'd vowed to drop 30 pounds in an off-season. Were he Terry Forster or Dick Radatz back in their hefty heydays, nobody would have batted an eye. But Bonds's words came toward the conclusion of one of the most controversial seasons in baseball history.

Over the course of the year, 12 major leaguers were suspended for violating the game's drug policy. Though most of the men were second-tier talents like Alex Sanchez and Agustin Montero, one name stood out. On August 1, it was announced that Orioles first baseman Rafael Palmeiro had tested positive for a banned substance (the steroid stanozolol). Only four and a half months earlier, Palmeiro had sat before Congress and made the strongest statement of any of the four active players called to testify. "Let me start by telling you this," he said. "I have never used steroids. Period. I don't know how to say it any more clearly than that. Never."

Now that Palmeiro had been deemed a fraud, it would be difficult to take ballplayers seriously again.

Even those with 756 home runs.

TWENTY-ONE

SHADOW DANCING

WHEN HE WOKE UP on the morning of March 7, 2006, surely Barry Bonds thought this day would be no different than any other. Why should it be? With rare exceptions, the life of a professional athlete is a testament to regimentation and repetitiveness. Bonds would drive to Scottsdale Stadium, lift some weights, eat a little breakfast, scowl at the media, walk out to the cage.

He had no idea what was in store.

At 1 P.M. Eastern Standard Time, *Sports Illustrated*'s website posted a portion of an excerpt from an upcoming explosive new book by Mark Fainaru-Wada and Lance Williams. In *Game of Shadows*, the two *San Francisco Chronicle* investigative journalists closed the door on any lingering doubts (if there were any) of Bonds's cheating by reexamining his history with remarkable precision—names, dates, drugs all included. Most damaging were details from Bonds's "sealed" grand jury testimony of December 4, 2004, when he told prosecutors that he had no idea what Greg Anderson and Company were dumping into his body.

"I have never, ever seen this bottle or any bottle pertaining that says de-potestosterone," Bonds said when prosecutor Jeff Nedrow showed him a jar of one particular steroid.

What about Clomiphene? he was asked.

"I never heard of it," responded Bonds.

And Erythropoietin, aka EPO?

"I couldn't even pronounce it."

Modafinil?

"I've never heard of it."

Bonds was also asked about an entry on Anderson's calendar, which read: "Barry 12-2-02 T, 1CC, G—pee."

"T could mean anything," Bonds replied. "G could mean anything. And pee could probably mean anything."

Wrote Fainaru-Wada and Williams: "Nedrow seemed pleased. It had been a slow process, but the prosecutor understood why it had taken so long: When you know what a witness knows, and they won't tell you what you know they know, it takes more time. . . .

"[Bonds] left the room confident that he had asserted control over the government's inquiry, just as he controlled his baseball team and, for that matter, most of the people in his life. His reputation had been preserved and his well-guarded secret had not been revealed. But as the government would learn, Bonds and his inner circle hadn't been so discreet about his use of performance-enhancing drugs."

In short, Bonds had lied to a grand jury, and most everyone in the room knew it. With this revelation now available to readers nationwide, there was speculation of jail time; of baseball's greatest all-time player going up the river on charges of perjury. Adios, Barry.

Yet even as the *Sports Illustrated* issue containing the full 14-page excerpt hit mailboxes over the ensuing week, Bonds was blessed with—of all things—relative indifference. After one day of "Kill Barry!" uproar, the world seemed to move on. "I don't worry about that stuff," Bonds told reporters with a passive shrug of the shoulders. "We can react about baseball questions or we don't have a conversation. That's my reaction."

And so it went.

Bonds's testicles had shrunk to the size of peanuts? *Ho-hum.*

Bonds popped more pills than Robert Downey Jr.? *Big whoop.*

Bonds's closest friends were named Winstrol and Deca-Durabolin? *Yawn.*

There were other headlines to be written. National Football League owners extended the collective bargaining agreement. The Dubai-based DP World dropped out of a deal to operate several American ports. Matthew McConaughey and Sarah Jessica Parker had a new romantic comedy. March Madness was coming.

Commissioner Bud Selig suggested he might finally look into the whole Bonds-drug thingamajig, but he also might fly to Vegas for the weekend, or head home and rent *The Cable Guy*.

By the time Bonds made his spring training debut in a game against the Angels on March 9, it was as if *Game of Shadows* had come out years ago. He stood along a railing and signed autographs for dozens of fans, not one of whom seemed bothered by the latest developments. When he was announced for his first at-bat, there were boos, but an equal smattering of cheers. ESPN announced it would still air its upcoming Bonds's reality program, *Bonds On Bonds*. Willie McCovey, the legendary San Francisco slugger, went so far as to protest the validity of the charges. "We're supposed to live in a world where you're supposed to be innocent until proven guilty," McCovey said. "He hasn't been proven guilty of anything."

Under normal rules, this was the point where a reporter interjects, "But Willie, the proof is un-*friggin'*-deniable!" Alas, nobody did. There was a spring-training game to watch. Hot dogs to eat. Sodas to slurp.

Members of the Giants—by now well versed in the art of saying nothing—supported Bonds by refusing to take the bait. "We should be focused on baseball," said Steve Finley, the new Giants center fielder. "That's what most people are concerned about."

Remarkably, he was right.

THE DEBATE OF IMMORTALITY

> When you come to the ballpark, you're walking into a place
> that is all deception and lies.
> —BARRY BONDS

IT IS SIX YEARS from now. Maybe seven. You are one of the nation's 500-plus Hall of Fame voters, and your ballot has just arrived in the mail. You urgently open it, anxious to see one name. You knew he would be there, of course. Everyone knew he would be there. But to actually view the 10 letters printed on the official piece of paper is daunting.

Before making a decision, you break out the National Baseball Hall of Fame guidelines. Under the heading "Method of Election" is a list of criteria for eligibility. One sentence stands out: *Voting shall be based upon the player's record, playing ability, integrity, sportsmanship, character, and contributions to the team(s) on which the player played.*

Barry Bonds. Yes or no?

Yes. "Look at what he's done defensively and offensively," says Rick Hummel of the *St. Louis Post-Dispatch*. "Throw out 300 home runs from his suspicious years if you'd like, and he's still got 400. He's an unbelievable talent."

No. "What bothers me more than the steroids is that he lied and lied and lied about it," says Dale Hoffman of the *Milwaukee Journal Sentinel*. "Character goes a long way when it comes to entering the Hall. And he hasn't shown any."

Yes. "No matter what suspicions we've had, he's still had a great career," says Mike Kiley of the *Chicago Sun-Times*. "Look at his numbers, his production. Despite the churlish attitude, Bonds makes baseball look easy."

No. "There's no way I'll vote for him," says Bill Livingston of the *Cleveland Plain Dealer*. "The biggest record in sports is the home run record. It's sacred. And he cheated. I won't vote for any of these steroid guys. What they did to the game is terrible."

Yes. "In an age where everybody took [steroids] he was still 20 percent better than anyone else," says Joel Sherman of the *New York Post*. "And if we establish that he wasn't taking until the late 1990s, that's still a Hall of Fame career."

No. "If I had a pill that would make me Ernest Hemmingway, maybe I'd take it," says John Erardi of the *Cincinnati Enquirer*. "But I didn't have that opportunity. I believe very strongly that we're put on this earth with certain gifts, and the idea is to maximize them properly. Unlike scuffing or corking, performance-enhancing drugs physically change who you are. It's crossing a line that should never be crossed. I'm a purist. Barry Bonds goes against everything I believe."

When Bonds finally does appear on the Hall of Fame ballot he will be, statistically speaking, the most qualified candidate in the long history of the game. No one else has exceeded 500 home runs and 500 stolen bases, hit 73 home runs in a single season, or won seven MVP awards. Entering the 2006 season, Bonds was 48 home runs shy of breaking Hank Aaron's all-time mark. Among baseball journalists, there was a general belief the Giants star would require two more years to make history—that no 42-year-old man coming off three knee surgeries could be *that* productive.

What gets overlooked in this discussion are the two decades Bonds spent silencing the unbelievers. Accused of being a terrible outfielder, he went on to win eight Gold Gloves. Derided as a postseason choker, he compiled a World Series for the ages. Considered the game's second-best player behind

Ken Griffey Jr., he proceeded to dwarf The Kid's statistics and accomplishments. Hence, it should surprise no one if, come September 2006, Bonds is twirling his bat, jiggling his fingers, and cocking his elbow in the name of immortality. "I believe he'll do it," says J. T. Snow, the longtime Giants first baseman. "If Barry wants something badly enough, he'll always find a way."

In the early days of the 1974 season, as Hank Aaron prepared to overtake Ruth, he encountered the sort of hatred only the strongest of human beings could have withstood. His children were threatened. His wife was threatened. His *life* was threatened. Each time Aaron took the field, he glanced toward the stands and wondered, "Is today the day somebody is going to kill me?" It had been six years since the murder of Dr. Martin Luther King Jr. in Memphis, and the racist South was still racist. When Aaron sent a baseball beyond the left-field wall of Atlanta-Fulton County Stadium on April 8, 1974, he struck a blow not only for the Braves, but for sports, for civil rights, for humanity. As a result, baseball rightly saluted Aaron as a hero; as a man whose skill, decency, and integrity made him an ideal holder of the game's noblest achievement.

But what about Bonds? Surely commissioner Bud Selig has already pondered his uncomfortable options when the record is broken. Will Selig stop the action, walk to home plate, and salute the Giant as a wonderful man, a worthy successor to Hammerin' Hank and an example of all that's good and righteous about the game? With nearly everyone inside baseball in silent agreement that Bonds has abused performance-enhancing drugs, does Selig do his best to put a happy face on an awkward moment? Or does he skip the night all together, as he did when Bonds bypassed McGwire's single-season mark in 2001? Does he pretend it never happened, and hope it all just disappears?

The moral dilemma confronting Hall of Fame voters is even greater. For those veteran scribes who have covered the game for more than a decade, there is a singular reward for missed wedding anniversaries, absentee parenting, and the never-ending road trips from Milwaukee to Detroit to Cleveland to Cincinnati. It is the honor of being a Hall of Fame voter—of deciding whether a man is worthy of immortality.

The Hall of Fame has endured its controversies, but never one like this.

While voters occasionally debate the merits of Pete Rose, the all-time hit king was banned from the game for life, rendering his Cooperstown worthiness a moot point. Bonds, on the other hand, will appear on the ballot, calling into question the very purpose of the Hall of Fame. Is such a place constructed solely to honor on-field greatness, or does character play a part?

"It might be the greatest debate the Hall has endured," says Bill Madden, the *New York Daily News* baseball writer. "There are so many arguments to be made on both sides of the issue. Nobody can argue that Bonds wasn't a terrific player. But a lot of us can argue that he's not worthy of being inducted."

To earn a spot in the Hall, a nominee must be selected on at least 75 percent of ballots. In a random poll of 80 Hall of Fame voters contacted for this book, 58 said they would definitely select Bonds on the first ballot. That's 72.5 percent—not quite enough.

Does this signal that Bonds is doomed for failure? No. What it means is the questions and doubts swirling through the minds of voters must be answered in a satisfactory manner.

If steroids were not outlawed in baseball through most of his career, did Bonds truly cheat?

Those in the slugger's corner correctly argue that, because it took the game until 2003 to officially declare steroids against the rules, Bonds never broke any of Major League Baseball's guidelines. "There was no legislation," says Hummel of the *Post-Dispatch*. "So if he was using, he had every right to do so."

Hummel makes a strong point. However, the anti-Bonds faction notes that all baseball ordinances fall under the laws of the United States of America. With that in mind, Bonds's possession and use of steroids without medical need is illegal as documented in the Controlled Substances Act. "You can't break the law and expect to be honored," says Daniel Habib of *Sports Illustrated*. "It makes no sense."

**If Bonds was one of many players of his generation to abuse perfor-
mance-enhancing drugs, why should he alone suffer?**

As baseball continues to increase the intensity of its testing policy and
the severity of its punishments, this will become less of an issue. "If baseball
does this the right way," says Scott Ostler of the *San Francisco Chronicle*,
"then eventually you would hope anyone who takes steroids will get caught."

Until then, however, there are only two options for Hall voters: Let absolutely everyone with Cooperstown-worthy statistics in, regardless of suspicions; or use all available knowledge, however damaging. Bonds's steroid
abuse is undeniable. So is that of Jose Canseco, Rafael Palmeiro, Mark Mc-
Gwire, Ken Caminiti, and Jason Giambi. "There are a lot of stars who have
surely used steroids without getting caught," says Bob Klapisch of the *Ber-
gen Record*. "But that's not a good enough reason to ignore those we know
have used. If you've clearly cheated, that must be considered."

**Hasn't baseball always been a sport where players use every possible
advantage?**

Here, the oft-cited example is Gaylord Perry, the Hall of Fame pitcher
who, over a 22-year-career, proudly perfected the spitball to baffle and be-
fuddle major league hitters. "Perry and Bonds are one and the same," says
one veteran writer who requests anonymity. "They both broke the rules. So
why does Perry get in?"

Now 67 years old and living on his farm in Williamston, North Carolina,
Perry was inducted into the Hall thanks to 314 wins and the game's best
spitball. But while saucing up a baseball was, technically, cheating, Perry
says there's a difference between him and Bonds. For one, Perry never
broke the law. "It's not even in the same category," says Perry. "Corking bats
and putting stuff on the ball is a bunt compared to the grand slam of cheating—steroids. You're talking about putting stuff into your body that causes
major health problems and alters your physical makeup. Spitballs are crafty.
Steroids are illegal."

Adds Bob Feller, the Hall of Fame pitcher: "You use steroids, you don't
deserve the honor of being among us."

If steroids were so important, wouldn't every weight lifter be a major league star?

"There's nothing harder in sports than hitting a baseball," says Evan Grant of the *Dallas Morning News*. "It'd be wrong for people to overlook Bonds's results just because of steroids."

Though Grant does not overstate the difficulty of connecting with a 95-mph fastball, his words—uttered by many who cover the game—discredit the power and effectiveness of performance-enhancing drugs. As noted earlier in this book, former Giants second baseman Jay Canizaro said steroids made him feel superhuman—immensely powerful, and able to spend long hours in the gym without fatigue. The advantage over the competition is huge.

Human growth hormones, meanwhile, are steroids times 1,000. They supply an even greater amount of energy and strength, and also have been shown to enhance vision. Is Bonds's legendary eye for the ball truly legendary? Or simply altered? We'll never know.

Wasn't Bonds a Hall of Famer before he cheated?

The answer to this is an undeniable *yes*. Entering the 1999 season, when he first used steroids, Bonds had already become the only player in history to eclipse 400 home runs and 400 stolen bases. He was an eight-time All-Star and three-time MVP who won Silver Slugger awards in seven of eight seasons.

The question voters must ask themselves is whether statistics are enough. In this area, history is on Bonds's side. From Ty Cobb to Steve Carlton, the Hall is filled with bigots, sexists, homophobes and (in Perry's case) cheaters. They are in not for their personal values, but because they were the best of the best of the best. By that standard, Bonds belongs.

If there is one thing we know for certain about Barry Bonds, it's that he's destined to leave the game the way he played it—alone. On any given day, Bonds can cruise through the Giants clubhouse without uttering a word to teammates. His closest associates—his publicist, his trainer, his videographer—are paid employees. Will the relationships last when the paychecks cease?

Should Bonds earn entrance into the Hall of Fame, it's hard to fathom who will serve as his presenter. With his father deceased, there remain only a small handful of people who consider Bonds a true friend. Willie Mays is one. Bobby Bonilla is another. He will return to the stadium as a retiree, and few—if anyone—will greet him with joy and sincerity.

"Life is more than how you play a game," says Andy Van Slyke, his former teammate. "It's how you influence the people around you while you have the chance. Barry might be the greatest player who ever lived. But if there's a Hall of Fame for decency, he doesn't earn a vote. And that's sad. Very, very sad."

ACKNOWLEDGMENTS (AKA "THE FLEMING FACTOR")

AS A FRESHMAN AT Mahopac High School in 1986, I found myself permanently situated near the front of the school bus—home to zit-faced geeks in turtlenecks. On one particular morning, Scott Wunderlich and I engaged in a back-and-forth game of sports trivia.

"Who," I asked, "led the Rams in rushing in Super Bowl XIV?"

From behind, I heard a voice quietly utter, "Wendell Tyler." Turning around, I was shocked to see Dave Fleming—*the* Dave Fleming—answering my question.

In the 10 years that we lived less than a half mile away on Emerald Lane, those were the only two words Dave had ever directed toward me. Yet I recall the exchange as if it were a week ago. Mahopac's star jock was wearing a blue T-shirt and jeans. His brown hair was parted down the middle. The seats were green, and his had a piece of silver electrical tape covering a penny-size hole. I suppose Dave's car was in the shop, because to see a senior of his stature alongside a loser like myself was rare.

I bring this up not to spark interest in Mahopac's favorite son (Dave went on to pitch in the majors for four and a half seasons), but because, two decades later, that simple conversation inspired the philosophy behind this book. In the course of researching *Love Me, Hate Me*, I interviewed 524 subjects, a number of whom had but a singular memorable experience with Barry Bonds. A person might not recall what was served for breakfast this morning, but he will always relish the time Anita Baker walked by and nodded; or Manute Bol stepped on his loafer; or George Peppard borrowed a pen.

This phenomenon is officially anointed "The Fleming Factor."

I made it my goal to interview not simply the Sid Breams and Dusty Bakers from Bonds's life, but to find anyone and everyone with a story. The real estate agent who sold Bonds a house. The bartender who served him beers. The housekeeper, the dog walker, the nosy neighbor, the gardener. If you've spent more than three minutes with Bonds, I likely contacted you.

So first and foremost, I'd like to thank all the people who returned my phone calls and spoke candidly about a most fascinating and controversial figure. I'd especially like to tip my cap to the 26 Sun Devils, 58 Pirates, and 98 Giants who were willing to break baseball's unofficial code of silence and chat freely. An extra-large dose of gratitude goes to two of Bonds's former San Francisco teammates: Brian Johnson, whom I now consider a friend, and Jay Canizaro, whose honesty will forever be appreciated. From the Pirates, Gary Varsho, R. J. Reynolds, and Andy Van Slyke stood especially tall.

Writing a book is a nightmare. I noted such in the acknowledgments section of my first biography, and it remains true. Yet with the right support staff, it can turn into something magical. An author is not an island, but the point man on a team. My agent, David Black, has shown me the power of positive, hands-on representation. If others in the book biz are Alex Van Dyke, he's Wesley Walker. I am equally indebted to David Hirshey and Nick Trautwein, two excellent, virtuous men who represent HarperCollins with class, decency, and untouchable skill.

A writer is nothing without his editors, and I have had my ass kicked by quite a few. Michael Lewis of the *Daytona Beach News-Journal* is not only one of the best wordsmiths I have ever encountered, but a helluva friend. I would be lost without L. Jon Wertheim and Stephen Cannella, two former *Sports Illustrated* colleagues whose support and insight are invaluable. Chris Knutsen surely wishes me a one-way trip to hell (or Delaware), but I am most grateful for his patience and deft touch. I hired two reporters for this massive endeavor, and both Casey Angle and Ian Begley dove into a sewage bin of tattered notes, faded clips, and indecipherable memos with aplomb. Huge thanks.

I would be remiss not to thank my longtime friend Paul Duer, the all-time scoring leader at Sylvia Lane. Paul's nose for righteous information is vital.

Early in the process, I was inspired by conversations with two of the great sports biographers of our time: Leigh Montville, author of *Ted Williams*, and Mark Kriegel, author of *Namath*. Double thanks for the boosts.

My former bosses at *Newsday* were incredibly understanding when I asked for time off. I am especially grateful to Barbara Schuler and Pat Wiedenkeller, the two most supportive, insightful editors I will ever work for.

Promoting a book is challenging, and luckily I have been represented by some of the best in the biz. Norma Shapiro of Waterworks, Inc., is incomparable, and Leah Guggenheimer has treated me not as a client, but as a brother. I knew I was in good hands when Laura Cole, my Florida regional manager, read the manuscript and said, "Bill could not have done this." Stanley Herz, executive, author and president of the Somers Rotary, spreads the word as well as anyone I have met

Throughout the summer of 2005, I did most of my writing at the Panera in Wayne, New Jersey. General Manager Tim Fyock provided a warm smile and a corner table seven hours per day—even when my lone purchase was a $1.09 Mr. Pibb. His staff of merry sandwich makers, including Wes, Beth, Evelyn, and Godfrey, made the time pass pleasurably. Equal thanks to Mike and Sandi Friedman of Camp Vacamas, who supplied a corner office, rent-free. Big ups to the staffs of the New Rochelle Public Library and the Eastchester Starbucks, and an eternal note of gratitude to Joy, Taj, and Linda at the *Sports Illustrated* library.

Were I to list every player, coach, reporter, friend, and colleague who assisted, the acknowledgments would stretch 12 chapters. But without some, this book doesn't work: Russ Bertetta of Junipero Serra High School, Sally O'Leary and Jim Trdinich of the Pittsburgh Pirates, Blake Rhodes and Jim Moorehead of the San Francisco Giants, Jim Lachimia, Gil Pagovich, Richard and Maggie Monaghan, Kristen Go, Iefke d'Aguiar, Elaine Murphy, Jenna Hislop of the Beaufort Chamber of Commerce, Jill Murray, Greg Kuppinger, Dr. Michael Sinkin, Rebecca Tollen, Henry Schulman of the *San Francisco Chronicle*, Pedro Gomez and Rob Tobias of ESPN, Jay Horwitz and Ethan Wilson of the New York Mets, Jeff Evans of Arizona State and the Texas Rangers, Doug Foster, Dave Gregorio, Chloe Weil, Chris Costa (for the Serra yearbook), and John Oates. A special nod to Bev Oden—researcher, friend, and survivor. Thank goodness you're still here.

I have missed far too many family events these past two years, and for this I beg forgiveness. My parents, Joan and Stan Pearlman, remain the best role models and friends a son could ever imagine. Without their support and encouragement, I would have never followed my dream of becoming a writer. Thanks to Richard, Susan, Jessica, Laura, Rodney, Leah, Jordan, and Isaiah for all the understanding.

To my daughter, the incomparable Casey Marta, gracias for the cuddles, the giggles, the smiles, the hugs, the kisses, the Peter Criss references, and—most important—the perspective.

And then there is my wife. When she agreed to marry me some four years ago, Catherine was surely unaware that all my sentences would begin, "When Barry Bonds . . ."; that her home office would be converted into a Bonds-related crack den; that I would wake her at 3 A.M. with excited shouts of "I reached Curtis Wilkerson! I reached Curtis Wilkerson!"; that a book would take precedence over, say, our anniversary.

Luckily, I married the most loving, supportive, understanding, good-natured partner a person could ask for. Earlie, thanks for enduring two years of hell. You are my oxygen.

NOTES

CHAPTER ONE: 70

8 **Giants first base coach Robby Thompson** Josh Suchon, *This Gracious Season*, p. 349.

10 **On September 15, after he posted 94 strikeouts** Jeffrey Parson, "Pitcher Spent Most of Season in Texas," *Wichita Eagle*, October 5, 2001.

12 **"I'll never forget that"** Dave Newhouse, "Straight from Barry," *Tri-Valley Herald*, February 13, 2002.

CHAPTER TWO: **BIRTH OF A BALLPLAYER**

16 **Those traits were pioneered by Barry's grandfather** Lance Pugmire, "A Bonds to Recall," *Los Angeles Times*, October 18, 2002.

17 **Located 50 miles southeast** George Sullivan, *Bobby Bonds: Rising Superstar*, pp. 16–17.

18 **Or they'd head to a field** George Sullivan, *Bobby Bonds: Rising Superstar*, p. 17.

18 **"I wouldn't want to"** George Sullivan, *Bobby Bonds: Rising Superstar*, pp. 16–17.

19 **Bobby once scored six touchdowns** Ron Fimrite, "Getting It All Together," *Sports Illustrated*, April 8, 1974.

20 **"My mom's family put"** Steven Travers, *Barry Bonds: Baseball's Superman*, p. 28.

21 **In addition to an $8,000 signing bonus** George Sullivan, *Bobby Bonds: Rising Superstar*, pp. 26, 27.

21 **Seven months later, . . . Bobby reported** George Sullivan, *Bobby Bonds: Rising Superstar*, pp. 29–30.

21 **One time, after he singled** George Sullivan, *Bobby Bonds: Rising Superstar*, p. 32.

22 **When Pat and Barry returned** George Sullivan, *Bobby Bonds: Rising Superstar*, p. 34.

23 **While Bobby's statistics were not eye-popping** George Sullivan, *Bobby Bonds: Rising Superstar*, pp. 40–41.

24 **Pat became a regular customer** Dave Anderson, "The .300-100-100-30-50 Man," *New York Times*, October 5, 1990.

24 **Though he did not change** Jeff Savage, *Barry Bonds: Record Breaker*, pp. 13–15.

25 **It wasn't until the next morning** George Sullivan, *Bobby Bonds: Rising Superstar*, p. 45.

26 **One day during batting** George Sullivan, *Bobby Bonds: Rising Superstar*, p. 48.

26 **As Ira Berkow of the *New York Times* wrote** Ira Berkow, "Willie Will Be There," *New York Times*, July 28, 1983.

28 **His best friend was** Richard Hoffer, "The Importance of Being Barry," *Sports Illustrated*, May 24, 1993.

29 **"I would rather watch"** Jeff Savage, *Barry Bonds: Record Breaker*, p. 18.

31 **Shortly thereafter he pleaded** Ron Fimrite, "Getting It All Together," *Sports Illustrated*, April 8, 1974.

32 **"I resented him"** Kevin Cook, "Barry Bonds Interview" *Playboy*, July 1993.

CHAPTER THREE: SERRA

36 **Founded in 1944 to provide** *Junipero Serra High School Student-Parent Handbook*, 2004–05, p. 7.

38 **"I was the only black kid at parties"** Dave Newhouse, "Straight from Barry," *Tri-Valley Herald*, February 13, 2002.

41 **"I had never played anything but mud football"** I. J. Rosenberg, "Sanders, Bonds Swap Some Stories," *Atlanta Journal and Constitution*, May 14, 1992.

44 **On page 40 of Serra's** *Junipero Serra High School Student-Parent Handbook*, 2004–05, p. 40.

45 **According to Serra lore** Russ Bertetta et al., *Pride, Passion & Padres: The History of Serra Sports*, p. 108.

45 **His performance led to a glowing headline** Merv Harris, "Heredity and Heart Earn a Title for Serra," *San Francisco Examiner*, May 7, 1980.

46 **"It's easy to start a rumor"** Ron Fimrite, "They Still Invest in Bonds," *Sports Illustrated*, September 7, 1981.

48 **One clocked him at 9.5 seconds** Dick O'Connor, "The Next Bonds," *Peninsula Times-Tribune*, May 27, 1982.

49 **"In my 14 years"** Art Rosenbaum, "The Family Bonds Are Still Strong," *San Francisco Chronicle*, September 14, 1981.

CHAPTER FOUR: **ARIZONA STATE**

52 **Born and raised in Phoenix** Jim Brock and Joe Gilmartin, *The Devil's Coach*, pp. 62–65.

52 **"If my team won, my job"** Jim Brock and Joe Gilmartin, *The Devil's Coach*, p. 28.

53 **During one of his first** Mike Digiovanna, "Easy Does It," *Los Angeles Times*, October 7, 2001.

54 **On the first day of practice** John W. Fox, "To CV Grad Brown, Homer King Bonds Was a Prince, Too," *Binghamton Press & Sun-Belletin*, October 10, 2001.

54 **Years later, Brock told *Sports Illustrated*** Hank Hersch, "30/30 Vision," *Sports Illustrated*, June 25, 1990.

55 **"My dad would call me in college"** Interview with ESPN SportsCentury.

55 **In an NCAA West II Regional** Staff writers, "'83 BYU baseball team reunion set for 4-19," *Desert News*, April 12, 2003.

59 **The taunt was a bad idea** Ira Berkow, "Baseball Amateur of the Year," *New York Times*, November 8, 1984.

62 **He graduated in 2001** Bob Lutz, "Even in His Hutch Days, Bonds Hard to Figure," *Wichita Eagle*, September 28, 2001.

63 **"Our big goal"** Bob Cuomo, "Penalties Spur Arizona State, Coach Says," *Los Angeles Times*, February 9, 1985.

63 **With a handful of major leaguers** Richard Obert, "After Slamming Home Runs in Three Stright Games, Barry Bonds Is Within One of 500," *Arizona Republic*, April 17, 2001.

64 **Dr. Robert Voy, chief medical officer** Franz Lidz, "Nardil and ASU," *Sports Illustrated*, April 8, 1985.

66 **Pittsburgh had actually preferred Larkin** Fred Mitchell, "Interest Building in Bonds," *Chicago Tribune*, September 14, 1986.

66 **That week, the Pirates flew Bonds** Ross Bernstein, *Barry Bonds: Sports Heroes and Legends*, pp. 22–23.

CHAPTER FIVE: **A PRODIGY TURNS PRO**

71 **"James Bond was agent 007"** Alan Robinson, untitled, Associated Press, March 4, 1986.

74 **As *Time* magazine's Ed Magnuson** Ed Magnuson, "Baseball's Drug Scandal," *Time*, September 16, 1985.

74 **The team's owner, Dan Galbreath** *The Pittsburgh Pirates Encyclopedia*, pp. 474–75.

75 **"I went in there thinking"** Charles P. Pierce, "A Dues Guy First and Last," *National Sports Daily*, June 17, 1990.

77 **Years later Barry liked to spin** Bob Cohen, "Bonds on His Own," *Washington Times*, June 11, 2004.

80 **When he was a second grader** Steve Rushin, "Playing for Laughs," *Sports Illustrated*, September 21, 1992.

84 **"I don't care"** Dan Le Batard, "Bonds: A Lonely Man Behind the Loud Façade," *Miami Herald*, June 4, 2001.

CHAPTER SIX: THE MONTREAL SUN

87 **A Swedish immigrant and aspiring cosmetologist** Kristian Gravenor, "Bonds of Passion," *Montreal Mirror*, October 19, 2000.

87 **"I wound up going to another club"** Kevin Cook, "Barry Bonds Interview" *Playboy*, July 1993.

89 **When asked by Pohla Smith** Pohla Smith, untitled, United Press International, April 14, 1988.

89 **"Barry Bonds has got a chance"** Paul LeBar, untitled, Associated Press, April 9, 1988.

95 **"Come sit at my locker"** Dan Le Batard, "Bonds: A Lonely Man Behind the Loud Façade," *Miami Herald*, June 4, 2001 .

95 **"He's a great talent"** Pohla Smith, untitled, United Press International, April 14, 1988.

95 **"Sun has more patience"** Kevin Cook, "Barry Bonds Interview," *Playboy*, July 1993.

96 **"He always told me"** S. L. Wykes, "Barry Bonds' Ex-Wife Tells of Abuse Since '89," *San Jose Mercury News*, December 7, 1995.

98 **"I never wanted to break the bank"** Associated Press, March 11, 1989.

100 **"All I've been hearing"** "Pirates Notes," *The Sporting News*, September 4, 1989.

CHAPTER SEVEN: OF FINANCES AND (PLAYOFF) FLOPS

102 **Wrote Bob Hertzel** Bob Hertzel, "Bonds Should Flex His Biceps Instead of Jaws," *The Sporting News*, March 12, 1990.

102 **"It used to be I'd"** Alan Robinson, untitled, Associated Press, March 22, 1990.

103 **"Bonilla is sunshine"** Bob Hertzel, *The Sporting News*, December 3, 1990.

103 **His father, Roberto** Thomas Boswell, "Pirates' Big Find Finds Himself," *Washington Post*, May 18, 1988.

104 **On April 30, *Los Angeles Times* writer** Bob Wolf, "Pirates Look Like the Real Thing on This Trip," *Los Angeles Times*, April 30, 1990.

104 **"Now everything's falling into place"** Alan Robinson, untitled, Associated Press, May 30, 1990.

109 **"I'm not kidding anybody"** Staff reports, "Choked Up," *Orlando Sentinel*, October 10, 1990.

109 **As the Pirates lost the next** Alan Robinson, untitled, Associated Press, October 6, 1990.

109 **"Jeff King's supposed"** Alan Robinson, untitled, Associated Press, October 11, 1990.

111 **With total revenue of $44 million** Doron P. Levin, "Pirates' Owner Pleading Poverty," *New York Times*, October 7, 1990.

112 **"The Pirates can't keep crying"** Associated Press, November 20, 1990.

112 **Shortly thereafter, Bonds told** Hal Bodley, "Bonds Promises to Haunt Pirates," *USA Today*, January 31, 1991.

112 **"The atrocities are almost"** Gene Collier, "Bonds vs. Bucs," *Pittsburgh Press*, February 1, 1991.

114 **"Barry's yapping and causing"** Interview with ESPN SportsCentury.

114 **"Don't fuck with me"** Steven Travers, *Barry Bonds: Baseball's Superman*, p. 61.

115 **In an interview with *Playboy*** Kevin Cook, "Barry Bonds Interview," *Playboy*, July 1993.

116 **Among the promotions** Tracy Ringolsby, "Bonds Is Own Worst Enemy," *Orlando Sentinel*, March 10, 1991.

116 **Bonds hired a New York–based** Chuck Moody, "Bonds Bids for Second MVP Award," United Press International, August 24, 1991.

116 **When Nikolai was old enough** Steve Wilstein, "Q&A with Barry Bonds," Associated Press, June 6, 1993.

117 **Wrote Mark Maske** Mark Maske, "Pirates Cash in on Maturing Bonds," *Washington Post*, August 25, 1991.

118 **"Everybody's looking for me"** Brian Schmitz, untitled, *Orlando Sentinel*, October 17, 1991.

CHAPTER EIGHT: THE WRIGHT STUFF

121 **"Pittsburgh has been good"** William Ladson, "Q&A with Barry Bonds," *Sport*, March 1992.

122 **"Just don't insult"** Alan Robinson, untitled, Associated Press, March 19, 1992.

122 **From the moment Bonilla** Joe Sexton, "Bonilla Learns That He Can't Go Home Again," *New York Times*, June 5, 1992.

122 **The next day, Bonds**   Joe Sexton, "It's Race, Not Money, Says Bonds," *New York Times*, June 6, 1992.

123 **On April 5, 1968, the day**   Paul S. Korol, "A Brief History of the Hill," *Pittsburgh Senior News*, February 4, 2002.

124 **One year later, after**   James Harney, "Bias in the Skies," *USA Today*, May 30, 1991.

125 **A reputation for client swindling**   Jerry Crasnick, *License to Deal*, p. 267.

125 **"This is a business that's almost"**   Jerry Crasnick, *License to Deal*, p. 24.

127 **"Baseball superstar Barry Bonds"**   Ray Loynd, "Review: Moment of Truth: Broken Pledges," *Daily Variety*, April 11, 1994.

127 **"They're a great team"**   Mark Whicker, "Bullish Bonds Can Market His Toughness," *Orange County Register*, July 14, 1992.

128 **"He's not done anything"**   Bill Plaschke, "Dodgers Answer Critics," *Los Angeles Times*, July 17, 1992.

128 **On the morning of game one**   Rod Beaton, "Bonds Plays for Pay," *USA Today*, October 7, 1992.

128 **Facing the pressure**   Rick Hummel, "Leyland Says Bonds Is Trying Too Hard," *St. Louis Post-Dispatch*, October 8, 1992.

129 **"Barry had put a lot"**   Fred McMane, "Leyland Says It's Wrong to Single Out Bonds," United Press International, October 8, 1992.

129 **On the afternoon of October 6**   Jeff Schultz, "NL Championship Series," *Atlanta Journal and Constitution*, October 8, 1992.

130 **"Father knows best"**   Jerome Holtzman, "Bonds Signaling He's Back in Gear," *Chicago Tribune*, October 10, 1992.

131 **"That made me feel great"**   Hal Bodley, "Heart-to-Heart Gets Bonds on Track," *USA Today*, October 12, 1992.

133 **"We're going to lose"**   Bob Smizik, "The Big Hurt," *Pittsburgh Post-Gazette*, October 12, 1997.

133 **Though Belinda was technically**   David Comer, "Belinda Is Liking Life with Rockies," *Centre Daily Times*, July 9, 2000.

133 **When Cabrera played**   Matt Michael, "Playoff Hero a Big Mac Favorite," *Post-Standard*, October 22, 1992.

134 **Cabrera was signed**   Jeff Schultz, "Atlanta's Newest, Most Unlikely Hero," *Atlanta Journal and Constitution*, October 16, 1992.

135 **"This loss"**   Tim Kurkjian, "The Cruelest Game," *Sports Illustrated*, October 26, 1992.

CHAPTER NINE: A HAPPY HOMECOMING

138 **Throughout his 20s**   "On the Record: Peter Magowan," *San Francisco Chronicle*, September 28, 2003.

143 **"Barry Bonds is to be paid $43.75 million"** "Letters to the Green," *San Francisco Chronicle*, December 12, 1992.

145 **Barry showed up** C. W. Nevius, "Bonds Brings His Act to Spring Training," *San Francisco Chronicle*, February 22, 1993.

147 **On an early March morning** C. W. Nevius, "Bonds Sent Message Early On," *San Francisco Chronicle*, August 24, 1993.

149 **"As far as anyone can"** Richard Hoffer, "The Importance of Being Barry," *Sports Illustrated*, May 24, 1993.

149 **"If you ask me"** www.baseballalmanac.com.

150 **"People ask me what"** Scott Ostler, "All Bonds Needs Now Is a Mural," *San Francisco Chronicle*, May 3, 1993.

150 **"This is Barry Bonds"** Scott Ostler, "All Bonds Needs Now Is a Mural," *San Francisco Chronicle*, May 3, 1993.

150 **He was the first Giant** Ross Newhan, "Bonds Is Top All-Star Vote Getter," *Los Angeles Times*, July 3, 1993.

150 **In an NBC News/*Wall Street Journal*** Roper Center at University of Connecticut, "Question Number 093," *Public Opinion Online*.

151 **The incident tarnished Clark's reputation** Peter Richmond, "God's Will," *National Sports Daily*, August 3, 1990.

154 **Sun had told police** Janet Kornblum, "No Charges Filed Against Bonds in Aug. 24 Altercation with Wife," *San Francisco Examiner*, September 23, 1993.

154 **"It's a nightmare"** Marc Topkin, "Braves, Giants: Teams Going Separate Ways," *St. Petersburg Times*, September 19, 1993.

CHAPTER TEN: YOU CAN'T LIVE WITH 'EM . . .

158 **According to a lawsuit filed by Peace** Dave Joseph, "Woman Linked to Cowlings Files Paternity Suit Against Bonds," *Sun-Sentinel* (Fort Lauderdale), November 23, 1994.

158 **"But Barry and Sun's breakup"** S. L. Wykes, "Bonds' Pact, Worth Millions, Approaches On-Deck Circle," *San Jose Mercury News*, March 25, 1995.

159 **Bonds's attorneys** "Names & Faces," *Orlando Sentinel*, September 25, 1994.

160 **"We gave him $47 million"** Untitled, *San Jose Mercury News*, January 24, 1994.

160 **Then, in late February** Tim Keown, "Bonds on Racism," *San Francisco Chronicle*, February 26, 1994.

160 **"All you get is crud"** Leah Garchik, "Personals," *San Francisco Chronicle*, March 23, 1994.

160 **In the suit, the owner** Jorge Valencia, "Bonds Wins Lawsuit; No Defense Needed," *Riverside Press-Enterprise*, January 30, 1998.

160 **In July, a poll**   Marc Topkin, "Bonds Not Ready to Cash In," *St. Petersburg Times*, July 13, 1994.

160 **"Those boos Barry Bonds received"**   John Steigerwald, "Color Blind Fans Who Booed Bonds Were Realists, Not Racists," *Pittsburgh Post-Gazette*, July 16, 1994.

162 **"Mr. Bonds has tightened"**   "Bonds' Wife Gets Raise," *Commercial Appeal*, October 2, 1994.

162 **According to Sun, Barry kicked**   S. L. Wykes, "Barry Bonds' Ex-Wife Tells of Abuse Since '89," *San Jose Mercury News* December 7, 1995.

162 **"In a majority of dissolution cases"**   Harriet Chiang, "State's High Court Upholds Bonds Prenup," *San Francisco Chronicle*, August 22, 2000.

163 **"It'll never be"**   Mark Camps, "Dusty Left to Wonder What Might Have Been," *San Francisco Chronicle*, February 23, 1995.

163 **Nobody was hit harder**   Ronald Blum, "Bonds Top Money Loser During Strike," *Lakeland Ledger*, March 1, 1995.

163 **Looking to put in**   John Hunneman, "Just Ten Years Ago," *North County Times*, November 1, 2005.

164 **"You guys could"**   Mark Camps, "The Sequel," *San Francisco Chronicle*, April 8, 1995.

165 **"Even when the fog"**   David Montero, "A Baseball Original," *Ventura County Star*, June 11, 1999.

167 **"I don't care"**   Nancy Gay, "Weary Bonds Taking Stock," *San Francisco Chronicle*, September 15, 1995.

167 **"Whether he has meant"**   C. W. Nevius, "Trade Bonds and Bring Back the Fans," *San Francisco Chronicle*, July 1, 1995.

168 **"The great Barry Bonds"**   Dan Le Batard, "Bonds: A Lonely Man Behind the Loud Façade," *Miami Herald*, June 4, 2001.

CHAPTER ELEVEN: **ARRIVAL OF AN ENEMY**

175 **"I could have stood"**   C. W. Nevius, "Selfish Bonds is Not Worth Giants' Money," *San Francisco Chronicle*, September 21, 1996.

175 **"I wouldn't recommend"**   Jerry Crasnick, "Bonds New Member of 40-40 Club," *Denver Post*, September 28, 1996.

175 **"Bonds is turning into"**   C. W. Nevius, "Selfish Bonds is Not Worth Giants' Money," *San Francisco Chronicle*, September 21, 1996.

175 **the Mets for first baseman**   Marty Noble, "Persuing Bonds Market," *Newsday*, "October 18, 1996.

176 **"Was Brian Sabean possessed"**   "Letters to the Green," *San Francisco Chronicle*, November 16, 1996.

176 **Buster Olney of the *Baltimore Sun*** Buster Olney, "Giants Get Lightweights for Williams," *Baltimore Sun*, November 17, 1996.

176 ***Newsday*'s Jon Heyman** Jon Heyman, "Deal a Giant Blunder," *Newsday*, November 17, 1996.

177 **Two days after the trade** David Bush, "GM Defends Williams Deal," *San Francisco Chronicle*, November 16, 1996.

177 **"When Matt Williams got traded"** "Barry Bonds Says Giants Lied to Him," Associated Press, February 13, 1997.

178 **"a tightly coiled spring"** Franz Lidz, "Stepping Up," *Sports Illustrated*, February 15, 1999.

179 **He bashed New York fans** Mark Kriegel, "Now At-Brat," *New York Daily News*, March 20, 1994.

179 **Kent spent his offseasons** Jeff Bradley, "Lone Star," *ESPN the Magazine*, March 3, 2003.

179 **"They've hated each other"** Ray Ratto, "If Nothing Else, Giants' Duo are Great Theater," *San Francisco Chronicle*, June 28, 2002.

180 **Speaking before the United Way** "Bonds Pleads for Donors," *Ethnic News-Watch*, February 26, 1997.

181 **"A lot of what Barry"** Benoit Denizet-Lewis, "Bow to the King," *SF Weekly*, September 6, 2000.

181 **The press praised Bonds** Burt Graeff, "A Giant Step Toward Maturity," *Cleveland Plain Dealer*, April 13, 1997.

181 **"For the first time"** Tim Keown, "Giants' Mix is Boon for Bonds," *San Francisco Chronicle*, May 28, 1997.

182 **"I shouldn't be allowed"** Nancy Gay, "Bonds Takes Blame for Loss to Marlins," *San Francisco Chronicle*, June 3, 1997.

182 **At 3:30 the next afternoon** Larry LaRue, "Taking Stock of Bonds," *Tacoma News Tribune*, June 29, 1997.

183 **He attributed the surge** Mark Gonzalez, "Credit Dad with Putting Pop Back in Bonds' Bat," *San Jose Mercury News*, September 19, 1997.

184 **"This is not a baseball field"** Ed Price, "'Football Stadium' Rankles Bonds," *Palm Beach Post*, October 1, 1997.

CHAPTER TWELVE: EXPANSION

185 **Held on the evening** David Higdon, "The Name is Bonds . . . Mr. & Mrs. Barry Bonds," *In Style*, March 1998.

187 **Immersed in his** Mark Fainaru-Wada and Lance Williams, "The Truth About Barry Bonds and Steroids," *Sports Illustrated*, March 13, 2006.

187 **She told the *San Francisco Chronicle*** Lance Williams and Mark Fainaru-

Wada, "Doping Scandal Swirls at Feet of a Giant," *San Francisco Chronicle*, March 20, 2005.

188 **There was speculation that Bonds**   Mark Fainaru-Wada and Lance Williams, "The Truth About Barry Bonds and Steroids," *Sports Illustrated*, March 13, 2006.

190 **Born developmentally disabled**   Chuck Squatriglia, "Last Game for 'Ballpark Marge,'" *San Francisco Chronicle*, June 27, 2003.

191 **"I know it was a little unorthodox"**   Ben Walker, "Ultimate Respect," Associated Press, May 29, 1998.

191 **Just how feared**   Henry Schulman, "Bases-Loaded Walk Still Talk of Town," *San Francisco Chronicle*, May 30, 1998.

192 **David O'Brien of the *Sun-Sentinel***   David O'Brien, "Marlins Help Bonds Reach 400-400 Mark," *Sun-Sentinel* (Fort Lauderdale), August 24, 1998.

192 **"I have nine writers standing"**   David O'Brien, "Marlins Help Bonds Reach 400-400 Mark," *Sun-Sentinel* (Fort Lauderdale), August 24, 1998.

193 **In his 1999 book**   William F. McNeil, *Ruth, Maris, McGwire and Sosa: Baseball's Single Season Home Run Champions*, p. 187.

195 **"McGwire is a hero"**   Bob Hunter, "McGwire Fills the Bill as a Genuine Sports Hero," *Columbus Dispatch*, September 10, 1998.

195 **"We knew his son"**   "What the Columnists Wrote," *Memphis Commercial Appeal*, September 10, 1998.

196 **"I've gone 0-for-4 before"**   Tim Keown, "Bonds Lets Chance to Be Game's Hero Slip Through Hands," *San Francisco Chronicle*, September 29, 1998.

CHAPTER THIRTEEN: BIG

197 **The high concentration**   Bob Finnigan, "Living Large," *Seattle Times*, January 4, 1998.

199 **When asked by Rick Hurd**   Rick Hurd, "Barry Bonds' Plea: I Want to Stay a Giant," *Contra Costa Times*, February 26, 1999.

202 **Three times in his life**   Lance Williams and Mark Fainaru-Wada, "Drugs, Records Seized During Raid on Barry Bonds' Trainer, Sources Say," *San Francisco Chronicle*, November 25, 2003.

202 **Even one year later**   Mark Fainaru-Wada and Lance Williams, "The Truth About Barry Bonds and Steroids," *Sports Illustrated*, March 13, 2006.

202 **"They played San Carlos Little League"**   Lance Williams and Mark Fainaru-Wada, "Drugs, Records Seized During Raid on Barry Bonds' Trainer, Sources Say," *San Francisco Chronicle*, November 25, 2003.

202 **"short, squatty, roly-poly"**   Lance Williams and Mark Fainura-Wada, "Drugs, Records Seized During Raid on Barry Bonds' Trainer, Sources Say," *San Francisco Chronicle*, November 25, 2003.

202 **Not much is remembered** Lance Williams and Mark Fainura-Wada, "An Unlikely Cast of Characters at Center of Doping Scandal," *San Francisco Chronicle*, February 15, 2004.

203 **The first steroid Anderson** Mark Fainaru-Wada and Lance Williams, "The Truth About Barry Bonds and Steroids," *Sports Illustrated*, March 13, 2006.

203 **A study conducted** Henry Schulman, "Bonds Defies Age-Power Argument," *San Francisco Chronicle*, April 2, 1999.

205 **"Only air is invincible"** Rob Gloster, "Bonds Says Hardest Part of Injury Will Be Watching Games," Associated Press, April 21, 1999.

206 **"We knocked on every single door"** Jon Heyman, "Bonding with Barry," *Newsday*, July 8, 2001.

207 **The key to the early comeback** "Bonds Endures Big Pain to Return," *Palm Beach Post*, June 13, 1999.

CHAPTER FOURTEEN: ACROMEGALY

209 **Into the arctic water** "Ballpark Dive Gets Worker in Hot Water," *Cal-OSHA Reporter*, January 28, 2000.

210 **His plan was a stroke** John Bloom, *Barry Bonds: A Biography*, p. 55.

212 **"Bonds's most appealing attribute"** "Barry Bonds," *People*, May 4, 1992.

213 **Prior to the season, Bonds** Mark Fainaru-Wada and Lance Williams, "The Truth About Barry Bonds and Steroids," *Sports Illustrated*, March 13, 2006.

218 **Heading into a series** Henry Schulman, "Manager Said L.A. Intended to Hit All-Star," *San Francisco Chronicle*, July 4, 1998.

218 **When San Francisco clinched** Frank Ahrens, "A Giant Star in Own Galaxy," *Washington Post*, October 3, 2000.

220 **As he drifted off** David Lennon, "Bonds Is a Bust," *Newsday*, October 9, 2000.

CHAPTER FIFTEEN: THIS GRACELESS SEASON

221 **On January 19, 2001, a story** Joe Roderick, "Lack of Loyalty Bugs Bonds," *Contra Costa Times*, January 19, 2001.

222 **"[Roderick] should be sued"** Josh Suchon, *This Gracious Season*, pp. 45–47.

222 **One thing was clear** Josh Suchon, *This Gracious Season*, pp. 50–51.

225 **He also backed Republican candidates** Dale Maharidge, "What You Need to Know About Pete Wilson," *Mother Jones*, November/December 1995.

226 **When Major League Baseball chose** Jon Heyman, "Bonding with Barry," *Newsday*, July 8, 2001.

227 **"I straight"** Henry Schulman, "Bonds' Flub Boosts Brewers," *San Francisco Chronicle*, April 16, 2001.

228 **"Bonds spent the season"** David E. Early, "Bonds on Bonds," *San Jose Mercury News*, September 30, 2001.

228 **"The best setting would be"** Henry Schulman, "500," *San Francisco Chronicle*, April 18, 2001.

229 **"The home run record"** Dan O'Neill, "Bonds Is Chasing a Record That Doesn't Matter Anymore," *St. Louis Post-Dispatch*, June 24, 2001.

232 **A typical day was** Daniel Brown, "Bonds Gets Chance to Make Splash in Batting Practice," *San Jose Mercury News*, May 2, 2001.

233 **"Ask God"** Josh Suchon, *This Gracious Season*, p. 113.

233 **This, even after a scout** Jeff Bradley, "Pushing 70?" *ESPN the Magazine*, June 11, 2001.

234 **Jay Mariotti, the *Chicago Sun Times* star columnist** Jay Mariotti, "The Rebirth of Barry Bonds," *The Sporting News*, June 4, 2001.

234 **It would be two more years** Lance Williams and Mark Fainaru-Wada, "How the Doping Scandal Unfolded," *San Francisco Chronicle*, December 21, 2003.

235 **According to the book** Mark Fainaru-Wada and Lance Williams, "The Truth About Barry Bonds and Steroids," *Sports Illustrated*, March 13, 2006.

236 **On July 3, 2001, Kyle Tucker** Kyle Tucker, "Someone Needs to Take Baseball Off All the Juice," *Macon Telegraph*, July 3, 2001.

237 **Bonds was woken up** Bob Nightengale, "The Quest for 70," *USA Today Baseball Weekly*, October 3, 2001.

238 **"It's impossible to root"** Jason Whitlock, "Bonds Can Symbolize Resilience," *Kansas City Star*, September 17, 2001.

239 **"For months Bonds has"** Ann Killion, "Bonds' Pursuit Welcome Distraction," *San Jose Mercury News*, September 22, 2001.

239 **When Bonds hit his 61st** Tom FitzGerald, "The Golden Retiever," *San Francisco Chronicle*, September 14, 2001.

240 **In the first inning, Bonds** Josh Suchon, *This Gracious Season*, pp. 330–31.

241 **"I don't get discouraged"** Frank Blackman, "Bonds Exorcises a Personal Demon," *San Francisco Examiner*, September 14, 1998.

241 **Nicknamed "Urkel"** Jeff Miller, "More Than Comic Relief," *Orange County Register*, June 27, 1996.

244 **"What's there to celebrate?"** Josh Suchon, *This Gracious Season*, pp. 354–55.

245 **Jon Miller of FOX Sports Net** Josh Suchon, *This Gracious Season*, p. 358.

246 **"This begins to leave"** Josh Suchon, *This Gracious Season*, p. 360.

CHAPTER SIXTEEN: A WINNER AT LAST

250 **In a December study** Michael Hiestand, "Bonds Can't Get Web Hits," *USA Today*, December 18, 2001.

254 **Bonds toured the mill** Kelly Egan, "Bonds Pays Holman Bat," *Ottawa Citizen*, January 27, 2002.

254 **On the morning of April 7, 2002** "PNC Park Groundskeeper Killed in Accident," Associated Press, April 8, 2002.

255 **Around this time, Dave Newhouse** Dave Newhouse, "Straight from Barry," *Tri-Valley Herald*, February 13, 2002.

256 **"It's no secret"** Tom Verducci, "Totally Juiced," *Sports Illustrated*, June 3, 2002.

256 **"Not long after"** "Bonds Admits to Supplements Use," United Press International, July 11, 2002.

257 **"The doctors right now"** "Giants Notebook," *San Francisco Chronicle*, July 14, 2002.

261 **When asked by the *Washington Post*** Charles Krauthammer, "The Strike That Will Kill Baseball," *Washington Post*, July 5, 2002.

261 **And on the afternoon of August 9** Deanne Fitzmaurice, "Behind the Scenes with Barry Bonds," www.sportsshooter.com, August 31, 2002.

261 **Wrote Schulman in the *Chronicle*** Henry Schulman, "600!" *San Francisco Chronicle*, August 10, 2002.

262 **"Have we lost our sense"** John Romano, "Bonds Will Join the Elite, So Why Don't We Care?" *St. Petersburg Times*, August 9, 2000.

263 **"If he's not back next year"** Henry Schulman, "Giants Lose; Bonds Says Keep Kent," *San Francisco Chronicle*, September 13, 2002.

264 **On September 28** Dan Brown, "Giants Grab Wild Card," *San Jose Mercury News*, September 29, 2002.

264 **"This isn't the Bonds"** John Shea, "This Bonds Is Different from the Past," *San Francisco Chronicle*, September 30, 2002.

CHAPTER SEVENTEEN: **MR. NOCTOBER NO MORE**

268 **As the Giants took BP** Tom Verducci, "Stairway to Heaven," *Sports Illustrated*, November 6, 2002.

271 **"It's a good thing"** Thom Loverro, "Bonds' Prodigious HR Was a Juicy Moment," *Washington Times*, October 22, 2002.

272 **Afterward, Bonds was cornered** Steve Fainaru, "Bonds Continues His Postseason Power Play," *Washington Post*, October 23, 2002.

275 **"When Bonds jerks reporters around"** Gary Peterson, "Bonds Can't Even Stand to Be the Guest of Honor," *Contra Costa Times*, October 26, 2002.

277 **Little did they know that** Tom Verducci, "Stairway to Heaven," *Sports Illustrated*, November 6, 2002.

Chapter Eighteen: **Death of the Father**

280 **On the night of November 9, 2002** Filip Bondy, "Power of Bonds Scandal to Japan," *New York Daily News*, November 16, 2002.

281 **Bonds was even glib** Ray Ratto, "Aging Process Hitting Bonds," *San Francisco Chronicle*, February 19, 2003.

281 **Near the end of the 2002 season** Howard Bryant, "A Tainted Era," *Boston Herald*, June 18, 2003.

282 **In the midst of Bobby's decline** Howard Bryant, "Beauty and the Beast," *Boston Herald*, March 30, 2003.

283 **In the April 13 edition** Henry Schulman, "Start Gives Bonds Time to Work Out Kinks," *San Francisco Chronicle*, April 13, 2003.

284 **"I'm just not here"** Joe Roderick, "Schmidt Leaves Team After Mother's Death," *Contra Costa Times*, April 23, 2003.

284 **Making his first start** Josh Suchon, "A Giant One for Mom and Dad," *Oakland Tribune*, May 1, 2003.

285 **"I've never played baseball"** Henry Schulman, "Bonds May Skip All-Star Game to See Father," *San Francisco Chronicle*, June 11, 2003.

286 **"Our prince of petulance"** Greg Cote, "Bonds' Rips of Ruth Are Blasphemous," *Miami Herald*, July 16, 2003.

287 **"If you've ever ushered"** Gary Peterson, "Bonds Inspires with a Heavy Heart," *Contra Costa Times*, July 25, 2003.

288 **"My dad wants everybody"** Nick Peters, "Bonds Gets Emotional After Visiting Dad," *Sacramento Bee*, August 20, 2003.

288 **That night at Pac Bell** Jorge L. Ortiz, "Welcome Back, Barry," *San Francisco Chronicle*, August 20, 2003.

288 **Because he had been escorted** Mark Purdy, "A Father Got to See His Son Play Ball," *San Jose Mercury News*, August 21, 2003.

289 **"Mother Bonds understands"** Jim Alexander, "Greats Honor Bonds," *Press-Enterprise* (Riverside, CA), August 29, 2003.

289 **"Bobby was a great"** Michelle Meyers, "Legends Pay Respects to Baseball Great," *Alameda Times-Star*, August 29, 2003.

289 **On one of the shelves Barry** Joe Roderick, "Bonds, Giants Lower Their Magic Numbers," *Contra Costa Times*, September 17, 2003.

290 **Bonds spoke in hushed tones** John Shea, "Emotional Return for Bonds," *San Francisco Chronicle*, August 31, 2003.

290 **The 150–160 beats** John Shea, "Emotional Return for Bonds," *San Francisco Chronicle*, August 31, 2003.

291 **"A Burlingame lab that specializes"** Dana Yates, "Star Athlete Lab Raided," *San Mateo Daily Journal*, September 4, 2003.

292 **Unknown at the time**   Mark Fainaru-Wada and Lance Williams, "The Truth About Barry Bonds and Steroids," *Sports Illustrated*, March 13, 2006.

292 **"Sports insiders speculate"**   Dana Yates, "Sports Lab Probe Deepens," *San Mateo Daily Journal*, September 5, 2003.

294 **When approached by reporter Matthai Chakko Kuruvila**   Matthai Chakko Kuruvila, "Officials Silent Regarding Search of Trainer's Home," *San Jose Mercury News*, September 7, 2003.

294 **In the piece, writer Jim Schmaltz**   Jim Schmaltz, "What Fuels Baseball Superhitter Barry Bonds?" *Muscle & Fitness*, June 1, 2003.

294 **When interviewed by the *New York Post***   Steve Serby and Kevin Kernan, "The Insiders: The Post Takes You Behind the Locker-Room Doors," *New York Post*, September 14, 2003.

295 **"We should all understand"**   Dave Albee, "Barry's Softer Side Is Showing," *Marin Independent Journal*, September 14, 2003.

CHAPTER NINETEEN: A TARNISHED LEGACY?

297 **"I have complete and utmost confidence"**   John Shea, "Aaron Says Bonds 'Clean as a Whistle," *San Francisco Chronicle*, October 23, 2003.

297 **As he approached Babe Ruth's**   Tom Stanton, *Hank Aaron and the Home Run That Changed America*, pp. 139–41.

298 **"During my last two years"**   Jim Van Vliet, "Aaron Fairly Sure Bonds Is the One," *Sacramento Bee*, August 24, 2002.

298 **"Both said, 'You represent'"**   Chuck Johnson, "Legends Encourage Bonds," *USA Today*, February 24, 2004.

299 **"Bonds' historic honor didn't"**   Ann Killion, "Tough Year Clouds Bonds' Record Award," *San Jose Mercury News*, November 19, 2003.

299 **"Federal investigators seized"**   Lance Williams, Seth Rosenfeld, and Mark Fainaru-Wada, "Details Emerge in Raid on Bonds' Trainer," *San Francisco Chronicle*, November 23, 2003.

300 **For investigators, the contents**   John McCloskey and Julian Bailes, *When Winning Costs Too Much*, p. 66.

301 **At November's general manager meetings**   Carl Steward, "'Barry Bonds Rules' was a Giant Farce," *Alameda Times-Star*, November 22, 2003.

302 **"I am saddened by the news"**   Curt Anderson, "Bonds' Trainer Among Four Charged in Scheme to Distribute Steroids," Associated Press, February 12, 2004.

302 **On March 2, Fainaru-Wada**   Lance Williams and Mark Fainaru-Wada, "Bonds Got Steroids, Feds Were Told," *San Francisco Chronicle*, March 2, 2004.

303 **Cardinals outfielder Reggie Sanders**   Joe Henderson, "Reward McGriff for Doing It Fairly," *Tampa Tribune*, March 4, 2004.

303 **Richard Pound, the chairman**   "Baseball Testing a Joke, Pound Says," *Ottawa Citizen*, March 5, 2004.

303 **Former Pirates teammate Andy Van Slyke**   Christian Red, "Van Slyke: I'm Certain that Bonds Used 'Roids," *New York Daily News*, May 5, 2004.

303 **Even Reggie Jackson**   Sam Borden, "Jackson Said His Frustration Led to Speaking Out on Steroids," *New York Daily News*, March 12, 2004.

303 **When reporter Paul Giblin**   Joe Roderick, "In Wake of Allegations, Bonds' Teammates Stick by Him," *Contra Costa Times*, March 3, 2004.

304 **As he walked away**   Richard Justice, "Race Creeps into Bonds Flap," *Houston Chronicle*, March 7, 2004.

304 **Cruising the stands**   Steve Fainaru, "Giant Company," *Washington Post*, April 13, 2004.

305 **"It's embarrassing when you"**   Richard Sandomir, "Broadcasters Don't Know How to Deal with Steroids," *New York Times*, April 20, 2004.

306 **Bonds told Gordon Edes**   Gordon Edes, "Giants' Bonds Is in a Blasting Zone," *Boston Globe*, June 18, 2004.

306 **"I ain't white"**   Gerry Callahan, "Arrogant Bonds Off Base by Playing Race Card," *Boston Herald*, May 14, 2004.

308 **On June 24, the *Chronicle***   Lance Williams and Mark Fainaru-Wada, "Track Star's Testimony Linked Bonds to Steroid Use," *San Francisco Chronicle*, June 24, 2005.

308 **"I ain't never met"**   Janie McCauley, "Furious Bonds: 'I Ain't Never Met Tim Montgomery,'" Associated Press, June 24, 2005.

309 **In a fascinating *Sports Illustrated* breakdown**   Tom Verducci, "A Season Like No Other," *Sports Illustrated*, May 17, 2004.

309 **"To have Hank there"**   John Shea, "Bonds Blasts 2 HRs as Aaron Watches Giants Win," *San Francisco Chronicle*, August 30, 2004.

310 **"Barry Bonds . . . keeps his eye on the ball"**   Bill Plaschke, "He Has at Least One Doctor's Seal of Approval," *Los Angeles Times*, September 18, 2004.

310 **Beneath the headline**   Lance Williams and Mark Fainaru-Wada, "What Bonds Told Balco Grand Jury," *San Francisco Chronicle*, December 3, 2004.

310 **As if this were not damaging**   Lance Williams and Mark Fainaru-Wada, "Giambi Admitted Taking Steroids," *San Francisco Chronicle*, December 2, 2004.

310 **Two months earlier**   Lance Williams and Mark Fainaru-Wada, "Bonds Used Steroids in 2003, Trainer Says on Secret Recording," *San Francisco Chronicle*, October 16, 2004.

311 **In the October 4 issue**   Tom Verducci, "Severing Bonds," *Sports Illustrated*, October 11, 2004.

312 **Bonds, who insisted on controlling**   David Grann, "Baseball Without Metaphor," *New York Times Magazine*, September 1, 2002.

312 **"I believe Barry Bonds"**   Rick Reilly, "No Doubt About It," *Sports Illustrated*, December 13, 2004.

CHAPTER TWENTY: THE PICNIC TABLE MONOLOGUES

315 **On February 12, Geraldo Rivera**   *At Large with Geraldo Rivera*, FOX News, February 12, 2005.

316 **Along with admitting his own**   Jose Canseco, *Juiced: Wild Times, Rampant 'Roids, Smash Hits and How Baseball Got Big*.

324 **"He is America's victim"**   Mike Vaccaro, "Time For Him to Leave for Good," *New York Post*, March 23, 2005.

325 **As a sixth grader, he placed**   Lynnbrook High School website, lhs.fuhsd.org.

325 **"Against Bonds's wishes"**   Valley View School website, www.valleyview school.org

325 **Never was this truer**   John Shea, "Fans and Bonds Enjoy Giants' Lovefest, Then Team Shows It Can Win Without Him," *San Francisco Chronicle*, April 6, 2005.

326 **"For one afternoon"**   William C. Rhoden, "Bonds Heard It from Crowd, and It Sounds Good," *New York Times*, April 6, 2005.

327 **On April 9, the** *San Francisco Chronicle*   Lance Williams and Mark Fainaru-Wada, "Bonds Working with Anderson," *San Francisco Chronicle*, April 9, 2005.

327 **"I just wanted to give you an update"**   www.barrybonds.com, April 23, 2005.

329 **Unbeknownst to the Giants**   Daniel Brown, "Bonds' Status Earns Him Leeway and Major Perks," *San Jose Mercury News*, May 17, 2005.

329 **"The reality is that he's"**   Daniel Brown, "Who's the Boss Here?" *San Jose Mercury News*, May 15, 2005.

330 **"I don't sign for white people"**   Ron Kittle and Bob Logan, *Ron Kittle's Tales from the White Sox Dugout*, p. 8.

330 **"Who is Ron Kittle?"**   Richard Roeper, "Bonds' Tirade at Kittle Not a Convincing Defense," *Chicago Tribune*, June 13, 2005.

330 **"My outlook is still positive"**   Laurence Miedema, "Bonds Continuing Rehab in Southern California," *San Jose Mercury News*, July 5, 2005.

331 **"I did pretty well today"**   Beth Harris, "Bonds Works Out with Giants," Associated Press, September 5, 2005.

332 **"Four-twenty stretch"**   John Shea, "Return of the King," *San Francisco Chronicle*, September 13, 2005.

334 **"I'm going to be skinny"**   Janie McCauley, "Bonds Realistic That Career Is Winding Down," Associated Press, September 17, 2005.

CHAPTER TWENTY-ONE: SHADOW DANCING

336 **Most damaging were details**   Mark Fainaru-Wada and Lance Williams, "The Truth About Barry Bonds and Steroids," *Sports Illustrated*, March 13, 2006.

337 **"I don't worry"**   Lisa Olson, "Bonds Begins Mood Swings," *New York Daily News*, March 10, 2006.

338 **Willie McCovey, the legendary**   "McCovey Sees Racism," *Chicago Tribune*, March 9, 2006.

BIBLIOGRAPHY

Bernstein, Ross. *Barry Bonds: Sports Heroes and Legends*. Minneapolis: Lerner Sports, 2004.

Bertetta, Russ; Rick Eymer; Bob Fitzgerald; Steve Johnson; Joe Hession; John Horgan; John Murphy; Joe Nolan; and Randy Vogel. *Pride, Passion & Padres: The History of Serra Sports*, San Mateo, Calif.: Junipero Serra High School, 2004.

Bloom, John. *Barry Bonds: A Biography*. Westport, Conn.: Greenwood Press, 2004.

Brock, Jim, and Joe Gilmartin. *The Devil's Coach*. Elgin, Ill.: David C. Cook Publishing Co., 1977.

Bryant, Howard. *Juicing the Game: Drugs, Power, and the Fight for the Soul of Major League Baseball*. New York: Viking, 2005.

Canseco, Jose. *Juiced: Wild Times, Rampant 'Roids, Smash Hits and How Baseball Got Big*. New York: Regan Books, 2005.

Carroll, Will. *The Juice: The Real Story of Baseball's Drug Problems*. Chicago: Ivan R. Dee, 2005.

Crasnick, Jerry. *License to Deal: A Season on the Run with a Maverick Baseball Agent*. New York: Rodale, 2005.

Einstein, Charles. *The Third Fireside Book of Baseball*. New York: Simon and Schuster, 1968.

Einstein, Charles. *Willie's Time: Baseball's Golden Age*. New York: Lippincott, 1979.

Fainaru-Wada, Mark, and Lance Williams. *Game of Shadows*. New York: Gotham, 2006.

Falkner, David. *Nine Sides of the Diamond: Baseball's Great Glove Men on the Fine Art of Defense*. New York: Times Books, 1990.

Feinstein, John. *Play Ball: The Life and Troubled Times of Major League Baseball.* New York: Villard Books, 1993.

Finoli, David, and Bill Ranier. *The Pittsburgh Pirates Encyclopedia.* Champaign, Ill.: Sports Publishing LLC, 2003.

Gravenor, Kristian, and John David Gravenor. *Montreal: The Unknown City.* Vancouver: Arsenal Pulp Press, 2003.

Greenwald, Hank. *This Copyrighted Broadcast.* San Francisco: Woodford Press, 1999.

Gutman, Bill. *It's Outta Here! The History of the Home Run from Babe Ruth to Barry Bonds.* New York: Taylor Trade Publishing, 2005.

Hall, Donald, with Dock Ellis. *In the Country of Baseball.* New York: Fireside, 1976.

Hillman, James. *The Soul's Code: In Search of Character and Meaning.* New York: Warner Books, 1997.

Kittle, Ron, with Bob Logan. *Ron Kittle's Tales from the White Sox Dugout.* Champaign, Ill.: Sports Publishing LLC, 2005.

Lorant, Stefan. *Pittsburgh: The Story of an American City.* Pittsburgh: Esselmont Books LLC, 1999.

Mahany, Effie C. *Through the Years in San Carlos: A Narrative.* San Mateo, Calif.: San Carlos Villagers, 1967.

McCloskey, John, and Julian Bailes. *When Winning Costs Too Much: Steroids, Supplements and Scandal in Today's Sports.* New York: Taylor Trade, 2005.

McNeil, William F. *Ruth, Maris, McGwire and Sosa: Baseball's Single Season Home Run Champions.* Jefferson, N.C.: McFarland & Company, Inc., 1999.

Muskat, Carrie. *Barry Bonds.* Philadelphia: Chelsea House Publishers, 1997.

Oberlin, Loriann Hoff; Jenn Phillips; and Evan M. Pattak. *Pittsburgh: Insider's Guide.* Helena, Mont.: Falcon Publishing, 2000.

Peters, Nick. *Tales from the Giants Dugout.* Champaign, Ill.: Sports Publishing LLC, 2003.

Plimpton, George. *Home Run: The Best Writing About Baseball's Most Exciting Moment.* San Diego: Harcourt, 2001.

Rambeck, Richard. *Barry Bonds.* New York: Child's World, 1995.

Richeal, Kip. *Pittsburgh Pirates: Still Walking Tall.* Champaign, Ill.: Sagamore Publishing, 1993.

Salin, Tony. *Baseball's Forgotten Heroes: One Fan's Search for the Game's Most Interesting Overlooked Players,* Lincolnwood, Ill.: Masters Press, 1999.

San Francisco Chronicle Staff. *Unforgettable!: The Giants' Spectacular 2002 Pennant-Winning Season.* Chicago: Triumph Books, 2002.

Savage, Jeff. *Barry Bonds: Record Breaker.* Minneapolis: Lerner Sports, 2002.

Scher, Jon. *Baseball's Best Sluggers.* New York: Sports Illustrated for Kids Books, 1997.

Schott, Tom, and Nick Peters. *The Giants Encyclopedia*. Champaign, Ill.: Sports Publishing LLC, 2003.

Schuerholz, John, and Larry Guest. *Built to Win: Inside Stories and Leadership Strategies from Baseball's Winningest GM*. New York: Warner Books, 2006.

Schwarz, Alan. *The Numbers Game*. New York: Thomas Dunne Books, 2004.

Sinclair, Mick. *San Francisco: A Cultural and Literary History*. New York: Interlink Books, 2004.

Stanton, Tom. *Hank Aaron and the Home Run That Changed America*. New York: HarperCollins, 2004.

Suchon, Josh. *This Gracious Season*. San Diego: Winter Publications, 2002.

Sullivan, George. *Bobby Bonds: Rising Superstar*. New York: G. P. Putnam's Sons, 1976.

Thrift, Syd, and Barry Shapiro. *The Game According to Syd: The Theory and Practice of Winning Baseball—From One of the Game's Most Successful Innovators*. New York: Fireside, 1990.

Travers, Steven. *Barry Bonds: Baseball's Superman*. Champaign, Ill.: Sports Publishing LLC, 2002.